HENRY KISSINGER

ROBERT D. SCHULZINGER

HENRY KISSINGER

Doctor of Diplomacy

COLUMBIA UNIVERSITY PRESS
New York

Columbia University Press
New York   Oxford
Copyright © 1989 Columbia University Press
All rights reserved

Library of Congress Cataloging-in-Publication Data

Schulzinger, Robert D., 1945–
Henry Kissinger : Doctor of Diplomacy/Robert D. Schulzinger.
p.   cm.
Bibliography: p.
Includes index.
ISBN 0-231-06952-9
1. United States—Foreign relations—1969–1974.
2. United States—Foreign relations—1974–1977.
3. Kissinger, Henry, 1923–
I. Title.
E855.S365   1989
327.73—dc20
89-32183
CIP

Casebound editions of Columbia University Press books are Smyth-sewn
and printed on permanent and durable acid-free paper

Printed in the United States of America

For my wife, Marie, and for Leonard Dinnerstein
In appreciation of their support

CONTENTS

Illustrations follow pages 92 and 172

PREFACE

Enough time has elapsed since Henry Kissinger directed American foreign policy for Presidents Richard M. Nixon and Gerald R. Ford to offer fresh perspectives. Some of the issues with which he had to deal, such as detente with the Soviet Union, relations with China, and war and peace in the Middle East, to name a few, remain key topics of discussion in the highest echelons of the American government.

Henry Kissinger goes beyond earlier accounts of Kissinger's foreign policy and is based, to a considerable extent, upon sources unavailable to previous scholars of American diplomacy in the early 1970s. Although Kissinger's own papers at the Library of Congress and some of his more significant files as National Security Adviser or Secretary of State are still beyond the reach of those who explore the issues which we associate with the man, many new insights may be gained by examining the papers of Presidents Nixon and Ford, which did open in the 1980s.

The manuscript has also benefited from some material declassified under the Mandatory Review system at the Presidential Libraries or Freedom of Information Act (FOIA) requests. Anyone who has used such documents knows that obtaining them is a frustrating process with unpredictable results. In the case of research for this book, my Mandatory Review requests produced more material from the Ford Library than from the Nixon Presidential Materials Project of the National Archives. FOIA documents for this subject, requested by other scholars, appeared in the *Declassified Documents Reference Service*. Inquiries made in the Carter administration produced useful records regarding the 1969–70 bombing of Cambodia and the 1970–73 efforts to destabilize the government of Salvador Allende in Chile. The Reagan administration, however, was less forthcoming in producing recent foreign policy and national security data.

Congressional documents have also complemented the manuscript sources for this study. The special circumstances of the time—the collapse of the cold war consensus, growing congressional opposition to the war in Vietnam, and lawmakers' disgust with Watergate—focused legislative attention on the foreign policy issues of the era. A revolution in presidential/congressional relations over foreign policy produced a far richer vein of congressional hearings, studies, reports, and debates than was the case for most other periods of post-World War II foreign affairs.

Henry Kissinger also utilizes the voluminous journalistic accounts and memoir literature of the time, which dwarf most other treatments of recent United States foreign policy. The public's appetite for stories of Kissinger's exploits seemed nearly limitless in the 1970s, and reporters and their editors were happy to serve all that readers could swallow. I once took a ruler to the pages of the *Readers' Guide to Periodical Literature* to compare the attention the popular press devoted to Kissinger to that which they accorded his predecessors as National Security Adviser or Secretary of State. Coverage of Kissinger, the most celebrated diplomat of the post World War II era, exceeded that of all earlier occupants of the offices he held by sizable or even enormous margins. As Secretary of State, he received 2.5 times the publicity of John Foster Dulles, his nearest competitor, 4 times that of Dean Acheson, 7.2 times that of Christian Herter, 11.7 times more than Dean Rusk, and 15 times as much as William Rogers. While National Security Adviser, Kissinger attracted more attention than Rogers did as Secretary of State—3.5 times the amount. The disparity with previous National Security Advisers was equally telling. Popular journals ran 10.8 times as many stories about him as they did about McGeorge Bundy and 8.5 times as many as they did about Walt Whitman Rostow.

Just as significant were the sorts of journals which wrote about him. Of course he was a staple of the coverage of, say, *U.S. News and World Report*, *The Nation* or *The New Republic*, but so were Acheson or Dulles. Stories about Kissinger, though, also regularly appeared in the most unlikely places. *The Ladies' Home Journal*, *Vogue*, or *Harper's Bazaar*, for example, all featured articles about him. They had all but ignored the Security Advisers or Secretaries of State who had served earlier Presidents.

To be sure, unlike many who had occupied high foreign policy positions in the government before him, Kissinger courted the press and encouraged the attention he received. Moreover, he was also discussed in the flood of journalistic analysis and executive branch memoirs that resulted from the constitutional crises caused by the illegal entry on June 17, 1972, into the Democratic National Committee headquarters at the Watergate complex, and President Nixon's attempts to cover up the affair.

Not to be overlooked either, and much more informative than one might assume at first glance, are Kissinger's own *White House Years* (1979) and *Years of Upheaval* (1982). They are far longer and more detailed than those of other National Security Advisers or Secretaries of State. They are also personal, selective, and sometimes defensive.

White House Years, Years of Upheaval, and other memoirs are important sources for *Henry Kissinger,* but I have treated them as what they are, reminiscences. As such, they are most useful for summoning the participants' later recollection of how they felt or thought, rather than what they did or said. When quoting conversations recorded in memoirs, I have noted that these are recollections. Customarily, I have used contemporary documents, where available, to establish the precise words and deeds of men and women at the time.

Many institutions and individuals have helped me since I began this project. The Council on Foreign Relations supported early research for this book with a Foreign Affairs/National Endowment for the Humanities Fellowship in 1981–1982. The Council on Research and Creative Work at the University of Colorado provided a Faculty Fellowship and several grants-in-aid to help the research from 1981 to 1988. The Committee on University Scholarly Publications of the University of Colorado helped defray the cost of reproducing photographs and cartoons.

Yale University invited me to serve as Cardozo Visiting Professor of History in the spring of 1987. At that time I offered a seminar on The Age of Kissinger where I tried out many of the ideas of this book on a spirited and intelligent group of fifteen undergraduates. I am particularly grateful to one, Marcel Bryar, for his insights into the process of arms control.

The staffs of the Nixon Presidential Materials Project of the National Archives and the Gerald R. Ford Library helped me find many of the documents which inform this book.

Several friends and colleagues deserve thanks for criticizing drafts of the manuscript: Bruce Kuklick, Robert Pois, Leo Ribuffo, Michael Schaller, Gaddis Smith, and Howard Smokler.

I also thank my father, Maurice Schulzinger, who read drafts with the eye of an interested nonacademic.

Kate Wittenberg, the history editor at Columbia University Press, has earned my appreciation for her infectious enthusiasm for this work which made completing it a pleasure.

My greatest debts are to the two people to whom the book is dedicated. Leonard Dinnerstein encouraged me to start it, offered invaluable suggestions for sources, criticized the manuscript, and pressed me to finish. Without his help, much of what is best in these pages would not be here. My wife, Marie, simply makes everything I do better.

INTRODUCTION

Henry Kissinger's Record

Henry Kissinger dominated American foreign policy during the most crucial period after the beginning of the Cold War. Along with Richard Nixon and Gerald Ford he presided over the end of direct global military intervention and the emergence of the Soviet Union as an equal to the United States. He commenced détente with the Soviets, a new relationship with China, and brought the United States into the Middle East as the major player.

Throughout it all Kissinger achieved celebrity unlike that accorded any previous American diplomat. The Gallup Poll listed him as the most admired man in America in 1972 and 1973. He won a Nobel Peace Prize in 1973. Egyptians called him "the magician" for arranging a disengagement of Arab and Israeli forces after the 1973 Mideast war. By that time, even his clothes made an impression; twice he made the best-dressed list. His shuttle diplomacy twice won him an award as "professional traveler of the year." Popular magazines were fascinated with him and his work. The *Ladies' Home Journal* commissioned actress Gina Lollobrigida to prepare a photo essay on him, and it reprinted portions of a book by a French journalist who developed a crush on him. Journalists followed him and women companions before 1974 and him and his wife after his marriage in March of that year. Nancy Maginnes Kissinger became a celebrity in her own right, dispensing advice on marriage, clothes, and foreign policy. There even was a story about his dog. Not surprisingly, cartoonists loved him: In their drawings he flew in a cape—Super K; he held the globe in his hand; he lifted it overhead; he held it on his shoulders; he tamed lions; he charmed diplomats; he snarled at congressmen; he flattered presidents; he was likened to Gulliver tied to the ground by Liliputians. After leaving office he made an impact on literature too, appearing as a character in novels, stories, plays, and even an opera.[1]

And yet. Much of this enthusiasm for Kissinger and his diplomacy faded by the end of the Ford administration. Kissinger became an issue in the election campaign of 1976 with both Ronald Reagan, the Republican challenger to President Ford, and Jimmy Carter, the Democratic candidate, assailing Kissinger's conduct of American foreign policy. Fifty percent of the public polled in 1976 had a favorable impression of him, down substantially from the eighty percent who approved in 1973.[2] The debacle of Vietnam took its toll, as did the inability to fulfill the early promise of détente with the Soviets. By the end of the Ford administration, the United States had not completed a Mideast settlement. The new relationship with China appeared stalled. Nor did Kissinger completely escape the aftermath of the Watergate scandal. Reports that he authorized wiretaps on the telephones of subordinates and journalists dogged him for years. By the end of the Ford administration he became almost forlorn, wondering aloud whether American democracy could sustain a "realistic" foreign policy and concerned that his countrymen could not tolerate equality with the Soviet Union.[3]

"Miracle worker or stunt man?" was the title of an assessment of Kissinger's record in early 1977.[4] That question has pursued him ever since. His reputation in the years after leaving power has fluctuated wildly, depending on the point of view of writers and politicians. His own two volumes of memoirs of the Nixon administration, *White House Years* (1979) and *Years of Upheaval* (1982), were the most extensive and illuminating of those of any American diplomat, and they went far to remind readers why he captured the public imagination in the early seventies. Yet one year after the second volume appeared, journalist Seymour Hersh published a scathing indictment of Kissinger's performance as Nixon's National Security Adviser.[5] Hersh focused on personal failings, claiming that Kissinger's insecurities and ego led him to abuse subordinates, deceive equals, and fawn over superiors.

Memoirs of other participants in the politics of the Nixon years painted different pictures of Kissinger. President Nixon himself drew Kissinger as less the initiator of a new foreign policy than a servant of a President who himself wanted détente with the Soviets and a new relationship with China.[6] Presidential speechwriter William Safire, once a target of wiretaps, also diminished Kissinger's accomplishments in comparison with Nixon's. Veterans of Watergate like H. R. Haldeman and John Ehrlichman weighed in with their own accounts of Kissinger as a shameless self-promoter.[7]

Diplomats of the time also provided their reminiscences. Raymond Garthoff, part of the negotiating team for the SALT agreements, wrote extensively on détente with the Soviet Union in a massive 1,000-page book.[8] He argued that Kissinger helped undermine the eventual appeal of détente by sloppy diplomatic work. He paid insufficient attention to details in the beginning of the relationship and let himself get sucked into anti-Soviet hysteria at the end. Garthoff's boss at the Arms Control and Disarmament Agency, Gerard Smith, wrote his own memoir, *Doubletalk*, in which he too concluded that Kissinger was excessively concerned with the political ramifications of diplomacy at the expense of real, long-term progress.[9] U. Alexis Johnson, the political undersecretary of the Department of State for many of the Nixon years and a professional foreign service officer, expressed the resentments of many of his colleagues when he accused Kissinger of ignoring the advice of professionals.[10]

But Kissinger had his defenders among his colleagues. While Kissinger was still in office Marvin and Bernard Kalb published *Kissinger*, a highly laudatory biography. Kissinger's onetime subordinate William Hyland, who later became editor of *Foreign Affairs*, published *Mortal Rivals*, a history of U.S.–Soviet relations from Nixon to Reagan, in which he praised Kissinger for having conducted relations between the two powers better than anyone who came after.[11] Other onetime subordinates who went on to high positions in subsequent administrations, like Winston Lord who became ambassador to China, or Lawrence Eagleburger who became Undersecretary of State, continued to praise Kissinger.

Kissinger's political rivals also moderated some of their earlier hostility. Ronald Reagan, after becoming President, discovered previously hidden virtues in Kissinger. He appointed him to head a special Bipartisan Commission on United States policy toward Central America in 1983.[12] Kissinger had not stressed western hemisphere problems while in office, but President Reagan believed that he carried such weight with the public that his views on any foreign policy subject would form a favorable impression. Later, when the Reagan administration moved toward strategic and intermediate missile control, they once more called upon Kissinger's expertise. Reagan also consulted Kissinger as he prepared for summit conferences with Soviet leader Mikhail Gorbachev. Again, the onetime critic of Kissinger's détente came to believe that his experience in dealing with the Soviets had proven invaluable.

Where does this absorption with a onetime obscure Harvard professor of government and international relations originate? Is it, as he and numerous defenders asserted, because of his remarkable record of achievement? Did he create a "structure of peace," as he claimed? Did he base United States foreign relations on a firm foundation of "maturity,"and on an accurate assessment of the extent and limits of Washington's power? Did he marry the European diplomat's worldliness to American optimism and idealism in a mostly successful effort to convince foreign policy experts and sensible members of the elite public that the United States had to play its appointed role as a great power? Does his appeal rest on the resumption of relations with the People's Republic of China after twenty-three years, the movement toward capping the arms race and détente with the Soviet Union, successfully disengaging the combatants in the 1973 Arab–Israeli war, and extricating the United States from Vietnam? Do his American supporters keep up their praise because of the honors heaped upon the former Secretary by Europeans with longer memories than Americans of how foreign policy should be conducted?[13]

Yes, in many, but not all, ways. Some of his achievements were real, especially in opening relations with China, pursuing détente with the Soviet Union and recognizing the relative decline of American power. Notable as these accomplishments were, they paled when set against his carefully contrived image as a genius of international relations. When the Egyptians designated him "the magician" they meant to praise, not tease, him. At the height of his renown in 1973 American supporters also seriously thought that his diplomacy approached the miraculous. Such hero worship had its inevitable costs. By the end of his tenure in office, the magic was gone and Kissinger seemed more illusionist than miracle worker. The praise heaped on him earlier rang hollow. His diplomacy seemed conventional, not innovative; the gap between his promise and his actual achievements provoked a natural dillusionment.

Kissinger was an ordinary diplomat in the sense that he stressed commonplace themes developed by foreign affairs professionals in the years following World War II. His very conventionality was a source of strength in propelling him to the top. His career represented the culmination of the influence of academic expertise on foreign affairs. His scholarly work of the 1950s and 1960s neatly summarized the realist tradition dominant in American universities after 1945. Kissinger was a masterful popularizer of themes developed by a corps of thinkers who advocated thoughtful United States participation in world affairs. As National Security Adviser and Secretary of State, Kissinger tried to balance the competing demands of theory and the practical necessities of daily foreign policy. Kissinger spoke of realist theory to provide academic justifications for policies tailored to political needs. This was an irresistible combination for scholars interested in the real world.[14]

Kissinger seizes the imagination because he engineered the most significant turning point in United States foreign policy since the beginning of the cold war. Just as Dean Acheson designed the structure of United States foreign policy in the early cold war, Kissinger created a framework for post-Vietnam diplomacy. Moreover, he became enmeshed in a changing environment for foreign policy officials. It was Kissinger's great opportunity as well as his personal misfortune to come to power as the twenty-year-old consensus over American foreign policy collapsed in the calamity of the Vietnam war.[15] As members of the foreign policy elite no longer shared a common urge to contain the Soviet Union, Kissinger advanced other goals for the United States. He succeeded for a while with some—détente with the Soviet Union, better relations with China, a cease-fire in the Middle East, for example—but he failed to foster a new consensus.

Congress became quarrelsome as members questioned the authority of the executive to direct foreign affairs. Kissinger discovered that he did not have the field to himself when he claimed special foreign affairs wisdom. This intrusion by outsiders on what had become the domain of the executive led Kissinger to some of his most celebrated manipulations of public opinion.[16] Many of Kissinger's justifications to favored journalists for his conduct tried to reduce support for competitors, for example, other White House staff members, Secretary of State William Rogers, Senator Henry Jackson, presidential candidate George McGovern.

A clear picture of Kissinger's foreign policy must be focused through the prism of his relations with Presidents Richard Nixon and Gerald Ford and their staffs. The advisory role is crucial for understanding the modern American government. Presidents and advisers needed one another. Nixon relied on Kissinger to provide legitimacy with foreign affairs experts, while Kissinger, in turn, used his connections to the presidents to assert his political acumen and toughness. Kissinger's relationship with Ford was unique in United States diplomatic history. An unelected president, untrained in foreign affairs, took instruction from a man near the height of his authority. The Secretary of State provided Ford with instant acceptance among the foreign affairs community. Ironically, however, Kissinger's very prominence became his undoing in 1975–76. Threatening to over-shadow a new president seeking election in his own right, the adviser became a liability.[17]

Other factors also account for continued interest in Kissinger. De-tractors focused on mistakes, duplicity, immorality, self-promotion, and maybe even crimes. Upon his departure from office in January 1977 the *New York Times'* liberal columnist, Anthony Lewis, found "it all very puzzling" that "the National Press Club produces a belly dan-cer for him and gives standing applause for his views on world peace. Harlem Globetrotters make him an honorary member. Senators pay tribute to his wisdom." For Lewis "secrecy and deceit were levers of his power." His "secret is showmanship. Henry Kissinger is our P. T. Barnum." For critics his career stood as a moral caution, a measure of "the price of power," as Hersh put it.[18]

Critics charged that Kissinger's accomplishments as National Se-curity Adviser and Secretary of State were illusory, inflated far be-yond reality by a press, that, Lewis wrote, Kissinger "played as Dr. Miracle plays the violin."[19] Detractors noted that the war in Vietnam lingered far longer than anyone expected in 1968 and that the settle-ment reached in Paris from October 1972 to January 1973 could have been obtained years earlier with far less loss of life. In the Middle East, they complained that Kissinger's remoteness from the issue combined with his systematic undermining of the position of Secre-tary of State William P. Rogers contributed to the outbreak of war in 1973. Only thereafter did he play a public part in resolving the tension between Israel and its neighbors. By that time the problems had become even more intractable. His 1973 and 1974 shuttling be-tween Israel, Egypt, and Syria, according to this view, only arrested further deterioration in a desperate situation. Further east, in Iran, he continued the flawed policy of heavily arming the forces of Shah Mohammed Reza Pahlevi. Within two years of Kissinger's departure from the State Department, the Shah's government lay in ruins, tak-ing with it United States influence in a strategic area. A combination of personal pique and misapplied geopolitical ruminations led the United States toward a senseless "tilt" toward Pakistan during the December 1971 war between Pakistan and India over the indepen-dence of Bangladesh (the eastern province of Moslem Pakistan). Even his opening to China has been roughly treated by the critics. Hersh, whose detestation of Kissinger surpassed his contempt for Richard Nixon, denigrated the Security Adviser's role in reversing the futile policy of isolating China. Instead he credited Nixon for taking the lead in adopting ideas about China that had percolated through the foreign affairs establishment over the previous decade.

Detractors pointed to Kissinger's personal flaws. Adversaries indicted Kissinger as the compleat courtier who flattered Nixon to his face while vilifying him behind his back. A stern taskmaster to subordinates, Kissinger was accused by Hersh of lacking the one quality that makes a difficult boss bearable to his staff—loyalty to employees. He was charged with playing one off against another, keeping the majority in the dark, speaking against them to other officials, and encouraging the FBI to tap their telephones and watch their activities. Other White House staff members in the Nixon and Ford administrations often believed that he promoted himself at the expense of the President. Kissinger's role in the resignation of Richard Nixon provides additional examples of deviousness and skirting the law.[20]

Questions of illegality arose regarding Kissinger's role in the secret 1969 bombing of Cambodia, the 1970 invasion of that country, and the Christmas bombing of North Vietnam in 1972. His actions toward the elected Socialist government of Salvador Allende in Chile also provoked charges that he violated minimal standards of law and decency. Adversaries complain that he helped the Central Intelligence Agency "destabilize" Allende's government after it failed in illegally blocking his election.[21]

Many of these criticisms highlight inexcusable shortcomings. Some diplomatic breakthroughs that appeared promising at the time—the Vietnam negotiations, détente with the Soviet Union, and even the Middle East Shuttle—dimmed or even collapsed by 1976. The "structure of peace," so heavily promoted in 1972, lay shattered by 1976.[22] He ignored economic and social developments abroad until very late in the Ford administration; by then he could do little about them. He also made things harder for himself and his foreign policy by his personal failings. His personal relations with staff members of equal rank were poor, and he was a tyrannical boss. As a bureaucratic warrior, he won short-term, tactical battles; but eventually he lost, in need of the help of the very people he had bested earlier. This bureaucratic conflict badly affected foreign policy. He tried to do too much, all by himself, which came back to haunt him when he needed allies. On a larger canvas, his indifference to legal requirements undermined self-respect at home and United States prestige abroad. His resentment of congressional participation in foreign policy made the quest for a consistent, legal and popularly based foreign policy all the harder.

Yet Kissinger's real diplomatic achievements have not been surpassed. Secretary of State George P. Shultz, commenting in the midst of public uproar on the Reagan administration's sale of arms to Iran, noted, "there's only one Henry Kissinger. They broke the mold after they made him." Anthony Lewis, one of his sharpest adversaries while he was in power, acknowledged in 1984 that "for all the inhumanity on his record, he dealt wisely with the Russians."[23] Kissinger understood as few American National Security Advisers or Secretaries of State have, the extent and limits of American power.

For all of the complaints about his indifference to human rights abroad, he avoided some interventions. Détente placed U.S.–Soviet relations on a firmer footing, even if it was oversold. The opening to China may have been long in coming, but Kissinger made the most of his opportunities. It stands as one of the major diplomatic reversals in modern history. In the years since Kissinger's visit to Beijing, the United States and China have become partners. Even Ronald Reagan, an opponent of the opening to China, went there as President, confirming the strength of the new relationship. Kissinger's shuttle diplomacy in the Mideast set in motion the process that culminated in 1977–79 in the Camp David agreements and the Egyptian–Israeli accord, the only peace treaty signed between Israel and an Arab state to date. Kissinger succeeded, at least for part of his tenure, as few had before and none since, in persuading Americans to acknowledge the nature of their interests in world politics.

ONE

The Adviser

Little in Henry Kissinger's career before January 1969 quite prepared him or the world for the meteoric trail he blazed across the sky. Born on May 27, 1923, in Fürth, Germany to a Jewish school teacher, Louis Kissinger, and his wife Paula Stern Kissinger, Henry's childhood and youth were rocked by the Nazis' rise to power. In 1933 the authorities, in one of their first acts, fired Jewish teachers from the public schools; so Louis found work in a Jewish vocational school. Three years later he lost that job too. Under the Nüremberg laws of 1935, Jewish children were expelled from public schools, so Henry entered a Jewish school in 1936. In August 1938, the family fled Germany, first for London but soon settling in New York City's Washington Heights on the northwest corner of Manhattan. There Henry entered George Washington High School in September. He did well academically, graduating in 1941. He then attended City College of New York until February 1943 when he was drafted into the U.S. Army.[1]

To this point he had followed a path not unlike that of other bright children of Jewish refugees from Hitler. Some friends from the time describe him as a shy loner, occasionally distrustful of others. This may or may not have derived from having to flee his homeland in such a threatening atmosphere. Many adolescents growing up in outward security are shy and anxious. Perhaps adding to his discomfort was his noticeable Germany accent, which, of course, he never lost. Yet there were other refugee children on Washington Heights then, so German-inflected English, by itself, probably did not call undue attention to a student. His brother Walter, younger by one year, did easily pick up an American sound. Walter later liked to joke "I listen" when asked to explain why he lost his German accent while his famous brother had not.[2] Yet it is safe to say that memories of the Nazi nightmare never left Henry. He developed a taste for order, an awareness of people's capacity for cruelty, and a need to protect himself.

By all accounts, Kissinger bloomed during his years in the Army. Tested and found to have superior intelligence, he quickly became known for his skill at lecturing troops on the reasons for the war. There his German accent probably helped his listeners believe that he knew what he was talking about when he spoke of European events. Later, as both professor and official, his accent often proved an asset, lending European gravity to his statements, whether they deserved them or not. His wartime lectures brought him to the attention of Fritz Kraemer, another German refugee in the U.S. Army whose duties included teaching soldiers the Allies' war aims. Kraemer became Kissinger's first patron.

First, Kraemer helped his protegé enter army intelligence. There Kissinger worked with the occupation authorities restoring order to the town of Krefeld in North Rhine-Westphalia. Kraemer proudly recalled, "I could only marvel at the way this twenty-one-year-old did the job." Kissinger stayed in Germany for two years after the end of the war, first in the army and then as a civilian employee, working as a Nazi hunter and as a lecturer to officers. The teaching he did went well, setting a pattern for his later academic career. He easily addressed older men who outranked him, and he developed a flair for discussing current events with participants.[3] Action and application, not analysis or profound thought, characterized his work then as an academic and in power.

Kraemer also helped Kissinger select Harvard over CCNY when he was ready to return to college in 1947. "A gentleman does not go to a local New York school," Kraemer told his protegé, who entered Harvard as a sophomore in 1947. There he met his next patron, William Y. Elliott, a professor of government with ties to Washington. In 1950 the twenty-seven-year-old Kissinger, now married to the former Anne Fleischer and living off campus, presented Elliott with a 377-page senior thesis entitled "The Meaning of History: Reflections of Spengler, Toynbee, and Kant."[4]

Over the years Kissinger's friends chuckled over the audacity of a twenty-seven-year-old senior summarizing humanity's activities in 377 pages. His friend John Stoessinger recalled the "interest and envy" he and other graduate students felt toward Kissinger and the rarity of his summa cum laude.[5] Perhaps, but other Harvard undergraduate theses were notable for their grandeur of scale combined with their conventionality of intepretation. Who but a twenty-seven or an eighty year-old would have nerve to assimilate everything that has happened in a single piece?

Kissinger did not publish his youthful observations, but scholars took note once he became a public figure. His longtime friend Stephen Graubard praised this "spirited" work that "challenged any number of academic orthodoxies."[6] Another, younger scholar, Peter Dickson, noted the germ of great ideas on international relations here. "Kissinger's political philosophy," grounded in a reading of Immanuel Kant, "constitutes a major break with the rationale of all postwar policy, which rested on the notion of America as a redeemed nation, as the guarantor of freedom and democracy."[7]

Kissinger remained at Harvard for graduate study under Elliott's sponsorship. In 1951 he became executive director of the Harvard International Seminar, which brought to the university young foreign nationals "who are on the verge of reaching positions of leadership in their own countries."[8] Here he shepherded several future foreign statesmen through six weeks of summer sessions, establishing valuable contacts.

He also worked on a dissertation on the concert of Europe following the Congress of Vienna of 1815. His work reflected the growing appeal of "realism" as a mode of studying international relations. Reflecting the influence of notable realists like Hans J. Morgenthau or George F. Kennan, Kissinger chided Americans for their moralistic approach to foreign affairs. His doctoral dissertation on the aftermath of the Congress of Vienna appeared to favorable reviews in 1956 as *A World Restored: Metternich, Castlereagh, and the Concert of Europe.* In it he established a reputation as one of the foremost students of realism. *A World Restored* was not really a history of the Congress of Vienna—British diplomat Harold Nicolson had provided an excellent survey in 1946. Rather, Kissinger's book was a paean to the achievements of a conservative diplomat, Austria's Klemens von Metternich.

Kissinger praised Metternich as a "scientist of politics." He became "Prime Minister of Europe," by "coolly and unemotionally arranging his combination in an age increasingly conducting policy by 'causes.'"[9] The Austrian foreign minister acknowledged that the multinational Hapsburg empire might be at a disadvantage in the struggle with the nationalist forces unleashed by the French Revolution. In the long run, the age of dynasties may have passed, but Metternich was determined to make sure that conservative regimes managed the

changes for their own benefits. Kissinger admired the way in which
Metternich created a system of alliances that managed to last for half
a century or, by some reckonings, fully one hundred years. The Concert
of Europe he managed was quite different from the reactionary Holy
Alliance pursued by Czar Alexander I. The Russian autocrat wanted
to end all change, which Metternich considered impossible. He preferred to lead conservative states into a series of accommodations with
revolutionaries, draw their fangs, and preserve the domination of old
regimes.

After completing his Ph.D. Kissinger and his mentor Elliott had
expected that Harvard would offer him an appointment as an assistant professor. No tenure track job was forthcoming, however, so
Kissinger had to decide between an academic career (he had offers
from both the University of Chicago and the University of Pennsylvania) and moving into the foreign policy world. Hamilton Fish Armstrong, editor of *Foreign Affairs* published by the Council on Foreign
Relations, had looked into Kissinger as a possible managing editor
in 1954. That fell through, but Kissinger had made a strong impression. Now, in 1955 the New York–based Council on Foreign Relations
employed Kissinger as rapporteur, or recording secretary, on a study
group investigating the implications of Secretary of State John Foster
Dulles' 1954 call for a strategy of "massive retaliatory power" against
the Soviet Union. The prospect of Washington using its atomic weapons at the slightest provocation sent tremors through the foreign policy establishment. Accordingly, the Council on Foreign Relations asked
Gordon H. Dean, once the chairman of the Atomic Energy Commission,
to head a panel on the proper use of nuclear weapons. The study group
did not know quite what to do with this intractable subject, and the
chairman told the assistant "Good luck, Dr. Kissinger. If you can make
anything out of the efforts of this panel we will be eternally grateful." [10]

Two years of discussions in a study group helped produce *Nuclear
Weapons and Foreign Policy*. Kissinger's job was to summarize the
debates and weave conflicting points of view into a coherent discussion of American nuclear strategy. The book insisted that apocalyptic
talk about nuclear weapons making foreign policy obsolete was out
of order. Dulles had erred in promising massive retaliation—a largely
empty threat. Only American policymakers took it seriously, and by
doing so they stopped thinking clearly about the implications of nuclear weapons. Better to accept the uncertainty of what might happen
if the United States were compelled to rely on conventional weapons
than to embark on a futile effort to end all threats. [11]

The core of *Nuclear Weapons and Foreign Policy* was not about the atomic bomb, but a plea for the contribution of serene and imperturbable experts to direct foreign policy. Kissinger, like other realists, berated Americans for their naive hope that all international issues could be quickly resolved by an exercise of American goodwill. He lamented that the United States lacked a "strategy," so Americans were always shocked by what happened in the world. Unless they could be persuaded to settle down for the long haul, they would constantly be shocked by alterations in the world around them. "The basic requirement," he wrote, "is a doctrine which will enable us to act purposefully in the face of the challenges that confront us. Its task will be to prevent us from being continually surprised."[12]

Nuclear Weapons and Foreign Policy did well in every respect. Some 17,000 copies were sold in the first year. Anchor-Doubleday brought out an abridged paperback edition in 1958, cutting most of the tedious descriptions of weapons systems in Europe and retaining the strictures against American naivete in foreign affairs. Gordon Dean offered a foreword in which he acknowledged the heaviness of the professor's prose. Some reviewers stressed the same point. Edward Teller, the legendary "father of the H-bomb" and just beginning his career as a military strategist, took Kissinger to task for the dullness of his prose and his airy dismissal of the massive use of nuclear weapons. Still, Teller could say, "everyone on this side of the Iron Curtain who will study *Nuclear Weapons and Foreign Policy* will learn of a better way to contribute to the safety of the free world."[13]

Kissinger's career flourished after the success of *Nuclear Weapons*. He returned to Harvard as associate director of the Center for European Studies. He became the most frequent academic contributor to *Foreign Affairs*. Armstrong, the editor, printed ten pieces by Kissinger on strategy, the organization of American foreign policy, conventional weapons, and relations with European allies. Throughout, he concentrated on the incapacity of Americans to think strategically. His fellow citizens persisted in the erroneous beliefs that foreign policy issues could be completely resolved, that "peace" was a final state of well-being, rather than a dynamic, virtually endless process, and that the United States could someday achieve the goal of perfect security. All of these delusions distracted the public from a true appreciation of the role of experts to manage America's foreign relations.[14]

Another, even more important, patron emerged at this time, as Kissinger met Nelson Rockefeller. David Rockefeller had served with Kissinger on the nuclear weapons study group and Nelson first met him at an arms control conference in Quantico, Virginia, in late 1955.

In the spring of 1956 Nelson Rockefeller approached Kissinger to coordinate a Special Studies Project sponsored by the Rockefeller
Brothers Fund. Editing a series of proposals that set the foundations
of Nelson Rockefeller's 1960 campaign for the Republican presidential nomination, Kissinger became further enmeshed in the network
of influential figures in the foreign policy establishment.[15]

When John F. Kennedy won the White House in the election of
1960, it seemed that realist national security managers had triumphed.
Kissinger played a small role in the campaign. Even while working
for Nelson Rockefeller, a Republican, Kissinger promised advice "on
a personal basis" to the Democratic Advisory Committee on Foreign
Policy.[16]

After the election, the President chose as his National Security
Adviser McGeorge Bundy, dean of arts and sciences at Harvard, an
eastern establishment Republican and son of Henry L. Stimson's chief
aide, Harvey Hollister Bundy. For a time in 1961 and 1962 Kissinger
could be found in Washington as a consultant to Bundy and the rest
of the NSC staff on the development of long-term strategy. But the
relationship never flourished. Kissinger objected to the administration's handling of the Berlin crisis of June-July 1961. He opposed the
call-up of reserves, because it "gives a psychological advantage to the
Soviets. If they relax pressure for a while or if they build up the crisis
very slowly, there will be a clamor to release the reserves." He advocated patience in an administration committed to action. "My view
is that at this stage the major emphasis should be on measures which
can be sustained for a long time." Six months later the State
Department complained to Bundy that Kissinger was stepping on their
toes. On a visit to Israel, the Harvard professor told the press that
"recent Russian arms deliveries to the UAR have provoked a crisis
in the Middle East." Such talk by a private citizen, albeit a consultant to the NSC, made the Department's work harder. By mutual
agreement, Bundy let Kissinger's consultantship lapse in February
1962.[17]

Back in Cambridge Kissinger engaged in the most sustained intellectual work of his career. In it he retailed the conventional wisdom of international relations. He returned to the question of nuclear
strategy in The Necessity for Choice (1961), published by Harvard's
Center for International Affairs. Here the adversary remained massive retaliation, as Kissinger advocated the current strategy of "flexible response" favored by the Kennedy administration. He noted that
the deficiencies of massive retaliation required that the United States
express the willingness to use every weapon in its arsenal.[18] Some-

times the military might respond to supposed Soviet threats with local armed forces, as it had during the Korean War. At other times the United States might play only a subsidiary role, send advisers and trainers to help local governments suppress their domestic leftist insurrections. At the time of writing *The Necessity for Choice* such an experiment had been in progress for three years in Indochina. Finally, Americans had to be prepared to use nuclear weapons on battlefields and for limited objectives. Without this possible threat looming over the Soviets, Kremlin planners would never acknowledge that the United States might use its huge arsenal of strategic weapons.

So far Kissinger expressed common beliefs that the United States somehow had to demonstrate leadership in world politics. Unfortunately, traditional American partners in Europe proved unwilling to follow. The middle 1960s saw a succession of shocks: Washington consulted little with its allies during the Cuban missile crisis of 1962; it scuttled the joint Anglo-American Skybolt missile project in December 1962; the Multilateral Force, to be made up of ships from all NATO navies was sunk by inadequate consultation with European governments in 1965. Finally, in 1966 Charles de Gaulle stunned Washington with the announcement that France was withdrawing from the military arms of NATO.

Faced with such dramatic shifts in the alliance the Council on Foreign Relations, for the most part made up of Atlantic firsters, commissioned Harlan van B. Cleveland, formerly ambassador to NATO, to chair a major research enterprise on the relationship between the allies and Washington. The Ford Foundation came through with $1.1 million to fund this gathering of academics and officials. Eventually ten volumes appeared, with Kissinger joining several other well-known realist professors in writing individual studies.

Kissinger's own contribution to the Atlantic Policy Studies was *The Troubled Partnership* (1966), a book that elaborated the themes expressed over the previous generation. He explained privately that "what I am trying to say . . . is that the technical issues of nuclear control seems to me less important than encouraging responsible attitudes on both sides of the Atlantic."[19] Later, in power, he continued to battle bureaucratic rivals who favored what he termed "technical solutions" over his own seldom-defined "responsible attitudes." In the book, he chided Americans for their preemptory style, their refusal to consult with their allies, and their arch dismissal of the "obstinacy of one man"—the critique of contemporary international relations offered by French President de Gaulle.

Customary American opinion in the Kennedy and Johnson admin-

istrations dismissed de Gaulle as an embittered old man, resisting the
relentless tide of history with his outworn appeals to French nationalism and European pride. For Americans the future lay in "integration"—a path blocked by French resistance to British membership
in the Common Market—and less, not more, nationalism. In the long
run, these Americans observed, de Gaulle would be considered nothing more than a quaint reminder of the burned-out flame of the na-
tion-state.

Kissinger encouraged Americans to pay closer attention to what
de Gaulle and other Europeans had been saying over the past decade.
If the United States were somehow able to treat its allies as partners,
Europeans might actually develop a sense of responsibility for world
politics. Unfortunately, he wrote, "the United States . . . has fallen
into the trap of dealing with its allies, except Great Britain, almost
psychotherapeutically. It has tended to confuse periodic briefings and
reassurance with consultation."[20]

Kissinger's life changed once more in 1964. His marriage of sev-
enteen years unraveled and he moved out on his own. With the end
of the Kennedy administration he was welcome once more in
Washington, briefing the Johnson administration on his travels and
views. Whenever he met a foreign leader or an American ambassador,
he fired off a report to the National Security Adviser, the Secretary
of Defense, or the President. Once he reported that President de Gaulle
was likely to be "more obstinate" in opposing American efforts toward European integration. The French leader believed, Kissinger reported, "that the major problem was to keep Germany under control.
[He] found it very important to remain the most attractive country
for the Soviet Union to deal with." France wanted to "anticipate [and
therefore blunt] United States bilateral attempts at détente."[21]

He became a skilled infighter, courtier, and gossip. While happy
to consult for the White House, Kissinger could be catty about his
contacts in the government. He reported to former Secretary of State
Dean Acheson on "the boredom of present-day Washington. There are
too many clever tacticians and too few reflective people." Kissinger
also knew how to flatter. He went on to say to the former Secretary
of State that "one sees no young Dean Achesons anywhere and I wonder whether we are still capable of producing them. What will happen to our clever young men when they are still clever young men at
the age of 70?" Name dropping helped too. He once told Acheson that
"while in Paris a few weeks ago, I spoke with a man who had an
appointment with De Gaulle right after you. He told me that De Gaulle

said, 'Voilà, un homme!' . . . It is, of course, no surprise to your admirers."[22]

All the while, Europeans began shaking their heads in disbelief, amazement, and eventual disgust at the waste of United States resources in Vietnam after 1965. At first most NATO countries, with the exception of France, had been supportive of, or at least acquiescent in, America's Vietnam policy. Then, in 1966, as the end seemed nowhere in sight, a subtle shift took place among the West Germans and British. When Kissinger spoke with German Chancellor Ludwig Erhard in early 1966, the German leader urged the resumption of bombing of the North "lest America appear weak and indecisive." Yet in the next breath the German leader expressed serious misgivings that "American involvement in Asia would reduce its interest in Europe." Erhard encouraged Kissinger to tell Defense Secretary Robert McNamara that it was "out of the question for Germany to send uniformed personnel to Vietnam." The British Labour government of Harold Wilson strove to support the Americans, but found that its 1966 and 1967 efforts to mediate the war through the government of Poland met with continuous rejection by Washington.[23]

As for France, it often seemed to Americans that Paris could not forgive the United States for having taken over the "mission civilatrice" from France after the unraveling of the Geneva accords of 1954. De Gaulle also faulted American conduct in the war. In December 1966 he visited Southeast Asia and told a cheering throng in Phnom Penh, Cambodia, that the United States had waged "Unjust war, immoral war."[24] Official Washington shrugged. To Secretary of State Dean Rusk, the French president simply vented the frustations of a generation of French statesmen, angry at seeing their own imperial dreams fade in the bright light of the American empire.

For realist writers like Kissinger, European complaints carried more weight. Kissinger warned about French animosity toward United States policy in Vietnam. "France was far from neutral," he told the White House. "Most senior officials in the French foreign office would welcome American embarrassment with a kind of schadenfreude."[25] What good was defeating the Communists in Vietnam, if the NATO alliance dissolved? How could the United States intimidate the Soviets in Europe or the rest of the world if the American leaders could think only of Vietnam? Something had to be done to stop this tail wagging the dog.

Kissinger traveled twice to Vietnam in 1965 and 1967 as part of government-sponsored tours designed to generate support for the war

among influential academics.[26] In 1965 Kissinger went to Vietnam for
the Foreign Intelligence Advisory Board. He promised the National
Security Adviser "to be at your disposal if you wish to discuss my
impressions." While there two Catholic priests shared with him "some
of the most interesting [observations] that I have had in Vietnam."
One informed him that "no Vietnamese thought anything of betraying even his seemingly closest friend and did not seem to hold a grudge
against those who had betrayed him. . . . [The Vietnamese] love in-
trigue and are professional opportunists." Later Kissinger spoke with
a psychiatrist who told him that "Vietnamese seem incapable of
drawing independent conclusions. . . . The reason seems to be that
their whole society is oriented toward the Confucian principles of
submission and acceptance of authority."[27]

While Kissinger was in Saigon the *Washington Post* reported that
he thought the South Vietnamese government was unpopular and could
not win. The Johnson administration disassociated itself from the
professor, and even suggested that the President had not known of
Kissinger's trip in advance. Privately Bill Moyers, Johnson's assistant, mollified the envoy. Explaining that he recognized the "anguish
an unwarranted press account can cause a fellow human being,"
Moyers assured Kissinger that he had fled from him in "the interest
of American policy." If he had not known before, Kissinger learned
how officials manipulated the press and how little they thought of
reporters—two lessons he applied in his own public career.[28]

The Harvard professor undertook secret negotiations to end the war
between August and October 1967. Two French acquaintances,
Raymond Aubrac and Herbert Marcovich, acted as intermediaries between Kissinger and North Vietnam's Mai Van Bo. In an operation
code-named PENNSYLVANIA, Kissinger relayed word from the
Johnson administration that the United States would stop the bombing if the North promised not to take "military advantage" of the
halt. Kissinger explained that the phrase meant that the United States
expected the North to refrain from "any increase in the movement of
men and supplies to the South." Hanoi refused this gambit, objecting
to American increases in the bombing while these talks went forward.
Kissinger replied that the North's attitude was "baffling." If we bomb
near Hanoi we are accused of bringing pressure. If we voluntarily
. . . impose restraint in our actions . . . we are accused of an ultimatum."[29]

Kissinger also reported to Nelson Rockefeller that the war was going
badly.[30] The objective for the United States was to conclude it quickly

while containing Communist gains. Throughout 1967 Kissinger offered Rockefeller suggestions on how to use the Vietnam issue in the 1968 presidential election. During the primaries, the New York governor would portray Richard Nixon as an unredeemable hawk. Once Rockefeller had secured the nomination, he would characterize President Johnson as an ineffectual bumbler, unable either to win the war or leave it.

The campaign did not follow this blueprint. Johnson stunned the nation on March 31 with his announcements that "I will not seek, nor will I accept the nomination," the end to some of the bombing of the north, and the opening of peace talks in Paris. Kissinger went to the French capital to study the negotiations that summer. By then Rockefeller had lost to Nixon, and Kissinger recalls having abandoned his immediate plans for a government advisory job. He contemplated a return to the semi-academic, semipolitical role he had followed previously in his work for the Council on Foreign Relations.

Back in Cambridge in the fall of 1968 he submitted his views on what was going on at Paris to Hamilton Fish Armstrong, editor at *Foreign Affairs*. Armstrong, a consummate Europeanist, had grown increasingly worried about what was happening to the United States in Vietnam. As he wrote in the summer 1968 *Foreign Affairs*, Americans cannot "ignore how much the Vietnam War is isolating us from other nations." He concluded that the United States could not prevail in Vietnam, because Americans had "failed to understand the people and society we were setting out to help." Intended to project American power abroad, Vietnam had instead become a debacle, not intimidating the Soviets while wrecking relations with the nation's European allies.[31]

Accordingly, Armstrong was happy to print Kissinger's own recommendations for ending the war. The professor thought that the fighting was more likely to peter out than end formally. The United States would not volunteer to exit Vietnam without assurances from the North that it would depart also. Hanoi was unlikely to offer such a pledge without pressure from its allies in the Soviet Union or China. The key to ending the war therefore lay in the hands of the two great Communist powers. A war on the periphery of the basic arena of the cold war could only be resolved if the principals in the East–West struggle made headway in reducing their own tensions. Once more he faulted Americans for a "diplomatic style marked by rigidity in advance of formal negotiations and excessive reliance on tactical considerations once negotiations start."[32]

Kissinger's proposals resembled Richard Nixon's. A year earlier candidate Nixon had answered Armstrong's call for his review of American policy in Asia. In "Asia After Vietnam," Nixon paid close attention to the recently completed eight volume Council on Foreign Relations survey of *The United States and China in World Affairs*. Scholars and officials had pledged flexibility in dealing with China since the old attempts at isolating Beijing had clearly failed. It was Washington that had been isolated from its allies. China's behavior had not altered and the Nationalists on Taiwan had not been encouraging. As Robert Blum put it in *The United States and China in World Affairs*, Americans had the uncomfortable feeling of "supporting as the government of China a regime with no foreseeable prospects of extending its authority beyond Taiwan and the nearby islands."[33] A "two China" policy of recognizing both the Communists and Nationalists seemed like the best way out of the morass. Sooner or later the United Nations was likely to seat the Beijing government, so the best the United States could hope for would be to retain some sort of recognition for Taiwan. If the U.N. accepted two Chinas, then the rest of the world would too.

Nixon elaborated these themes in "Asia After Vietnam," which appeared in the fall 1967 issue of *Foreign Affairs*. He suggested that over the long term the United States would have to come to terms with Beijing, once the irritant of Indochina were removed. Like other foreign policy experts, Nixon acknowledged the disorienting effects of American involvement. Designed to send a message to potential adversaries, the war had sown dissension among friends. The aim, therefore was to quit the battlefield without having been forced to leave. He lamented that the legacy of Vietnam "will be a deep reluctance on the part of the United States to become involved once again in similar interventions on a similar basis." Greater realism toward China was called for.[34]

Foreign policy experts worried as much about domestic dissent over the war in Vietnam as they did about the complaints from other nations. Since the late forties a broad consensus had arisen over fundamentals of foreign policy. While, of course, the two parties had bickered over which was better able to wage the cold war, both acknowledged the apparent need to confront the Soviet Union with a huge military and to enlarge the power of the President to direct foreign policy. Now that consensus had eroded. As moderate a figure as Senator J. William Fulbright, chairman of the Foreign Relations Committee, had broken with the prevailing assumptions in 1965 after the United States had occupied the Dominican Republic. He had suggested that presidents since Harry Truman had exaggerated the threat from the Soviet Union to augment the power of the White House in foreign affairs. He recommended that modern American foreign policy pay less attention to the use of force and the confrontation with revolution.[35]

Congressional dissent, while important, was not the only thing bothering foreign policy managers. Lyndon Johnson had become unwelcome on college campuses after 1966. Newspapers and television networks flooded readers and viewers with stories about the difficulty Johnson, Secretary of State Rusk, Secretary of Defense Robert McNamara, and Commanding General William C. Westmoreland had when they predicted a speedy end to the war in Vietnam. The moral authority of the executive branch seemed to have been overthrown. The entire structure of post–World War II foreign policy rested upon public acceptance that the President and his advisers knew best. With that gone, no President could have his way in foreign affairs.[36]

Nixon resolved to restore the dominance of the President once he took office. Public criticism had to end or be neutralized, Congress had to submit once more to the executive, and, most important, the President himself had to once more become the central figure in foreign affairs.

As in so many aspects of his presidency, Nixon would emulate, and, he hoped, surpass the achievements of the Kennedy administration. Then Secretary of State Rusk had not been an especially important figure. Instead the President had relied on the counsel of his brother Robert, the Attorney General, McGeorge Bundy, the National Security Adviser, and Robert McNamara, the Secretary of Defense. Rusk's stature rose under President Johnson, as did that of Bundy's successor as National Security Adviser, Professor Walt Whitman Rostow of MIT. But in both the Kennedy and Johnson administrations, the Presidents had found the counsel received often conflicting and confusing. Moreover, the President's own directives were often lost in the bureaucracy.

Kennedy, who had decided to seize control once he entered the White House, had grown frustrated with the bureaucracy. At the beginning he had asked Professor Richard Neustadt how to take charge quickly. Neustadt, who had studied the transitions between recent presidential administrations, was quick to oblige in the winter of 1960–61 with a quick course based on his book, *Presidential Power*. Although the book became almost a bible for the transition team, it had proved more difficult than expected to put into practice the professor's prescriptions about an activist presidency. Neustadt had objected that President Dwight Eisenhower had relied upon a staff system more appropriate to winning a war than running the White House. He said that Ike, unlike Truman before him, "seem[ed] both unsure of his objectives and unwilling to persist, for long in any given course."[37]

But Kennedy had found it easier to assert the need for presidential preeminence than to accomplish it. Secretary of State Rusk had proved especially disappointing. Some of Kennedy's advisers, writing in the nostalgic haze of Camelot and subsequent disillusionment with Rusk's behavior as the war in Vietnam escalated assert that the President planned to drop him in a second term. Pierre Salinger, Kennedy's press secretary, suggests that Kennedy wanted more than he got from Rusk.

Whether Kennedy intended to drop Rusk may never be known, but the President's touchy relations with his Secretary of State and with gaining control of the unwieldy apparatus of the bureaucracy sounded alarms for Nixon, the first Republican to become President since Kennedy's death. For Nixon the apparent conflicts and confusion within the foreign policy apparatus presented an opportunity as well as a challenge. The risks were obvious—he might be stymied by bureaucratic inertia. If, on the other hand, he could successfully concentrate power in the White House, he might outstrip the record of two longtime rivals, Eisenhower and Kennedy. The formal use of the National Security Adviser by Kennedy and Johnson provided a model.[38] If the person tapped for the role could actually gain mastery over the foreign affairs apparatus, the President would have found his way to becoming the dominant figure in postwar foreign policy.

Nixon's envy of the Kennedy family was matched by his resentment of Nelson Rockefeller and the eastern establishment wing of the Republican party, which had always expressed disdain for the parvenu westerner. After his celebrated defeat for the governorship of California in 1962, Nixon had moved to New York City and purchased a cooperative apartment in the same building where Rockefeller made his Manhattan home. The New York governor snubbed the newcomer and in the 1960 presidential election Nixon had been forced into a humiliating capitulation to Rockefeller in the "compact of Fifth Avenue." In that document the Vice President accepted Rockefeller's and Kennedy's view that the Eisenhower administration's foreign policy had been too sluggish and restrained.[39]

Now in 1968 Nixon was ready once more to make his peace with Rockefeller. He wanted to mend fences with the establishment wing of the party, which had dominated Republican foreign policy since the Second World War. In his westerner's view, internationalist Republicans controlled the national media, influenced public opinion, and recruited the officials of the foreign policy apparatus. Kissinger had crystallized many of the themes of realist and internationalist advisers. Kissinger's strictures against sentimentality combined with his sensitivity to foreign opinion and his esteemed position among foreign affairs experts added luster to an administration of outsiders.

On November 25, Nixon selected Kissinger, Rockefeller's principal foreign policy expert, to head the National Security Council. Kissinger too modestly recalls "neither expectation nor enthusiasm" at the summons from Nixon.[40] He had, after all, sought some role in the new administration, feeding information on the Paris Peace negotiations to the Republican campaign. Nixon recalled that "he had been helpful during the campaign" and when campaign manager John Mitchell suggested that Nixon see Kissinger at the Pierre the President-elect obliged.[41] A few days after Nixon named him his National Security Adviser, Kissinger met with President Johnson and National Security Adviser Walt Rostow. He had been there a year before for an off-the-record discussion on Vietnam with Secretary Rusk, General Maxwell Taylor, Clark Clifford, soon to be named Secretary of Defense, and Rostow.[42]

Nixon's appointment of Kissinger won praise across the political spectrum. The conservative *National Review* called it "very good news." *Business Week* praised him because he "defies 'hard' and 'soft' labels." The liberal *New Republic* was happy that the Harvard professor "brings to his share of responsibility for foreign policy in the nuclear age a sophistication that Mr. Nixon lacks."[43] Here was a charge that formed the basis of much of the later fascination with Kissinger as the one true intellectual and sophisticate in an administration of philistines. As Adam Yarmolinski, one time Defense Department official in the Kennedy and Johnson administrations and now a colleague at Harvard told *Time* magazine, "We'll all sleep a little better each night knowing that Henry is down there."[44] *Newsweek* described him as "a tender hawk, a vigilant dove" and expressed the hope that his appointment "would help to bridge the gap between the President-elect and the halls of academe."[45]

From the beginning, Kissinger presented Nixon with his own views on the national security system. He urged that the adviser be more than a coordinator of various prescriptions emanating from the bureaucracy. To wait for State, Defense, Treasury, or Central Intelligence to present their plans and then choose among them would not make the President dominant in foreign policymaking. He would be a decision-maker, perhaps, but he would not originate policies.

Accordingly, Nixon and Kissinger looked for ways to make certain that policy went from the top down, not the other way round. One of the first memoranda Kissinger sent the President-elect outlined "a new NSC system." He noted that Johnson had relied upon a largely informal Tuesday lunch for which the "discussants are frequently inadequately briefed and often unfamiliar with the nuances of an issue." He complained of the absence of "any formal method for assuring that decisions are adequately implemented." In contrast, Eisenhower had employed a "highly formal system in which participants had the benefit of full staffed papers." Unfortunately, the very formality of the system took too much time and sometimes bogged down in triviality. Kissinger tried to combine the best of both. He recommended that the NSC become "the principal forum for issues requiring interagency coordination, especially where presidential decisions of a middle or long range are involved." He also advised creation of an NSC Review Group, which he would chair, to "examine papers prior to their consideration by the NSC." He recommended that the NSC scrap the current National Security Action Memoranda and replace them with National Security Decision Memoranda (NSDMs) and National Security Study Memoranda (NSSMs). The former would be used "to report presidential decisions" to agencies concerned. The latter, obviously, "would be used to direct that studies be undertaken" by the appropriate agencies. He also advised preparation of an "annual review of the international situation similar to the annual economic message" of the President to Congress.[46]

This was precisely what Nixon was looking for. The National Security Adviser-designate noted that "Nixon's decisions to the new role and structure of the NSC were influenced by his direct experience with the NSC machinery as it was used during the Eisenhower administration."[47] The NSC system envisaged by Kissinger had the advantage of concentrating power in the White House. At the same time it could keep the prying eyes of the press out of the business of foreign policy. The larger bureaucracies of the State and Defense Departments, consisting of thousands or tens of thousands of people who survived changes in administration, hardly had the particular interests of the Nixon administration at heart. They had developed a distressing tendency to speak privately to journalists whenever they wanted their views supported. Nixon, uncomfortable in public, longed to achieve popular success without confronting a skeptical press. Kissinger, with intelligence, a grand strategy, and connections in academia and the press was exactly the man to enhance the reputation of the White House.

On February 7, 1969 the White House announced that "the President . . . has indicated that the Council will henceforth be the principal forum for the consideration of foreign policy issues on which he is required to make decisions."[48] Specifically, Kissinger expected that the new system would provide "creativity . . . systematic planning, . . . determination of the facts, and a full range of options" for the president.[49] Kissinger persuaded Nixon that "above all, a foreign policy for the 1970s demands imaginative thought. In a world of onrushing changes, we can no longer rest content with familiar ideas or assume that the future will be a projection of the present."[50]

The task of concentrating power in the NSC became easier when it became apparent that Nixon preferred the counsel of the White House staff to the recommendations of his cabinet heads. Many of the latter had been selected to appease constituencies within the Republican party, while the staff owed its allegiance only to the President. For Secretary of State Nixon chose William P. Rogers, an old colleague from the Eisenhower administration. In 1952 Rogers, an erect New York lawyer, had discussed with Nixon what the latter should say on television as he fought to retain his position on the Republican ticket in light of the revelation that a group of Los Angeles businessmen had contributed $18,000 to a private fund to eke out Nixon's government salary. Rogers retained his friendship for Nixon and went on to become Attorney General in 1958. He had not been especially close to Nixon after his 1963 move to New York, but the two got along well enough. More important, perhaps, than their personal relationship, was the eastern respectability Rogers lent to Nixon's reputation. Well connected to the establishment, Rogers was a further bridge to that important element of the Republican party.[51]

Another potential rival for the preeminence of the White House and the National Security Adviser was the Defense Department, with its budget of more than $70 billion, its civilian staff of 35,000, and its armed forces approaching three million uniformed men and women. The major foreign affairs issues of the previous generation—NATO, Korea, nuclear weapons, relations with Cuba, and the war in Vietnam—had all seemed to involve the use of military force. Robert

McNamara's high reputation among politicians and civilian strategists, if not among military people, had polished the reputation of the Defense Department.

Nixon turned to Congress for someone who could preside over the sprawling defense establishment. Wisconsin Representative Melvin Laird, a twenty-year veteran of the House, had served on the Armed Services Committee, rising to the position as ranking minority member. As ranking minority member, Laird had become a force on a panel made up of fervent supporters of the uniformed services. Laird's worries over whether the services were getting enough of the new weapons systems that McNamara's Office of Systems Analysis had subjected to withering scrutiny, led him to some uncharacteristic notions about the future of American commitment in Vietnam. In 1967 the Wisconsin representative had come to believe that Vietnam had depleted America's armed forces, despite the $20 billion-per-year extra the United States had appropriated for the war. The "chew up," as it was called, of matériel, the cost of outfitting, transporting, feeding and paying a field army of 535,000 in Vietnam itself, and the subsidies provided the forces of South Vietnam, South Korea and the Philippines, had left very little for other commitments. Laird worried that overcommitment in Vietnam made it less likely that the United States would use its military forces anywhere else. With Laird urging a speedy end to involvement in Vietnam, Kissinger knew that the head of the Pentagon presented a potential rival for the NSC's preeminence in foreign policy.

While Laird could cause trouble, Kissinger took comfort that Nixon seemed to maintain control over the federal bureaucracy from the White House. His chief of staff, H. R. Haldeman, and his domestic counselor, John Ehrlichman, worried that cabinet secretaries would soon come to owe their allegiance to the needs of their departments, many of which were staffed by Democrats and liberals. Ehrlichman recalled that "conflict characterized the cabinet's teamwork from the beginning." Nixon discovered that "some of the men he'd selected for the Cabinet soon embarrassed him" so he "began to instruct them via his senior staff."[52]

Haldeman and Ehrlichman had both campaigned with Nixon in his losing bid for the White House in 1960 and in his disastrous race for the California governorship in 1962. They knew he tired quickly and could not tolerate alcohol, so they let him rest and banned whiskey in 1968. They knew he resented reporters, so they limited the access of the press. Their own positions depended on their ability to regulate the flow of traffic to the candidate, so they made sure staff members made appointments with the boss through them. Haldeman recalls that "Nixon was able to halt, through me, the unending flow of government officials who 'just had to see the President.'" The chief of staff noted another reason for a "wall" around Nixon. "This President had to be protected from himself."[53]

Nixon's isolation persisted throughout the transition period, even though it contradicted a campaign pledge to press "government by cabinet." Such a system, though, makes sense only in a parliamentary democracy. In an executive system such as the American presidency, it is nearly impossible for the Chief Executive to thresh out problems in a committee made up of the heads of departments. Rarely are all members of a cabinet veterans of years of political warfare, as they are in European parliamentary democracies. But the President's own staff often do have a sort of old soldier's feeling for one another. Nixon's cabinet met once, accomplished nothing, and was rarely summoned again.

This style suited Kissinger's own desire to be at the center of foreign policy action. What might interfere, though, was his realization that Nixon barely knew the Harvard professor, and what he did know did nothing to prove Kissinger's loyalty. He had been a Democrat, then a supporter of Nelson Rockefeller, and taught at Harvard, the bastion of the establishment Nixon both resented and longed to join. Kissinger had to prove his worth by demonstrating that he could make better choices than anyone else in the bureaucracy.

Kissinger's physical proximity to the President in the NSC offices in the White House helped. His position as special assistant to the President, which did not require that he go through the process of Senate confirmation also made his job easier. He did not have to interrupt his day to testify on Capitol Hill, but could cement his position with daily briefings of the President each morning at eight. He also made it a point to give few on-the-record press interviews in 1969 and 1970. Instead, he carefully cultivated reporters like Marvin Kalb and Bernard Kalb of CBS News and Richard Valeriani of NBC. When he became a public figure in the midst of his dramatic trip to China in July 1971, he had already established his bonafides with Nixon and could afford to embark upon a more open courtship of the molders of opinion. All that was in the future, though, in January 1969.[54]

Kissinger came to the office of National Security Adviser as a product of the post–World War II national security establishment. His academic work had been at the border between scholarly research and practical action in foreign affairs. He had taught at Harvard, making him worthy in Nixon's eyes. Kissinger had recognized that the war in Vietnam had extracted a huge cost from the United States among its allies and with its own citizens. It had to be ended to allow the United States to pursue other foreign policy interests. His commitment to permanent United States interest in world affairs reflected the wisdom of foreign policy experts who had come to question the way each administration since Truman had waged the cold war. In the fifties and sixties, Americans clung to the belief that the Soviets would someday be vanquished. Kissinger, on the other hand, sought to conduct the relationship over the long haul. The two should accommodate one another's basic security needs while competing in regions unlikely to spark major confrontations.

Kissinger brought to office the habits, concerns, and even suspicions of thirty years. A refugee, he feared for the stability of modern societies. An outsider, he depended on the patronage of the influential and powerful. He had learned how to flatter, how to fight, and how to gossip. Now his position rested on the favor of Richard Nixon, a man usually scorned by people whose help Kissinger earlier had sought. As the administration opened, the new National Security Adviser needed to prove himself to his new patron and carve out a distinct identity among subordinates who had served Nixon longer. He also felt the need to retain the goodwill of the academic, media, and foreign policy establishments that had given him his start. He and the new administration began, therefore, with the opportunity to change the way the United States conducted its foreign relations. Success would be a personal and political triumph. Failure to exert control and appear in command would be devastating.

TWO

Grappling With Vietnam, 1969–1971

On Richard Nixon's desk on the afternoon of January 20, 1969 was a memorandum from Henry Kissinger on the organization of national security. NSDM-2 (National Security Decision Memorandum-2) represented the culmination of the effort to concentrate authority over foreign affairs in the National Security Council staff and special assistant for national security affairs. All agencies of the government dealing with foreign affairs—State, Defense, Central Intelligence, Defense Intelligence, Treasury, and any other bureaus that might be concerned with overseas issues—had to coordinate their activities through the NSC. Nixon signed the directive ordering all agencies to route papers for the President through Kissinger's office. Moreover, the NSC could go beyond hammering out a common policy among the bureaucratic competitors to summoning information and policy from them.[1]

Kissinger hoped to assure that decisions flowed from the top down. Otherwise, were the NSC to rely solely on options originating with the other elements of the bureaucracy, the President would be at a substantial disadvantage. Lacking an independent source of judgment, evaluation, or direction, Nixon and Kissinger would find themselves fighting the same vortex that had sucked down previous presidents. If, on the other hand, they could make the professionals respond to *their* agenda, then the President would regain control.

Vietnam stood at the center of the current foreign affairs difficulties, and Kissinger and Nixon were resolved that the new administration would not suffer the same debilities as had made life miserable for Lyndon Johnson after 1966. Progress had to be apparent in the Paris Peace Talks, troops had to be withdrawn, casualties had to decline, the allies had to be mollified, the domestic peace movement had to be neutralized, and all the while the government of South Vietnam had to be convinced that Washington still backed it in its war. One of Kissinger's aides reported that the NSC chief wanted a negotiated agreement "that Hanoi would sign, that would get our POWs back and that would end our involvement. He would not even entertain the notion that we could get better terms or that Saigon could ever win the war." Nixon, on the other hand, believed, according to the same aide, that "the only way to end the war by negotiations was to prove to Hanoi and to Saigon that Saigon could win it." This was a neat trick, to persuade one group that the war was winding down while retaining the confidence of domestic hawks and foreign combatants.[2]

There was a window of opportunity at first, as Nixon encountered some goodwill in unexpected places. Dean Acheson, for example, found Nixon "a definite relief from LBJ, not from definable positive virtues, but from the absence of a swinish, bullying boorishness which made his last years unbearable. Also his women are less omnipresent than LBJ's." After meeting Nixon, Acheson went so far as to describe him as a "curiously appealing person. Against my better judgment, I find myself liking him."[3]

At the beginning of the new administration the Democrats' representatives—Averell Harriman and Cyrus Vance—were replaced by a staff headed by David K. E. Bruce, a longtime foreign service officer. Bruce was the consummate professional. He had served as Eisenhower's ambassador to France and Kennedy's to England.[4] Leading the American delegation to the peace talks required different skills. Patience for interminable diatribes from the North Vietnamese and National Liberation Front representatives, a subtle distancing from the South Vietnamese, and the ability to divine what Washington hoped to obtain taxed the strength of the official American representatives.

Their job was made all the more difficult by Kissinger's conclusion that the road to peace in Vietnam ran through Moscow and perhaps Beijing.[5] If Hanoi could be made to see that the Soviet Union attached more significance to improving its relations with the United States than it did to support for wars of national liberation, then it might become more tractable in the negotiations.[6]

In 1954, faced with apparent betrayal from his principal allies, Ho had little choice but to reach an agreement. The pain of not realizing the goal of a communist Vietnam could be eased though by the terms of the Geneva agreement, which promised an election throughout the country within two years of the treaty's ratification. The failure of the new republican government of South Vietnam created in 1955 to participate in the elections robbed Ho of his victory and helped foment the insurrection in the South that led to the eventual commitment of United States troops. Kissinger hoped that similar pressure might arise in the current talks.[7]

In 1969, however, the situation with all the Communist powers differed from the arrangements of 1954. Zhou Enlai, longtime premier of the People's Republic and regarded by some western China experts as something of a moderate, seemed to lose authority.[8]

The split between its two patrons surprised Hanoi. But the fissures in the Communist movement presented opportunities too. As a Vietnamese Nationalist, Ho worried about depending for patronage on China, Vietnam's traditional rival and occasional occupier. Early in the war, one observer commented, "the Chinese were interested less in revolutionary change in Southeast Asia than in a peaceful rear at a time when their attention was directed primarily at threats from Japan, Korea, and Taiwan." Nothing could be better for Hanoi's freedom of action than to force Moscow and Beijing into a bidding war for the honor of greatest supporter of the revolution in Southeast Asia.[9]

Into this complicated situation strode Kissinger and the NSC staff with plans for cutting Hanoi off from its sources of outside sustenance. Since Moscow provided the lion's share of the war matériel, the proper way to change the mind of Hanoi's negotiators would be to demonstrate the existence of détente between the United States and the Soviet Union. The process began in February 1969 with the opening of a "back channel" of negotiations between the White House and the Kremlin through the auspices of Kissinger and Anatoly Dobrynin, the Soviet Ambassador to the United States. Dobrynin was the dean of the diplomatic corps by virtue of having served in Washington since shortly before the Cuban missile crisis.[10]

In the beginning of the Nixon administration Dobrynin was to be the vehicle of signaling the Kremlin that the United States did not want differences over Vietnam to interfere with the continuation of a dialogue on strategic weapons. The Soviet ambassador seemed an excellent choice as a discreet messenger. By making certain that the principal arena of the negotiations took place in Washington rather than Moscow or some neutral site, the White House could have more direct control over the substance of the discussions. This was vital for Kissinger and the NSC who might have greater access to the President than did State Department officials, but whose small numbers prevented them from conducting a full-scale, long-distance dialogue. At its height the NSC staff numbered fewer than sixty with no more than five professionals working on relations with the Soviet Union and arms control.[11]

The small size of the NSC was one of its attractions for Kissinger. He would have to spend less of his precious time as a manager, a job for which he was temperamentally ill-equipped. Instead, he could devote himself to meeting personally with the President, something he did every morning. In these private conversations he treated President Nixon as a star pupil and budding statesmen. Nixon's wide travels had "formed the basis of a new American foreign policy," Kissinger claimed. No one had come to office better prepared. Kissinger explained to his superior that he had an excellent opportunity to graft Nixon's political skills to the adviser's grand strategic conceptions. Yet the NSC chief was not naïve. A disgruntled aide recalled how Kissinger liked to tell the story of meeting Mrs. Nixon at a reception and "making a special point of telling [her] how much he was impressed with her husband. His grasp of issues and his command." Then, eyes twinkling, Kissinger told one on himself. The First Lady frowned and said "Haven't you seen through him yet?" Nine months into the term Kissinger joked to aides that Nixon was "my drunken friend."[12]

Kissinger's special relations with the President charmed the press. Within six months adoring profiles appeared of Kissinger, the "man with the pressure cooker job," as he described it to friends. Journalists idolized his "omniscient, cosmic view of foreign affairs. His goal seems to be to look ahead so far that he will foresee all difficulties for years ahead and avert future catastrophes."[13] *Look* magazine described the "strategist in the White House basement" as a "political independent who likes to think of himself as a liberal."[14] The liberal *New Republic* extolled him as "the one indispensable man on the Nixon staff. . . . Nixon literally could not function without Henry Kissinger at his beck."[15] *Newsweek* assured readers that "Kissinger has firmly established himself as a predominate force in the shaping and implementation of U.S. foreign policy." The newsweekly decided that "in the blurry Milky Way of Nixonian Washington, Kissinger's star is one of the few to burn brightly."[16] An English reporter concluded the "stock Washington—or anyhow, Georgetown" explanation of Kissinger's eminence was "that he was the only serious intellectual the Republicans had."[17] John Osborne of the *New Republic* identified Kissinger as Nixon's "surrogate brutalitarian" shaking up the Department of State. Yet Osborne considered Kissinger's domination of the machinery more cosmetic than real. "One can only examine the process itself, and marvel that so many people go to so much trouble for so little demonstrable result."[18]

Others noted dangers in Kissinger's prominence. James McCarthy of the *Chicago Daily News* observed that his relationship with the President had "become almost too close and too personal . . . for effective operations of the NSC staff." Some of his subordinates left early in frustration. One complained that "Henry Kissinger is a one man show. . . . When a memo goes to the President from the National Security Council staff it carries one name and only one name— Henry Kissinger. It doesn't make any difference who wrote it. Some people don't like to work that way." Yet even some of the dissatisfied aides acknowledged that "Kissinger approaches genius in knowledgeability and expertise."[19]

Such preeminence aroused Congress. Senator J. William Fulbright, Chairman of the Foreign Relations Committee, resented the NSC chief's refusal to meet directly with the panel. He drafted legislation, never passed, compelling Kissinger and other presidential advisers to appear when Congress called. "No one questions the propriety or desirability of allowing the President to have confidential, personal advisers," he told a Judiciary Subcommittee. "President Nixon is certainly entitled to the private and personal counsel of Mr. Kissinger, but Mr. Kissinger in fact is a great deal more than a personal adviser to the President." Fulbright cited reports that Kissinger had a "hammerlock on foreign policy." He noted that "Mr. Kissinger has become the instrument by which President Nixon has centralized the management of foreign policy in the White House as never before." Whether the policy was good or bad, "the result is that the people's representatives in Congress are denied access not only to the President himself but to the individual who is the President's chief foreign policy adviser, the principal architect of his war policy in Indochina."[20]

Others who had served previous presidents admired Kissinger's domination of the process. Former Secretary of State Dean Acheson, who had had his own bad experiences with Congress, preferred Kissinger's insulation from Senatorial scrutiny. He predicted that Fulbright's request for Kissinger's consultation would cause "useless

friction within the government of the United States, hamper the conduct of one of its most vital functions and increase the harrassment
and difficulty for the President."[21] Former Secretary of State Dean
Rusk agreed that Kissinger is "acting in a very personal sense for the
President himself."[22] On the other hand, former ambassador Averell
Harriman explained that "Dr. Kissinger is certainly assuming some
of the responsibilities of the Secretary of State."[23]

Meanwhile, Kissinger used the back channel to explain directly to
Dobrynin the nature of American strategy in the war. He stressed to
him "that a fundamental improvement in U.S.–Soviet relations
presupposedSoviet cooperation in settling the war."[24] The United States
wanted Moscow to explain to Hanoi that Washington could not be
driven forcibly from Vietnam. The cost to the reputation of the country for steadfastness seemed too high, despite the complaints from
the European allies that the preoccupation with Vietnam had diverted Washington's gaze from the more important issues of European security.

But Kissinger also wanted Dobrynin to let the North know that
the United States stood ready for an accommodation. The Johnson
administration's negotiating position had been that the United States
would not leave until the North acknowledged that it was in the South
and withdrew its troops. Kissinger indicated to Dobrynin that Nixon
was not going to wait forever.[25] The Soviets should let the Vietnamese
know that the United States did not want them to take advantage of
the diminution of the American combat role, but they would not be
expected to match the withdrawals man for man.

Dobrynin reported the American view to North Vietnam, but Kissinger worried that without forceful action the Communists would
not be convinced that they had to do anything themselves to earn
further concessions. He feared most of all the appearances of weakness before the adversary. Since Ho had repeated for years that the
United States eventually would lose heart, the United States had to
raise the anxieties of the North if they did not cooperate.

Therefore, Kissinger and Nixon worked out a strategy of applying
more military pressure with fewer troops. "Vietnamization," became
a formula for beefing up the firepower of the South's armed forces.
In 1969 the United States shipped $1 billion in weapons and matériel
to the South. The combat role of the American soldiers shifted as well.
No longer did the army and marine corps soldiers aggressively pursue "search and destroy" tactics of tracking down Vietnamese revolutionaries. Instead, reducing losses to American forces became the

goal of U.S. commanders. Insofar as U.S. troops did enter the field they accompanied the soldiers of the Army of the Republic of Vietnam (ARVN), offering instruction in rooting out guerrillas and hoping to draw the North Vietnamese armed forces into fire fights. Once large concentrations of North Vietnamese troops did make their presence known, the Americans could call for the awesome fire power of artillery and carrier-based fighter bombers.

As the level of violence in the ground war diminished the air war became more destructive. In 1969 over a million tons of TNT fell over the battlefields of the south, another half million rained down on North Vietnam, and a new theater, Cambodia, opened for the air war. Until 1968 Cambodia had remained poised in a precarious neutrality. The "playboy Prince," Norodom Sihanouk, had maintained a delicate neutrality in the war, one that had spared his principality some of the devastation of its eastern neighbors, Laos and Vietnam. Nonetheless, Cambodia shared a border with Vietnam, and the North had made use of the relative safety of Cambodia to move supplies into the South without fear of aerial attack. For commanders like General Creighton Abrams, who took over direction of American forces in Vietnam in 1969, Cambodia presented an additional thorn as a sanctuary for North Vietnamese and NLF troops. In February Abrams cabled the Joint Chiefs of Staff that "recent information, developed from photo reconnaissance and a rallier give us hard intelligence on COSVN HQ [central office for Vietnam headquarters] facilities" in Cambodia.[26] The ARVN commanders also resented the inability of their forces to pursue suspected North Vietnamese across the border into Cambodia and sometimes Laos. The Vietnamese fretted that the sight of enemy soldiers scurrying across the border to safety demoralized the unmotivated ARVN conscripts who did not want to fight in the first place. Both the American and the South Vietnamese commanders speculated without much basis in fact that Cambodia hid a special command station for all Communist troops in the South. If the Americans could find and destroy that headquarters the Communist operations would be crippled throughout the South.

Pleas for heavy bombing, hot pursuit across the border and a full-scale invasion of Cambodia had formed a standard part of the generals' request lists forwarded to President Johnson through Defense Secretaries McNamara and Clark Clifford in 1967 and 1968. Plans for bombing and invading Cambodia reached the President's desk monthly, but Johnson denied each request.[27] He feared that new antiwar agitation might sweep over the White House, China might enter the war, the Soviet Union might make trouble for the United States in Europe, or Cambodia's Sihanouk might throw in his lot with the Chinese if the United States violated the unstated agreement that the war would be limited to South and North Vietnam.

Nixon and Kissinger, however, labored under no such prior restraints. As long as the Soviets and Chinese knew that the United States did not threaten them directly, and that an attack on Cambodia was, ironically, a prelude to eventual American departure from Vietnam, then they would raise no significant objection. In March 1969 General Earle Wheeler, Chairman of the Joint Chiefs of Staff, requested permission of Secretary of Defense Melvin Laird for B-52 strikes against targets in Cambodia. An operation called MENU began, with strike, codes named BREAKFAST, LUNCH, DINNER, and SNACK authorized weekly. In April Wheeler went further and requested "ground and air preemptive operations in Cambodia to a depth of 10 km." Laird was skeptical about the usefulness of the strikes, and in October he told Wheeler that "before any further operations are mounted the target areas should be reviewed in depth, both for military advantage and political risks, particularly the risk of hitting Cambodian personnel." But Nixon thought the bombing worked. The Joint Chiefs reported that "the enemy is suffering human and material losses. . . . Military risks continue to be minimal as well as political risks, so long as Cambodians are not injured."[28]

Nixon reasoned that Sihanouk might have some interest in an American campaign to rid the country of northern Communists. Certainly the Cambodian army, trained and equipped by the United States and France, welcomed the prospect of ridding the country of North Vietnamese. The eastern neighboring Vietnamese had been the traditional adversary of the Cambodians, in much the same way that China had been the scourge of Vietnam for centuries. Hotblooded army officers berated Sihanouk for his lax disregard of Cambodia's national pride. One of them, Colonel Lon Nol, was the chief of staff who displaced Sihanouk with a coup d'état in March 1970, immediately prior to a major American invasion of Cambodia.

Sihanouk of Cambodia proved a hard nut to crack. In later justification of the bombing Kissinger claimed that Sihanouk approved the action by nods, winks, and refusing publicly to denounce the United States. Kissinger wrote "Sihanouk not only did not object; he treated the bombing as something that did not concern him since it occurred in areas totally occupied by North Vietnamese troops and affected no Cambodians; hence it was outside his control and even knowledge."[29]

Such bland assurances were disputed by Sihanouk himself from his exile in China after his overthrow by Lon Nol. The prince's protestations diminished as the alliances shifted in Southeast Asia after the eventual fall of Cambodia to the Khmer Rouge (Communist) forces in 1975. After a bloody revolutionary regime killed nearly three million of Cambodia's six million people, Vietnam invaded Cambodia, replaced the brutal Pol Pot government with one friendly to Vietnam, and Sihanouk joined forces with Pol Pot and other anti-Vietnamese forces to regain power. Ironically, the United States also supported Pol Pot, because he opposed the Vietnamese. When Sihanouk came to the United States in 1981 looking for support in his guerrilla war against the Communists, he dropped his objections to the secret bombing campaign of 1969–1970.

William Shawcross, a British journalist, claimed in *Sideshow: Kissinger, Nixon and the Destruction of Cambodia* that Sihanouk objected bitterly to the bombardment. Sihanouk told him "In the sixties Cambodia survived because Lyndon Johnson rejected all the requests of his military that the United States invade Cambodia and remove Sihanouk. . . . But Nixon accepted those ideas. I did not know about the B-52 bombing in 1968. In 1968, I had told Chester Bowles, *en passant*, that the United States could bomb Vietnamese sanctuaries, but the question of a big B-52 campaign was never raised."[30] The kernel of Shawcross's charge, however, is that Kissinger and Nixon opened Pandora's box with their policies. They upset the uneasy balance in the principality and enraged the local Communists. Soon the Khmer Rouge were rallying peasants to their side by pointing to the deadly rain of bombs from the Americans. Moreover, the bombardment did not eradicate the headquarters of the North Vietnamese, probably because none existed there. Few shipments of weapons were blocked by the bombing, which served principally as a morale booster for the South Vietnamese. American commanders, however, were distressed that the infiltration from the North continued unabated.

Obscured in the debate over the effects of the bombing was the bureaucratic controversy at the time as to the wisdom of the approach. Secretary of Defense Melvin Laird led the objections on mostly pragmatic grounds. He complained that the Cambodia campaign was likely to lengthen the war, while what was needed was a speedy conclusion. Odd as it may seem for the head of the Pentagon to worry about the use of military force, Laird based his fears on the overextension of American forces around the globe. Over a third of the Pentagon budget was going for equipment and salaries used by the forces

in Vietnam, while the purchases for new weapons had been starved.
Moreover, Senator Mike Mansfield, the Democratic Majority Leader
in the Senate, had introduced legislation in 1969 calling for the withdrawal of United States forces from Europe because the NATO allies
had not paid their fair share of the cost of keeping them there. Laird
argued that expanding the air war into Cambodia was likely to increase calls by Congress to quit Europe, while at the same time Europeans were likely to complain more about the waste of American
resources in Asia. He told the President that "Congressional concern
must be seen as a real constraint [and] escalating acts on our part
would not help reach a negotiated settlement."[31]

Curiously absent from the discussions over the Cambodia bombing
was Secretary of State Rogers. Kissinger believed that the State Department's role consisted solely in the public negotiations at Paris.
The conduct of the war itself was a matter for the White House. When
Rogers heard of the bombing campaign, he was furious for having
been excluded. In fact, Rogers accepted Kissinger's reasoning that the
bombing of Cambodia kept North Vietnam off balance and encouraged the southern forces. But at the same time Rogers worried about
the future. He wondered if the Cambodian government was strong
enough to withstand the natural public outcry if the bombing became
public.[32] His anxieties proved to be prophetic over the next year.

From the very beginning Kissinger feared leaks from anyone other
than himself. In April 1969 he opposed conducting a study of the
Johnson administration's decision to halt the bombing. Nixon proposed it as a way of damaging the Democrats. Yet Kissinger pointed
out that such a study would require interviewing the participants.
"There was always a good chance," he told the President, "that one
or more of the personalities involved would leak to the press the fact
that the administration was conducting such a study."[33] The President would not let the matter drop. A few months later he ordered
"as complete a report as we can possibly get on the Bomb Halt from
all vantage points, what we learned in the campaign, what we heard
in the campaign, what the record shows, the conversations of Rusk,
etc. . . . The same goes for the Cuban missile crisis, and the Diem
murder."[34]

Keeping the bombing campaign out of the press obsessed the White
House. In part the covert nature of the air raids rested on Kissinger's
geopolitical theories. The other side had to be kept off balance. Sihanouk's tacit support could be guaranteed only by keeping quiet about
the bombing.

Most of all the bombing was kept secret to avoid an outcry from the antiwar movement. For the first six months of the new administration a certain reservoir of goodwill or at least patience persisted among the majority of the public. The antiwar movement itself had been mauled by the 1968 election, but protesters renewed their call for demonstrations against the war in the spring of 1969.[35]

The White House took extraordinary pains to keep word of the bombing out of the newspapers. The pilots who flew the raids heard from their briefing officers that their targets were inside South Vietnam. Those few officers who were let in on the secret were instructed to file correct reports of the attacks directly to the White House National Security Council. They were instructed to doctor the reports sent to the Pacific command in the Philippines and the military headquarters for the war in Saigon. A few technicians had to be appraised as well, because the coordinate on the maps used by the B-52s had to be altered to mislead the computerized navigational system. Navigators on the giant warplanes sometimes thought they were releasing their deadly cargo over South Vietnam, while in fact they flew twenty miles or so to the west and attacked positions inside Cambodia.

This violation of the traditional canons of accuracy in military reporting finally got the administration into trouble. One of the technicians who changed the coordinates complained to William Beecher of the *New York Times,* who broke the story in the spring of 1969. His report also included statements from diplomatic officials implying that the Cambodian government knew what was happening and approved the effort to rid the country of North Vietnamese.[36] Sihanouk, of course, denied that he was privy to the American assaults, for fear of further alarming his indigenous Communists and ruining his reputation for neutrality.

In Washington the White House was furious with the reports and assumed that leaks from "liberal academics" and doves in the NSC staff had been responsible for making life miserable with the antiwar movement. Kissinger himself stood accused of having been the source of the information for complicated reasons of his own. Nixon feared that his adviser, recognizing the limits of the bombing achievement, had whispered in the ear of the *Times*man in the hope of retaining the goodwill of the generally antiwar newspaper reporters. According to Haldeman Nixon railed that he was "being sabotaged by bureaucrats in the administration." Ehrlichman reports that the President objected to the technical violations of secrecy, but was more restrained than Kissinger who "fanned Richard Nixon's flame white hot."[37]

Kissinger himself was in a quandary when the story broke. On the one hand the National Security Adviser thought that making the bombing public might put additional pressure on North Vietnam. Not that Hanoi had been unaware, of course, of what had been falling on its soldiers as they moved weapons to the front. But a public acknowledgment that the United States was attacking North Vietnam might make Hanoi understand that Washington would not be forced out of the war. That alone might make as positive an impact on uncommitted public opinion as the news of the bombing might have negatively on the antiwar movement.

FBI Director J. Edgar Hoover described Kissinger as overwrought when he called from Key Biscayne about Beecher's article on the Cambodian bombing. The Security Adviser characterized the piece as "extraordinarily damaging" making use of "secret information." He asked Hoover to "make a major effort to find out where that came from." A few hours later Hoover phoned back speculating that Morton Halperin of Kissinger's staff might have been Beecher's source. The FBI Director proceeded to insult both as "so-called arrogant, Harvard-type men." Kissinger, the former Harvard professor, sensed his own vulnerability. He thanked Hoover for the information and, with an eye on the rest of the White House Staff, promised to "destroy whoever did this."[38]

This was not the only time Kissinger had suspected Halperin. In September 1969 Nixon pressured Kissinger to stop detrimental leaks to the press. Columnist Joseph Kraft reported a result of Nixon and Kissinger doing everything themselves: "many men—including top NSC people—with important business are 'shut out.'" Nixon asked Kissinger, "Did anyone on your staff talk to Kraft on these lines?" Kissinger replied, "I have no way of knowing the source." He allowed that "it could well be that Mort Halperin contributed. However, I have no evidence." Kissinger himself had spoken to Kraft "prior to publication of the article and it was obvious that he had been given some erroneous information." Kissinger tried to suppress the article but the best he could do was "get him to tone down the treatment somewhat."[39]

The publication of word of the attacks had not done any real damage to the American military effort, since the bombing had not achieved its goal in the first place of stopping the transportation of supplies. Whatever benefits would come from the public perception of greater

American "toughness." The National Security Adviser may have been whistling in the wind, because his only patron, the President, was obviously at wits' end at the newspaper reports. They meant that the White House could not guard its most sensitive secrets, could only embarrass Secretary of State Rogers, maybe to the point of goading him into a public fight with Kissinger and Nixon. Moreover, Nixon worried that Kissinger might be disloyally trying to distance himself from failed efforts. Given his suspicion of intellectuals, the eastern press, Harvard, and that vague thing, the establishment, and recalling his rough treatment at Nelson Rockefeller's hands Nixon could easily see Kissinger as a cat's paw of all his enemies.[40]

For his part Kissinger wanted to demonstrate his loyalty to Nixon, for without him he could not do anything. Accordingly he agreed with Haldeman to monitor the telephone conversations of some of his aides suspected of having spoken to the *Times*. Kissinger explained that "the idea of wiretapping has always been distasteful to me . . . but the divulging of sensitive information in violation of trust was, and is, also distasteful to me." Kissinger therefore permitted his deputy, Colonel Alexander Haig, to visit the FBI. J. Edgar Hoover reported to Attorney General John Mitchell that "Haig, who is assigned to Dr. Henry A. Kissinger's staff, came to this Bureau to advise that a request was being made on the highest authority . . . that telephone surveillance" be placed on four NSC staffers, Morton Halperin, Anthony Lake, Winston Lord, and Roger Morris.[41] Haig told a congressional committee in 1974 that "Dr. Kissinger gave [the names] to me, but I must say I had the distinct impression that I was confirming a decision already conveyed to the Bureau."[42] Haig reported that contents of the tapped conversations was provided in personal meetings between the FBI officers and "either Kissinger and myself. Subsequently there were written memoranda addressed to both Dr. Kissinger and the President."[43]

The Cambodia bombing shook Halperin. No longer did he believe that the Nixon administration looked for a graceful way to leave the war. His respect for Kissinger also plunged. He wondered whether his superior was more interested in securing the good opinion of his patron than in developing a sensible strategy for ending the war. Halperin told other staffers of his misgivings and strongly dissented to Kissinger about the bombing. Kissinger, aware that Halperin had made his unhappiness known, and concerned that the Californians in the rest of the White House staff would have trouble distinguishing Halperin, an Ivy League intellectual, from Kissinger felt the need for protection. He also worried that his own ties to previous Democratic administrations made him suspect. Kissinger explained that had partisanship gone too far "I would have been subject to tapping because I was a friend of both Jack and Robert Kennedy. I had worked for [Undersecretary of State Nicholas deB.] Katzenbach. . . . In 1967 I conducted negotiations with the North Vietnamese for [Averell] Harriman and Katzenbach." He told Senator Edmund Muskie that "there is no doubt that some of my colleagues in the White House were very upset that I alone of the senior officials in the White House had brought on my staff individuals who had been closely identified with the previous administration or administrations [Lake and Halperin]. . . . There is also no doubt that the admiration of Mr. Hoover for the Kennedy family was very limited."[44]

While hoping on the one hand to show Nixon and Haldeman that no one on his staff had been the culprit, Kissinger did not stop with taps on Halperin's telephone. Roger Morris and Anthony Lake, two junior foreign service officers who had close ties to former Johnson administration officials, also had their families' intimacies revealed to the eavesdroppers' devices. The taps revealed no evidence that the aides had said anything to journalists that indicated they had been the sources of the leaks. Nixon explained to John Dean at the height of the Watergate coverup: "Lake and Halperin, they're both bad. But the taps were too. They never helped us, just gobs and gobs of material: gossip and bullshitting."[45] Kissinger himself reported that he could tell Nixon that whoever had informed the reporters the source had not been the NSC staff. When a Senator later asked Kissinger "Was the Beecher source ever discovered?" the Secretary of State replied "no."[46]

By the time the information reached Nixon that the professional staff had not been the source of the press leaks another, greater, problem had arisen in the conduct of the war. On April 30, 1970 Nixon announced that hundreds of United States troops were leading another twenty thousand ARVN regulars across the border into Cambodia in another effort at finding the elusive headquarters of the Communist forces in South Vietnam. He railed that "if when the chips are down, the world's most powerful nation acts like a pitiful, helpless giant, the forces of totalitarianism and anarchy will then threaten free nations and free institutions throughout the world. . . . If we fail to meet this challenge all other nations will be on notice that despite its overwhelming power, the United States, when the real crisis comes, will be found wanting."[47]

Kissinger helped plan the invasion but drew back from Nixon's overheated rhetoric. The NSC staff presented options on April 22. Members of the Washington Special Action Group agreed to a military move into Cambodia, but divided over whether American troops should participate. Secretary of State Rogers demurred while Secretary of Defense Laird and the Joint Chiefs of Staff favored the use of GI's. Kissinger saw advantages in toughness. He presented the plan to go ahead to Nixon at Camp David. Morris recalls Nixon saying "If this doesn't work, it'll be your ass, Henry." Turning to his friend Charles "Bebe" Rebozo Nixon went on, "Ain't that right, Bebe."[48] Kissinger then pleaded with the President to leave the formal announcement up to the Pentagon. It should be just another military operation, not a major presidential initiative. This advice ignored, Kissinger awaited the storm.

Kissinger strolled through the Rose Garden with Nixon and Ronald Ziegler, White House Press Secretary, listening to his boss explain a line of "cold steel—no give." He agreed that the supportive congressional leadership had shown "enthusiasm." They were "ballsy," Nixon said, and that was "not just routine."[49]

Soon, however, Kissinger's behavior in the Cambodian invasion alarmed Nixon. He demanded that Haldeman "get K. off the press." He "takes too long" with reporters. The President thought his Security Assistant was "not good with the cabinet—he can't handle Rogers and Laird." Just as Kissinger bolstered Nixon's opinion of himself, his patron wondered "where can K. get ego gratification?" The rest of the staff "have to point K. to where he can be of help." Maybe he could speak to "Wall Street" or "congressmen."[50] In return, Kissinger told Haldeman how to handle Nixon. Rogers and Laird "must talk affirmatively to the President," Kissinger advised. They should not "emote or discourage the President." Above all "don't bring problems to the President."[51]

The invasion touched off the most massive antiwar demonstrations on college campuses of the Vietnam era. Kissinger told Gerald Astor, Look's senior editor, that Vietnam was not one of the "greatest moral issues." Instead student antiwar protesters had been led astray because "they lack models, they have no heroes, they see no great purpose in the world."[52] The students' rebellion provoked a miniature rebellion among the NSC staff, with three key aides Halperin, Lake, and Morris resigning in protest. Kissinger demanded loyalty to the policy. "We are the President's men and we must behave like them!" he told his staff. The resignations of the three key aides "represented the epitome of the cowardice of the Eastern establishment." He told friends that "there is a great need to rally around our leader, because only then will plans for getting out of Vietnam succeed."[53]

At this time Nora Beloff turned an English journalist's eye on Kissinger. She noted that "Many people, at home and abroad, assumed that when Kissinger spoke of 'an honorable peace' he was disguising an American decision to give up and give in. It came as a shock to discover that he really did believe that the Saigon regime was an essential partner in any future settlement, and that consequently the war must go on for the time being."[54]

Another reporter, Joseph Kraft, found the real Kissinger an elusive figure. He wrote that "Kissinger tries to come on as the secret good guy of the Nixon foreign policy establishment. Actually when set against the dovish temper of the country . . . he works to legitimize the President's hard-line instincts on most international issues." Because of his unerring ability to express the President's wishes while maintaining credibility with the press, Kraft labeled him "the second most powerful man in the world." Kraft described how "Inevitably, Kissinger was drawn to the hardliner who showed least disposition to yield. Between the President and Kissinger there was established a professional and psychic bond far deeper than previous presidents developed with their chief foreign policy assistants."[55]

The *Nation* concluded that "in Nixon's domestic war strategy, Kissinger's role is that of pacifying the intellectuals." The liberal weekly reported on Kissinger's meeting with academics and opinion leaders in the wake of the Cambodian invasion. He calmed the audience with, "We are trying to end the war. . . . The trend line is down and I assure you it will continue to go down." But he pleaded with liberal critics of the war to be patient lest a right wing backlash overwhelm the country. "If we had done in the first year what our loudest critics called on us to do," he explained, "the 13 percent that voted for Wallace would have grown to 35 or 40 percent; the first thing the President set out to do was to neutralize that faction." He even suggested that he and Nixon had been the liberals' secret benefactor. "This administration has been the best protection of those who most loudly deplore our policy."[56] One antiwar protester who met with Kissinger later told a *Washington Post* columnist "he's got this weird thing for us who operate out of the morality bag; he sees himself as the conscience of the administration."[57] Yet he presented a different face to the President. While contemplating success in the Vietnam negotiations, he became vindictive. "As soon as we harvest Vietnam," he predicted, we "should turn on the liberals and attack them. We could destroy them then."[58]

John Osborne of the *New Republic* also thought that "his main contribution to Vietnam and Indochina policy has been the provision and bid for a negotiated settlement." He noted forty seven meetings between Kissinger and antiwar students or professors in 1970–71. The reporter concluded that Kissinger arranged these get-togethers in part to "moderate hostility to him in the academic community." But he also took the National Security Adviser at his word when he observed that he stressed the need for "a reconciliation of society." Osborne was persuaded that Kissinger seriously believed that "the war will prove to be a greater national tragedy than it already has if the reconciliation that he tries to prepare and further with his meetings is not accomplished." Osborne reflected widespread uncertainty about how supportive Kissinger was of the Cambodian invasion. "What is known," Osborne reported," is that he was visibly and unusually uncomfortable when he explained and justified that 'incursion.' . . . [H]e was unhappy not so much with the action itself as with the belligerent rhetoric in Nixon's announcement of the action."[59]

Several of Kissinger's former Harvard colleagues berated him for betraying his academic calling by remaining in office after the invasion. He received them politely, but there was no meeting of the minds. He reflected that "they were as passionate as they were ill-informed."[60] He found the turmoil at universities symbolic of more than disagreement with the war policies of the Nixon administration. He told a reporter that "the unrest on the campuses has very deep, maybe even metaphysical causes, for it seems to me that it is a result of the seeming purposelessness of the modern bureaucratic state. . . . It is the result of thirty years of debunking by my colleagues and by myself by which the academic community has managed to take the clock apart and doesn't know how to put it back together again."[61]

The meeting with the academics ended Kissinger's formal relations with his erstwhile colleagues. He had taken a two-year leave from Harvard, and the university was notably reluctant to allow its professors more time away from their offices. Moreover, his position with the Californians in the White House had become nearly untenable with the outburst of complaints over the Cambodian war. Having staked out a reputation for toughness within the administration, he was not interested in restoring good relations with the professoriat who had very little power anyway. In the future his principal sponsors would be either within the administration itself or journalists to whom he could whisper secrets.

Militarily, the invasion of Cambodia yielded little. The American forces found no headquarters, and the ARVN regulars did not seem any better in the neighboring country than they had been for the last several years at home. The promise to remove the troops from Cambodia by the end of June took its toll too. If there was a headquarters, which no one could prove with any certainty, it could easily enough be hidden temporarily while the North Vietnamese waited for the Americans to depart the field. By the time the expeditionary force left at the end of June General Creighton Abrams, the American commander in Saigon, ruefully had to report that no headquarters had been destroyed.

The diplomatic results of the invasion seemed more promising. The outcry in the United States was not matched by similar outpourings of rage elsewhere. European allies continued to demand a speedy end to the war, but they seemed persuaded by Kissinger's and Nixon's assurances that they were moving as fast as possible to limit the commitment of American forces. The French government of President Georges Pompidou, hosting the Paris peace talks, abandoned the hostile rhetoric of its predecessor, Charles de Gaulle.

The fall of 1970 saw the bombing of the North and South increase. Kissinger publicly announced that he hoped that the government in Saigon, recently bloodied in Cambodia, would take heart from the increased destruction of the North.

But 1970 was an election year. Hawkish Democrats like Senator Henry Jackson (Wash.), Armed Service Committee Chairman John Stennis (Miss.) or House Armed Service Chairman Mendel Rivers (S.C.) could be counted upon to back whatever Nixon or Kissinger decided to do in Indochina. Yet many other Democrats were not so docile. Senate Majority Leader Mike Mansfield had called for a deescalation of the war in 1967. He believed that the United States had committed too many resources abroad, and in 1969 introduced a resolution demanding the removal of most of the American forces from Europe and Korea. Arkansas Senator J. William Fulbright had been a major dissenter from the War in Vietnam beginning in 1965. His hearing of February 1966 concentrated on the inadequacies of the assumptions underlying the continuous confrontation with revolutionary nationalism.

In 1970 the Foreign Relations Committee was at it again. Senator Stuart Symington (D.-Mo.) convened a series of hearings on the extent of United States overseas promises. For three months the Committee on Foreign Relations heard scores of witnesses denounce the current commitment of hundreds of thousands of United States forces in Europe, the Middle East and Asia. Symington, who formerly had a reputation as one of the foremost supporters of the commitment of United States forces overseas, now thought that the cost was too high. He joined with Senator Fulbright to complain that the American economy could not bear the cost of its war and its overseas bases. Whenever the stock market went down during the hearings, opposition senators gloated. A ten-point slide in the Dow Jones industrial averages drew from Fulbright that "the United States cannot afford" all of its overseas commitments.[62]

Ridding Congress of such obstreperous critics and replacing them with safe Republicans who could be counted upon to keep quiet and support the administration's initiatives became the goal of the 1970 election efforts of the Nixon White House.

Nixon used Kissinger to neutralize talk that Ho Chi Minh had a superior grasp of the situation. A reporter wrote that the North Vietnamese leader believed that the 1970 congressional elections could be a lever against the Americans. If he waited, Nixon would be forced to make concessions. The writer went on in awe about Ho's "uncanny ability to predict successfully what LBJ and RN would do . . . even before they know themselves." Nixon and Kissinger wanted the press to refer to them, not Ho, as men who predicted the future better than others. Nixon ordered Kissinger to see that this sort of reasoning was "knocked down now."[63]

Democrats capitalized on Nixon's stridency. Senator Edmund Muskie, the vice presidential candidate in 1968, delivered the official Democratic message to voters on the Sunday before the voting. Seated before a roaring fire, and speaking in a calm, reassuring voice, Muskie's craggy face and huge frame provided a sharp contrast to the administration. Nixon found that his carefully constructed attempts to appear as a moderate, skilled diplomat were overturned. When the final votes were counted, the Democrats had gained eleven seats in the House, while the Republicans had seized two from the Democrats in the Senate. The President had hoped for a far better showing, but he was able to note that the White House now had an "ideological majority" in the Congress that would assemble in January 1971.[64]

Muskie's strong appearance before the election indicated that the former vice presidential candidate was the front runner for the Democratic nomination in 1972. If he continued to project an image of quiet competence in contrast to the emotional excesses of the Nixon administration, the Democrats, as the majority party, might regain the White House in 1972.

Problems seemed likely to increase, however. None of the leadership positions had changed in the new Congress. Senator Mansfield was still the Majority Leader, and his complaints about the cost of maintaining a forward foreign policy, with the large commitment of troops in Europe and Vietnam, would only mount. Fulbright still chaired the Foreign Relations panel, and nothing that had happened over the past four months had altered his perception that the war had to end quickly. Younger senators like Idaho Democrat Frank Church, Oregon Republican Mark Hatfield, or Massachusetts Democrat Edward M. Kennedy insisted that the American role in the war must end soon.[65] They would reintroduce legislation abrogating the Gulf of Tonkin resolution of 1964. They planned as well to take a hard look at the money flowing from Washington to Saigon. They wanted to reduce the number of missions flown by United States bombers in the South, and end bombing completely in the North. They grew restive at the slow pace of the Paris peace negotiations, and complained that the United States should show more good faith. They wanted the official negotiators to lean more on the Saigon government, and directly respond to the proposals of the NLF and the North Vietnamese.

Perhaps worst of all from the point of view of the White House, the congressional elections of 1970 demonstrated that public patience was wearing thin. Elected in 1968 to end the war as quickly as possible, with as few American casualties as possible, by the end of 1971 Nixon found himself as the official responsible for the continuation of the war. Nixon alerted Kissinger to the "attempt to keep the war up front as an issue" when the television networks led with reports on the high level of combat in Vietnam.[66] During the Laotian incursion of 1971 Kissinger helped organize the campaign to convince the public the "President will not go out of Vietnam whimpering." If there were no breakthrough by November the United States should play its "hole card—bomb North Vietnam totally. . . . Turn right all the way."[67]

Kissinger also continued skirmishes with Roger and Laird. He tried to prevent them from joining the meetings with President Thieu in Midway in June 1971. He decided to "ease into it" with Rogers and explain that "the President asked [Kissinger] to go" to Midway. He hoped the same strategy might work with Laird too.[68] Kissinger also resented congressional efforts to force the pace of diplomacy. "Setting a deadline is totally inconsistent with cease-fire negotiations and release of POWs," he complained to Nixon. If such mischievous resolutions passed Congress the "enemy's incentive would be eliminated."[69]

Yet praise from Congress prompted Nixon to have Kissinger offer special access to the White House. Nixon's staff reported that Senator William Saxbe, upon returning from a tour, believed "we're going to be out of combat—and VN itself—faster than a lot of people expect." A pleased President scrawled "good—thank him for RN. K.—have him in for a report."[70]

Vietnam policy publicly took a back seat in the summer of 1971, as other issues competed for attention from Kissinger and Nixon. Détente with the Soviet Union proceeded, the *New York Times* published the Pentagon Papers, and, most of all, planning went forward for the trip to China. The convergence of all of these events made Kissinger more than usually testy about any outside interefence with his work. Alexander Haig, Kissinger's deputy, explained his boss's attitude upon the release of the Pentagon Papers. The *Times* had committed a "criminally traitorous" act. Publication "doesn't hurt us— it *does* hurt the war. It *will* cause terrible problems with South Vietnam." The key for the Nixon administration was "to *keep out of it*."[71] Charles Colson took a tougher line. He advised administration spokesmen to "point out that the bad guys and spies are all left wing Democrats. . . . Those who got us into trouble can't be trusted to get us out of trouble."[72]

Kissinger's fury was mainly directed toward the State Department official who delivered the Papers to Daniel Ellsberg. The administration was "too soft on Cook. Why did he show [the document] to Ellsberg? What was his right to know?"[73] Kissinger believed that the Pentagon Papers altered the prospect for diplomacy. "Now everything's domestic politics," he mourned. He feared he would "never have a chance again" if the present Paris conversations failed. Talking with Nixon and his other aides made Kissinger want to sound tough and avoid any suspicion of Ivy League effeteness. Thus he was pleased to note that the Papers revealed Hubert Humphrey's "yellow streak." The country now saw "his Chappaquidick." Ehrlichman was more politically astute. He greeted the possibility of the Supreme Court ruling in favor of the *Times* with equanimity. He told the President it was "OK to try but fail [to block publication] soon." The public would see that we had "done our part." After that, "let it come out." In his view "it's going to come out anyway" and it is "worse to keep it in."[74]

Even after the Supreme Court ruled in favor of the *Times* Kissinger opposed releasing the remainder of the documents to friendly news-papers. "Maintain the principle of security of the government," he advised. "Don't give the Papers out."[75] Sometimes Kissinger's com-bative secrecy alarmed even his own staff. The controversy over the Papers provoked Haig to side with Rogers in the ongoing dispute with the National Security Adviser. The Secretary of State "is right" Haig said. "Kissinger should not have seen Harriman" to discuss the status of the talks with the chief American negotiator in 1968.[76]

Kissinger used the opening to China to quiet congressional rest-lessness over Vietnam. While briefing the bipartisan leadership of the House and Senate on his return from China he warned that "any speculation regarding Vietnam—in any way—will be totally *coun-terproductive.*"[77] In the euphoric days after his return from China Kis-singer predicted a 50 percent chance of a Vietnam settlement in Au-gust. He suggested "we have to hang on somehow." The key was American support for Thieu. Kissinger promised "we will not over-throw him." That was "not in the American character."[78]

Throughout the summer of 1971 Kissinger flew to Paris to continue a secret dialogue with North Vietnam's Le Duc Tho and Xuan Thuy. The Communists proved difficult interlocutors. They reiterated ear-lier positions: They did not require the immediate end to the Saigon government or "Thieu-Ky clique," as the Communists insisted on calling the authorities to the infinite annoyance of the Americans. But the government had to go eventually. Xuan pressed harder, however, for the United States to leave immediately and stop aiding the Saigon authorities. They in turn had to pledge to open their regime to a co-alition with the NLF. More galling yet to the Americans and South Vietnamese was the refusal even to discuss continued northern pres-ence on the southern battlefields. Xuan would not acknowledge that there were any of his nation's troops in the south, so Kissinger's pleas that he at least promise to send no more troops against the ARVN made no impression. Xuan stressed that there was no such thing as two Vietnams, so it made no sense to speak about an invasion from Hanoi.

Kissinger thought, however, that he detected a loosening in the Communist position. Le Duc Tho seemed to indicate that although he would make no commitments regarding the future of Communist forces in the South, the important subject was the presence of the Americans there. Once they left, he implied, then the North would be much more accommodating to Washington's requests for a speedy end to the fighting.

Unfortunately for the American conception of what the North Vietnamese would and would not accept, Le Duc Tho never acknowledged, either publicly or by winks and nods, that he was engaged in the same enterprise as the Americans. The idea that the private conversations might yield some sort of grudging admiration between the two sides never seemed to enter his mind. While Kissinger hoped that the bargainers might sit down to resolve a complicated issue, treat one another with respect as had gentlemen of old, and keep their passions studiously outside the negotiating chamber, Le thought otherwise. He maintained that the United States had come to Vietnam as an aggressor and the only way to resolve the issue peaceably would be for the Americans to acknowledge their "crimes" by getting out.

To Kissinger, whose model for diplomatic arrangements was the concert of Europe system of the nineteenth century, this behavior was inexplicable. Here was the United States, an incomparably greater power than France and certainly than of Vietnam, asking for some face-saving gesture. Instead of leaping at the chance of ridding his country of the Americans, Le seemed bent on humiliating them. By late 1971, Kissinger had accordingly concluded that the only way Hanoi could be made to negotiate seriously was to be faced with the prospect of the United States using its overwhelming military power, especially its heavy bombers, to bring Hanoi to its knees. Maybe then the North's negotiators would acknowledge the right of a great power to leave the war on its own terms.[79]

By the end of 1971, therefore, Kissinger had failed to isolate Vietnam from the debate over the future of American foreign policy. He enjoyed notable success with the press, but many members of Congress and the public were impatient for results. His position within the Nixon administration was also precarious. The President needed him; but other aides did not fully trust him. Kissinger too was on the spot. He had promised much with his reorganization of the apparatus of foreign affairs, but few tangible results could yet be seen. Something had to happen in the next year to burnish the reputation of the Nixon administration in foreign affairs. Otherwise, the political clock would make it impossible for the White House to show progress in time for November 1972.

THREE

The Perils of Détente

One of the most fruitful areas of possible foreign policy success lay in improving relations between the United States and the Soviet Union. Over the years Henry Kissinger, as one of the principal realist analysts of foreign relations, had outlined elements of the East–West conflict. Realists had dissented from some tactics used by American diplomats during the cold war. He had complained that Americans expected to vanquish the Soviets. "Managing" the relationship was a more realistic outcome.

George F. Kennan's famous 1947 dissection of "The Sources of Soviet Conduct" indicated that the United States must subtly apply containment until the Soviets changed their ways. After 1948, Kennan had dissented sharply from the militarization of the confrontation. He opposed the NATO alliance and left the State Department in 1950.[1] Kissinger never was so bold in the fifties and sixties as to suggest scrapping NATO in the interests of accommodating the Soviets. Where Kennan called for the neutralization of central Europe and the simultaneous removal of United States and Soviet troops from the region, Kissinger recommended more modest adjustments in the working of the western alliance.[2]

As part of the Atlantic Policy studies of the Council on Foreign Relations Kissinger dealt with the challenges to the American stake in Europe posed by French President Charles de Gaulle's call for a Europe united from the Atlantic to the Urals. France under de Gaulle moved toward its own accommodation with the Soviet Union, regardless of the wishes of the United States. The French President traveled to Moscow in June 1966 to broker the end of the cold war.

C. L. Sulzberger of the *New York Times* called the warm reception in the Kremlin, the first of a western leader in the Soviet inner sanctum since the November 1917 Revolution, an "icebreaker." The French president projected a Europe free from American influences, one where the Soviets would relax their grip on their Eastern European neighbors.[3]

At the same time, a new government in West Germany altered Bonn's view of East–West relations. The grand coalition of Christian Democrats and Social Democrats, which put the Socialists' leader Willy Brandt in charge of the foreign ministry, looked to normalize relations with East Germany, Poland, and the Soviet Union. After Brandt became chancellor, he expanded his Ostpolitik with a visit to Poland in which he acknowledged the validity of the Oder-Neisse river line as the boundary between Poland and East Germany. The Soviet-backed Polish government had adopted the Oder-Neisse line at the end of the Second World War as the official boundary, but the Federal Republic had never acknowledged a border that included much traditional German territory. Brandt traveled to Warsaw in 1969 and indicated that Bonn now accepted the permanent boundaries of postwar Poland. In 1969 Brandt offered the Soviets a nonaggression pact between NATO and the Communist world.[4]

Kissinger had studied some of these developments as part of the Atlantic Policy Studies. These volumes had attempted to create a new United States policy toward the alliance. Kissinger suggested that the United States pay respectful attention to European concerns. Kissinger likened Washington's relations with the Atlantic allies to that of a father with grown children. The United States, he wrote, "can always take the attitude that, since their interests are identical he [the father] will continue to control all the resources." He indicated that Washington could either maintain the Europeans on a short leash and run the risk of their resentments festering or it could allow them some additional freedom in the hope that greater independence would eventually result in closer ties among equals.[5]

The Johnson administration took tentative steps in the direction of reducing tensions with the Soviets. When Soviet premier Alexei Kosygin attended the special United Nations General Assembly session in the aftermath of the six-day Arab–Israeli war in June 1967 he met Johnson at Glassboro State College in southern New Jersey. The two leaders agreed to open discussions on reducing their nuclear arsenals despite the differences over the Middle East and the war in Vietnam.[6]

When the Nixon administration took over, arms control talks had reached a critical point. The United States had reached the technological point of developing an effective antiballistic missile system. Although Secretary of Defense Robert S. McNamara in one of his last acts before leaving the Pentagon for the World Bank in December 1967 had stopped production on the ABM, the Johnson administration kept the option alive in its last year.

Kissinger understood the dangers in an ABM—that it might encourage the other side to embark upon a vast increase in the number of missiles to flood the ABM. But technological developments often proceed despite political opposition. President Nixon begged Congress to continue work on the ABM to provide his negotiators with a "bargaining chip" in the arms control negotiations with the Soviets. Senator Albert Gore (D.-Tenn.) derided such reasoning and called the ABM "a weapon in search of a mission," but in August 1969 the Senate approved the ABM by one vote.[7]

The nuclear arms race had interested Kissinger since writing *Nuclear Weapons and Foreign Policy* in 1957. For the most part he argued that strategic nuclear weapons were not actually for use but for deterrence. He amplified these notions in *The Necessity for Choice* (1961). Here he suggested that smaller, tactical nuclear weapons had a battlefield role, but the larger strategic bombs had a use mostly as threats to terrorize a civilian population or leadership. Most American strategists who helped develop the notions of Mutual Assured Destruction in the 1960s took pains to make the Soviets aware of their calculations. The strategy of mutual deterrence could work only if both sides accepted it as a valid approach. If the Soviets could be made to see that their interests were served by a deterrence strategy, then they might have certain interests in common with the United States. Kissinger did not, however, press arms control as vital to this process. Kissinger thought that the arms controllers took too seriously the danger of a nuclear war. While possible, nuclear war was unlikely and had been so since 1949 when the Soviets had developed their own atomic weapons. As he charged in 1961 "the most vocal and passionate advocates of arms control have . . . [too often] given the impression that simply because the goal is important it can be reached easily." He urged Americans to acknowledge that "without arms control stability will be more difficult to achieve. But it probably can be achieved even then."[8]

In the late 1960s détente appeared as both a relaxation of tension between two suspicious adversaries—the classic definition of the term in traditional diplomacy—and a common interest in keeping other, lesser powers from upsetting the nuclear balance. Proliferation of weapons outside the hands of the major powers became a problem in 1962 when France exploded its own independent "force de frappe" and in 1964 when the People's Republic of China touched off a device of their own. Both of these countries had tenuous alliances with one or another of the nuclear giants, but neither Washington nor Moscow could trust its ostensible partner. How much worse would the situation be if nuclear weapons spread to nations in the southern hemisphere or the Middle East bound to neither of the colossi![9]

Central to Kissinger's notion of détente was the idea that the Soviet Union would not go away or change its social system. For Kissinger internal developments were less important than a country's external policies. The Soviets, for their part, had to repudiate Nikita Khrushchev's boast to the west "we shall bury you." A "mature" relationship between East and West meant that each acknowledged the legitimate interests of the other. The two would try to reach accommodations where they could and try not to let their disagreements spread to poison remaining areas of concern. Kissinger expressed these sentiments as early as the 1950s when he decried Americans for their excessive "empiricism" in foreign affairs. Too many American diplomats came from legal or business backgrounds where "nothing is true unless it is objective! And it is not objective unless it is part of experience." Schooled in the art of drawing up contracts from business deals American diplomats conduct "deliberations . . . as if a course of action were eternally valid, as if a policy which might meet exactly the needs of a given moment could not backfire if adopted a year later."[10]

Political successes came as Moscow and Washington acknowledged the need for arms control. Kissinger moved in an atmosphere of congressional skepticism regarding the antiballistic system. Restless Republican senators, looking for a middle ground between opposing the Safeguard and breaking with the White House, explored a mutual moratorium with the Soviets on testing and deployment of strategic weapons. Fearful of losing control of the process, Nixon ordered Kissinger to "contain this kind of nonsense." Democratic Senator Edmund Muskie observed that "the illusion of national security offered by the ABM offers no sanctuary against hunger, poverty and ignorance. Hunger and poverty are more dangerous than Communism." Nixon told Kissinger that this was "unbelievable nonsense from a national 'leader'!"[11]

Lobbies of scientists led by the Federation of American Scientists, or the Council for a Liveable World, predicted disaster if the United States deployed its ABM. The Soviets were bound to do the same. ABM systems could not knock out every incoming missile, so each side would have an incentive to build more missiles and flood the adversary's defenses. More destabilizing still was the prospect of the side behind in the development of the ABM toying with the idea of a preemptive strike before the other's defense system was operational. All of these objections led Senators Frank Church (D.-Ida.), Albert Gore (D.-Tenn.), Edward M. Kennedy (D.-Mass.), Edmund Muskie (D.-Me.), Walter Mondale (D.-Mn.), and John Sherman Cooper (R.-Ky.) to oppose the ABM.[12]

Kissinger and Nixon resented the congressional interference even as they acknowledged the accuracy of the criticism. Nixon described the ABM as vital as a bargaining chip in the arms negotiations. He announced that far from "complicat[ing] an agreement with the Soviet Union," a modified ABM would "give the Soviet Union even less reason to view our defense efforts as an obstacle to talks."[13] The NSC chief dismissed concerns about the supposedly destabilizing effects of the ABM, since "Soviet leaders and military theorists had never espoused the western academic notions that vulnerability was desirable or that the ABM was threatening or destabilizing."[14] At the same time he feared having American arms policy dictated by Congress. He scoffed that "we could sell an ABM program to the Congress apparently only by depriving it of military effectiveness against our principal adversary." Later on he exploded that "congressional insistence and bureaucratic demoralization resulted in 1975 in a unilateral decision" to scrap the one ABM site permitted by the 1972 SALT agreement.[15]

He looked backed fondly to the time when members of the national legislature in the aftermath of the Second World War had excused themselves from questioning the need for any weapons proposal brought forth by the military or the administration. Earlier members of Congress had in fact been interested in weapons systems only when they could be built in their districts. This was fine for Kissinger, for it meant that Congress saw its role as the parochial defense of local interests. Once, however, representatives and senators began commenting on the international implications of individual weapons, the President's control over foreign policy quickly eroded. Were Congress successful in blocking the ABM or the MIRV (Multiple Independently Targeted Reentry Vehicle), the legislators would take the bit between their teeth and question other foreign policy actions.

To avoid this unhappy state of affairs Kissinger pressed arms control at the presidential level. He told Congress that interference with the deployment of the ABM or MIRVs would wreck delicate conversations. Kissinger scoffed that congressional meddlers pressed the administration to "abandon our ABM without reciprocity . . . and postpone our MIRV deployment as a unilateral gesture—in short to forego both our missile defense and the means to defeat that already deployed by the Soviet Union."[16]

Kissinger carefully cultivated his position as a broker between Nixon and the arms control community. He pressed for a "presidential boost" for the advisory committee on arms control headed by New York lawyer and Council on Foreign Relations figure John McCloy. Kissinger acknowledged that McCloy "has largely succumbed to the pressures of the present activists on the committee." Still, a meeting with Nixon would prevent "obvious prettification [sic] of [the committee's] activities," which "would have adverse consequences on the Congress."[17]

Meanwhile, Gerard Smith, head of the Arms Control and Disarmament Agency who was meeting the Soviets in Vienna to conclude an agreement with them regarding arms, argued that the ABM should not stand in the way of an effective settlement of the more important question of the number of missile launchers. Smith told his counterpart Vladimir Semenov that both sides recognized that the ABM was an ineffective weapon that frightened its owner as much as potential adversaries.[18]

Unfortunately, by the time of the Nixon administration the ABM had taken on a life of its own. Smith in Vienna continually signaled his opposite numbers that the United States wanted some way out of the morass of both powers investing heavily in destabilizing weapons. He wrote President Nixon that his opposite number, Semenov, "strikes me as a man bent on serious business. . . . He spoke of nuclear war as a disaster for both sides—of the decreased security as the number of weapons increases—of the costly results of rapid obsolescence—of the dangers of grave miscalculation—of unauthorized use of weapons—and of hostilities resulting from third power provocations."[19]

While Smith, as a State Department functionary, conducted the official negotiations with Semenov over the future of the strategic missile systems of each side, Kissinger pressed forward with his own quiet talks with Soviet ambassador Anatoly Dobrynin. The "back channel" negotiations over arms had several advantages from the White House point of view. They kept Congress outside the process.

Since Kissinger had not even publicly acknowledged that he was supervising the conversations, Congress could not intervene with embarrassing questions. Moreover, the Nixon administration maintained the doctrine of executive privilege prevented the personal advisers of the President from testifying before Congress.

The back channel to Dobrynin also allowed Kissinger to outflank the State Department. He told the Soviets that the final decisions rested in the White House, which could overrule any initiative from the State Department. Confidential conversations let Kissinger inform Dobrynin that the United States could be more flexible privately than was possible in public sessions. Kissinger indicated that the two powers had several things that bound them more to each other than to any other powers. Their very strength and interests everywhere around the world set them apart. Unlike their allies and the lesser powers in the Third World, the United States and the Soviet Union alone had the capacity to destroy the planet with their nuclear forces. They, not their allies, could project forces far beyond their shores.

In May 1971, the back channel brought positive results. Kissinger and Dobrynin divided the issue of ABMs (the primary Soviet concern) and offensive arms (the foremost American issue). They announced that their countries would "concentrate this year on working out an agreement for the limitation of the development of antiballistic missile systems. They have also agreed that, 'together with concluding an agreement to limit ABMs, they will agree on certain measures with respect to the limitation of offensive strategic weapons.'" In other words, Kissinger decided that it was easier to reach a firm commitment banning further deployment of ABMs, which did not yet exist, than it was to draft a treaty setting limits on nuclear weapons already deployed. As one observer noted, "left unresolved in the 'back channel' discussions were the specific limitations to be placed on offensive arms."[20] Some conservative Republican lawmakers carped at the new position. Senator Strom Thurmond (R.-S.C.) wrote his constituents that the United Sttaes had yielded to a Soviet demand to limit ABMs before deciding on offensive arms. "The Soviets have won their point, for all practical purposes," he said. "The U.S. is therefore set out upon a dangerous course." Nixon exploded "this is not our posture." He asked Kissinger to "straighten Thurmond out."[21]

As agreement seemed assured, Nixon and Kissinger turned their attention to their domestic rivals. The President mused to his National Security Adviser that "we have to break the back of the establishment and Democratic leadership" on the questions of SALT, defense, and the Soviet ABM.[22] Congress was not the only target. Nixon and Kissinger agreed on how to handle the press. When releasing news of the breakthrough over SALT and ABM, we "can't say [the Soviets] gave all and we gave nothing." Nixon told the cabinet "Kissinger and I have often talked" about the negotiations. "Getting this far is a result of doing the long hard process, developing U.S. position—fighting for it, knowing what we want and going for it." Nixon described the agreement as a "significant first step." It "could be [a] decisive step [but this is] not a time for euphoria."

Nixon and Kissinger wanted the information tightly controlled. They warned the cabinet "don't tell them [the rest of the bureaucracy] anything." The Russians were "very sensitive" about leaks, so American officials must "close down the curtain." The President told everyone other than Kissinger "don't speculate on where" the negotiations would go next. Leave that to Kissinger, because uninformed talk would "tie hands." The negotiators "need flexibility." Kissinger went further, explaning that "no cabinet members should speculate on what is in the agreement." As Nixon put it "the less said regarding what is going on the better. The more we talk, the less chance of an agreement."[23]

Closed lips did not last long. In early June, Secretary of State Rogers announced the probability of a trade deal with the Soviets—to which a jealous Kissinger complained about the "incurable disease of quick headlines."[24] While keeping others out of negotiations with the Soviets, Kissinger became involved in setting the defense budget. In late July Nixon lectured Kissinger about the need to "cut defense in the right way." The President complained that "never has a country spent more for less defense than does America." A few weeks later Kissinger bemoaned the fact that there is "still no reorganization of the services" and "no strategic concept."[25]

Kissinger's conversations with Dobrynin allowed the President to signal a new approach. While Nixon felt constrained by his previous public statements to appear as committed as ever to vanquishing communism, he could signal through Kissinger his appreciation of the shared concerns of the superpowers. When the time was ripe, Kissinger implied, the President would drop old cold war categories in favor of mutual recognition of common approaches to the rest of the world.

Kissinger envisaged a world order with five centers of power—the United States, the Soviet Union, Western Europe, Japan, and China. The economic and strategic positions of these five enabled each to play a major role on the world stage. The trick was to convince the Soviets that a stable world could be built on these five foundations. For fifty years successive Soviet leaders had behaved like touchy outsiders, certain of the hostility of the non-Communist world. Kissinger hoped to persuade Dobrynin and Leonid Brezhnev, the Communist Party chairman, that the United States in the 1970s had reverted once more to the cooperative stance of the Second World War.

Central to Kissinger's notion of détente was the urge to "raise the Soviets' learning curve," as the professors of strategy put it, regarding the shape of the world's pattern of competition. The major powers were supposed to agree to respect one another's primary spheres of influence, their immediate neighborhoods. The United States was to be regarded as supreme in the western hemisphere and the Soviets in Eastern Europe. Outside these primary areas of interest in the Middle East, Africa, and Southeast Asia, the two powers were supposed to act with restraint. While they might pursue their own interests, they could do so only insofar as they did not alarm the other superpower.

Kissinger never made clear precisely the sort of behavior in the Middle East, Southeast Asia and Africa the United States would consider nonthreatening to the precarious balance of power. Was moral and monetary support for an insurrectionary movement acceptable? Was the stationing of troops overseas within the rules? Was the assassination of foreign leaders inside the boundaries of the rules of the game of superpower competition? Kissinger never said.[26]

The United States would not commit itself beforehand to stating the norms of acceptable behavior outside the two spheres of influence. When, however, the Soviets did things that violated explicit and tacit understandings, the United States would then complain that the rules of détente had broken down. Kissinger believed in some subtle forms of "linkage," or the tying together of apparently unrelated issues in world politics. Accordingly, the United States would connect the agreements over trade with those on arms control; Soviet behavior in the Middle East and Africa would become part of the conversation on the level of troops each side maintained in Eastern and Western Europe.

Linkage was not always applied evenly. Ever testy and impatient with lawmakers who did not defer to his supposed grasp of international relations, Kissinger reacted furiously when Congress tried to link American favors to the Soviet Union to the Kremlin's willingness to loosen its grip on its own citizens. He derided as the worst sort of legislative grandstanding the 1973 efforts by Washington Senator Henry Jackson and Ohio Representative Charles Vanik to deny the Soviets' most favored nation status until they permitted the uninhibited emigration of their dissatisfied citizens. He charged them with "recklessness" and demanded to know "if baiting Moscow led to increased Soviet adventurism, which of our crusaders for human rights would support our determination to resist it."[27]

Kissinger complained of "the unwillingness of many nations to face the facts of interdependence. The application of ever more restrictive trade practices, the insistence of the unfettered exploitation of the national advantage, threatens the world with a return of the beggarthy-neighbor policies of the thirties." There was little or no proven connection between the application of U.S. trade laws and another nation's behavior. Most of all, the extension of benefits to the Communists was meant as an economic and political benefit to the United States. Denying these benefits would diminish trade without helping emigration. Kissinger reported to the Senate Committee considering the Jackson amendment in 1974 that the Nixon administration had favored "quiet representations on the issue of emigration. We were never indifferent nor did we condone restrictions placed on immigration. . . . We believed, based on repeated Soviet statements and experience, that making the issue a subject of state-to-state relations might have an adverse effect on emigration from the USSR as well as jeopardize the basic relationship which had made the steadily rising emigration possible in the first place. We were convinced that our most effective means for exerting beneficial influence was by working for a broad improvement in relations and dealing with emigration by informal means."[28]

On August 15, 1971 Nixon announced a sweeping new set of economic proposals. He slapped controls on wages and prices for the next six months. Thereafter, any upward adjustments in prices or wages would have to be approved by a federal panel. On the international front, he notified the membership of the International Monetary Fund that the United States no longer would redeem its dollars for gold. Ending the gold link effectively devalued the dollar. The price of the American currency was allowed to find its own level versus the currencies of the other major trading powers. Over the next five months, the value of the dollar fell fifteen percent against other currencies.[29]

An economic decision had been taken without much input from Kissinger. It came less than one month after his dramatic trip to China. At that time the allies had also complained that their wishes were being systematically ignored. The journey to Zhou Enlai had indicated that the United States was so powerful militarily that it did not have to consult with its partners. In the military balance between East and West there could be no other players than the United States, the Soviets, and the Chinese. Allies were ignored because they were so insignificant. Economically, on the other hand, the swift Nixon reversal meant that the United States was so weak it could not let its allies know of its intentions.

Kissinger found himself in the uncomfortable position of having to justify a policy he had not created on a subject he did not fully comprehend. One former aide joked that "being economics adviser to Henry Kissinger was like being military adviser to the Pope." Another noted at the time "Henry will get involved when economic problems threaten his political and military strategies. He just doesn't think he has to bother with details of economic issues on a regular basis."[30]

Things got worse in the fall when Nixon appointed former Texas Governor John Connally, a conservative Democrat, to be Secretary of the Treasury. Connally's ascendency to one of the premier spots in the cabinet represented Nixon's choice as a potential successor. He might foretell a shift of other conservative Democrats into the Republican Party. Unlike other cabinet secretaries, whom Kissinger could intimidate or dominate, Connally had the security of a political base in Texas. Nixon needed him more than Connally needed Nixon. Kissinger discovered that Connally could present an economic policy that served political ends but also would alarm partners in Europe and Japan.

Throughout the fall of 1971 Connally delayed setting a new value for the dollar in terms of other nations' currencies. Japan and the Europeans wondered if the new Treasury Secretary indeed sought an equitable solution to the trade imbroglio. Former National Security Adviser Walt Rostow reported that Kissinger and other officials were "much upset" with Connally. According to Rostow, the Treasury Secretary's rivals believed that "Connally appears to be using the bargaining leverage acquired by President Nixon's economic program . . . not to negotiate a settlement with our major partners but to raise a series of ultimatums. . . . [H]e is overplaying his hand; he has no clear and viable idea of the disputed matters of money and trade. . . . " According to Henry Brandon of the *London Sunday Times*, European objections aroused Kissinger who "suddenly realized" their distress "could imperil American foreign policy on the central diplomatic front." The National Security Adviser consulted economics professors Richard Cooper of Yale and Francis Bator of Harvard who recommended that the United States refrain from pressing the Europeans too hard. They advocated a quick return to negotiated fixed exchange rates.[31]

Armed with this report and fearful that Connally had accumulated power at the expense of the State Department and National Security Council, Kissinger urged Nixon to pay attention to the problem. Kissinger alerted the President to "the dangers of further delay in a monetary settlement, the damage that could develop to world trading relationships and to American trading security interests." By late November Nixon had come round to Kissinger's view that an international agreement was necessary.[32]

Facing these challenges to his political authority, Kissinger wanted to demonstrate that relations between the United States and the Soviet Union were directed by the White House. Bureaucratic rivals had parochial interests. The Arms Control and Disarmament Agency under Gerard Smith wanted credit for controlling the arms race. As Smith described the team assembled to negotiate with the Soviets, "while the delegates held different views on a number of major issues, the surprising thing was the degree of harmony that existed between personalities who had long been used to 'running their own shops,' whether it was a weapons laboratory, a military service or a major embassy."[33] From Smith's point of view the purpose of the negotiations at Vienna was to reach an agreement on arms. "We should avoid wasting time on obviously inequitable propositions—especially when that time is being better used by the other side," he recalled in frustration over the long experience in Vienna and Helsinki.[34]

For Kissinger arms control talks had the larger purpose of assuring each side of the other's good intentions. Success in SALT would mean that the United States and the Soviet Union had finally come to acknowledge the rights of one another to peaceably inhabit the same planet.

To keep the negotiations focused on the political aims of creating good feelings between the United States and the Soviet Union was the goal of the White House. For Kissinger, pursuing a strategy of virtually endless competition with the Soviet Union, it hardly mattered which side had the formal military balance. Neither was likely to press that advantage to the point of actual warfare. Accordingly, it was more important that an agreement be reached between the two sides, demonstrating that the relationship could be managed, than it was to make sure that every military precaution was taken. He patronized Smith's concerns for his delegation: "It was only human that they wanted to play a central role at the turning points which they and their dedication had made possible. It was not their fault that the key decisions were political, involving domestic and foreign policy considerations for both sides. At the same time we could not slow our efforts to resolve deadlocked issues simply to maintain the morale of our delegation."[35]

For his part Smith felt undercut by the White House during three hard years of negotiations. He assembled a team of experts who knew the intricacies of the strategic balance between the two sides. Smith wanted to be more cautious on the technical questions, while less mindful of the political repercussions of the talks. Accordingly, he pressed Washington to drop the ABM as a highly dangerous system. If it actually were deployed it might end forever the chance to get a handle on the arms race. Smith, a technician, considered Nixon and Kissinger excessively concerned about appearances and political advantage. He thought that they pressed the ABM in order to appear tough before hardline members of Congress and conservative spokesmen. Such pandering to the baser instincts of nationalism was unworthy of sophisticated politicians. Smith feared that politicians, trying to carry water on both shoulders, would be unable to make the hard choices necessary for reaching an agreement. He recalled the frustrations of learning too late about the back channel negotiations of Kissinger and Dobrynin by likening it to an epigraph from Frederick the Great, "If I had thought my coat knew what my plans were, I would take it off and burn it."[36] When Kissinger first let him know that he had been speaking to Dobrynin for over a year and showed him a draft of the May 1971 announcement he sputtered that "the drafting was imprecise and the 'agreement to agree' would be criticized." For Smith, Kissinger's position would result in endless conversations without reaching a formal treaty.[37]

Smith took a tougher position regarding missiles actually in place. He took seriously technical points raised by the military. They worried that the Soviet Union, which relied on greater destructive power of their bombs to make up for the American advantage in accuracy of warheads, might look for high limits on total numbers of missiles. Under these circumstances they could overwhelm the United States forces.

Smith stressed the importance of arms control for its own sake. If the world did indeed stand poised on the edge of disaster with only the fallible judgment of political leaders in Washington and Moscow preventing a holocaust, then it was important that the numbers of missiles and warheads each side possessed be accurately measured and limited. The technical experts of ACDA and the Vienna negotiating team were then the only appropriate officials to conduct the conversations. Kissinger, working out of the White House with the assistance of just forty staff members, simply did not have enough information. His notoriously poor relations with the Defense Department made the isolation of the NSC all the worse. Smith bewailed the "doubletalk" he heard coming from the White House. Every proposal he made to the Soviets seemed undercut by counteroffers originating with the White House and NSC.

Kissinger thought Smith was nitpicking. In the battles for bureaucratic preeminence the National Security Adviser wanted the NSC to win. Objections that his staff was too small or that it did not possess enough technical information made no impression. When Smith and ACDA complained that the NSC lacked information to make informed judgments, Kissinger believed they missed the point of reaching an agreement with the Soviets over arms. The actual details were less important than the fact that the two sides could come to terms on armaments.

Under this view arms control was important primarily as a signal that détente worked between the United States and the Soviet Union. When an actual Strategic Arms Limitations Interim Agreement was hammered out during the summit meeting between Richard Nixon and Leonid Brezhnev in Moscow in May 1972, Kissinger believed that the facts of signing was more important than the contents. Smith thought that the cavalier disregard for the work he had done in Vienna produced a worse agreement. One would have come eventually, he opined, but the rush to make the President look good at the summit produced a treaty that gave the Soviets advantages they did not deserve. "I questioned whether we should accept an SLBM (Submarine Launched Ballistic Missile) freeze on terms that to many would look so unequal."[38]

Smith berated Kissinger for having wasted time "in a foolish quest for an ABM arrangement." He was irritated that the National Security Adviser would not make available to him copies of the translator's notes of his conversations with Brezhnev. The ACDA head confessed that he was "flabbergasted that Kissinger had once again gone off on his own and bypassed the delegation and other officials with SALT responsibilities." Nixon expressed himself forcefully regarding

Smith's complaints. They were "bullshit," recalled the astonished diplomat, and he should keep his objections confined to "matters of substance."[39]

When Smith pointed out that Brezhnev's position, accepted in May by the administration, contained principles "that could cause trouble in the future" Nixon told him to mind his own business. Kissinger, for his part, waived these dissents with his customary swipes at the nitpicking of professionals unconcerned with political appearances. When it came time to explain the agreement freezing the number of ICBM's each side would have, he joked to an adoring press corps in Moscow, "Well, some of the great minds of the bureaucracy, which is not necessarily saying a great deal, [laughter] have addressed this question."[40] Kissinger suggested that Smith, representing the needs of his service, overlooked the importance of arms control as a vehicle, not an end in itself.

Arms control was to be a process, the continuation of which was as vital as any actual agreement. If the President could sign papers with the general secretary of the Communist party of the Soviet Union, as occurred during the Moscow summit of May 1972, that alone had greater impact than any particular clause.

Even before the Moscow trip, staff members cautioned that specific agreements would be hard to arrange. Peter Flanigan told Nixon in late April that "the Russians have taken positions that reflect either extreme financial naïveté or unreasonable demands" in discussions over grain, lend-lease, and liquified natural gas. He believed that "the Russians are not anxious to be in a position to sign substantial agreements during the Moscow visit."[41]

The White House walked a delicate line between promoting Kissinger as a star and having him detract from the President. Nixon used Kissinger, while some other staffers resented the Security Adviser's growing preeminence. In November 1971 Nixon asked Haldeman to "tell Kissinger to hold some time open between China and Russia for major appearances" on behalf of the new foreign policy. At the same time Patrick Buchanan of the press office warned that we "have to avoid the mythology of Kissinger building up" with the China trip and the new relationship with Russia. Raymond Price, a speechwriter for the President, recalls that from the beginning Kissinger carried to "compulsive extremes" an irritating habit of "incessant backbiting of anyone who in any way might be perceived as his rival for power or influence. While cordial enough to their faces, he was ruthless behind their backs." Price found Kissinger "a master of bureaucratic manipulation." He was also, however, "an exceptional negotiator, a prodigious worker. He was deferential toward the President, genial toward his peers, rude and tyrannical toward his aides."[42]

As they fretted over Kissinger's growing popularity, the rest of the White House staff suffered from Kissinger's war with the Secretary of State. Haldeman noted that "Kissinger has to quit running Rogers down." He promised Nixon he would "try to keep Kissinger on an even keel versus Rogers." That would not be easy. Kissinger kept demanding a "strategy of how to handle Rogers." He ordered Haldeman: "absolutely don't show him [a] communiqué" worked out with European allies. Kissinger explained that "the problem is that Rogers will blow his top on everything he doesn't do. Whenever he's called in in advance he puts the President through hell. So [I] have to wait until the last minute to tell him."[43]

Nixon and Kissinger carefully played down expectations before the Moscow summit to assure maximum impact of Nixon's visit. The President told Kissinger that "what I am concerned about is not that we will fail to achieve the various goals about which there has been speculation but that when we do make the formal agreements there will be no real news value to them." The President considered it "vitally important that no final agreements be entered into until we arrive in Moscow." To dampen euphoria he suggested that Kissinger "begin a line of pessimism" regarding the SALT negotiations. Already news stories had appeared predicting the amount of money the administration would request from Congress to implement SALT. Such forecasts discounted the President's and Kissinger's accomplishments. Nixon warned that "our critics who oppose summitry in any event" will try to "make it appear that all of this could have been achieved without any summit whatever, and that all we did was to go to Moscow for a grandstand play to put the final signature on an agreement that was worked out by Gerry Smith, State, etc."[44]

At the Moscow summit President Nixon and Party Secretary Brezhnev signed three important documents: The Anti-Ballistic Missile Treaty, the Interim Agreement on the Limitations on Strategic Arms (SALT-I), and the Basic Principles of U.S.–Soviet relations. Kissinger and Nixon played the major role in these prominent agreements. The Secretary of State had far less impact. At one point he complained to H. R. Haldeman that he "might as well go home," so useless did he feel. The President's Chief of Staff "hit him on a personal basis." You "just can't do this," Haldeman pleaded. After some prompting, Kissinger agreed to "find something for Rogers to do on his own—maybe move him over as the commercial negotiator." But he was not to have any part in the primary blueprints of détente. When the final session with Brezhnev over SALT took place, Kissinger, not Rogers, accompanied Nixon. As the Security Adviser put it, Brezhnev would not want Foreign Secretary Andrei Gromyko there, so why should Rogers take part?[45]

The ABM accord pledged each party to build not more than two ABM sites, one guarding a missile base and the other protecting the capital or National Command Authority (NCA). SALT limited both sides' offensive ballistic missiles to the number projected under United States construction programs, but scaled back the more ambitious Soviet deployment schedule. It led the Soviets to scrap some older ICBM systems. Yet the agreement had serious shortcomings. At the urging of the Joint Chiefs of Staff, who believed that the United States had a technological edge, it did nothing to restrict the development of Multiple Independently Targeted Reentry Vehicles (MIRVs), with which a single ICBM could destroy three, five, and eventually ten targets. A new arms race ensued between the two powers over these systems. SALT also let the two sides proceed with other qualitative improvements in missiles, especially in their accuracy. The closer missiles approached their targets, the easier it was to destroy an opponent's weapons. Hence, increased accuracy made a first strike more feasible. SALT-I was also silent on aircraft and cruise missiles. The agreement had a term of five years, with a stipulation that each would try within that period to develop a full-fledged treaty. The Basic Principles of U.S.–Soviet Relations represented a Soviet effort to be considered an equal. Nixon and Brezhnev agreed "there is no alternative to . . . peaceful coexistence." Both acknowledged "the principle of equality and the renunciation of the use or threat of force."[46] These innocent-sounding words came back to haunt Kissinger and other advocates of détente.

When Nixon and Kissinger left Moscow they stopped in Teheran before heading home. There they held two days of meetings with Shah Mohammed Reza Pahlevi, which cemented a strategic connection between the United States and the shah. These fateful meetings had catastrophic repercussions for both participants. The Americans agreed to increase dramatically the number of uniformed advisers in Iran and promised the shah virtually unlimited access to the most advanced weapons in the U.S. arsenal. For his part, the shah agreed to become the principal protector for western interests in the Persian Gulf. Nixon and Kissinger promoted these arrangements as part of their grand strategy of reducing overt United States commitments, while maintaining large American interests. Iran looked like a good surrogate. "I need you," Nixon plaintively told the monarch at the end of their conference.[47]

The State Department bureaucracy, however, was far more prescient than Kissinger or Nixon in this matter. Iran experts and arms sales professionals worried about the blank check offered Iranian military buyers. By permitting the shah to purchase whatever he wanted, the United States seemed ready to abdicate its own assessment of appropriate defense needs. Once more, Kissinger tried to silence the skeptics. He explained in a NSDM that the President had decided it was in American interests for the United States to encourage Iran to buy only U.S. military equipment. As Iran specialist Gary Sick observed: "In the President's name, Kissinger formally served notice on the bureaucracy that, henceforth, discussions on purchases of U.S. military equipment would be left primarily to the government of Iran." Kissinger later explained to Nixon that "we adopted a policy which provides, in effect, that we will accede to any of the shah's requests for arms purchases from us (other than some sophisticated advanced technology armaments—and with the very important exception, of course, of any nuclear capability)."[48]

These decisions, made in the euphoric afterglow of the Moscow summit, proved disastrous. Nixon and Kissinger created a monster they could not direct and could barely influence. Within eighteen months, the shah became the major power in the region. In the aftermath of the 1973 Arab–Israeli war, he led the movement toward higher oil prices, becoming wealthy beyond even his dreams. No longer was he a surrogate for the United States. Instead, he demanded and received more and more weapons. Over the next several years, the shah, flushed with oil revenue, hastened the modernization of his country. This process, in turn, fanned the animosity of traditional religious elements threatened by modernization. A revolution boiled beneath the surface, and within seven years of the 1972 meeting, the shah was overthrown and the U.S. position was wrecked.

All of this was in the future, though, when Nixon and Kissinger returned to Washington in early June with the ABM Treaty, the SALT-I agreement, and the Basic Principles of United States–Soviet Relations. Taken together, the three set the ground rules for détente between the United States and the Soviet Union. Only one of these documents (the ABM pact) was an actual treaty of the sort requiring constitutionally mandated action by the Senate. The treaty sailed through the Senate on August 3, 1972, winning approval with an affirmative vote of 88 to 2.

On the other hand, the interim agreement, or SALT-I, and the Basic Principles, neither of which required congressional approval, set off a sulphurous debate. By the time both houses of Congress adopted joint resolutions favoring SALT-I at the end of September, much of the original public euphoria over the fruits of the Moscow summit had dissipated, and critics challenged Kissinger's interpretation of détente and arms control.

During the summer the administration tried to steer a middle course between a new arms race and the euphoria of détente. Nixon wrote to Haig on June 20, "when Henry gets back tell him we must . . . stay right on the tightrope—hold the hawks by continuing adequate defense. Hold doves by pointing out that without SALT arms budget would be much larger."[49]

When the Treaty, Interim Agreement, and Basic Principles reached Congress in June they revealed profound disagreements among lawmakers over who should control foreign policy and the nature of détente. Observing the formal courtesies, Kissinger stepped back and let Secretary of State William Rogers present the case publicly for ABM and SALT. The official report to Congress on the two agreements came from the Secretary's office, and Rogers testified in public sessions before Senate and House Foreign Relations and Foreign Affairs Committees. Secretary of Defense Melvin Laird, who, like Rogers, had had little direct input into drafting the agreements, presented the case before the open sessions of the Armed Services Committees.

Kissinger, relishing his role as the broker of the final accords, offered the closed-door, executive session briefings on the administration's positions. He stressed the political importance of the summit and SALT. "The agreement on the limitations of strategic arms is not," he reported, "merely a technical accomplishment, although it is that in part, but it must be seen as a political event of some magnitude."[50] Kissinger wanted to shift American attention away from sterile questions of whether the United States or the Soviet Union was "ahead" in the number of nuclear weapons. He told Senator Jacob Javits (R.-N.Y.), one of the principal backers of SALT, that "beyond a certain level of sufficiency, differences in numbers . . . are not that conclusive."[51]

Kissinger praised the SALT agreement to Congress as "without precedent in the nuclear age; indeed in all relevant modern history."

He defended détente, because "we are compelled to coexist. We have an inescapable obligation to build jointly a structure for peace. Recognition of this reality is the beginning of wisdom for a sane and effective foreign policy today." He also presented a gloomy warning should the two powers "continue along well worn paths." Drawing on his professional experience, he explained that "history is strewn with the wreckage of nations which sought their future in their past." "Catastrophe" he concluded, could come from "fear of breaking loose from established patterns." He drew a frightening lesson from the end of European order in the early twentieth century. "The paralysis of policy which destroyed Europe in 1914 would surely destroy the world if we let it happen again in the nuclear age."

Kissinger claimed that he and Nixon had carefully combined concrete proposals with a new climate between the two superpowers. "Past experience," he noted "has amply shown that much heralded changes in atmospherics, but not buttressed by concrete progress, will revert to previous patterns, at the first subsequent clash of interests." He informed Congress of the hope "that the Soviet Union would acquire a stake in a wide spectrum of negotiations. . . . We have sought, in short, to create a vested interest in mutual restraint."

Kissinger stressed the role of SALT in the broader political process of détente. "The SALT agreement does not stand alone," he said. "It stands, rather, linked organically to a chain of agreements and to a broad understanding about international conduct appropriate to the dangers of the nuclear age." Kissinger told Congress how "technically demanding and politically intricate" the negotiations had been. "The composition of forces on the two sides was not symmetrical," he lectured. The Soviets favored "systems controlled within its own territory while the United States had turned increasingly to sea-based systems."

Even in the briefing Kissinger rebutted charges that the United States had come out second best. "Who won?" was an immature inquiry. "It is inappropriate to pose the question in terms of victory or defeat," he reminded lawmakers. If they persisted, however, they should understand that "the current arms race compounds numbers by technology. The Soviet Union has proved that it can best compete in sheer numbers. This is the area which is limited by the agreement. Thus the agreement confines the competition with the Soviets to the area of technology. And, heretofore, we have had a significant advantage."[52]

But Kissinger failed to persuade congressional skeptics that "sufficiency" in nuclear weapons was good enough. Led by Senator Henry Jackson (D.-Wash.), the detractors of détente focused on the ambiguities of the interim agreement. Jackson lectured Defense Secretary Laird that "the total number of ICBM missiles [listed in SALT] represents a unilateral position on our part and does not represent a bilateral understanding with the Russians. . . . In all of my experience, I must say that I have not heard of an agreement which involves such a serious substantive matter as the whole of our land-based strategic force not being set out in detail in the agreement. This kind of ambiguity can breed suspicion and lead to an unstable situation rather than to a more stable one. So if I do nothing else, I am going to try to nail down, line by line, the exact meaning of these agreements."[53]

During the Armed Services Committee hearing Jackson hammered away at what he considered the deficiencies in the interim agreement. He charged that Kissinger, in his haste to reach an understanding before Nixon left Moscow, had specified the number of missiles the United States would maintain without demanding that the Soviets do the same. The Washington Senator berated Paul Nitze, the Defense Department's expert on arms control, "All you are saying is that there is no ambiguity about the fact that the number is not specified. That is not the point. Without a specific number, there is definite uncertainty and ambiguity because the Soviets cannot be held to a specific number of ICBM launchers."[54]

SALT-I was not a treaty, however, so it would have taken more than the votes of one third of the Senate to prevent its ratification. Jackson probably did not have a majority of the upper house opposed to any further SALT conversations, since arms control had a popular constituency outside Congress. Therefore, instead of trying to block SALT, Jackson sought to make sure that Kissinger followed Jackson's design for American force structure in future negotiations.

Jackson developed an amendment to the Joint Resolution expressing congressional support for SALT. In it the Senator seized upon the Basic Principles of "equality," readily accepted by Kissinger, to mold the SALT process to Jackson's liking. The Senator turned the notion of equality from a Soviet phrase denoting western acknowledgment that Moscow was a legitimate state with rights equivalent to those enjoyed by the United States, something Kissinger believed improved the atmosphere. Instead, Jackson substituted the affirmation that equality demanded that the missile forces of the two powers should be equal in every particular. His amendment to the Joint Resolution insisted that in the forthcoming set of SALT negotiations Kissinger maintain "the principle of United States–Soviet equality reflected in the antiballistic missile treaty." The amendment warned that pending a permanent limit on offensive arms set by treaty, the United States would consider new Soviet deployments endangering American weapons to be contrary to United States interests. The amendment also called for continued development of the next generation of American missiles.[55]

Some forty senators joined Jackson in sponsoring this amendment. For those concerned that Kissinger had promised more than détente could deliver, the amendment seemed a good way of hedging a bet. What could be more innocent than an appeal to "equality" between the United States and the Soviet Union?

Yet supporters of SALT, led by Senators J. William Fulbright and John Sherman Cooper (R.-Ky.), perceived that the Jackson amendment wrecked Kissinger's arrangement. The National Security Adviser had been able to reach an agreement with Moscow precisely because U.S. and Soviet forces were "asymmetrical." The United States relied on a triad of land-based ICBMs, submarine launched ballistic missiles, and manned bombers. For their part, the Soviets had invested almost exclusively in land-based ICBMs. Fulbright and Cooper wanted Kissinger to be able to exploit these asymmetries in future discussions. They altered Jackson's amendment to drop references to the specific weapons the United States would develop in response to new Soviet deployments.[56]

On the Senate floor Fulbright took the lead in resisting Jackson's request that the United States match the Soviet Union launcher for launcher, missile for missile. According to Fulbright, Kissinger had a better, intuitive understanding of "equality" than did the Senator from Washington. The commonsense approach meant "overall equality of nuclear weapons—equality of capacity to develop new ones. . . . I do not believe that what the senator from Washington is really saying is that—regardless of the degree of superiority we may have in the fields of airplanes and the capacity to deliver nuclear weapons from forward bases, or our superiority in other areas—these are excluded from his concept of equality and that all the Senator is contemplating when he uses the word 'equality' is in the number of intercontinental missiles." Jackson shot back that "it is amazing for the Chairman of the Foreign Relations Committee to tell over forty members of the Senate that they do not know what equality in intercontinental missiles is about."[57]

Jackson's objections turned the debate away from Kissinger's accomplishments at the Moscow summit into a discussion of the future of arms control. In it lawmakers came closer to Jackson's skepticism than Kissinger's optimism. Much of Jackson's language remained in the Joint Resolution. While Congress did not threaten specific weapons in retaliation for Soviet moves, it did go on record favoring formal equality of forces. The Resolution also indirectly chided Kissinger for not going very far toward *reducing* armaments. It called for the beginning of Strategic Arms *Reduction* Talks (a Jackson locution later adopted and popularized by President Ronald Reagan). Finally, Congress insisted that any new treaties contain "concrete agreements," a recognition of Jackson's disappointment with the slipperiness of Kissinger's numbers.

Congressional resistance to SALT-I dimmed the glow of détente. By the fall of 1972 Kissinger had gone part of the way toward better relations between the United States and the Soviet Union. He had correctly diagnosed the problems in the relationship and sought to go forward on a basis of equality. But his eagerness for an agreement carried seeds of destruction. He had rushed through a political arrangement, beyond the advice of the technical experts. He had promised that the fact of an arrangement was more important than its specific contents. As long as Kissinger could focus attention on the fact that the United States and the Soviet Union, despite their differences, were engaged in a political *process* which *could* contain the arms race, he controlled the political debate. When Senator Jackson managed to turn attention to specific details, however, Kissinger's consensus over arms control broke down.

FOUR

Breaching the China Wall

Henry Kissinger's greatest achievement was the opening of relations between the United States and the People's Republic of China. His success was all the sweeter because it was unexpected. Not an expert on China himself, he adopted the positions taken by Americans who had studied the problem the most carefully. He was at his best in weaving China into the pattern of relations running from Washington to Hanoi to Moscow and Western Europe. His flexibility altered the balance in the war in Vietnam and changed the domestic debate over foreign affairs. For years after his 1971 trip to China, Americans regarded it as a model of the sort of dramatic gesture that could change the international environment overnight.

For nearly twenty years after 1949 no American politician dared to speak openly about unfreezing relations between Washington and the People's Republic of China. When Secretary of State Dean Acheson predicted to the Senate Foreign Relations Committee in 1949, at the time of the Communist victory, that official Washington would "wait until the dust settled" before recognizing the new government, no one expected the dust to swirl for twenty more years. The Korean War, McCarthyism, a Sino–Soviet alliance, China's development of an atomic bomb, the war in Vietnam, and the Cultural Revolution combined to make American leaders distrust their own countrymen as well as the Chinese.[1]

During the Eisenhower, Kennedy, and Johnson administrations, the thought of restoring ties with Beijing could only revive memories of an angry China Lobby accusing State Department officials of serving the Communist cause by their accurate reporting of the strengths of the Communist revolutionaries and the weaknesses of the Nationalist government of Chiang Kai-shek. American participation in the war in Vietnam rested at least in part on the fear that domestic pressures would become overwhelming should a Communist revolution succeed in another Asian country. Secretary of State Dean Rusk rested the case for American involvement in the war in Vietnam on the belief that the Chinese Communists exported a virulent strain of revolutionary anti-Americanism. If the National Liberation Front and the North Vietnamese mounted a successful revolution, it would signal other revolutionaries around the globe. Rusk expressed the fear of "one billion Chinese armed with atomic weapons" as a reason for United States support of the government of South Vietnam.[2] The Johnson administration did, however, continue talks with the government of China through the mediation of the Polish government in 1968. Washington hoped to resolve issues remaining from the Chinese revolution—the question of private American claims against China, the fate of prisoners from the revolutionary period and the Korean War, and the possibility of exchanging journalists and academics.

When Kissinger became National Security Adviser in January 1969, these talks had gone on for fifteen years, with little progress noted on either side. China was engulfed in the Great Proletarian Cultural Revolution, Mao Zedong's effort at purging the Communist party and People's Liberation Army of anyone who might challenge his preeminence. To outsiders it seemed as if one quarter of humanity had gone mad. The Chinese appeared to combine a paranoid fear of the rest of the world with extraordinary hatred of one another.

Early in the administration Nixon and Kissinger wanted to use a possible opening to China as a subtle threat to the Soviet Union. Nixon told the National Security Adviser that "I think that while Gromyko is in the country would be a very good time to have another move toward China made." While Kissinger explored a new relationship with Beijing, Nixon feared the ire of conversatives. Therefore he encouraged Kissinger to meet with prominent supporters of Nationalist China like Senator Karl Mundt (R.-N.D.) or former Republican Representative Walter Judd of Minnesota.[3]

Meanwhile, China made progress in gaining legitimacy in the rest of the world. Ever since the Bandung conference of 1956 China had been a leader in the movement of nonaligned nations. It had condemned both the United States and the Soviet Union for their "hegemony" over the remainder of the world, and had competed with India for a place at the lead of the newly independent nations of Africa,

the Middle East, and, most of all, Asia. The Chinese had formal diplomatic relations with over fifty countries in 1969.[4]

European allies of the United States, including France and Great
Britain, maintained diplomatic relations with the People's Republic.
Pressure mounted in Europe, Africa, and Asia to seat Beijing in the
United Nations. The policy of isolation of China advocated by the
United States since the fifties seemed to attract fewer supporters every
year. Some American allies hoped that China might become a vast
market for agricultural and manufactured goods. Without formal ties
to China, the United States might lose an opportunity for its own
merchants to tap a limitless sea of buyers of western products.[5]

Most of all, China appeared to have broken decisively with the Soviet
Union by 1969. The Soviet alliance, signed in 1950, had broken down
in the middle 1960s. Donald Zagoria, a scholar of the Sino–Soviet
split writes that "as tension between Russia and the United States
attenuated in the late 1950s, the main factor cementing the Sino–
Soviet alliance gradually disappeared. While China sought to pursue
an even more active anti-American policy than it had conducted earlier, Russia began gradually to seek ways of reducing tensions with
the United States, tensions which might lead to war."[6]

For American observers of the quarrel, the confrontation between
the two Communist giants challenged dearly held assumptions about
the cold war. Since the end of the Second World War containment
of the Soviet Union had gone hand in hand with containment of communism. American policy-makers had not distinguished between the
Soviets and other Communist states. If they did not believe, as most
of them did, that communism was a conspiracy directed from Moscow,
they held fast to the notion that Communists everywhere shared a
basic hostility to the United States and the interests of its allies. They
believed that the two social systems had irreconcilable differences,
and the struggle was likely to end with one or the other triumphing.

Kissinger, however, had taken a different view of the cold war. He
did not believe that the United States or the Communist powers would
"win" the confrontation. Such a view reflected an "immature" wish
for an end to foreign policy involvement.[7] The Sino–Soviet split added
credence to Kissinger's beliefs that modern international relations were
an intricate web rather than a fight between good and evil.

Kissinger's historical perspective was not a common view, though.
With the Chinese now charging that the Soviets were hopeless revi-
sionists who had betrayed the basic revolutionary tenets of Marxism,
some American officials were puzzled. For Dean Rusk it meant that

China represented an even graver threat than the Soviets had. In January 1965 he explained to a top secret meeting of the Senate Committee on Foreign Relations why the Sino–Soviet split forced the United States to action in Vietnam. As historian Warren Cohen recounts, Rusk believed that "It was urgent for the United States to demonstrate that the militant Chinese line would fail, that the Soviet line of peaceful coexistence was right. Otherwise, Communist nations might adopt China's belligerent approach and the Russians themselves might be forced to follow."[8]

For liberal critics of American involvement in the war in Vietnam the Sino–Soviet rift represented an entirely different problem and opportunity. As liberals began to break with the Johnson administration over the conduct of the war, they had to contend with the legacy of the Kennedy administration. JFK had proclaimed that the next confrontations between the United States and its Communist adversaries would take place outside Europe, in what Mao began to call the Third World. From the perspective of convinced cold warriors the split between the Soviets and Chinese proved the validity of Kennedy's predictions that the arena of confrontation had shifted away from Europe to small wars of national liberation in the former colonial areas.

To liberals who shared Senator J. William Fulbright's belief that the cold war categories had hardened attitudes, the split suggested another approach. Communism was no longer "monolithic." The challenge posed by the Soviet Union in the forties and fifties had been a national rather than an ideological threat, and the United States might profitably deal with some regimes calling themselves Communist. If the split between the two Communist powers was real, then the United States might be making a terrible mistake in the war in Vietnam. It might, as Fulbright or George F. Kennan, the father of containment, contended at a celebrated set of 1966 hearings before the Senate Foreign Relations Committee, be forcing the North Vietnamese into greater radicalism than they otherwise would assert.[9]

Realists like Kissinger also doubted that ideology was very important in international relations. Power, geography, economics and military might took precedence. As Kennan proclaimed in his discussion of the "Sources of Soviet Conduct," the Soviet Union was expansionist but traditional Russian nationalism, not Marxism, guided its moves. From this viewpoint, the Cultural Revolution in China might be more a manifestation of traditional Chinese xenophobia than an attempt to create a new sort of revolutionary zeal for the rest of the world. Realists hoped that the United States might be able to reach some sort of accommodation with China, one that recognized the nation's distrust of foreigners. At the same time the United States could avoid thinking that the Chinese were out to conquer East Asia.[10]

Many of the realist themes Kissinger had voiced in the late fifties were echoed in the reversal of elite opinion about China that took place in the middle 1960s. While administration officials avoided any talk of improving relations, members of Congress were not so reticent. Senator Fulbright's Foreign Relations Committee held hearings in March 1966 designed to "bring China into the world community of nations."[11] The chairman presented "some limited positive steps which the United States might take toward improving relations with China. It would do the United States no harm in the short run and perhaps considerable good in the long run to end our opposition to the seating of Communist China in the United Nations."[12]

The Council on Foreign Relations spent the middle of the sixties producing a massive $1.1 million study of The United States and China in World Affairs.[13] The Asia Society and journalists seeking entree into a previously closed China spent time looking at Chinese politics and society. The conclusions reached by the United States and China series provided a foundation for a new elite interpretation of the proper shape of relations between the two countries. Scholars lamented that the United States had tried for twenty years to isolate China. They reckoned that this policy had passed the point of diminished returns. Now the United States was isolating itself more than China as more and more western, non-Communist nations opened relations with the revolutionary state. As the Communists stayed in power for over a generation, the prospect that their success was a fluke became more and more unrealistic. Now the United States was not even doing anything for its friends on Taiwan. The Nationalists there had ceased to believe American assurances that Washington had their best interests at heart. Chiang Kai-shek and the Nationalists were now resigned to permanent exile on Taiwan.

Prescriptions for a two-China solution came more from strategists of global politics than from China specialists. The former, like Kissinger, preferred to consider external relations to what went on within a state's borders. Many of the latter noted how deep the divisions ran between the two Chinas and warned that the Communists deeply distrusted the United States. For Kissinger the split between nationalists and Communists was far less important than the breakup of "the Moscow–Beijing axis." Now the United States was in an ex-

cellent position to revise the terms of the cold war. Under the new
ground rules, ideology would be replaced by the traditional struggle
of nations and great powers for preeminence. The United States and
the Soviet Union would each seek allies around the globe. China, oc-
cupying a middle position could become the Americans' counter to
the Soviets in East Asia. Should the United States prove able to "play
the China card" as it was called, Washington would feel less exposed
and vulnerable in Asia. Indeed, good relations with China would make
the war in Vietnam less important to Washington's overall policy.[14]

An opening to China might also turn up the heat on North Vietnam.
Here was something that struck a responsive chord with Kissinger,
as it fit in neatly with a comprehensive end of the Vietnam War. The
Vietnamese had come to count on the Chinese supporting them out
of the necessity of revolutionary solidarity, not out of any affinity for
the Vietnamese. Indeed, China had been Vietnam's traditional imperial enemy. North Vietnam had profited from the division between
Beijing and Moscow by playing one Communist rival off against the
other. If the United States were able to reconcile itself to China, North
Vietnam might lose that opportunity. If the United States succeeded
at the same time in improving relations with the Soviet Union, then
the North might be thoroughly isolated. Under such circumstances,
Americans would have freedom of action, while the North Vietnamese would be highly vulnerable. Even if the North did not alter its
negotiating position to be more accommodating to the Americans,
the United States would *think* it was in a superior position to them.

What could Beijing derive from an improvement in relations with
the United States? On its face China did not appear interested in better relations with Washington. From the rhetoric emerging from the
Cultural Revolution, no power on earth was more evil than the United
States. Mao Zedong held that Americans were responsible for most
of the oppression in Asia and the rest of the world, while at the same
time Americans were only "paper tigers" who won through bluster
and intimidation what they could not achieve through real strength.
Turning outsiders into devils was nothing new in Chinese history. When
the Chinese felt themselves weak and vulnerable to others, they became the most xenophobic.[15]

The Cultural Revolution revived many of these concerns, as the
Chinese felt threatened by the American presence in Vietnam. At the
same time, important Chinese leaders, fearful of the course of the revolution and desperate about their own futures, looked for an end to
isolation. Zhou Enlai, China's prime minister who had a long career

as a diplomat, believed that an opening to the West would reduce some of the vulnerability and lessen the excesses of the upheavels of the revolution. He claimed that China should not isolate itself from the rest of the world. If China's revolution were indeed as threatened as the Red Guards claimed, Zhou believed that China needed friends.

Fear of the Soviet Union also contributed to the Chinese desire for a rapprochement with the United States. The Soviets shared a 2,000-mile border with China, and were not likely to go away. Serious fighting flared in March 1969 as Chinese forces ambushed a Russian company making a routine patrol on an island in the Ussuri River, claimed by both China and the Soviet Union. The Beijing *People's Daily* demanded "Down with the New Tsars" in an editorial assailing "the armed provocation by the Soviet Revisionist clique against our country." The Soviets had engaged in "a frenzied action . . . taken out of the need of its domestic and foreign policies at a time when it is beset with internal difficulties."[16] Over the remainder of 1969, nearly 400 border skirmishes took place between Chinese and Soviet forces. If China continued to have poor relations with its northern neighbor, pragmatism dictated that it seek friends outside. A war with India in 1965 had broken China's connection to the other giant power of Asia. The North Vietnamese were too unpredictable. The wounds were still sore from Japan's attempt to create a Pacific empire anchored on China. That left the United States as a potential ally.

America possessed several assets from China's point of view. Its remoteness from Asia indicated that Americans might stay across the Pacific. The dreary history of the war in Vietnam might further discourage future United States leaders from participating in Asian politics. The Nixon doctrine, announced in Guam in July 1969, indicated to Asians that the United States no longer had the will and stamina to fight in Asia unilaterally. President Nixon promised three things: 1) the United States would keep its treaty commitments; 2) it would "provide a shield if a nuclear power threatens" an ally; and most significantly, 3) "in cases involving other types of aggression we shall furnish military and economic assistance. . . . But we shall look to the nation directly threatened to assume the primary responsibility of providing the manpower for its defense."[17] If Americans seriously intended to stay on their side of the Pacific, they would no longer present a threat to China. At the same time, the Chinese could envy the industrial and military might of the United States. America could become a source of investment, goods, and military assistance for the Chinese. The Soviets might find themselves isolated the same way the

Chinese had been for the previous generation. An opening to the United States would vindicate China's position that it could remain an active force between the two superpowers.

Maybe most important of all, an end to the breach with the United States would go a long way toward solving the problem of Taiwan. As a condition of patching up relations with the United States, Beijing would demand that the Americans draw away from the Nationalists. The United States would also make legitimate China's emergence into international organizations—the United Nations and its specialized agencies.

For Kissinger, still feeling his way in the new administration, relations with China had to be handled delicately. Public opinion regarding China had not substantially altered. Republicans in Congress still believed that Beijing stood behind the North Vietnamese. The China Lobby still had important congressional representatives like Senator Barry Goldwater or Congressman John Rhodes (R.-Ariz.). They had supported Nixon's election in the belief that his long-standing opposition to Asian Communism would prove itself by his backing the Nationalists on Taiwan. Nixon himself had offered conflicting signals about his Asian policy. In "Asia After Vietnam," his 1967 article in *Foreign Affairs*, he had likened China to a black American ghetto. He suggested that the United States must induce China to change, "but any American policy must come to grips with the reality of China." As is the case of blacks huddled in America's inner cities, "in neither case can we let those self-exiled from society stay exiled forever." A combination of sternness (containment) and conciliation (détente) would lessen the problems emanating from Beijing.[18]

Nixon did not know how China might respond to an offer of better relations. Kissinger leaned toward the view that the realities of China's position in the world forced it toward seeking an end to its crushing isolation. But could he be certain? The threat from the Soviet Union on China's northern border impelled China to look for allies, but would Mao Zedong accept the fact of vulnerability? His Cultural Revolution seemed to fly in the face of pragmatic assessments of a realistic balance of power. His taunts at American weakness might be simple bragadoccio designed to mask a chilling sense of China's own weakness. On the other hand, Mao might actually believe his own rhetoric. In which case he would consider an American overture a surrender. A rebuff to a direct approach to China from Washington would make the new administration appear weak, something it considered the worst sort of mistake in international affairs. Domestic conservatives would be outraged if they thought the United States were approaching China. They would be contemptuous if the opening did not seem to work. Allies who had staked their position in Asia on support for the United States would resent the thought that the new United States administration had decided to befriend China without letting its traditional partners know what was going on. Most of all, any public atempt to heal twenty years of bad feelings without consulting the Nationalists on Taiwan would ignite a firestorm. If, however, the administration alerted the Nationalists to its intentions, Chiang Kai-shek's government would do its best to scuttle a deal.

Whatever happened, the staff of the National Security Council under Kissinger had to keep a tight rein on relations with China. Leaks alarmed the administration. If the State Department handled the opening to China word would invariably reach other nations before a final arrangement could be made. Informing Secretary Rogers of the plans or letting his officers handle the details was bound to lessen White House control over the operations. Kissinger and the White House could keep the operation quiet until it showed signs of bearing fruit.

Injecting China into the balance of power of East Asia required some difficult adjustments. No one knew how Japan might react to the addition of another pro- or at least not anti-American nation in the region. Kissinger did not seem to care about Japanese concerns. Where else would they go if the United States opened good relations with China? Would not Tokyo believe that greater stability in East Asia benefited them? Yet Alexis Johnson, onetime ambassador to Tokyo and now Undersecretary of State, believed that "Kissinger had a disdain for the Japanese [which] threw a devastating wrench into our relations with Japan on the question of China."[19] The Japanese might follow the American lead, establish commercial relations with China, and use their greater proximity and cheaper supply of labor to outstrip the Americans in the newly opened China market. Worse still, signs of a growing entente between the United States and China might reawaken old Japanese nationalistic fears. Feeling abandoned by the United States, aware that the pull of ideology had weakened and that the Americans were basing the calculations on old-fashioned measurements of power, the Japanese might assert themselves independently. While it was not likely the Japanese government would rearm in the near future, that remained a real long-term possibility. If an opening to China resulted only in Japan acting as an independent force, little would have been gained for the United States.

Kissinger also had to navigate carefully around difficulties in South Asia. India, once close to China, had fought a bitter war with the Communist state in 1962. Now India had grown close to the Soviet Union. Prime Minister Indira Gandhi had relied on Soviet support for India's industry and Soviet weapons for its army. A tacit ally of the Soviets, India had taken sides in the dispute between Moscow and Beijing. Should Kissinger succeed with China, India was likely to believe that the great powers of the region had combined against it.

This problem was complicated further by India's resentment that the United States had grown too close to Pakistan. India had looked to the Soviet Union for weapons after the United States had become the major arms supplier to Pakistan. Despite Beijing's revolutionary rhetoric, China had supported Muslim Pakistan in its 1965 war with India. Here was a straw in the wind for outsiders looking for China to signal an end to its commitment to revolution. Kissinger, ever skeptical of revolutionary zeal, applauded. India, however, saw the Chinese embrace of Pakistan's ruler General Mohammed Ayub Khan only as an indication that China was an enemy. Unity between China and the United States would frighten India even more.[20]

Finally, Kissinger had to worry about the effect of the opening to China on relations with both Vietnams. He had hoped that better relations with China would wean Beijing from its allies in the North. Kissinger hoped Hanoi would consider the reversal of alliances a slap in the face and become more amenable to United States suggestions for ending the war. The Communists in the North might, however, be just as likely to consider better relations between Beijing and Washington a sign of weakness on the part of the Americans. Instead of reducing their own demands they might raise the ante. Somehow Americans had to make it clear to the North that Beijing had deserted them.

Kissinger faced similar problems when Saigon learned of the new friendship. South Vietnam probably would explode at news that the United States had approached the Chinese. The government of President Nguyen Thieu knew as well as anyone that American efforts in the war rested at least in part on hostility toward China. Should the United States and China appear to end their differences, fewer reasons would remain for America to continue to aid the South. Thieu's government feared that overtures to Beijing meant that the United States actually was putting the Nixon Doctrine into effect before the end of the Vietnam War. The United States seemed to say that now, before the war had ended on acceptable terms, it was acknowledging that it had no military interest in East Asia.[21]

The Warsaw conversations received very little public attention throughout 1970. Insofar as outsiders considered the talks, it seemed as if they accomplished little. The official position of the United States government was that the conversations were designed simply to untie the several knots left over from the revolution. No one told the public that the actual intention of the discussions was to open formal relations between the United States and China.

All that changed on April 6, 1971, when the Chinese Sports Federation invited an American Ping-Pong team to visit the mainland. Except for Americans sympathetic to the Chinese revolution, no ordinary United States citizens had been permitted by the Communists to visit the mainland. Columnists greeted the invitation with astonishment. *Time* magazine enthused over "the Ping heard round the world."[22] A week later, the United States relaxed the 21-year-old embargo on trade with China. American citizens could now travel more easily to the mainland. Almost immediately journalists scrambled to be part of the team that would cover the historic trip. Eventually some fifty reporters covered the visit by about a dozen young Americans to the mainland where they were soundly defeated by the best table tennis players in the world. The Americans were treated to tours of China's finest attractions—the Great Wall and the Forbidden City—and lectures on how the thoughts of Chairman Mao helped an athlete smash a table tennis ball with greater force.

Back in Washington the trip to China by the young Americans appeared to mean something but it was not clear what. No word went through Warsaw that the Chinese actually were seeking better relations with the United States through this visit. It might just as easily mean that China was attempting to circumvent the traditional channels of diplomacy, something the White House could not stand for.

To Kissinger the invitation to people-to-people diplomacy was an encouraging sign, as long as it were not taken too seriously by the administeration's liberal critics—if they took it to mean that private citizens had the right and obligation to conduct relations without regard to the official wishes of the government in Washington. Already Senator Edward M. Kennedy (D.-Mass.) had told 2500 people at the National Committee on U.S.-China Relations that the United States should open consular offices and extend full diplomatic relations. He recommended dropping relations with Taiwan and seating the PRC in the U.N.[23] Kissinger informed a favored journalist that Nixon "worked quietly, step by step, behind the scenes" instead of making "a speech and a big deal" out of the movement toward China. The National Security Adviser told a delighted Nixon that he wanted reporters to note that "what makes the President so formidable is his turning their theory of protracted war against" the Chinese who had invented it. Kissinger wanted newspapers to give "another hypo to the fact" the Chinese had invited the United States Ping-Pong team.[24]

Of course China might be offering a different sort of signal with its invitation to the Ping-Pong players. The more "moderate" of the Chinese leadership might be attempting to notify Washington that those Chinese who were unhappy with the course of the Cultural Revolution wanted outside help. Then it would appear that the United States held the whip hand. "We knew something big was about to happen, but we were baffled as to what channel would surface it," Kissinger recalled.[25] His job was to determine precisely what the Chinese had in mind. His own inclination in the spring of 1971, however, was to distrust the Chinese motives. He believed that a visible offer to the Ping-Pong players represented a squeeze play. The Chinese wanted to force the United States into negotiating with them.

However much Kissinger might resent being placed in the uncomfortable position of having to respond to Ping-Pong diplomacy he could appreciate the political advantages. Democratic and liberal critics of the administration's Vietnam policy would be thrown into disarray by responding to the Chinese. Better relations between Washington and Beijing would refute critics who said that the United States was so bogged down in Vietnam that it could not attend to pressing issues elsewhere in Asia. On the contrary, an opening to China could be described as proof of the effectiveness of the Vietnam policy of the Nixon administration. By refusing to exit Vietnam quickly in 1969, the United States had demonstrated its resolve. Now, if China wanted a good relationship with the Americans, it would mean that they could overlook the United States in Vietnam. The administration could waive the taunts of its critics, and reply that it was China that had backed down.

The administration could also score heavily with voters not committed to either Democrats or Republicans. This vast middle ground did not follow foreign affairs closely. They paid little attention to the intricacies of the war in Vietnam and the international situation. They wanted the war to end and for the United States to appear successful in the world at large, but did not go much beyond these simple requirements. A dramatic overture to China would certainly capture public attention, demonstrate the firm control over foreign policy exercised by the President, and silence critics. The only people likely to complain were traditional conservative anti-Communists committed to supporting Nixon and the Republicans, anyway. The remaining, middle ground of the public could only be impressed with the remarkable drama of two old adversaries coming together.

If drama and public appeal were the major components of the new relationship, Kissinger could pay more attention to appearances of détente than to the content of what the two powers had to say to one another. Kissinger easily could accept that a closer relationship with China would ruin friendship with the Nationalists on Taiwan. The Koumintang had become a political liability by 1970. Even the prospect of a two-China solution seemed passé by 1970. Neither of the Chinese governments would participate in the United Nations if the other belonged as well. Each year the PRC gained more votes in the General Assembly, and the United States was able to prevent its seating only by persuading barely more than one third of the nations that the issue should be considered an "important question" requiring the approval of two thirds of the members. Nationalist China looked as if it was going to be evicted from the world body with or without United States acquiescence. By opening relations with the People's Republic the United States might actually salvage a desperate situation for the Nationalists. Washington could convince Beijing that it could make no military move against Taiwan so long as it had good relations with the United States. The result might allow Taiwan to continue as an independent and prosperous unit, even if its political future seemed grim.

Kissinger also did not believe it was appropriate to press the Chinese too hard about the war in Vietnam. Once more the fact of the two meeting spoke more eloquently to the new position of the United States than did anything the Chinese might agree to formally. If the two powers were seen by the rest of the world to be coordinating their activities despite their differences over Vietnam they would produce a clear message. Their joint appreciation of a Soviet challenge, their belief that stability in Asia was important to both of them, could not but convince the rest of Asia and Vietnam that both of them had drawn away from their respective allies. As was the case in negotiating arms control agreements with the Soviets, Kissinger came to believe that critics had too narrow a view of what should be accomplished in meeting with adversaries. The National Security Adviser preferred to believe that the fact of meeting China superseded any particular agreements reached. Accordingly, critics were able to complain that the deals reached in Kissinger's trip of July 1971 and Nixon's visit of February 1972 left matters far too vague between the United States and China. Kissinger responded, however, that these "churlish moments" revealed only an envious desire to share the glory. "We had not previously been overwhelmed by volunteers offering to support our policy," he noted with a twinkle.[26]

The trip to China came about through the intervention of Pakistan's President Mohammed Ayub Khan. He believed that Pakistan could score heavily in its battles with India by becoming the matchmaker. Pakistan had sizable disadvantages on the subcontinent. India had a population of 600 million compared to Pakistan's 150 million. Worse, Pakistan was divided into two provinces separated by 2,000 miles of India. Both sections of the country were inhabited by Moslems, but the richer, less numerous westerners dominated the poorer, dark-skinned Bengalis of the east, who outnumbered them 100 million to 50 million. The Moslem East Bengalis had organized a political movement, the Awali League, under the leadership of Sheik Mujibar Rahman, to contest the presidential election of 1971. West Pakistan leaders feared that Sheik Mujibar received support from rival India. But the government of Pakistan could strengthen its position on the subcontinent by bringing the Americans and Chinese together. China already had good relations with Pakistan, as did the United States. If the two of them were allied, the Soviets' support of India would appear less threatening. China had been more belligerent toward India over the previous fifteen years than the Soviets had been toward Pakistan. The United States also had a reputation of greater willingness to project its power outside its borders than did the Soviets. If these two more active powers were united in their support of Pakistan, that country would not need to fear the prospect of Indian support for the dissatisfied Moslems of their eastern province.[27]

So it was that President Khan relayed to Kissinger word that Zhou Enlai was eager to receive him in Beijing on July 9. The National Security Adviser quickly accepted the offer, foreseeing enormous gains for the United States, the Nixon administration, and himself. The final invitation for Kissinger to visit Beijing made him lyrical. "That was great" he told Haldeman. He felt "ecstatic—one of the great moments here." It was all the sweeter, he pointed out in the next breath, because there would be "no advance notification to Congress."[28]

Very soon though, Kissinger found Rogers at his heels. Haldeman heard the National Security Adviser complain that "Rogers is trying to stop Kissinger as the negotiator with the Chinese." In retaliation the National Security Adviser suggested that the White House "change signals—don't tell Rogers till *after* K. is there," in Beijing.[29] This was good advice, but Kissinger seemed overwrought. Haldeman wanted to use Alexander Haig to "keep K. calmed down, because there's nothing we can do" about Rogers's objections to his exclusion. Haig finally told the Secretary of State when Kissinger was enroute from Pakistan to China. Domestic politics also intervened. Nixon insisted that "Kissinger must get out of Chou [sic] that no Democrat is to go to China before the President."[30]

The White House foresaw Kissinger's emergence as "the mystery man of the age" upon his return from China. Some of that elusiveness helped the President's reputation, so Haldeman ordered that "he will kill it if he has *one* word of background. There are to be no backgrounders whatever. He has to quit seeing anyone from the *Times* or the *Post* including columnists—except Joe Alsop." Besides, "Rogers will be easier to handle if K. doesn't background."[31] Aside from this one backgrounder, Kissinger was to set up an "*absolute* wall" around himself. He "must *not see* on *any* basis the New York Times, the Washington Post, CBS, or NBC."[32]

Kissinger's trip to China did more than anything else to establish his and Nixon's reputation as diplomatic dramatists. On July 9 he dropped out of sight on a trip to Pakistan, claiming a stomach ache. On July 15, President Nixon announced that Kissinger had just returned from China. After his conversations with Zhou Enlai, Kissinger was everywhere. Cover stories in *Time* and *Newsweek* vied with portraits of him on each of the evening news shows. He became Henry the K, Superkraut, and the Modern Metternich.[33] *U.S. News and World Report* believed that "Kissinger's secret mission to red China has few parallels in the annals of U.S. diplomacy. . . . The mission gave a new dimension to the remarkable career of Mr. Kissinger." A "White House insider" confided to *U.S. News* that "I believe he is as much an expert on China as he is on Europe." The breakthrough to Beijing seemed to confirm his standing as "the smartest guy around." Kissinger's second visit to China in October 1971 brought even more praise from the press. The thirst for stories about Kissinger became almost insatiable. The *Ladies' Home Journal* ran a major article on Kissinger's two private secretaries who accompanied him to China. "Pretty," having "the leggy curves and radiant faces that draw men across crowded rooms," they were "the two most indispensable women in the life of 48-year-old Henry Kissinger . . . who literally has the whole world on his mind." Kissinger gallantly characterized them as "magnificent representatives of young American womanhood."[34]

His meteoric rise into public consciousness opened divisions between him and President. While Nixon appreciated Kissinger's ability to improve his standing with liberal and moderate columnists and editors he worried that "we're losing our base on foreign policy." Haldeman told Kissinger "start talking to the conservatives." He should stress that the "President is *not* liberal, he's conservative." Nixon thought that the "press *wants* a blurred image—indecisive—they know that defeats us."[35]

While Kissinger was still in China, Nixon outlined the politicians who would be notified before his televised speech. "Only our friends" should be told. "Don't inform any of the Left or the establishment," he ordered Haldeman. He wanted no members of Congress in on the secret "except possibly Mansfield."[36]

Nixon told the nation that Kissinger had flown to China. Immediately, it became obvious that the United States had scored a great triumph. Jaws dropped in Hanoi, which now believed that one of its major backers had become a partner to the Americans. In Moscow, too, officials were astonished. Their worst fears of encirclement seemed to be realized. The Chinese, whom they had come to consider mad adventurers over the previous ten years, had at least limited their effectiveness by the very extremism of their actions. Now, however, they seemed to play the international game with exquisite finesse. That would make them all the more dangerous.

Nations friendly to the United States were equally surprised, but they were mostly jubilant at the reversal of alliances. For Europeans the news was especially welcome. The British, for example, had maintained diplomatic relations with the People's Republic since 1950, and London wondered how long the United States could keep up the fiction that the Nationalists on Taiwan represented an effective government for China. Britain had reluctantly gone along with the United states in voting to exclude China from the General Assembly of the United Nations and wondered how long they would be able to maintain that ridiculous position. An American accommodation with China would lift a great burden from the shoulders of the British. They might even be able to upgrade their mission to Beijing to a full embassy, should the Americans drop ties to Taiwan. In such an event, the British would do the same thing. France was even happier with the news of Kissinger's trip for it seemed to confirm the Gaullist view of world politics. The great blocs were breaking down. In West Germany the trip appeared to be evidence that two powers, one Communist and the other not, could coexist.[37]

While in Beijing Kissinger met Zhou Enlai over three days and became infatuated with the Chinese leader's grasp of world politics. Kissinger described Zhou as "one of the two or three most impressive men I have ever met. Urbane, infinitely patient, intelligent, subtle," the Chinese leader was as skeptical of the value of ideology as was the National Security Adviser.[38] Instead, an old man now, Zhou seemed obsessed with the judgment of history on himself, the revolution, and its leader Mao. He intimated to Kissinger that only a breach in China's impregnable isolation could stop the depredations of Mao's Cultural Revolution. He also explained the long-standing connections between the United States and China. They had more in common with one another than their different political systems would indicate. Most of all, of course, they were bound together by their resentment and fear of the Soviet Union. The Soviets directly threatened China's northern border Zhou reported, but the Americans had their own reasons to be afraid of the Russians.

Zhou indicated that the balance of power in Asia was at stake. He urged Kissinger to accept China as another player in the game of nations in Asia and not consider it an unruly upstart requiring containment. Zhou proposed a partnership between China and one of America's recent friends in the region, Japan. China probably would be in a better position than Japan to acquire friends throughout the rest of Asia because of the memory of the Second World War. In the previous decade Japan had substituted a booming export economy for its militaristic expansion of the decades prior to the Second World War. In much of South and Southeast Asia the result was the same, with local officials highly suspicious of Japanese control over their economies. Accordingly, political cooperation between such South and East Asian powers as Korea, the Philippines, or Indonesia and Japan had proved elusive. China, on the other hand, had the same experience of Japanese domination as did the other Asian states. Only its revolutionary ideology had disqualified China from leading other Asian states in the fifties and sixties. Now that Zhou agreed to abandon an emphasis on revolution, Beijing would become a better candidate to lead the rest of Asia.[39]

The main order of business between Zhou and Kissinger was preparation for Richard Nixon's upcoming visit to the People's Republic. For Kissinger the journey had to be choreographed to show the President in the best possible light. He could not be seen as a supplicant paying tribute to the Chinese empire. It was hard to avoid this impression, for the symbolism suggested that the United States was apologizing for twenty years of fruitless antagonism. Concentrating on the Soviet threat might be one way of shifting attention away from an apparent American capitulation. The realities of détente with Moscow, however, intruded. Kissinger did not want to offer Moscow any reason to complain that its two main rivals were planning a preemptive attack.

Nothing was more troubling than the future of U.S.–Taiwan relations after Nixon's visit. Kissinger pressed Zhou to allow some sort of two-China solution, but the old revolutionary made no promises. For the Chinese Communist party, Taiwan was an integral part of China. Much of the party's appeal was to city folk and intellectuals, people who had suffered directly from the depredations of the imperial powers. As nationalists, the Communist leaders could not afford to appear as anything other than staunch upholders of China's full territorial integrity. Accepting any sort of special status for Taiwan would mean that the Communists effectively accepted the results of the 1895 Sino–Japanese War, which had first stripped Taiwan from Chinese control. Allowing special status for Taiwan would also undermine Beijing's goal of recapturing other territories not under Beijing's aegis. The British lease on Hong Kong, for example, was due to expire in 1997 and Beijing wanted to be sure that when the British left full Chinese sovereignty would be restored in the Crown Colony. The most Kissinger could get from the Chinese on Taiwan was a pledge that each side could present its views when Nixon arrived.[40]

Vietnam also played an important part in the July negotiations. Kissinger wanted to make Zhou realize that it was in China's interest as much as that of the United States to permit Washington to save face in the war. Should the Communists rout the South Vietnamese the United States would appear to be the very paper tiger Mao Zedong had accused it of being in the early 1960s. China, looking for an ally in the fight against the Soviets, could hardly rely on the roar of a stick figure. The National Security Adviser encouraged Zhou to make the North Vietnamese more malleable.[41]

Zhou, for his part, did not need much persuasion. China's long-standing rivalry with Vietnam opened his eyes to the dangers of untrammeled Vietnamese success. In 1954, at the Geneva conference called to end the first Indochina war between France and the Vietminh, China and Zhou had urged Ho Chi Minh to accept a partition of the country rather than pursue the war. Now, in 1971, the North seemed poised on the edge of another victory. The United States was asking China to urge similar restraint. The danger for China lay in going too often to the well. Zhou did indicate, however, that the two could reach common ground on Vietnam. Both wanted the war to end. Both looked

Henry Kissinger, airborne, at work as National Security Adviser. (Courtesy NP, NA)

At an early meeting of the National Security Council, Kissinger is in the foreground (l.). President Richard M. Nixon, opposite, is flanked by Secretary of State William P. Rogers (l.) and Secretary of Defense Melvin R. Laird (r.) and Chairman of the Joint Chiefs of Staff Gen. Earle G. Wheeler (far r.). (Courtesy NP, NA)

President Nixon confers in the White House with his principal aides, John D. Ehrlichman, Kissinger, and H. R. Haldeman. (Courtesy NP, NA)

President Nixon with a new confidant, Treasury Secretary John B. Connally, Jr., September 1971. (Courtesy NP, NA)

With President Nixon, strolling through the Kremlin during the Moscow summit, May 1972. Behind them are two of Kissinger's deputies, Generals Alexander M. Haig (l.) and Brent Scowcroft (r.) (Courtesy NP, NA)

President Nixon and Kissinger meet at the White House with a prominent congressional critic of détente, Democratic Senator Henry M. Jackson of Washington (second from l.) (Courtesy NP, NA)

With Premier Zhou Enlai in Beijing, July 1971. (Courtesy NP, NA)

North Vietnam's Le Duc Tho (center l.) makes a point during the Paris talks on Vietnam. (Courtesy NP, NA)

In Hanoi with North Vietnam's Prime Minister Pham Van Dong after the Paris accords are signed. (Courtesy NP, NA)

Israel's Prime Minister Golda Meir (l.) visits the White House after the 1973 Mideast war. (Courtesy NP, NA)

Chief of Staff Alexander Haig, Kissinger, and presidential lawyer James St. Clair (l. to r.) confer during the Watergate crisis. (Courtesy NP, NA)

for stability and predictability throughout Asia. Both deeply suspected the motives of highly revolutionary states like North Vietnam.
The trick was to persuade the North to go along.[42]

Fatigue, excitement, obsession for detail all combined to make
Kissinger more difficult to handle than ever when he returned from
China. He appeared "dead on his feet," and Alexander Haig took him
to dinner "just to block his evening" and prevent his saying something rash to the press.[43]

Preparations for Nixon's visit took place in Washington in a troubled atmosphere. The President continued to urge Kissinger to protect his right flank by meeting with former Representative Walter
Judd, but no briefing took place. As Patrick Buchanan, one of the most
conservative staff members put it, "it would just give Judd a forum
to spout off from." Alexander Haig, consulted on behalf of Kissinger,
laconically wrote he was "against" the idea. Kissinger did meet with
Billy Graham at the President's request. Nixon wanted him to provide a briefing to twenty–twenty-five "highly influential people within
the conservative ranks" who could be organized by the evangelist.[44]

The public reaction displayed "much more spontaneous excitement than expected, including that from strong Conservatives." Dean
Acheson arranged for a messenger to hand deliver to the White House
"hearty congratulations on the greatest secret operation since the development of the atomic bomb." The former Secretary of State fed
the growing perception that the Adviser outshone the President, hoping "that your chief will know what he wants to achieve when he
keeps the date you have made for him." Only Buchanan of the press
office appeared "depressed" because he thought "we're in the hands
of the Chinese, hostage to them." Rogers reported that the foreign
response was "better than expected" except for Japan. Prime Minister
Esako Sato felt the "rug pulled" from under him. He had a "terrible
problem" with the new relationship with China. His discomfiture
would likely wash over to the American Congress, which would again
complain that the administration conducted too secret a foreign policy.[45] Yet favorable congressional comment was sweet music in the
White House. John Stennis (D.-Miss.), a favorite Democrat, praised
Nixon's "courage and nerve." He said the trip reflected neither an
alliance with China nor one against Russia. "It is peace we seek and
this must be made clear to all." A pleased Nixon scrawled "K, excellent, tell him" in the margin of his daily news summary. He asked
for special presidential "notes of thanks to those who are all out" in
their support. He wanted them sent only to "Republicans and Stennis
types."[46]

Nixon alerted Kissinger that Clare Booth Luce, longtime backer of Chiang Kai-shek, had proclaimed the breakthrough as "the greatest international happening" in twenty-five years. Even Mike Mansfield, the Senate Democratic Majority Leader, supported the secrecy of the negotiations because of their "delicate nature." He predicted that the trip will "increase the prospect of a settlement on Vietnam." Republican challenger Pete McCloskey, launching his presidential campaign in New Hampshire, predicted that the opening to China would have no effect on the war in Vietnam. He also challenged the reasons for the secrecy of the announcement. Nixon ordered "get our friend [Rep. Jack Kemp (R.-N.Y.)] after him on this."[47]

After a few days, the White House staff tired of Kissinger's stories of his historic breakthrough. As the National Security Adviser briefed the cabinet, Haldeman scribbled: "He was there 49 hours. He says he spent 20 hours with Chou [sic]. He says he spent every waking hour with Chou. Therefore: he slept 29 hours. Or 15 hours sleep each night. Not bad! This is now the 28th time I've heard this."[48]

As Haldeman seethed, Kissinger explained to the congressional leadership the need for secrecy. "Only the President, Bill [Rogers] and I knew the whole picture," he claimed. The Chinese were "very concerned about too much public speculation." Therefore, he warned, a "great amount of self-discipline on our part is essential." J. William Fulbright, chairman of the Foreign Relations Committee promised to do what he could. "I completely agree with what you're doing," he said. "I don't want to do anything to handicap" it, but it will be "impossible to stifle the committee." Majority Leader Mansfield concurred that "both sides" of the leadership were "walking on eggshells." He promised "understanding . . . because of the delicacy and promise of the situation."[49]

Some of the greatest satisfaction came from drawing congratulations from political adversaries. Edward Kennedy's "effusive statement of praise" drew attention from Charles Colson. He told Nixon "as an old Kennedy watcher, I can say that it was an extremely generous statement by Kennedy's standards. . . . It must have pained him to do it."[50]

Amidst all this Democratic praise, Kissinger worried if opposition politicians might try to upstage the President by traveling themselves to China before Nixon's visit. He thought it "worth a try to talk them out of it on the grounds [we] will welcome them after the President." If Democrats insisted on going soon, Kissinger threatened "at least be sure to hold Mao in reserve" for the President.[51]

The prospect of Nixon's trip to China altered calculations about

détente with the Soviet Union. With Beijing open to a new relationship with the United States, Kissinger calculated that the Soviets
needed Washington more. While planning the announcements of the
impending trips to Moscow and Beijing Kissinger suggested "if we
don't get a summit [with the Soviets] then do China this year" instead of 1972 "as originally conceived."[52]

The White House feared that the wrong sort of publicity could scuttle
Nixon's trip. When James Reston spent six weeks in China in the
summer he requested an interview with Kissinger on his return. Nixon
ordered that "K. is not to see him at all," because "Reston's motive
is clearly to sabotage the trip." The *Times* reporter warned that he
did not expect the Chinese to make concessions to Kissinger or Nixon.
He also said that "it might have crossed his [Nixon's] mind" that the
trip "might help his political interests in 1972."[53]

Lack of consultation with allies made difficulties. The Japanese had
gone out on a limb for the United States by maintaining relations
with Taiwan despite the commercial attractions of China. The sudden
opening to China hurt them where it mattered most, in their export
industry. Alexis Johnson grumbled that "I am afraid that the scin-
tillating Kissinger mind let itself get mesmerized by the charm and
urbane intelligence of the cosmopolitan Zhou Enlai. . . . The resulting policy was . . . lopsided. Japan, for the foreseeable future our
most important ally in Asia by far, was shoved rather obviously on
to the back burner."[54] European allies also found themselves in the
uncomfortable position of learning afterwards what the United States
was doing. As a scholar, Kissinger had noted that the gravest threat
to the NATO alliance was the United States tendency to confuse informing allies after the fact with true consultation.[55] While Europeans might applaud the aims of Nixon's trip to China, they could not
but fear that the unilateral American approach denigrated their importance in world politics.

Throughout the fall Washington worried about things that could
interfere with the President's trip. Nixon's schedulers resented that
he would be at the mercy of his hosts. "The Chinese will control
everything!" lamented one. "What are Henry's instructions?" he begged
to know. Dwight Chapin, the President's appointment secretary, feared
that the National Security Adviser and the Chinese might place the
President in uncomfortable surroundings. Chapin believed "one of the
most helpful things from our standpoint would be to get plugged in
on some of the various planning meetings regarding Henry's trip which
are now going on."[56] Kissinger wanted Pat Nixon included in the
presidential visit to China. He agreed that "people contact is more

important than meetings in terms of public reaction here" and "PN is one way to get 'people pictures.'" The White House gave Kissinger "running room" to "raise the PN question" with the Chinese. He should keep in mind that "if she goes, then the President doesn't have to go out into the people—if not, he'll have to."[57]

Kissinger's October trip was scheduled at the time the U.N. prepared to vote on the ouster of Taiwan and the seating of the People's Republic in the world body. Rogers voiced concern. The Secretary of State knew that "in spite of Kissinger's trip, our U.N. position was doomed to fail. We would have lost this fall." Still, it did not look good for the National Security Adviser to be a supplicant in Beijing as the world body voted to expel the Nationalists. Rogers lost whatever equanimity he had upon Kissinger's return from Beijing. He complained to the White House that the "trip to Beijing couldn't have been at a worse time." The NATO allies had voiced objections. Rogers said it was "important [for him] to be phased in on everything." Nixon, on the other hand, warned it was "just as bad or worse to go after the U.N. vote with Taiwan out." The President told Kissinger that "it's set now. We can't do anything about it." Kissinger had already scheduled a meeting with Soviet Foreign Minister Gromyko to announce the forthcoming Moscow summit. For him to back out of a planning trip to Beijing would be "too big a risk vis-à-vis the Chinese." Public reaction to the expulsion of Taiwan was muted much to Kissinger's relief. His self-satisfaction irked other staffers. "Don't let him get too cocky now, for his own good," Haldeman noted. "He's made some boo boos too."[58]

Kissinger was surprised that a liberal like Edward Kennedy criticized the administration for abandoning Taiwan at the U.N. He called John Kenneth Galbraith, a longtime Kennedy supporter and former Harvard colleague, who agreed that it was "just cheap politics" for Teddy to have made his "flip on Taiwan." Kissinger thought it was better politically that the expulsion had come in 1971 than later, during the election. Now was the time to "kick the cannibals," the third world countries, who had led the ouster. He advised in response that the "main thing is to kick senators for demagoguery" on the Taiwan issue. Dissatisfaction with the Third World could be an excuse to diminish administration backing for foreign aid. "People are opposed to" foreign aid anyway, he reported.[59]

In December Washington was shocked again as war broke out between India and Pakistan over East Bengal. India assisted the Bengalis in establishing an independent Bangladesh. The United States supported its friends in Pakistan: partly because Kissinger believed they would win, partly because he feared they would lose badly, and partly because he wanted to reassure China, Pakistan's other patron.

The tilt toward Pakistan raised questions about Kissinger's comfortable relations with the press. John Osborne of the *New Republic* described him as "the most skillful backgrounder in Washington and one of the most frequent visitors to the rear section of the President's plane." That was where officials riding with the President went to use the single restroom on Air Force One. In the process they confronted the pool of about five reporters who always traveled with the President. Kissinger was a master of dropping hints about United States policy on condition that he not be identified. Osborne smiled that "our Henry just loves to background: the practice gives play to his wit, feeds his abundant vanity, and in his own opinion serves essential purposes of diplomacy." In this case, Kissinger told a *Los Angeles Times* reporter that if the Soviets did not restrain India in the war with Pakistan "the entire matter [of the Nixon visit to Moscow] might be reexamined." Kissinger then went over the reporter's typescript and changed the phrase to the far more threatening "the entire U.S.–Soviet relationship might well be examined." This alteration was too much for the *Washington Post*, which thought it improper to be the vehicle of threatening the Soviet leadership. It identified Kissinger as the source, explaining "We are now convinced that we have engaged in this deception and done this disservice to the reader long enough."[60] Despite such pious sentiments the *Washington Post* did not stop using information provided on deep background. Over the next several years, however, readers came to know that someone identified as "an administration official traveling with the President" or "a State Department official traveling with Secretary of State Kissinger" customarily was Kissinger.

The India–Pakistan war brought relations between Rogers and Kissinger to their lowest point yet. Even in the summer, Kissinger declared that he had to "remain involved" in the India–Pakistan dispute. He told Nixon "I can't turn it over to Rogers. We can't be frivolous about this," because it is "the one area that will screw up the trip" to China. When India declared a cease-fire Rogers sensed a "PR coup, but we should keep it for the President" rather than let Kissinger make the American announcement. "Rogers is going ape" Haldeman reported. Rogers' sympathy for India enraged Kissinger who was "so blinded now that he can see no good in Rogers."[61]

Kissinger defended himself as "caught in a dilemma with Nixon." He lamented that "the President doesn't want details." Kissinger therefore had to do the job himself, which provoked "endless battles with State when things blow up." The India–Pakistan war was a case in point. He returned from India and informed the President that war would break out. Nixon turned the issue over to Rogers with instructions to cut foreign aid to India in the event of war. Instead, Rogers had turned relief funds over to the United Nations. To Kissinger this meant that "State refused to take the President's direction." Worst of all, "Rogers never said he disagreed with the policy, but sabotage went on underneath." Nixon believed that Kissinger should not rebut press charges about the "tilt" toward Pakistan. "It looks self-serving" for Kissinger to publish the record of the many offers the United States had made to India. Instead "a State Department White Paper" might help the cause more.[62]

Nonetheless, Kissinger's diplomacy triumphed when President Nixon bounded down the steps of Air Force One in Beijing on February 21, 1972. At the bottom of the gangplank stood Zhou Enlai. When Nixon reached out a hand to Zhou he erased an eighteen-year-old slight, Secretary of State John Foster Dulles' refusal to shake Zhou's hand at the 1954 Geneva conference. That picture set the stage for the entire visit. Photos of the President and Mrs. Nixon visiting the Great Wall of China, Nixon and Kissinger speaking with Zhou and Mao, a live broadcast of the toast at the mammoth Great Hall of the People all dominated the headlines at home.

In Beijing, Kissinger was more active than Secretary of State Rogers. The National Security Adviser arranged a meeting with Mao Zedong and fashioned the final communiqué.[63] A belief that appearances superseded substance dominated his actions. The fact that a final document agreed to by both principals emerged was the most important thing. Kissinger helped prepare groundrules for handling the press while in China. Newspapers should note the different world views of Americans and Chinese. "We stress peace, they stress justice. We stress stability, they stress conflict." He set the standards by which to judge the meetings. First, and perhaps least important, were "the agreements we make there." As in the case of the developing détente with the Soviet Union, Kissinger thought atmosphere surpassed specific accomplishments. "Their judgment of our leadership" was the key to the future of U.S.–Chinese relations. "Do we have a world outlook, a sense of the Pacific, of history? Are we reliable?" Nixon foresaw a problem with the press if no communiqué resulted from the meeting. Who would brief journalists then? "The principals [should] stay away from it," Nixon said. "The President can't do it, Ziegler can't do it, Kissinger has to do it. But he should have [Assistant

Secretary of State for East Asian Affairs Marshall] Green with him—not Rogers."[64]

Kissinger's preeminence during the China trips provoked other staff members to guard Nixon's image. One commented that the press had "built HAK to the point where people wonder if he makes foreign policy or the President."[65] Kissinger chafed under White House restraint on his press contacts. He "needs to sing," Haldeman told the President. "How about letting him do the *Times?*" he asked. Nixon agreed, but added "when Kissinger does see the *Times* he should do the editorial board" rather than a single columnist. The President advised "don't let K. be picked off by one little guy."[66]

Critics like Seymour Hersh derided Kissinger's efforts as the worst sort of show business self-promotion.[67] For the Security Adviser, however, such carping obscured the very real successes of the trip to China. It mattered less what was said about great power rivalry, Taiwan, the Soviet Union or the war in Vietnam than the fact that the two powers were talking at all. Kissinger, therefore, was willing to adopt Chinese language in the final communiqué issued in Shanghai on several issues of concern to China. The United States stipulated that there was only one China. Both Beijing and Taipei agreed that there was a single country. The American language held that the Chinese themselves would resolve the issue. At the same time, however, the United States insisted that the issue be resolved peacefully.

Kissinger also helped draft the language about the world views of the two powers. They agreed that both powers were interested in Asia. They agreed that "neither should seek hegemony in the Asia–Pacific region" and, in a warning to the Soviet Union, said that "each is opposed to efforts by any other country . . . to establish such hegemony." They went on to criticize Soviet behavior elsewhere by affirming that "both sides are of the view that it would be against the interests of the peoples of the world for any major country to collude with another against other countries, or to divide up the world into spheres of influence."[68]

Kissinger succeeded in drawing the Chinese into an American view of the Soviets. Détente with them would be possible now that the more polycentric view of the world had been stressed in Shanghai. He was less successful, though, in persuading the Chinese that they should pressure the North Vietnamese. One had to read between the lines of the communiqué to see that the United States had separated Beijing from Hanoi. That conclusion was inescapable, nonetheless. China agreed, in the midst of the war, to open liaison offices in

Washington and Beijing. Obviously Beijing valued its budding relationship with the Americans more than its revolutionary solidarity with the North Vietnamese.

Some conservative Republicans were so outraged by the new direction that they considered challenging Nixon for the nomination in 1972. Representative John Ashbrook of Ohio complained that "we have set up the framework to abandon 15 million people [on Taiwan] to the tender mercies of a regime that during its tenure in office—its 23 years of enlightenment and progress—has managed to slay . . . 34 million of its own citizens."[69] He entered the New Hampshire presidential primary in March in the hopes of unseating the President. He got only 7 percent of the vote.

Kissinger was the most important figure in generating political support for the Shanghai communiqué. "Deep-freeze Rogers," Nixon ordered. He designated Kissinger to "see all the conservatives, because the President can't see them and be quoted." The President told his Security Adviser to "call Reagan. Tell him it's left-wing enemies in State" who had spread reports that Nixon and Kissinger had sold out the interests of Taiwan.[70] Kissinger told the cabinet upon return: "This couldn't have been done at a lower level. The Chinese had to ask themselves: Do these people have a view of the world we can live with? Are they reliable enough as a people—and as leaders—to carry this out for a period of time?" These themes, rather than details, were important. "When the words of the communiqué are long forgotten," he went on, "it may be considered a historical turning point if . . . they now look on our whole society and see there is enough there to be what they want."[71]

His public relations performance did not fully satisfy the rest of the White House staff. Haldeman thought that the "main thing for us [to get] out of China is the President's position." Kissinger had not stressed that Nixon was "big league, has done it for years. [He is an] unusual world statesman." Above all Kissinger should "get off the issues and on the man." If the National Security Adviser proved lacking, "maybe put the Pandas on tour? Would it hurt them?" Haldeman wondered about gaining political advantage from the Chinese gift of two bears.[72]

Democrats were much more discomfited. They could not complain that Nixon was moving away from the old categories of the cold war, for many liberal Democrats had charged with Senator Fulbright that America had ignored changes in the world. The Sino–Soviet rift proved to liberals that communism no longer was a unified movement threatening the United States. If the United States could resolve its differences with China, Senator George McGovern argued, it could end the war in Vietnam too.

When Democrats did complain about the opening to China, they faulted the process, not the outcome. Secretary of State Rogers had been kept in the dark, a humiliating experience for the principal foreign policy figure in the administration. By concentrating the power in the White House and the NSC, Nixon and Kissinger had avoided congressional scrutiny and played directly to the public. Democratic liberals found themselves in the odd position of supporting Taiwan. The Nationalists had not been consulted at all by the United States. They justifiably believed that their interests had been sacrificed on the altar of great power accommodation. Senator Hubert Humphrey charged that "it is now clear that the rug has been pulled out from under the Taiwanese, though the people of the island of Formosa once aspired to determine their own destiny." The former Vice President, seeking the 1972 presidential nomination, also disputed Nixon's statement that no other nation's fate was being determined behind its back in the conversations. "It is apparent from the communiqué as I read it," Humphrey went on, "that concessions were made by the president and Dr. Kissinger, but not any, insofar as I have been able to interpret, by the Chinese."[73]

Kissinger accurately predicted the sources of Democratic opposition to Nixon's trip. The "Liberals will try to piss on it," he said, as an "election year gimmick." He imagined that Democratic members of Congress would resent an apparent lack of consultation. Such objections were sour grapes. In response, he recommended, "we say they're unmasking themselves. You're not against *what* we're doing, you're just against the fact *we* are doing it."[74]

Despite these political criticisms, the President's trip to Beijing was a tangible demonstration of the success of Kissinger's and Nixon's approach to revolution, the war, and the other great powers. The two men could not state with some authority that they had altered the course of U.S. foreign policy. They had broken the rigid categories of the cold war without appearing "soft." The United States remained in the war in Vietnam, was repairing relations with the Chinese while at the same time opening bridges to the Soviets. No previous administration had this record of achievement. Critics in Asia, Europe, and the United States could only mutter and look embarrassed as Nixon and Kissinger rewrote the script of post–World War II foreign policy.

FIVE

Liquidating Vietnam, 1972–1973

At the beginning of January 1972 Richard Nixon told Henry Kissinger he was "under terrible pressure on Vietnam." He proposed delivering an "all out speech" to the country on Vietnam "prior to Congress's return." Kissinger calmed his excited boss. "This is a mistake," he replied. It "will focus congressional" attention and make "Vietnam the key issue at the outset." Despite Nixon's anxieties, Kissinger assured him he was "in good shape on Vietnam." He should speak out on the war on the "latest possible" date, after Congress had reconvened. Nixon followed Kissinger's advice and waited until late January for a speech on Vietnam. Kissinger predicted that "the press will kick us on Vietnam, not because he thinks we're wrong, but because he knows we're right. He is furious because we're doing it [sic]."[1]

As the election of 1972 approached, the continuing war in Vietnam cast a cloud over the chances of the Nixon administration. For three years Nixon and Kissinger pleaded for time to end American involvement in the fighting, but now patience was wearing thin. The peace movement on college campuses had received a serious setback in 1970 when four students were killed by the National Guard at Ohio's Kent State University and another two were shot to death at Mississippi's Jackson State College. The stakes in opposing the fighting climbed now to the point where demonstrators risked their lives. Moreover, the President had announced that conscription would end in 1973, further undermining the appeal to the young of opposing American foreign policy.[2]

South Vietnam also presented serious difficulties to Nixon politically and to Kissinger diplomatically. Saigon feared abandonment by a United States hopeful of reaching a settlement with the North before the election. President Thieu reasoned that the Americans had come to consider South Vietnam a burden, not an asset. Nixon's trip to China in February had underscored the changing focus of United States foreign policy. While the United States sought to portray the opening to China as an attempt to wean Beijing away from Hanoi, the South worried that it indicated just as much that the United States was pulling away from Saigon. It seemed as if Kissinger, seeking to place American foreign relations in the context of the great power rivalry, had recognized that Vietnam paled in importance when compared to China.[3] Regardless of what Kissinger said to the South Vietnamese, America's opening to China proved Washington looked elsewhere in world politics. From here on, Kissinger probably would stress the relationship with the Soviet Union and China. Southeast Asia, once a showcase of American resolve to thwart the spread of Communism, now seemed a diversion from the more traditional arena of the cold war.[4] The United States should not be forced to leave by the superior perseverance of the NLF and the North Vietnamese. Instead, the United States should achieve victory on its own terms. That was the public stance at home. Did Kissinger believe it, though?

The signs that the United States would prevail were hardly encouraging in the spring of 1972. The ARVN had fled from Cambodia after the abortive invasion of 1970. An assault on Laos in the spring of 1971 had been an even greater fiasco. South Vietnamese forces had mounted no effective offensive, scampering home at the first sign of resistance from the Communists. Ground fighting inside the South also achieved little in 1970 and 1971. The best that could be said was that the Communist forces had not increased their control over the South. They still remained a force to be reckoned with. The ARVN had not become the sort of army that could win, and few American officials believed it ever would reach that state. The United States had diminished its own forces' role in ground combat. As more troops were withdrawn there were fewer American soldiers who could carry the fight to the NLF. But television pictures of American deaths or American families mourning their fallen sons also disappeared. Nixon's popularity soared as a result.[5]

Congress also was restless. The Senate passed the Church–Case amendment in April. It banned appropriations after December 31, 1972 "for the purpose of engaging U.S. forces, land, sea or air, in hostilities in Indochina."[6] After Nixon announced that the air force would continue to bomb the North as United States troops left the South, Frank Church excoriated the administration's refusal to set a firm date for the withdrawal of United States forces. "I thought that Vietnamization meant turning the war back to the Vietnamese. Not until we do that can I agree that the policy is a success."[7]

Kissinger therefore conducted diplomacy against the deadline of the 1972 election. The best he looked forward to in mid-1972 was indefinite stalemate in the war. The NLF seemed incapable of mounting another full-scale offensive in the South similar to their actions during the Tet New Year of 1968. Their reluctance to commit themselves indicated to American field commanders that they had exhausted their resources in one final, fateful bid. When it failed, the Communists expected the collapse of the South's government. That, at least, had not occurred in the four years since 1968.[8]

Kissinger hoped the South could continue without American military support. He relied upon the judgment of American generals who proclaimed that the forces of the NLF were not strong enough to overcome the South.[9] The international situation should also persuade Hanoi that it no longer could count on unquestioning backing from its major allies. The Chinese–American rapprochement had been a major setback for Hanoi's international efforts. China seemed to agree with the United States that the war in Southeast Asia no longer should come between the two powers. This acknowledgment represented an enormous shift in twenty-five years of Communist policy. Beijing had backed Hanoi in its war only to keep the Americans away from the southern borders of China. Beijing had always been suspicious of the motives of the Vietnamese. Much like the Soviets in the twenties and thirties who distrusted the bona fides of any revolutionaries outside their control, the Chinese wondered if the Vietnamese were more Nationalist than Communist.[10]

Kissinger also found encouragement in shifting Soviet attitudes. Moscow had backed away from Hanoi in the rush to reach an arms control agreement with the United States. Once Soviet leaders had considered the American involvement in the war to have been the first step in a global assault on Communism. Now the Kremlin believed that the Americans wanted out of Vietnam on the best terms they could get. Anything that avoided an outright humiliation of the United States would be acceptable as a settlement. The Soviets believed that the war had sobered the United States. The Soviets resisted forcing the United States to the wall. If cornered, the Americans might just stay in Southeast Asia out of spite. Accordingly, Kremlin policy in 1972 encouraged the North to offer the United States a way to save face.[11]

Kissinger responded well when Moscow agreed that North Vietnam should permit the Saigon government to retain a nominal role in the future of the southern republic. The National Security Adviser had different interests from Moscow's, but he believed he could turn Soviet efforts to American advantages. Any pressure they put on North Vietnam helped Kissinger's position.[12]

The Soviets, for their part, supported Hanoi's claim that the Saigon government, lacking real support among the Vietnamese, fronted for the United States. Soon after the Americans departed, the Saigon government would find itself at a political disadvantage, unable to recruit anyone to its side. It would fall under its own weight and the better organized Communists would come to power.

Moscow told Hanoi that this could happen, though, only if the North made enough concessions to get the Americans out of Vietnam. The Kremlin wanted Hanoi to grant some of the American claims. It could acknowledge that its troops were actually engaged in combat in the South, something the northerners had heretofore refused to admit. The Americans asked for a complete withdrawal of the northern forces. Hanoi rejected that proposal out of hand. The Soviets pressed them, however, to accept another American position. If the North would agree *not to raise* the level of its forces after an agreement, the United States would agree to remove its own. The Saigon government would then be left to drift and decline on its own.[13]

The Soviets took this moderate position even in the face of the American assault on the North's ports in May 1972.[14] For seven years, since the beginning of the bombing campaign in 1965, the United States had avoided attacking the port of Haiphong, the North's principal outlet to the rest of the world. The Johnson administration had placed the ports off limits to the bombers out of fear of provoking outsiders whose ships might be hit. The Soviets could react to the attacks on their shipping by retaliating elsewhere in the world. Western allies that traded with North Vietnam also might explode if American bombs hit their ships.

Nixon and Kissinger looked at the situation differently. First, Nixon had more faith in the judgment of the military. His most faithful constituency admired military strength, and conservatives believed that the war had gone badly precisely because Johnson had kept the military on a short leash. While Nixon at times accepted this argument,

Kissinger was more skeptical. Letting the military run the war left him in the cold. From this point of view he had no quarrel with Johnson's refusal to grant every request for additional bombing.[15]

Yet Kissinger also believed that the President needed to maintain the goodwill of his most ardent backers. The use of greater force had its domestic advantages even if it failed to persuade the North Vietnamese to accept American bargaining positions. It could, instead, convince supporters of the President that he had done everything possible to win the war. By playing the final card against the North, the administration hoped to alert all participants that the United States was willing to go the limit in its support of South Vietnam. The use of what H. R. Haldeman termed the "madman strategy" might even have some beneficial results with the North. Fearful that Nixon would stop at nothing to be able to declare a victory in the war, North Vietnam might become more conciliatory. If they did not alter their stance, the Americans still would not be at a disadvantage. The United States could simply assert that it had pressed the North to the limit and accept whatever agreement emerged from the talks going on in Paris.[16]

Kissinger thought that South Vietnam could also be pressured by the American bombing campaign. The United States signaled its friends in Saigon that it was willing to use more force in their behalf than ever before.[17] At the same time, America wanted out of Vietnam. If the southerners presented roadblocks to the conclusion of the agreement, Washington indicated that it would leave the southerners to their own devices if they refused to settle. Once the United States demonstrated its commitment to pressuring the North into letting the United States save face, the South could ask for little more. The United States promised President Thieu that Americans always stood ready to enter the war once more in force if South Vietnam were overwhelmed.

The lack of Soviet reaction to the bombing of the harbors of North Vietnam in May 1972 cheered Kissinger. While skeptics had fretted that the bombing would alienate Moscow without intimidating Hanoi, Kissinger predicted that détente would survive. Senator John Sherman Cooper (R.-Ky.), an outspoken dove, or Hugh Scott (R.-Pa.), the minority leader, feared that Moscow might actually freeze relations with the United States on the eve of Nixon's scheduled visit.[18] The easiest way they could respond to the Americans' attack on the North would be to forbid the American President from calling in Moscow.

As Kissinger hoped, the Soviets did not withdraw their invitation to Nixon. Moscow accepted United States assurances that the mines that damaged the Soviet vessels had hit them inadvertently. Moreover, the Soviets wanted to play host. They could demonstrate to the Chinese that the United States still considered Moscow the most important other power in the world. Moscow expected that the result of the bombing would be greater American enthusiasm for the candidacy of Richard Nixon. They would have to deal with him in a second term, and they wanted to derive the maximum advantage from his willingness to negotiate before the election.

With the visit to the Soviet Union a reality, Nixon and Kissinger claimed success in their effort to separate North Vietnam from its allies. China printed the full text of Nixon's remarks announcing the bombing. Kissinger later gloated that "the dour fanatics of the North Vietnamese Politburo could only interpret this as cool dissociation by their major allies."[19] Even if nothing else happened to diminish the North's stature in the Communist world, the United States could claim that Hanoi had been severely damaged by its May bombing. Paradoxically, northern weakness allowed Kissinger to offer greater concessions in the Paris talks. He could now accept some northern troops south of the seventeenth parallel because the United States had demonstrated clear military superiority. This alone should persuade the South that the United States would come to its aid against any future North Vietnamese attacks.

The North Vietnamese response in the summer of 1972 disappointed Kissinger. Instead of acknowledging that the United States possessed superior power and had a right to assist the South, NLF representative Madame Nguyen Thi Binh repeated that the United States should leave Vietnam. The private talks in Paris between Kissinger and Le Duc Tho seemed to go no better. Tho continued to have to refer issues back to Hanoi for final approval. Kissinger suspected that the delays in the North's movement toward accommodation rested on their assumption that the United States was desperate for a solution before the election. North Vietnam mistakenly thought that Nixon was politically vulnerable to the challenge from liberal Senator George McGovern. The Democratic nominee had barnstormed the country berating the President for wasting time in the peace negotiations. Kissinger believed that the North Vietnamese were playing into McGovern's hand. If they could hold out until the fall, then the United States would almost be forced to settle.[20]

During the summer negotiations Kissinger wanted to disabuse the

North of what he considered to be several false notions. He let them know that McGovern was unlikely to win. Public opinion polls put Nixon at 65 percent to McGovern's 30 percent in August. The imposition of wage and price controls in August of 1971 seemed to turn the economy in favor of the President. With inflation now reduced to 2 percent and the annual rate of growth of GNP up to 4 percent the President's popularity had risen.[21]

Kissinger wanted the North to acknowledge that opposition to the fighting attracted only a minority of the public. Most Americans had been pleased with the lesser American role. The death rate for G.I.'s had fallen to under 30 per week in 1972 from a high of over 300 per week in 1968. No longer was the war a staple on the television news. In the middle of 1972 the three evening network news shows reduced the amount of coverage of United States combat operations from an average of twenty-five minutes per week in 1969 to an average of ten minutes per week in the summer of 1972. Kissinger wanted the North to be aware that the antiwar movement commanded only a small minority of the public and had no influence with the administration.[22]

At home, Nixon's reelection campaign tried to discredit Democratic vice-presidential candidate Sargent Shriver. He had claimed that the Johnson administration's Vietnam negotiating team had been prepared to make more concessions in 1968 than Kissinger had done in the last three years. Haldeman noted that "Bill Jordan in Kissinger's shop was a staff man in Paris. He knows everything about it." He ordered "be sure of our facts, then don't let the issue die. Destroy Shriver." He hoped to "get a statement from Rusk or Rostow" contradicting Shriver. Nixon thought the campaign should stress that the Democrats were "playing politics with peace."[23]

At this time, Kissinger encouraged North Vietnam to settle before the election. If Nixon returned to power with any sort of enhanced majority, the President would never have any reason to accommodate. Now, before November, the North could at least hope that the President would want an agreement to show the electorate. Kissinger repeated his earlier assurances of American intentions. As he had stressed for three years, the United States wanted the South to have an opportunity to stand on its own.

Yet Kissinger displayed some flexibility when he indicated that the military and political sides of the war could be separated. In August Haig reported that "at the proper time Kissinger will pull the rug" out from under the POW issue. The politicians in Washington "must stay away until we know what he has." Washington had to be aware that "he may have a legitimate offer." The North might be prepared to "release a few now and a few when the bombing stops."[24]

As Vietnam diminished in international importance, Washington was principally concerned with the military aspects of the war. The United States wanted assurances that the North would not take advantage of its departure from the war. Kissinger reassured Le Duc Tho that the United States did not insist that the government of the South get everything it wanted. In fact, once the United States left Vietnam and the North promised not to augment its forces in the South, Washington would have little interest in the political shape of Vietnam.[25]

Kissinger promised that the United States would not interject its views into the future of a coalition government in Saigon. If the National Liberation Front became part of the government, the United States would do nothing to prevent it from exercising control over its ministries. Moreover, Kissinger implied to Le Duc Tho that the United States would accept some sort of partition of the South. Since the NLF forces could remain in place, they could retain their control over approximately forty percent of the country. The United States, however, would not permit the NLF to set up a provisional government in the areas it dominated. Should the NLF continue to call itself the Provisional Revolutionary Government, the United States would not stand aside. The NLF could not have it both ways by being included in the national government and also proclaiming itself a provisional government. Short of that, however, the United States was prepared to allow a coalition government in the South.

Kissinger acted as both advocate and mediator, pressing the United States position while letting North Vietnam know that he did not care greatly about the fate of South Vietnam. He wanted his negotiating partners to realize that the United States had other interests than Vietnam. All the while, however, the United States did not want to appear to have been driven from Vietnam.[26]

He therefore refused to dump President Thieu. If the NLF and the North wanted to satisfy themselves that the United States was going to leave the South, they could not also require that Thieu leave as well. For three years the North Vietnamese representatives to the private and public peace talks had proclaimed that President Thieu was only a puppet of the United States who represented no one but himself. They demanded that any future government of South Vietnam remove the "Thieu-Ky clique" and replace it with men sympathetic to the NLF.

Le Duc Tho repeated these demands in the summer of 1972, much to Kissinger's exasperation. It seemed to the Americans that the events of the past three months had done nothing to alter the North's intransigence. The leverage imposed by Moscow and the shock of Nixon's visit to China did not seem to have moved the North from its hard position. Most discouraging of all, Kissinger could detect no difference in the private talks from the public position of the North and the NLF.[27]

The North's inflexibility changed, however, in August. Le Duc Tho suddenly seemed able to negotiate on his own without referring every nuance back to the Politburo in Hanoi. Perhaps even more significantly, the North's spokesman for the first time acknowledged the possibilities in the American approach of separating the military from the political. While the United States would not say Thieu was its puppet, fully under the control of the American mission in Saigon, it also would not insist that the political and military issues be resolved together. For the first time Le Duc Tho seemed to acknowledge that the United States wanted to get out of Vietnam on the best terms it could arrange for itself. The Americans would not dump Thieu, but they might do the next best thing, which was to let him try to survive on his own without American backing. Only if the North Vietnamese pressed too hard to have Thieu removed from office before there could be an agreement would the United States get its back up. From the North's viewpoint the best thing it could do would be to allow Thieu to stay. That would give the Americans their opportunity to leave and would put the South Vietnamese government in a highly exposed position.[28]

As the Paris talks seemed to progress, Kissinger sought the limelight. Schedulers in the White House were told "if . . . you should have the occassion or opportunity to schedule Dr. Henry Kissinger, please keep two points in mind:

1. He should never be scheduled in conjunction with another White House staff member to make an appearance. He should appear by himself.

2. He should never be scheduled at any type of fund raising event. . . .

Please follow these above points explicitly."[29]

Such insufferable egoism moved other staff members to worry that Kissinger might overshadow the President during the campaign. Murrey Marder, a *Washington Post* columnist, asked "where does the massive Kissinger ego, which he mitigates somewhat by joking about it, expand next?" Marder reported that "White House insiders" had told him that Kissinger had been kept off television and radio by other staffers, jealously protective of Nixon. "Television exposure, especially live television, could preempt everyone else—including the President—on foreign policy." Charles Colson filed this column next to a demand from Haldeman that Kissinger's schedule "not conflict in any way with the President's calendar."[30]

As the election progressed, panic gripped officials in Saigon. They had never been happy with the process of peace talks. Their refusal to sit down with the NLF had delayed the opening of the first round of talks in the middle of 1968. It was only the Johnson administration's threat to move forward without them that had brought the South Vietnamese to the table along with the NLF. For the first three years of the Nixon administration Saigon had consoled itself with the thought that the North raised impossible conditions. As long as the Communist side refused to budge, the South could expect the United States to remain steadfast. The slightest evidence of movement on Hanoi's part, however, suggested that the United States could cut a deal with the North.

The South had not been kept fully informed regarding the private talks between Kissinger and Le Duc Tho. Naturally, their anxiety mounted as they heard Nixon and Kissinger explain that the military and political aspects of the war could be separated. Saigon represented the political side of the war. Should the United States and the North Vietnamese reach an agreement on the military side of the war, the South's government foresaw itself facing a bleak future bereft of United States support. After August 1972, it seemed from Saigon that the United States would put it in that position.[31]

Thieu depended on Kissinger and Nixon. As the North appeared to make more concessions in the fall of 1972, Saigon grew increasingly balky. The South's negotiator at Paris objected to provisions in the proposed agreement allowing the North to retain troops below the 17th parallel. Kissinger explained that the North would not be permitted to increase the number of its men. Presumably, the ARVN would then be in a position to wipe out the last pockets of NLF resistance. While the United States could not keep its troops in South Vietnam after the conclusion of the peace agreement, America could continue to supply munitions to the South.[32]

Yet the republic's negotiators did not perceive these advantages. If Kissinger was going to agree with the North Vietnamese, America had already decided that it wanted a solution. Saigon feared that whatever violations of the cease-fire took place, the United States would ignore them. America would have a vested interest in making certain that the cease-fire seemed to be working. Washington was unlikely to make an issue of any violations that were taking place. Despite Kissinger's assurances of help to the South Vietnamese, the United States could not be relied on to do much. America would be too concerned with the appearance of an agreement to care much about the substance.

Throughout September, Saigon feared that Kissinger was about to strike a deal overlooking their interests. President Thieu fulminated against the Americans. He objected that he had done what they had asked of him over the past several years, often against his better judgment, only now to be cruelly cast aside. He had pressed his generals to enter Cambodia and Laos as a token of the ARVN's greater willingness to fight only to see that his troops had been routed and morale had plunged.[33]

Sensing that Kissinger looked for a way to jettison South Vietnam, Thieu put up a series of obstacles to the proposed agreement. Not only did he complain about the possibility of the North retaining its forces in the South, he objected to recognition of the legitimacy of the NLF. Thieu believed that Kissinger was willing to let the NLF continue as a responsible quasi-government in control of 40 percent of the territory of South Vietnam. Once the NLF were recognized as a realistic power in South Vietnam, Thieu feared that it would never acknowledge the legitimacy of the official government of the South.

Thieu also put little stock in Kissinger's assurances that an international commission would monitor the cease-fire. Representatives from Canada, Poland, Indonesia, and Hungary were supposed to observe the cease-fire along with a mixed commission made up of members from the government and the NLF. Thieu was certain that Hanoi would ban entry of the mixed commission into their territory. At the same time he predicted that the NLF would not abide by the terms of the armistice.[34]

What could the South Vietnamese do to press the Americans? Aware that the Nixon administration wanted a solution to the war before the election, Thieu decided to make Kissinger squirm. The South simply would refuse any agreement unless the United States pledged greater support.

But Kissinger could play the pressure game as well as the South. He knew that the southerners had to rely on United States support. Their economy had been greatly distorted by the presence of hundreds of thousands of United States troops, and the South now had come to depend on the infusion of United States dollars to maintain the high living standards of their cities. Should the southerners continue to object to any agreement reached between the North and the Americans, the United States would proceed on its own with its arrangements.[35]

On October 26, two weeks before the presidential election, Kissinger achieved his greatest personal notoriety. He announced to a stunned news conference that the United States and North Vietnam were on the verge of an agreement. "Peace is at hand" he assured the world. The reaction in the United States combined high praise for Kissinger with skepticism that anything actually had been accomplished. Republicans naturally were gratified. The remaining cloud hanging over the reelection of President Nixon seemed to have been lifted. The Democratic challenger seemed to be in a state of shock. George McGovern could only mutter that he did not believe it. Even if Kissinger had been successful, he complained, the same deal could have been arranged three years earlier. The costs of the agreement, he implied, had simply been that an additional twenty thousand Americans had died in the three years since Nixon had come to office.[36]

When Kissinger returned to Washington in October he worried about the political impact of an agreement permitting North Vietnamese troops to remain in the South. Would "it look like we've given in to Jane Fonda?" he wondered. There even could be the "appearance of the President crawling" to Hanoi for a settlement before the election. Kissinger's rebuttal to these charges, as always, stressed process and freedom of action above specifics. Permitting the North to keep troops without resupply would "keep them still while we maneuver in the first six weeks" after a cease-fire. It also "puts a deadline on the discussions."[37]

Perhaps most surprising of the reactions came from the White House. It did not join the high chorus of praise for the work of the National Security Adviser. Instead, the President's closest personal and political assistants came to distrust Kissinger's zeal for the limelight. Chief of Staff Haldeman and Counselor Ehrlichman wondered if he was not trying to gain credit he did not deserve. What did "peace is at hand" mean anyway? Had he actually concluded an agreement with Le Duc Tho? If so, where was it? Why had the two men not called in reporters for a signing ceremony?[38]

Haldeman and Ehrlichman disdained the impertinence of another staff member trying to push himself to the head of the queue. They

believed that Kissinger had deliberately sought to have the date of
the announcement moved up before the election so he could receive
the credit for the impending victory. The President's California guard
did not think the outcome of the election was seriously in doubt by
the end of October. Kissinger, therefore, was only forcing his way into
the center of attention. He violated a cardinal rule of staff assistants.
He had called attention to himself and distracted it from his political
superior. Kissinger had even let it be known to the press corps that
the President could not have achieved the breakthrough. He indicated
that the President was so belligerent that he could not have picked
up the nuances of the North's position. He even seemed to accuse the
President of slowness of thought. Only he had the subtlety of mind
to discern the changes in the North's attitude.[39]

Kissinger's rivals in the bureaucracy found their suspicions confirmed over the next few weeks. Details of the new agreement, following the contours of the summer negotiations, excluded the South.
The United States accepted the continued presence of Northern troops
below the Demilitarized Zone in exchange for Hanoi's promise not to
increase its troops' strength. The United States and NLF pledged to
work for a coalition government in the South. Both the Communists
and the Americans sponsored a four-power supervisory commision to
oversee the cease-fire. Observers from Hungary, Poland, Canada, and
Indonesia would keep an eye on the military situation.

The South refused to have anything to do with the proposed settlement. The United States therefore backed off signing a document
before the election. McGovern, who had seemed on the brink of elim-
ination just two weeks before the announcement, now claimed that
no agreement actually was forthcoming. He charged that Kissinger
had only invented an accommodation to solidify his popularity. For
the White House assistants to the President, Kissinger's premature
revelation simply indicated his colossal egoism. They blamed him for
actually undermining the President's credibility with the voters. They
became even more incensed with the publication of a lengthy interview with Kissinger conducted by the Italian journalist Oriana Fallaci.

Fallaci had acquired a reputation over the previous few years of
being an intrepid interviewer who forced her respondents into making extraordinary mistakes. Kissinger's bout with the Italian reporter
confirmed the reputation. Kissinger gave no credit for the foreign policy accomplishments of recent years to the President. Instead, vio-
lating every principle of a good staff assistant, he likened himself to
the "cowboy who leads the wagon train by riding ahead alone on his

horse" to save the day from the mistakes of others. "The cowboy doesn't have to be courageous," he went on. "All he needs is to be alone to show others that he rides into the town alone and does everything by himself. This amazing, romantic character suits me precisely because to be alone is part of my style or, if you like, my technique." If he was the Lone Ranger, who was the President?[40]

Kissinger now seemed to have crossed the line between privately expressing unflattering opinions of the President to a carefully selected group of favored journalists, and publicly indicating that the achievements of the past several years had been accomplished despite the actions of the President. A furious H. R. Haldeman banned Kissinger from making further statements to the press without clearing them first with the White House. More distressing still to the National Security Adviser, who prided himself on his unfettered access to the President, the inner sanctum was off limits to him for the next month.[41]

The President also pestered Kissinger to show his toughness on Vietnam. Nixon chided Kissinger that his old friends at the Council on Foreign Relations continued to deride administration Vietnam policy. Hamilton Fish Armstrong wrote in the October 1972 *Foreign Affairs* that the "war in Vietnam has been the longest and in some respects the most calamitous war in our history." Nixon underlined Fish's contention that "it is a war that has not been and could not be won, a war which was pushed from small beginnings to an appalling multitude of horrors, many of which we have been conscious of only by degrees. The methods we have used in fighting the war have scandalized and disgusted public opinion in almost all foreign countries." Nixon scrawled in the margin "K—after the election give me your critique of this last bump from your friends in the foreign policy establishment."[42]

Worse was to happen inside South Vietnam in November. The Thieu government continued to refuse assent to any agreement with the North. It presented conditions completely unacceptable to the United States. The South demanded that the North remove all of its forces from the Republic. Thieu refused to offer any sort of acknowledgment of the legitimacy of the NLF. He did not want to permit it inside a coalition government. He reckoned that whatever the NLF certified, it would not pay any respectful attention to the coalition agreement. Thieu believed that once the Communists had been elevated to the position of equality in the government, the NLF would never recognize the Thieu's legitimacy.

Kissinger became fed up with Thieu in the fall. He promised "There will be peace. We have decided to have it and we will. It will come in a few weeks' time or even less, that is, immediately after the resumption of negotiations with the North Vietnamese. . . . There is no need to succumb to panic."[43] He believed that Saigon's leader simply abdicated responsibility for his own government's future. Kissinger now came to think that the process of Vietnamization had failed. The South really could not stand on its own, and its leaders knew it. Kissinger might sympathize with their plight, but he also realized that they were likely to drag the United States into an endless war. Now the United States had nothing more to gain from continuing its support for the South. The longer America remained the mainstay of the government of South Vietnam, the more likely the rest of the world would come to doubt that the United States had an appropriate view of its own self-interest. Kissinger now wanted to squeeze President Thieu. He wanted the South Vietnamese leader to acknowledge that America's own interests would take precedence.

He dispatched his deputy, General Alexander Haig, to Saigon to lay out the options. Kissinger and Haig met with Nixon to determine how to approach Thieu. Nixon would inform Thieu that "I have approved every section" of the letter Haig carried with him. Haig agreed to take a "hard line on Thieu." Kissinger ordered him to tell the South Vietnamese leader that "the President has been totally in charge of all this and will go ahead regardless" of anything Saigon did to block the deal. Thieu also should know that "if he takes on K. or the agent, he takes on the President personally."[44]

Haig bullied Thieu. He announced that the United States did not have limitless resources or patience to expend on Vietnam. He reviewed the history of détente of the previous several years to make Thieu realize that the United States had shifted the focus of its foreign policy. South Vietnam no longer represented the important matter for American foreign policy it had during the Johnson administration. Once the United States had improved its position with China and the Soviet Union, South Vietnam certainly was not going to interfere with the greater assertiveness of the United States. South Vietnam also would not be permitted to interrupt the repair of United States relations with its allies in Europe and Asia. They no longer expected the United States to dwell upon the war in Southeast Asia. Haig wanted Thieu to know that the United States was not going to sacrifice improvements in its standing in the world on the altar of the South's desire to survive.[45]

Haig offered barely concealed bribes to force Thieu into accepting the cease-fire agreement. Should he continue his objections, the United States could show just how tough it was. Having denied that the government of South Vietnam actually was a dependent of the United States, Haig now wanted Thieu to acknowledge that his regime could not make a move without Washington. Haig threatened that the United States was prepared to let the South founder if it continued to object to the peace agreement. He pointed out that the South's supposed leverage over the United States depended on American willingness to continue the fiction that Thieu was truly an independent figure. Once Washington decided to demonstrate its own assertiveness, Thieu's leverage would vanish. The United States would then *tell* Thieu what to do. If he refused to accept the arrangement worked out by the North and the United States, America would sign anyway. More important, the United States would publicly criticize Thieu for not having the courage to reach an honorable settlement to the engagement. The United States would decry the Republic's inability to govern. The Americans would stop looking the other way at tales of abuses and corruption inside South Vietnam. Instead, Haig implied that official statements on the war would come to resemble the complaints of the American antiwar movement. The United States government would no longer look the other way at the abuses of the South.[46]

In Washington, Kissinger and Nixon reacted to Haig's report that the South did not intend to stand aside. They decided that both Vietnams needed a demonstration of United States toughness. Hence the concerted bombing of North Vietnam that began in the days before Christmas 1972. For the first time the B-52s went into action against North Vietnam proper.

The bombing ignited some of the most vehement criticism of the war. In America antiwar critics charged that the President had finally dropped all restraints after securing his huge landslide. They cried that a "madman" was conducting a "war by tantrum."[47] They challenged his claims that a true accommodation had been reached at Paris. Instead, the President and the National Security Adviser had misled a docile electorate into believing that they had come to a meeting of the minds with the North. Now with nothing to hold them back, the administration's diplomats and warriors had decided to break the North's capacity to fight. In Europe too, liberal and social democratic friends of the United States who had kept their peace while Kissinger had negotiated during the summer erupted in fury at having been betrayed. François Mitterrand, the longtime Socialist leader of France exploded that Nixon was a "barbarian." Willy Brandt, the Social Democratic chancellor of West Germany charged that he had been misled by the United States. Harold Wilson, the Labour party prime minister of Great Britain, also thundered that the United States had broken its word.[48]

Kissinger kept up his dual role of spokesman for toughness within the administration while subtly hinting that he stood in the way of even more aggressive action. The *Nation*, disgusted by the renewed bombing, rebuked Kissinger for his "colossal effrontery" in denying that he had engaged in a charade. Instead, it editorialized, "between them, Mr. Nixon and Dr. Kissinger have kept the American people guessing at their pantomime for the past four years, in a game both deadly and deceptive." Even this liberal journal believed that Kissinger was better than Nixon, who had used his assistant's credibility with the press for electoral advantage. "Henry was pulling the emperor's chestnuts out of the fire, at the expense of his own credibility."[49]

Kissinger continued the negotiation in Paris with Le Duc Tho. He let Tho know that the United States now had no limits on what it would do. The United States was committed to an agreement. It wanted Tho to return all prisoners and make even more explicit commitments to allow the South to flourish. He expected the North not to add to its troop strength in the South. He expected the North to keep the NLF on a very short leash. They too had to recognize that the South was a legitimate government and they would not resume the war. He pointed out to Tho that the United States was willing to go into action once more over North Vietnam to keep the agreement. The Americans also stood poised to resume the war in the South if the cease-fire was violated repeatedly.

Time named Nixon and Kissinger Men of the Year for 1972, since "foreign policy reigned preeminent and was in good part the base for the landslide election victory at home." The "improbable partnership" of Nixon, "champion of Middle American virtues, a secretive, aloof yet old-fashioned politician, given to oversimplified rhetoric," and Kissinger, "Harvard professor of urbane intelligence" accomplished "the most profound rearrangement of the earth's political powers since the beginning of the cold war." *Time* outlined the successes—notably China and détente with the Soviets—but noted that it "was also, in its final days, a year of devastating disappointment . . . flawed by the ugly war from which, once again, there seemed no early exit."[50]

In Paris, Kissinger explained to Tho that the United States stood ready to help the North rebuild its economy. Taking a page from Lyndon Johnson's book, he promised $7.5 billion in aid for the region with $3.25 billion going directly to the North if only they would reach an agreement. He did, however, qualify his pledge of aid by reminding the North that "It should be understood that the Congress traditionally authorizes and appropriates considerably less than the amount which the President recommends and requests."[51]

Tho was willing, but what about the South? That was where Haig's pressure on Thieu became so important. Haig returned to South Vietnam with the same message he had carried earlier in the fall. Now, however, he had the proof necessary to persuade Thieu of America's future intentions toward the continued war in the South. If the North did not keep the agreement hammered out between Kissinger and Le Doc Tho, the United States had demonstrated its willingness to use the strongest weapons in its arsenal. On the other hand, were the South Vietnamese to object to the agreement and prevent its completion, Haig made it clear that the United States would stop aid immediately. It would go forward with the arrangements with North Vietnam and leave the South in the lurch. Faced with such pressure, the South capitulated on January 15.

At this point Kissinger was able to nail down the arrangement with Le Duc Tho. On January 23 the two initialed an agreement virtually unchanged from the one proposed in October. Asked if he thought that the bombing had brought the North to its knees, Kissinger replied: "I was asked in October whether the bombing or mining of May 8 brought about the breakthrough in October, and I said then that I did not want to speculate on North Vietnamese motives. I have too much trouble analyzing our own. I will give the same answer . . . but I will say that there was a deadlock which was described in mid-December, and there was a rapid movement when the negotiations resumed on the technical level on January 2."[52]

The North agreed to release the American POWs and not increase its troops in the South. Tho also accepted the proposal of a mixed armistice commission to supervise the cease-fire. They accepted the legitimacy of the South Vietnamese government, so long as it recognized that the NLF had a right to exist peacefully in the South. For its part, the United States finally recognized the legitimacy of Northern claims to be in the South. By not insisting that Hanoi withdraw all of its troops from the South before an acceptable peace could be arranged, Kissinger effectively acknowledged that the North had a say in the outcome. Most of all, the United States formally acknowledged that the political issues it had come to Vietnam to settle exceeded its grasp. With the return of its prisoners from the North the United States had received all it believed it could get from North Vietnam. While Kissinger expected the North to observe the cease-fire and pledged aid to the South if it were violated, he realized that the South would have to make its own bargains with the North. Kissinger acknowledged that "it is . . . obvious to any reader of the Saigon press and of their official communications that we did not accept all of their comments and that we have carried out precisely what the President has said . . . namely, that we would make the final determination when American participation should end."[53]

The White House was jubilant at the favorable reaction to the cease-fire. The press office rejoiced that "there is great admiration for the President which seems to grow as we move further from Washington." Most papers praised "the fact of the cease-fire, with little concern at the terms." Notably, "many editorials do point out that it was the bombing which did bring Hanoi back to Paris for serious negotiations." The *Birmingham Post Herald* praised Nixon and Kissinger for their "risk-taking, doggedness, and high diplomatic skill." The *Birmingham News* lauded "the patient, long-suffering efforts of the administration. . . . They represent, in fact, a much better bargain than Sen. George McGovern or other 'dove' critics were willing to settle for." The *San Diego Evening Tribune* thought that the "dogged insistence of Mr. Nixon on adherence to his policy . . . has given the democracy a fighting chance for survival in the alien climate of Saigon." A California radio station mocked the administration's detractors. "Their predictions were wrong and his actions were correct." The *Los Angeles Times* believed that "Protocols confirmed only when Kissinger returned from Paris a fortnight ago" had strengthened the October cease-fire agreement. The *Denver Post* considered the peace agreement "the most promising that could possibly have been extricated from the excruciating difficulties and complexities of the Vietnam dilemma." The Paris accord "is a tribute to the skill and statesmanship of Henry Kissinger and to the determination, spirit and persistence of President Nixon."[54]

So ended the Nixon administration's combat in Vietnam. It had reached an agreement in 1972–1973 similar to one it could have achieved in 1969. To its detractors, the additional three years of bloodshed meant that it had done nothing to end the suffering. They were not persuaded that Kissinger and Nixon had maintained the credibility of the word of the United States. For the principals in the

Nixon administration, however, the eventual cease-fire represented a real, if delayed triumph. The United States had not been forced out of Vietnam. It had arranged good relations with the Soviet Union and China, seemingly at the expense of the North. They had also acknowledged the effective limits of American power. They hoped that over the next several years they would be able to apply it selectively. The public sigh of relief at the conclusion of the war combined with the renewed mandate of election of 1972 would, they hoped, offer a new honeymoon in which they could have a free hand in foreign affairs.

SIX

Securing the Prize: Kissinger as Secretary of State

With the President's smashing reelection victory, the Nixon White House looked around for ways of assuring their authority over the next four years. Promoting Henry Kissinger to Secretary of State could focus public attention on the foreign policy accomplishments of the second administration. Observers had called for Kissinger's elevation in 1972. George Ball, Undersecretary of State in the Kennedy and Johnson administrations, and often a critic of Kissinger, thought elevating him to Secretary would "make the architect of our foreign strategy accessible to the Congress and the people." Beyond that, Kissinger's performance was in danger of going stale. "Anticlimax is fatal to effective theater, and, after Peking, there is nowhere the President can go (except the Moon) with anything like the same dramatic punch."[1]

Richard Nixon himself was especially concerned about the possibility of a second term letdown. He recalled the foreign policy perils of Eisenhower's later years. Secretary of State John Foster Dulles died in 1959. A vacuum at the top caused drift, as the administration seemed to lurch without direction from one foreign policy crisis to another. If it was not the Soviet's launch of the world's first space satellite, *Sputnik*, in October 1957, it was a revolution in Lebanon in 1958, or it was the success of Fidel Castro's insurgents in Cuba at the beginning of 1959. Nixon himself had gone from the heroics of his "kitchen debate" with Nikita Khrushchev in 1959 to the ignominy of his stoning by leftist Venezuelan students a few months later. By 1959, Democrats, preparing themselves for the 1960 election, had begun to challenge the capacity of the Eisenhower administration to see clearly the real foreign policy problems.[2]

Nixon also worried about his status as a lame duck. The only way to avoid a gradual diminution of his authority would be to shake up his administration at the very beginning of the second term. To that end, his chief aide, Bob Haldeman, astonished the members of the cabinet on the morning after the election victory by demanding that each submit resignations for review by the White House staff. All grumbled but complied.

Secretary of State William P. Rogers worried the most. He had been kept in the dark about all the major achievements of the past two years. He had not been taken into the White House's confidence about the opening to China and his advice had been ignored regarding preparations for the trip to Moscow in May 1972. The State Department had been shunted aside in the planning for arms control talks and for peace negotiations with the North Vietnamese. Throughout these humiliations Rogers stoically kept his peace.[3]

However much the staff wanted to replace Rogers, they also were uncomfortable about promoting Kissinger. In November the National Security Adviser was still under a cloud because of his interview with Oriana Fallaci. Moreover, he had not yet nailed down an agreement with the North Vietnamese removing the United States from the war. To relieve Rogers in favor of Kissinger before such a settlement were in place appalled aides and made Nixon think twice. The staff would find themselves hoping that Kissinger would succeed without being able to discipline him. Indeed, Nixon would have provided the reward without Kissinger first having won a victory.[4]

Kissinger's early appointment also might tie his hands in dealing with North Vietnam. As Secretary of State he would be desperate for an end to the war. He could not make any demands upon the North, for Hanoi would realize how eager he was to have an accommodation. They would press him to the limits, realizing how much he needed a signed accord. He would either accept their position or lose influence as Secretary of State. Moreover, as chief of the foreign policy apparatus, Kissinger could not have the time to continue the negotiations. (Events proved that fear to be baseless. Within less than a year he embarked on his celebrated shuttle between Jerusalem, Cairo and Damascus. Then too his critics complained that he betrayed arms control with his preoccupation with ending the Middle East War.) Finally, as Secretary of State, his talks with Hanoi would be conducted in the full glare of media exposure and publicity. Whatever advantages had been gained by the secrecy shrouding Kissinger's meetings with Le Duc Tho would vanish.

Once Kissinger nailed down the cease-fire in January 1973, however, there were no further barriers. The pressure to elevate him to the premier position in the cabinet became almost irresistible. His stock among the press continued to rise in early 1973. The peace with North Vietnam generated a chorus of adulation. *Time* and *Newsweek* featured him on their covers and praised him for having a greater grasp of the subtleties of foreign affairs than anyone else in the bureaucracy. Nixon and Rogers suffered by comparison. The President appeared too intransigent, too belligerent, and too insensitive to the needs of other nations to be accorded much respect as the major architect of the nation's foreign policy. Rogers' very good nature seemed to disqualify him for the job he held. He appeared to lack the toughness, even the duplicity, to get his way with other officials. The fact that Kissinger had outmaneuvered him since 1969 made him a less than attractive candidate to remain at the State Department.[5]

At this point Rogers became more of a liability to the Nixon administration. Once the press considered him ineffectual, his good manners, soft voice and careful tailoring did him no good. His reputation for rectitude paled when laid against the White House's record of accomplishment. Nixon had needed him as a shield against a suspicious press in 1969. New to power, the fledgling administration appeared on the defensive and needed Rogers to smooth the way. In light of détente with the Soviets and the end of the war in Vietnam, however, even the most liberal organs had to admit that Nixon and Kissinger had succeeded. In these circumstances self-confidence soared at the White House and Rogers became a far less valuable asset.

Kissinger's appointment as Secretary of State resolved many of these problems. The President, an unlikable figure to Washington reporters and columnists, could bask in the reflected glory of the National Security Adviser. Kissinger provided brilliance. His successes abroad—his trailblazing along Nixon's road to China, the SALT breakthrough, or the end of the Vietnam War—all made him the darling of liberal commentators. With Kissinger as Secretary of State the administration had the grudging admiration of a press that had been cultivated by Kissinger for four years.

Kissinger's stock rose in the middle of 1973 just as the President became embroiled in congressional investigation of the Watergate break-in of June 1972. Through the election campaign the administration successfully kept Watergate out of the public eye. Only in March did the issue again become topical to the public and press. James McCord, one of the burglars arrested in the Democratic National Committee headquarters, informed Judge John Sirica that the burglars had been paid by the Nixon administration's reelection committee. At the same time the Senate established a select committee to investigate abuses during the 1972 campaign. Under the chairmanship of North Carolina Senator Sam Ervin a bipartisan group of seven senators began to hold hearings on the Watergate break-in in May. The President's lawyer, John Dean, broke with the White House in April, began cooperating with the Justice Department prosecutors and promised to testify before the Ervin committee in May. An embattled President Nixon argued that the public and press attention to the news coming from the Ervin committee undermined his ability to conduct international relations. He accused liberals within the press and Congress of attempting to win through the courts and the Senate hearings what they had lost at the ballot box in November. Nixon claimed that the public itself was not interested in the tale unfolding in the Senate caucus room. He indicated that without the steady diet of sensational reports from the prosecutors or Senate the public would quickly become bored and would return their affection for the President's foreign policy.[6]

Watergate affected the timing of the announcement of Kissinger's appointment. "Watergate, some officials believe," reported the *Christian Science Monitor*, "may have been a catalyst in President Nixon's decision to make the change. It already has enabled him to say that he is 'getting the work out' in the departments where it belongs."[7]

As the Watergate investigation grew, Secretary General Brezhnev came to Washington to return President Nixon's call on Moscow. Kissinger had prepared for the new summit with a trip to the Soviet capital in April. Given full freedom by Nixon, he sought concrete agreements for signing in Washington. Brezhnev pressed for a declaration barring either side from using nuclear weapons first. Kissinger turned that aside and substituted what he later described as "a bland set of principles that had been systematically stripped of all implications harmful to our interests." At the Washington summit the two sides confirmed this deal with an agreement on the Prevention of Nuclear War. The two sides agreed that "an objective of their policy is to remove the danger of nuclear war and of the use of nuclear weapons." They stipulated that "each party will refrain from the threat or the use of force against the other." Finally, they agreed to "enter into urgent consultations" should their relations "appear to involve the risk of a nuclear conflict." The Soviets hailed this pact as the centerpiece of the June summit. Kissinger too described it as "a significant step toward the prevention of nuclear war" and possibly "a landmark in the relationship of the United States to the Soviet Union."[8]

In fact, the PNW Pact was the only concrete accomplishment of the second summit. Kissinger sought to dispel public anxieties that little had transpired. The *Philadelphia Inquirer* declared that "Agreements are Mostly Ballyhoo" and the *Washington Post* questioned "A-Pact: Policy Paper or Bold Venture?" Kissinger felt compelled to respond. He repeated his observations during the 1972 summit that détente was a process. "Whether the agreement proves to be meaningful or meaningless," he told a press conference at the end of the summit, "depends not on the document itself, but what Washington and Moscow choose to do about it. It can either be another piece of international paper or a bold venture in international affairs."[9]

The decision to appoint Kissinger as Secretary of State therefore took on additional importance in August. As the President's hold on the public imagination slipped, Kissinger became a more valuable asset. Reaction to the appointment was almost universally favorable. *Time* enthused there was now "A Super Secretary to Shake Up State." *Newsweek* chronicled "the Apotheosis of Henry Kissinger," praising him as "the White House genius in residence." *U.S. News* predicted that Kissinger's elevation would "give him the most powerful voice in foreign policy in recent U.S. history."[10]

Others praised the appointment for strengthening the State Department. "It's a good thing that Henry Kissinger is moving over from the White House to the State Department for the entirely impersonal reason that it is time to get American foreign policy back in the State Department." A foreign service officer exulted that "we'll consider ourselves God's chosen children for a couple of months—until the dust settles." Charles Yost, a former ambassador, explained he was "delighted that the President has decided to unite these responsibilities [National Security Adviser and Secretary of State] under one man, particularly one as able and experienced as Henry Kissinger." Robert Bowie, who worked for the NSC staff in the Eisenhower administration, also considered an impending end to the rivalry between State and White House "an improvement over the previous setup for the handling of foreign policy." Yet Bowie, who had been Kissinger's superior at the Harvard Center for International Affairs in the late fifties, was more prescient than many, and he foresaw dangers. He considered Kissinger too optimistic when he said that the need was mainly to "solidify what has been started" and "institutionalize the initiatives of the first term." Bowie thought he had to go much farther and "ultimately come to terms with the dominant facts of growing interdependence." The liberal *New Yorker* described Kissinger as a "prodigiously intelligent, articulate, talented, witty and imposing man."[11]

With the appointment of Kissinger the White House hoped his high appeal with the press would rub off on the President himself. The very people who criticized the President and his men for abuse of power believed that Kissinger's conduct of foreign affairs had been superb. Liberals for the most part approved of détente with the Soviet Union, arms control, and the opening to China. As chairman J. William Fulbright observed at Kissinger's confirmation hearings, "Dr. Kissinger is widely regarded as possessing a brilliant mind, and an iron constitution capable of endless travel and interminable conferences. His travels to China and Russia have helped change the climate of international relations, a change long overdue and for which I congratulate him."[12] The Foreign Relations Committee was highly supportive. Nixon's adversaries on Watergate tended to lean over backwards in their efforts to boost Kissinger. Some observers believed that senators questioning Kissinger were "predictably . . . cordial and respectful."[13] *New Republic* columnist Stanley Karnow thought that "senators chose . . . to skim the surface." He lamented that "even the more dynamic members of the committee are, despite their rhetoric, essentially less interested in challenging the President than in sharing his power in foreign relations, and they therefore treated Kissinger gently as a way of signaling their receptivity to a truce with the administration."[14]

Senator Frank Church (D.-Ida.) of the Foreign Relations Committee noticed that letters from constituents opposing Kissinger's elevation to Secretary of State fell into two categories. Some, hinting antisemitism, believed that only a native-born U.S. citizen should hold the office. Others objected to his foreign policy itself. Church responded to the first with a homily on "the glory of our country that an immigrant citizen can rise to so high a position." As for the second, Church could read the election returns as well as anybody. He thought that "any president is entitled to the services of the most skillful men he can find. . . . No one can deny that Henry Kissinger has demonstrated consummate ability in conducting negotiations for the President." If the policy was wanting, Nixon, not Kissinger, was the man in charge. "Responsibility should be placed where the power resides; in this case with the President."[15]

Events gravely disappointed the public relations and political experts at the White House. In the midst of Watergate nothing might have helped Nixon's standing. Instead of making the President look better for having chosen Kissinger, Nixon seemed weaker than his Secretary of State. As *The New Yorker* commented, Kissinger "is quite unlike most of the people President Nixon surrounded himself with in the White House. He has style, he has intellectual finesse, he has warmth and humor, he speaks the English language, he is without pretention, he is not mean spirited, he seems instinctively drawn to telling the truth, and he clearly wants to serve his country well."[16] For the first term Nixon had decided that to be his own principal diplomat he needed to have greater authority than the Secretary of State. With the benign William Rogers in charge it was easy for the President and his National Security Adviser to outshine the State Department. With Kissinger running things at Foggy Bottom, the President invariably would appear to pale in comparison to the new Secretary.

When Kissinger assumed his duties as Secretary in September he insisted on retaining his position as National Security Adviser to the President. No other White House official had also taken a job as head of a cabinet department. Certainly no National Security Adviser had ever tried to blend the two roles. On its face, consolidating the two offices under a single head defeated the purpose of the National Security System. The NSC was supposed to coordinate policy among the various groups within the bureaucracy. If the Adviser and the Secretary of State were the same person, the views of the State Department were bound to take precedence in the bureaucratic warfare. If the NSC continued to override the views of the foreign service and the permanent officials of the State Department, the Department might feel more ignored than ever. If, on the other hand, the Secretary of State continued to express views manufactured in the Department, he would find it impossible to act as the impartial arbiter in his role as Security Adviser.

Kissinger waived these objections aside in the summer of 1973. He could not conceive of accepting less than both positions. To have stayed at the White House without taking the State Department role would have kept him out of the spotlight he craved. To have yielded his role as head of the NSC while going to Foggy Bottom would have diminished his access to the President. He explained to skeptical senators that "the President will select whomever among his advisers he believes can best fulfill those functions of adviser and negotiator." He pointed out that "if the positions are separated, then the management of the interdepartmental machinery will be conducted in different capacities, and that range of activity would again be withdrawn from congressional discussion." He told Senator Stuart Symington (D.-Mo.) "Of course, the President would have it in his power, if he appoints another Assistant, to withdraw all foreign policy matters from Secretary Kissinger and have him empty the wastebaskets in the State Department. So that problem is not solved by separating the two positions. In fact, the danger is reduced by combining the two positions."[17]

Kissinger already feared that his onetime deputy, Alexander Haig, was surpassing him in the President's favor. Haig had taken over the position as Chief of Staff in the White House in May when Haldeman had been forced to resign. Kissinger believed that his own authority was strong enough with the press and public that he could avoid Rogers's fate. On the other hand he did not want to risk sharing power with a potential rival at the NSC. Any newcomer to the NSC would necessarily resent Kissinger's looking over his shoulder. He would become embroiled in the same sorts of disputes over priority that had soured relations between Kissinger and Rogers or Laird.

Within a few months it appeared to reporters that "State is being molded into Kissinger's image and not vice versa. From such incidentals as decor (he has substituted modern art for the landscapes and portraits favored by former Secretary William Rogers) to personnel (some 30 new ambassadors . . .) the department is taking on the Kissinger stamp."[18] Observers noticed "a new electricity throbbing through the long-torpid State Department." A foreign service officer exclaimed, "you can sense it ever since Kissinger took over. Before he arrived we were shuffling papers, doing busy work, not really accomplishing anything. Now you feel someone's in charge."[19] "Kissinger Tops White House Power Structure" noted an editorial that praised him as "the architect and builder of the most popular part of the Nixon record. As the man who ended the 'cold war' and cleared things for Mr. Nixon to Peking, Dr. Kissinger is the proudest adornment of the Nixon scene. Untouched (almost) by Watergate, he is the administration's most untouchable man."[20]

When Kissinger became Secretary of State he had the opportunity to put into effect the general coordinating functions of the National

Security Adviser. Although he had tried to become the originator and final arbiter of foreign policy, combining the functions had eluded him. Now, as Secretary of State, he had the chance to exercise both the planning of foreign policy and the execution. In his own mind the difficulties facing President Nixon with Congress and the public over the Watergate investigations proved a mixed blessing. Nixon's diminished public standing gave Kissinger some greater freedom of action. He had, however, enjoyed such freedom during the first term when Nixon needed his appeal to the Rockefeller wing of the party and his entree into the foreign policy establishment. As Nixon became ever more entangled in scandal, he came to resent Kissinger rather than find him a help. The more Nixon appealed to the press and public to defer to the White House over foreign affairs, the more outsiders came to elevate Kissinger above the President. Kissinger could go only so far in welcoming this adulation. While it fed his own sense of superiority and growing sense that the President was out of touch, he feared that Nixon might react badly. The President could easily decide that the gap between Kissinger's high reputation and his own low ranking with the public was unacceptable. Jealous, he might drop Kissinger from the cabinet. While that was not highly likely, Kissinger could suffer in other ways from the scandal. He worried that eventually the opposition to the President would wash over into foreign affairs. Once Congress received a taste of blood, it might be unstoppable.

In fact, Congress began its assault upon presidential foreign policy prerogative in the midst of the Watergate hearings. In June 1973 both houses voted to halt funding for bombing Cambodia where the war continued to rage. The two principal students of congressional control of foreign policy, Thomas Franck and Edward Wiesband, designate June 29 as "the Bastille Day of the foreign policy revolution."[21] Kissinger, on the verge of his greatest triumph, muttered about Congress's usurpations. He derided a "runaway legislative rabble." He wondered if the legislators actually would let him conduct the country's diplomacy. Nonetheless, he did little to reverse the Joint Resolution. He believed that it was a largely symbolic gesture. He wanted the public to forget about the war in Southeast Asia. He believed that there was very little the United States could do to affect the outcome of the war in Cambodia anyway, so a dramatic protest against the congressional action would raise more dissent than it would still. All Kissinger could do was object to what Congress had done, let friends know that he believed that foreign policy autonomy was slipping from the President's grasp, and warn that Congress was incapable of acting responsibly.[22]

In public, at least, Kissinger was more deferential to congressional desires for a greater say in foreign policy. He promised that he would try to consult more often as Secretary of State. "I cannot guarantee that we will always be able to accept the views of this committee," he told the Senate Foreign Relations Committee, "but we will certainly discuss our views fully and listen very carefully to the views of the Committee." He pledged "a regularized reporting and consultation process" to keep congressional leaders up-to-date. Nonetheless, he reserved the right to act without congressional foreknowledge "in cases of really overwhelming national security considerations." Then he hoped that somehow the old congressional deference to the views of the President might revive. When questioned whether he might recommend another covert operation like the secret bombing of Cambodia, he replied, "the circumstances that produced that situation were nearly unique. It [is] almost inconceivable that they could be repeated. However, should they be repeated, I would expect that relations between the executive and legislative branch would have reached a point of trust where your Committee would know about it."[23]

At the very beginning of his term as Secretary of State Kissinger had little time to consult with Congress. Two problem areas—Chile and the Middle East—erupted. Neither had received major attention from the State Department or NSC in the preceding four years. While National Security Adviser he had often complained about the inability of State to plan strategically. Officials there were preoccupied with the parochial interests of their regions of specialization and often failed to acknowledge the larger interests of United States foreign relations. They became advocates of their regions rather than proponents of United States national concerns.

To Kissinger's dismay the same thing happened to him. The more he concentrated on specific areas of the world the less he could set broad themes. Soon he was no more successful than the old-fashioned State Department officials in seeing the big picture.

The first regional problem that confronted the new Secretary of State was Chile where a socialist government headed by Salvador Allende Gossens had been in power since 1970. Allende had been elected to the presidency on his third try with 36 percent of the vote. Even before he took power the United States tried everything to stop the success of the socialist revolution. Kissinger ordered a review in the

President's name "of United States policy to cover the possibility of an Allende victory in the presidential elections." He wanted the State and Defense Departments, the CIA, and the Joint Chiefs of Staff to explain the "objectives of the Allende administration, [the] immediate and long-range threats to the United States, and possible United States course of action." Allende appeared to Washington as an unwelcome symbol to other Latin Americans. For the first time a Marxist government had been legally elected and taken office in the western hemisphere. If it prospered, the message to other Latin American nations might prove irresistible. Since the Kennedy administration's adoption of the Alliance for Progress, a multilateral foreign aid effort, in 1961, the United States had sought an alternative to Leftist control of Latin American governments by supporting the efforts of Christian Democratic politicians. The CIA had funneled hundreds of millions into the coffers of the Chilean CDP. Its leader, Eduardo Frei, who had directed the government since 1964, had depended on the largesse of the United States. Now Frei had passed from the scene, his party was in tatters, and the Socialists, whom the United States had sought to keep out of office, had triumphed. Should Allende succeed, he might prove a graver threat to United States interests than did Cuba's Fidel Castro. A democratically elected socialist government could become a model. If Chile pressed socialism, without the United States or the bloodshed and dictatorship of Cuba, other Latin states might follow.[24]

Kissinger presided over the Forty Committee, which supervised covert overseas operations of the intelligence agencies. "I don't see why we have to let a country go Marxist just because its people are irresponsible," he told one meeting in the summer of 1970. First the Committee attempted to prevent Allende from assuming office. United States CIA officials in Santiago helped the outgoing Christian Democratic party to have the Chilean congress deny the Socialist the presidency. Even though Chilean custom required that the highest vote-getter become the president, the law allowed legislators to choose from any of the contenders. The United States Ambassador, Edward Korry, cabled Washington after the first round election gave Allende a slight, one-percentage-point plurality that the election of "Communism . . . will have the most profound effect on Latin America and beyond; we have suffered a grievous defeat; the consequences will be domestic and international."[25]

Chile's congress followed tradition and duly elected Allende in October. At this point the United States pursued a second track of disrupting Allende's inauguration, and failing that, making his administration impossible. Before the Socialist leader could take the oath of office, Henry Hecksher, the CIA man in Santiago, helped arrange the assassination of the chief of staff of the armed forces, General René Schneider.

The general seemed to follow the traditional nonpartisan approach. He became a target for assassination as a ploy to discredit the Left. The CIA hoped that Chilean public opinion would turn on the Socialists and accuse them of engineering the murder, but the plan backfired. Instead of pinning responsibility on the Allende forces, Chile's congress, newspapers, and informed public correctly assumed that the nationalist right had been behind the murders. Whatever chance there was that Allende's elevation would be blocked ended in October when a hail of bullets cut down General Schneider.[26]

Back in Washington Kissinger presided over a stunned Forty Committee. The CIA in secret and other agencies of the United States government in public decided to substitute the stick for the carrot. Aid to the government of Chile abruptly stopped. The Agency for International Development withdrew its personnel and programs from the country. Credits from the Export–Import Bank dried up. Kissinger pressed the International Monetary Fund, the World Bank, and the Inter-American Bank for Development to halt loans to the Socialist government in Santiago.[27]

With less success, the United States discouraged allied governments in the western hemisphere and Europe from trading with or aiding the Chileans. These countries continued to trade with Chile, but a worldwide drop in the price of copper in 1971–1972 severely undermined the strength of the nation's economy, which depended heavily on the reddish-brown metal. Chile tried to counterpunch by withholding copper from the United States, something Korry described as "a conscious challenge to the tradition of the United States defense of its major business interests in Latin America." Still Korry, unlike Kissinger, wanted to "cultivate pragmatic relationships with Chile and avoid confrontation." *New York Times* columnist C. L. Sulzberger, one of Kissinger's staunchest allies in the press, visited Latin America in the spring of 1971 and also urged caution on the President and National Security Adviser. He dismissed Allende as "a clever but not profound man, energetic but undisciplined . . . a man being rendered giddy with success." Sulzberger recommended that Washington should "never allow any developments to precipitate a break in relations with Santiago."[28]

Despite these pleas for calm, the CIA followed a covert course of destabilizing Chile. It went outside the traditional Chilean party structure to fund groups dissatisfied with the Socialists. Middle-class homemakers, alarmed at the rising prices, commenced demonstrations funded by the United States. Independent truck drivers, who previously had prospered under a market oriented economy, saw their earnings erode when inflation hit 400 percent. They too received assistance from the CIA to mount public displays of discontent with the government. They struck, blocked roads, burned tires, and demanded that they be allowed to set their own fees.[29]

None of this agitation seemed to affect Allende's government. In 1972 congressional elections took place in Chile and the Socialists and parties allied with them managed to increase their share of the vote to 41 percent. The figure did not differ significantly from the 43 percent of the popular vote Nixon himself received in 1968 or the proportion of the congressional vote earned by Republican candidates over the previous twenty years. Experts in Washington panicked. It appeared as if the Socialists in Chile were maintaining their popularity and their legitimacy. Contrary to expectations, they had not suspended constitutional guarantees of civil liberties. Opposition parties continued to operate. Although their economic performance had been poor, the Socialists remained popular. Indeed, if there were any indications of a decline in the public appeal of socialist leadership it came from portions of the working class that feared that they had gone too slowly in pressing their agenda. Land reform and nationalization proceeded at a measured pace, with punctilious regard for the requirements of compensation. Radicals were disappointed that the standard of living of the poor had not risen to the heights of the elite. They demanded faster action, and, more ominously, insisted that they would take over the land if the government did not act. They wanted to be armed by the state to resist the forces of the rich. Leftists warned that the armed forces of Chile planned a coup d'état to evict the Socialists.[30]

As tensions rose inside Chile at the beginning of 1973, American officials worried that two contradictory outcomes might occur. Should Allende succumb to the blandishments of his most radical supporters, he could establish a Soviet- or Cuban-style dictatorship. A revolutionary government was one thing in Cuba, where there was no democratic tradition. Despite his Communist rhetoric, Fidel Castro could easily be assimilated into the long history of personal rule in Cuba. Chile, however, was entirely different. It had maintained democratic institutions since 1830. The Socialist government had come to power through constitutional means and it gave every indication of continuing to uphold them. Had the Allende government lost badly in the congressional elections, it would have yielded power to the right. In Washington, the very punctiliousness of the Socialists raised an even more menacing specter than the threat of a Soviet-type dictatorship in Latin America. If it appeared that the Socialists would willingly yield power to conservatives or Christian Democrats, part of the fear of Marxism might be eroded. Kissinger indicated that Marxist states were different from any other sort because the process of revolution was irreversible. The United States could not sit by and allow any people to choose Marxism. Even if they did so freely, Kissinger assumed that they could not then reverse themselves.

The democratic respectability of the Allende government lessened the impact of such fears. Kissinger scoffed at Allende's democratic credentials as a "myth . . . as assiduously fostered as it is untrue." Once more he berated liberals for succumbing to such fantasies.[31] He became alarmed at the prospect of a Marxist government turning over power peacefully to liberal or conservative parties that won elections. The model for the remainder of Latin America would be worse from the American point of view than revolution in Castro's Cuba. A dictatorship offered the non-leftist opposition little choice but to seek alliances with the United States and the CIA. Many Latin liberals or conservatives had strong nationalist sentiments that targeted the United States as the major block to their nation's development. They preferred to keep an arm's-length relationship from the United States, if that was at all possible. A revolutionary dictatorship provided them with no choice but to link arms with the United States. Similarly, Chile's military's history of avoidance of interference in politics made its officers reluctant to involve themselves in the future of the regime. Allende's refusal to arm the radicals who wanted more dramatic changes in the economy tended to confirm the generals' expectations that the Socialists would behave in responsible fashion. The military in Chile, proud of its traditional independence and isolation from the United States, wanted desperately to believe that the government would leave them alone.[32]

In the remainder of Latin America, military leaders also had a tenuous relationship with the United States. They welcomed United States weapons and training for their armed forces, but they did not especially want to follow United States political advice. Throughout Latin America military governments had been slow to support the Allies during World War II. Only the military governments of Central America, many of which had undergone actual occupation by the United States, were staunch supporters of the Allied cause during the war against Germany. Similarly many of the military governments of Latin and Central America had not enthusiastically endorsed the American crusade against Castro's Cuba. In Washington the military rulers of Latin America had an unsavory reputation for taking what they wanted from the United States but they did little to return America's favor. Accordingly, if given their choices, Americans would prefer to deal with anti-Communist civilian governments. These were the type that tended to insist on national prerogatives, were the most hospitable to the desires of multinational American corporations, and the most likely to develop their national economies.

Unfortunately from Kissinger's point of view, the choice of a non-Communist civilian government did not appear to be available in 1973. Even if the Chilean people changed their minds and voted the Christian Democrats back into power at the next presidential election in 1977, the model for the rest of Latin America would be devastating for American control. Moreover, the United States came under considerable pressure from the multinational firms taken over by the Socialist government. ITT, which controlled the telephone company of Chile, had operated profitably there since the 1930s. The compensation offered by the Socialist government for the telephone and electronic communications in the country did cover the cost of the installations plus a rate of profit of 10 percent.[33]

Still ITT was not satisfied with such an arrangement. In the first place payment was made in Chilean pesos, not readily convertible into American dollars. The Socialists of Chile claimed they were only taking ITT at its word when it said that it wanted to keep its profits inside the Latin American country. Yet ITT complained to the United States government that payment in Chilean bonds did not represent "prompt, adequate and effective compensation," the standard by which foreign firms and international lawyers customarily evaluated the justice of nationalizations by host governments. The Socialists understood something else from ITT's appeal to nineteenth-century standards of international law. It appeared as if the United States multinational actually was living up to the image of capitalist rapacity. Harold Geneen, president of ITT, seemed to insist that the company had the right to do whatever it pleased with its earnings. For years it had told a succession of Christian Democratic or conservative governments that the conglomerate had the interests of Chile's development at heart. Now, with its refusal to accept bonds in payment for the company, ITT indicated that it did not care to invest its profits further in improving Chile's economy.[34]

In fact ITT had every hope of further profiting from the development of industry and communications in the Latin American country. That was precisely why it objected to *any* nationalization plan. Even had it received full payments for all of its holdings in United States dollars it would have found the Socialists' program abhorrent. The standards of international law worked in the company's favor when it came to demanding payments in foreign currency, but the same standards worked against the company when it came to insisting on payments for future profits. These were not covered by the traditional requirements of compensation cases. If Chile's economy grew as expected over the next generation, ITT could make a fortune in telecommunications. The nation was growing ever more a part of the international market and it needed to expand its ability to get in touch with the banks, brokers, and importers of North America and Europe. The future possibilities for the American conglomerate seemed unlimited.

ITT resolved to fight Allende. It would overthrow the Socialists if possible. If not, they would make the Chilean economy suffer such extensive damage that no other country would see the Chileans as a model.

ITT wanted the assistance of the Nixon administration. To assure official backing for its campaign against Allende the conglomerate worked through its Washington lobbyist Dita Beard. This colorful figure had been a fixture of the Washington scene for a generation. She saw an opportunity to help her firm in the desperate pleas of the Nixon administration for money to support the President's reelection. Nixon wanted very much to hold the 1972 Republican National Convention in San Diego near his summer retreat at San Clemente. The city itself was reluctant to commit the $5 million required to host the party and keep an eye on the thousands of antiwar demonstrators expected to show up. Beard worked out a scheme for ITT to contribute $250,000 to the Committee to Reelect the President, which could then be used to foot some of the bill for the proposed convention. In return for this generosity ITT expected several favors from the administration. A long-standing antitrust suit accused ITT of fixing prices. Beard expected that Attorney General John Mitchell, who was heading the reelection campaign, would make certain that the antitrust division of the Justice Department would drop the suit. Moreover, Beard expected that the administration would come to believe

that it shared a common interest with the firm in Chile. Beard expected the CIA to funnel hundreds of millions of dollars through the
multinational to opposition factions in Chile. In 1971 and 1972 the
CIA obliged and the two coordinated their activities against the Socialist government.[35]

This frantic activity largely bypassed Kissinger's office within the
NSC. He never appreciated being shunted aside by the rest of the
foreign policy apparatus, and exclusion from planning over the future
of Chile did not improve his spirits. While he believed that Chile itself
had little strategic value for the United States—he once identified it
as "a pistol pointed at the heart of Antarctica"—he saw value in
demonstrating his own toughness against the Socialists. He had also
developed a visceral dislike of Allende and worried about the example
he could set in the remainder of Latin America.[36] Fighting to preserve
his own authority over the apparatus, he asserted the primacy of the
NSC. Attending meetings of the Forty Committee he previously had
spurned, he encouraged local CIA operatives to increase the pressure
on the Allende government.

By the summer of 1973 the CIA found a greater willingness to listen on the part of Chile's military. Despite Allende's refusal to pass
out weapons to leftists attempting to seize the land and the mines,
the military became increasingly alarmed. They expected that the Socialists at some point would suspend civil liberties guaranteed by the
Constitution. A purge of non-Socialist military leaders could come at
any time. Officers had made no secret of their social distance from
the rulers of the government and they certainly did not approve of
the widespread confiscations of land and factories. Unlike Central
American countries where the officer corps was sometimes made up
of young men of lower social classes who saw a uniform as a ticket
up, Chile's military leaders had always come from society's leading
families. When the chiefs of the three services contemplated the policies of the Socialists, they noticed that their own relatives had suffered the most at the hands of the government.

Moreover, the officers discovered to their dismay that their respect
for the traditional nonpartisanship of Chile's military won them few
friends. Their own relatives accused them of siding with the government. Despite pleas that their aloofness from politics followed the
best traditions of their services, conservatives accused the military
officers of ignoring real threats to the safety of the country. The Socialists, for their part, did not seem any happier with the officers'
attitude. Allende and his principal advisers believed that the military

should do more to demonstrate their loyalty to the government than simply assert that they would not overthrow it. Socialists feared that officers planted seeds of subversion among the troops. Conscripts of poorer backgrounds who were the young men most likely to support the socialist program, found themselves targets of conservative educational campaigns. They learned that the nation customarily had avoided radical solutions to social problems. They were told that Chile's Catholic background made it impossible for Marxism to take hold.[37]

As they puzzled over what should be done with the military, Socialists faced a deteriorating economic situation. The United States–inspired campaign of destabilization had worked. Copper prices continued depressed, while the international lending agencies remained aloof from Chile's development projects and its demands for foreign currencies. As a result, the public appeal of the Socialist government plunged. Allende had always represented the moderate faction of the Socialist party, hoping to maintain alliances with the Communists and even the Christian Democrats in support of the constitution. He had feared that the demands of the Left for a militant policy would irrevocably split the country. Now, in the summer of 1973, he veered to the Left.

At that point naval and army leaders mounted plans, with the CIA men in Santiago, to overthrow the Socialists. On the morning of September 12, troops loyal to the new junta surrounded the prime minister's residence, overpowered his loyal guard and either murdered Allende or forced him to take his own life. The military rounded up every Socialist, Communist, and left-wing Christian Democrat they could find and incarcerated them in soccer stadiums around the country. The new authorities executed as many as 10,000 people over the next few weeks. For its part the United States quickly recognized the new junta and promised to lift the sanctions imposed on Chile. The new military government would have America's blessing to borrow from the International Monetary Fund and the Inter-American Bank, and to seek credits from the United States Export–Import Bank.[38]

Kissinger was enthusiastic about the new military regime. While his own role in the ouster of the Socialists had been mixed, encouraging the destabilization program conceived within the CIA, he applauded the outcome. Kissinger had not taken the lead in evicting Allende. The CIA had been the principal force behind the coup. Within Chile itself conservatives, nationalists, and businesses tied to the United States and the world economy had reasons of their own for wanting to see the end of the Marxist experiment. The Chilean government would have been subject to serious pressures regardless of what the United States did. Allende might not have been able to withstand the eventual dissillusionment of the military no matter what the United States did. Regardless of what Kissinger himself did to hasten the downfall of the Socialists, he greeted the new government as a model for others in the hemisphere. The successful coup also confirmed his own belief that he had to act quickly to avert challenges to his authority in the national security bureaucracy.[39]

There was little public reaction in the United States to the coup in Chile. Events moved swiftly in the autumn of 1973, and the traditional United States disdain for Latin America forced attention to other subjects. Kissinger achieved his greatest personal triumph barely a month after the coup. The Norwegian Nobel Committee named him the co-recipient along with Le Duc Tho of the Nobel Peace Prize. The two were lauded for their work on the cease-fire of the previous fall. Kissinger was ecstatic, because he was joining such prominent American officials as Theodore Roosevelt and George C. Marshall.

Kissinger, more than these two officials, won the Prize without having achieved the highest official position. He considered the medal, the $100,000, and the right to make a speech before the assembled nobility of Scandinavia as validation of his approach to the war. Le Duc Tho, continuing the psychological warfare of the previous years, refused to accept his share of the prize. He repeated the charges of liberals and antiwar activists in the west that Kissinger had not really achieved peace but had merely prolonged the war. George McGovern expressed common liberal disappointment when he observed that "I would give the Nobel Prize to the men who warned against this tragic conflict, not those who came to clean up the wreckage after the accident."[40]

Some of Kissinger's former Harvard colleagues were puzzled about his winning the Peace Prize for the fragile settlement in Vietnam. Edwin O. Reischauer, former ambassador to Japan, said "Mr. Kissinger is a very appropriate choice for the Nobel Prize in terms of his general effort to find a greater balance in world politics. But to put him together with Le Duc Tho shows either that the people of Norway have a very poor understanding of what happened out there or a good sense of humor. There is no peace in Vietnam and the getting out was much too slow." Benjamin I. Schwartz, an expert on China, observed "I'm no fanatical enemy of Kissinger, but this is a bit much. I think he's done some good things, but the Peace Prize? There's no peace, and we stayed too long." Only John Kenneth Galbraith offered an unqualified, and characteristically wry, endorsement. "I have the impression they both worked hard to get the war over and both deserved the money. If they had gotten it over quicker they would have deserved more money."[41] The *Los Angeles Times* explained that "some of the surprise . . . was due to the fact that Southeast Asia is still not associated in most people's minds with peace." Nonetheless the award was won by "a professional and brilliant feat of diplomacy by two remarkable men."[42]

But the newly confirmed Secretary of State was undeterred by Le Duc Tho's unhappiness, liberal anger, or the hundreds of demonstrators who surrounded the hall in Oslo denouncing the award. For every opponent who found the North Vietnamese stance reasonable there were two former skeptics who concluded that Kissinger had been right all along about his counterpart. Now his critics had to acknowledge what the most prestigious international body had said. The fact that the award came from Scandinavia, where dissent from the war had been vocal, made Kissinger's triumph all the sweeter.

He began his tenure as Secretary of State in a seemingly impregnable position. He had won his Nobel Prize before he was in office two months. He was clearly the most notable and successful member of the administration. His relations with the press were better than those of any other official. The public responded well to his apparent knowledge of the ways of the world. Perhaps best of all from the point of view of dominating the foreign policy process, the President himself was deeply involved in the Watergate scandal. Since the announcement in July that the President had maintained a taping system Congress and the press had hounded the President and his White House associates. Kissinger therefore was poised to assert himself almost at will in the setting of foreign policy. He would get his chance, and indeed more than he wanted, over the next six months as a war between Israel and its Arab neighbors erupted on October 6 and threatened to involve the United States and the Soviet Union.

SEVEN

America Enters the Middle East

The Middle East stood beyond the major area of focus of Richard Nixon's and Henry Kissinger's détente policy in the first four years. The problem seemed both intractable and on the fringes of the competition between the United States and the Soviet Union. Kissinger therefore excluded the Middle East from the NSC's focus.

Two weeks after Kissinger became Secretary of State, however, fierce fighting broke out when Syria and Egypt attacked Israel. The October war threatened the security of the Jewish state, rocked the economies of the industrial West, and shook détente between the United States and the Soviet Union. As Steven Spiegel has written, "The October War completed the transformation of the Arab–Israeli dispute from a nuisance into a conflict central to American diplomatic and strategic concerns."[1]

Kissinger, facing the calamity of confrontation with the Soviet Union and the opportunity to make the United States the major power in the Middle East, rushed in as a mediator. Over two years, the Secretary of State shuttled from Jerusalem to Cairo to Damascus in search of an accommodation that would stabilize the area and promote the United States. In the end, his mediation accomplished disengagement between Israeli and Arab armies, but it also ignited furious opposition at home and abroad. The heady spirit of détente faded in the wake of economic difficulties and recriminations over responsibility for the mideast war.[2]

Both great powers had clients in the region. The United States supported Jordan, Saudi Arabia, and Israel, while Moscow put its money on Syria and Egypt. The Soviets had fully rearmed the two Arab states after their humiliation at the hands of Israel in the 1967 war. Egypt and Syria had fought a series of lesser engagements with the Israelis in the years after 1967. The death of Egypt's leader Gamal Abdel Nasser in September 1970 further complicated the situation. His replacement, Vice President Anwar Sadat was virtually unknown in the West. Americans could only predict that the new Egyptian president would try to follow Nasser's policies of confrontation with Israel, closeness to the Soviet Union, and movement toward unity with other Arab nations.

Kissinger had remained aloof from conversations over the future of the Middle East. As a Jew, he believed that anything he said on the issue could be misinterpeted as favoring Israel's position. He preferred to remain in the background and permit the State Department to have its way with the problem.[3] The department's professionals, happy to be out from under the thumb of the imperious National Security Adviser, eagerly sought to make a contribution to the development of a peace program for the Middle East.

But the Israelis dug in their heels. First they decided that Jerusalem could not be divided again. They asserted that their control over the city holy to three religions had been safer than had been the case during nineteen years of Jordanian rule after 1948. The Israelis accused Jordan of having reneged on their agreement to respect Jewish rights in the Holy City.[4]

Similarly, the Israelis commenced a program of fortifications of the West Bank, the Golan, and the Sinai peninsula. Israel did not assert claims to the captured territory but did create military settlements to provide protection against infiltration of Palestinian guerrillas.[5] The Labor government hinted that none of these settlements was permanent, but they would continue to create them until there was a prospect for face-to-face negotiations between the Arab states and Israel.

Europe discovered that its traditional connection to Israel ruined its relations with the Arab states. It came to believe that only an agreement between the two sides could improve Europe's standing with the Arab states. Naturally, Israelis rejected such advice. Despite the obvious achievements of Israel's armed forces and the contempt many Israeli military and political leaders expressed for the Arabs' capacity as soldiers, Jerusalem worried about the power of Arab nationalism. Noting that the Soviet Union had more than made up the losses in tanks, planes, and artillery of Egypt and Syria since 1967, the Israelis could not be content about their own security. Moreover, the Europeans, with the exception of West Germany, had virtually stopped their arms sales to the Jewish state. The United States, which before the Six Day War had been a secondary supplier of weapons, now provided the bulk of its military hardware. Dependence on a single nation for modern weapons augmented the Israelis' sense of vulnerability. Israel constantly worried that the United States might use its arms supplies as a lever to extract concessions in the peace process. As the Americans, with their large and influential Jewish population that supported Israel, had not expressed as much dissatisfaction with Israel's refusal to make concessions as had the Western Europeans, the prospects were good for future American grumbling.[6]

Thus, by 1970, Jerusalem had hardened its position. Unwilling to make concessions to bring its adversaries to the bargaining table, Israel's leaders preferred to believe that the three main "confrontation states" needed another dose of reality. Predictably, however, Israel's reluctance to compromise embittered the Arabs. Egypt and Syria were already virtual clients of the Soviet Union. Jordan, while still friendly to the West, hinted that it too could not wait forever. It reluctantly acceded to radical Arab pressure and yielded the right to speak for the inhabitants of the West Bank to the Palestine Liberation Organization. But it could not abide the PLO and worried that if the stalemate between Arabs and Israel continued for long, radical Palestinians would gain the upper hand inside Jordan itself.[7]

Kissinger, preoccupied with Soviet–American relations, the opening to China, and the Vietnam negotiations, had little time for such speculations. The problem of Middle Eastern nationalism fell beyond the usual limits of his geopolitics. He preferred to deal with established governments rather than movements. Inside the Department of State, however, Saudi Arabian arguments carried much weight. The American position in the oil-rich Middle East seemed to be held hostage to Israel's policies. Departmental officials resented what they considered to be the Israelis' arrogant disdain for Arab sensibilities. While the Israelis insisted that their residence in the region qualified them to understand the nuances of Arab statements, American Arabists winced. Americans who had spent decades in the region concluded that nationalistic sentiment among the Arabs was real and growing. One acute observer of the Department noted that "At State one heard of 'the erosion of American influence,' of 'deterioration' of the American position, of 'radicalization,' and of 'polarization.' "[8]

The Saudis feared that unless some progress were made in recovering the lands from Israel irresistible pressures would mount from radicals. Nasser and the other pan-Arab Nationalists had complained for years that reliance on Europeans or Americans for support could lead only to grief. Nationalists mocked the pretentions of conservative Arabs. Arab Nationalists held that the experience of the last three hundred years had represented a series of humiliations for a once-proud nation. The creation of a Zionist state in Israel had only deepened this sense of wrong. The Saudis and their American backers wanted to make sure that Arab nationalism made no further inroads by raising the specter of Jewish control over Islam's second holiest city, Jerusalem.[9]

To allay these anxieties among friendly Arab states, the State Department moved to arrange a settlement between Israel and its neighbors. Kissinger remained outside this process. His lack of involvement actually spurred State's efforts. Secretary of State Rogers, excluded for so long from the major issues of Nixon administration foreign policy, found an issue. Rogers believed that Kissinger had mistakenly concentrated all of his efforts on a U.S.–Soviet arrangement. The Secretary of State considered that the very difficulty of the problem made it necessary to solve. The dangers to the endurance of Kissinger's détente with the Soviet Union might come more from peripheral regions than from bilateral relations of the superpowers. Rogers considered that the National Security Adviser may have made a mistake in believing that Moscow and Washington could work out regional problems between themselves. Rogers thought that Washington should deal with the Middle East as well as with the Kremlin.[10]

As a war of attrition intensified along the Suez canal in 1969 and 1970, Rogers and the State Department explored the possibility of arranging a cease-fire. Rogers pressed Israel to state precisely what sort of military hardware it wanted from the United States. State believed that if the Israelis could finally generate a statement of what their security requirements were, the United States could better decide whether they could meet them. Otherwise, with Israel coming every year to Washington with a shopping list, no one could judge the merits of the request. The State Department offered assurances to Jerusalem that the United States would readily make up future losses. In return the Israelis had to promise to do their best to make sure that there would not be any new wars of attrition. They had to agree to make their best efforts at an accommodation with Egypt.

America's renewed interest in the future of the Middle East presented Jerusalem with a serious dilemma. On the one hand it welcomed American aid, and found Washington's views more supportive than those of the Western Europeans, and God forbid, the Soviets. On the other hand, simply because the United States was closest to the Israelis, Jerusalem had the least freedom of action. If the United States presented views that the Israelis rejected, the Jewish state would find itself without *any* supporters in the remainder of the world.[11]

All of this made Israel unusually attentive to Washington's point of view. The critical moment came in the summer of 1970 as war raged along the Suez canal. Every week the Israelis downed four or five planes and killed scores of Egyptian soldiers. More ominously for Israel, however, were its own losses. Most frightening of all to Israeli defense planners was the prospect of the installation of Soviet surface-to-air missiles along the Egyptian side of the canal. Israel had vowed to destroy SAMs before they became operational, but the government recognized the dangers involved in implementing such a threat. The most likely Soviet method of assuring the security of its weaponry would be to station its own soldiers in Egypt to operate the antiaircraft batteries. If Israel attacked or captured these modern weapons they would find themselves in the uncomfortable position of waging war on one of the superpowers.[12]

The United States saw nothing but trouble ahead in an outbreak of fighting between Israel and Soviet or Eastern bloc troops. State Department officials feared that the United States would lose whatever influence it had in the Arab world if it was forced into backing Jerusalem in a war with the Soviets. A new war also promised to bring Henry Kissinger back into the picture before the State Department had brokered a settlement. From a bureaucratic point of view, Kissinger's entry into the process might diminish State's autonomy. Kissinger would come too late and too inexperienced to the Middle East. If he entered after a new war, State Department experts feared that Kissinger could only prevent matters from getting worse. He could not promote the United States to the position of major outside power in the Middle East.

A combination of forces therefore worked toward an end to the war of attrition in the summer of 1970. In the United States the war between Israel and Egypt threatened to involve the Soviets. In Israel the costs had mounted and attrition had actually worked against Israel. The prospect of continuing the war, especially with a restless United States providing the aid did not appeal to the Israeli government.

Egypt too needed relief. Having burnished Arab honor, Nasser might be in a position to agree to a cease-fire with Israel. The most distressing aspect of his nation's situation was its growing dependence on the Soviet Union. He had to balance his pleasure at seeing the Israelis fighting the Soviets against his embarrassment over losing power over the direction of the future of the Middle-East. Nasser had come to believe that the Soviets really did not care for a settlement of the Arab–Israeli conflict along lines favorable to the Arabs, so much as they wanted influence in the region.

Both sides then were in a mood to accept American mediation in June and July of 1970. Secretary of State Rogers took the lead. Kissinger raised no objections and did not seek a detailed accounting of the Secretary's actions. The National Security Adviser thought that the prospects for agreement were remote and the chances that a settlement would promote America interests slight.

Given his freedom by Kissinger, Rogers traveled to the region and left behind a special representative to work out a cease-fire along the canal. To Israel the United States promised to keep the military pipeline open once a cease-fire were arranged. It offered the most modern fighters and fighter-bombers in the American arsenal—the F-5 Phantom jets—equipped with air-to-surface missiles. These weapons would be able to destroy the modern surface-to-air antiaircraft batteries left behind. The United States also promised to make certain that Egypt would not increase the number of planes, troops and antiaircraft batteries left along the West Bank of the canal. To Egypt the United States promised that Israel would not increase its fortifications along the canal. More than that, the United States undertook to get Israel's agreement to a political settlement. Nasser leaped at the chance of having Washington broker a political end to the Arab–Israeli dispute. He believed that the United States might succeed where the United Nations had failed.[13]

As part of a cease-fire agreement that went into effect on August 7 Secretary of State Rogers presented his own views on what a final agreement between Israel and its neighbors should look like. He offered the American interpretation of Resolution 242. First, there could be no piecemeal arrangements. All of the problems—territorial, security, and the future of the Palestinians—had to be solved together. If they were not, Rogers feared, each part of the problem would be held hostage to all the others. The result, he expected, would be endless dispute and no satisfactory conclusion. Second, Rogers believed in the exchange of captured territory for peace. The Israelis had to take the initiative, as they had the tangibles—the land—to turn over for the intangibles—goodwill.[14]

Israel's Labor government resented Rogers' suggestions about the eventual shape of the map of the Middle East. They believed that the American Secretary of State had prejudged the outcome. They wondered what good could come from a process that avoided face-to-face encounters between the two sides. They thought that Rogers had stripped Israel of its most important asset—its ability to stay put unless the Arab states agreed to meet with them. Israel also doubted whether the United States could maintain its position as an impartial mediator if it presented its own views.[15]

Israel's concerns about American impatience reflected a grasp of the intricacies of the American electoral cycle. Yitzhak Rabin, the ambassador to the United States, understood that the administration would mount no effective pressure on them during the election year of 1972. When Rogers announced his plan in August, Israelis predicted they had a period of eighteen months of intense pressure before the presidential campaign diverted attention from the Middle East. Customarily, these projections would have made sense, but it is harder to see the future clearly in the Middle East than elsewhere.

On September 28, 1970 President Nasser died from a massive heart attack. His replacement, Anwar Sadat, paled by comparison with the appeal Nasser exercised over the imagination of Arabs throughout the Middle East. Sadat vowed to divine what Nasser would have done and follow the same course. In relations with Israel, this meant no compromise.[16] An uneasy calm prevailed for thirty months.

Later, the first six months of the new American administration also was no time for a new démarche in the Middle East. Rogers was the lamest of ducks and Kissinger had other interests to preserve. The glow of the settlement with North Vietnam continued into the spring. Détente with the Soviet Union proceeded with increased trade, cultural exchanges and talks about expanding the SALT agreement of 1972. The National Security Adviser did not want to interrupt this pleasant picture with an embroglio over the Middle East. Nixon himself found the Watergate scandal taking more and more of his time. The Middle East, with its problems that did not seem amenable to any any sort of solution, could not provide the boost to his prestige that might end the public's fascination with Watergate.

By the middle of 1973 Sadat had despaired of having the United States successfully implement the Rogers plan. Israel had used the respite from the war of attrition to strengthen its lines in the Sinai. It threatened to remain in Egypt forever and keep Cairo from its sources of foreign exchange—the Canal and the newly opened oil wells of the Sinai. The loss of the latter was especially galling to Egypt, which deeply resented seeing its bitter enemy receive the benefits of the oil wells on its land.[17]

More frightening to Sadat were the sounds emanating from Syria. Damascus was highly suspicious of any Egyptian opening toward the United States. The Soviet Union had been Damascus's staunchest patron since the 1967 war, and the Syrian Ba'ath Party had come to believe that anything proposed by Europeans and especially by the United States served the interests of "imperialism and Zionism." President Hafez Assad publicly warned Sadat against succumbing to American blandishments with the suggestion that Egypt stood to lose its premier position in the Arab world.

On the other hand, he privately encouraged Sadat to mount a joint military operation against Israel to recapture the lost territory. Who knew, but if the Arab armies achieved complete surprise and the Israelis continued arrogantly to dismiss the Arabs' military abilities, Syria and Egypt might deal Israel a crippling defeat.[18]

Sadat anticipated few risks in joining Syria in an attack. He would have the support of Egypt's armed forces who were straining for the opportunity to redeem their lost honor. The Soviet advisers to the Egyptian armed forces also might enjoy seeing their pupils put into practice the lessons of the last few years. Even if Cairo failed to recover all of the lost territories, the shock to Israel of Egyptian armies crossing the Suez Canal would have excellent effects for the future.

On the morning of October 6, Yom Kippur, the holiest day of the Jewish calendar, Egyptian armies struck in force across the Suez Canal while the Syrians knifed into the Israeli-occupied Golan Heights. The government of Golda Meir received verified intelligence reports at dawn that the two nations were going to attack in hours, but Jerusalem did not issue a general mobilization order until the actual fighting began. Fearing the appearance of provocation and the expense of a general mobilization, Israel waited before calling up its reserves.[19]

Within a week the situation had become desperate and Israel appealed to the United States for aid to make up the losses. Now for the first time Kissinger became actively engaged in the Middle East. Leading both the State Department and the National Security Council, Kissinger no longer had to worry about rivals in other departments. He also appreciated the dangers to the United States of a conflict in the Middle East with the Soviet Union. He expected that the Israelis' plight might make them attentive to pressures for a settlement designed in Washington. In sum, the war presented the danger of the death of détente. But it also put forth the opportunity for the

United States to become the principal player in the Middle East.[20]

Kissinger had to sell the rest of the foreign affairs bureaucracy on his plans for injecting the United States into the process. First, he had to convince the Defense Department that the proper resupply of Israel would bind that nation more tightly to the United States. Unlike some of Israel's staunchest supporters in Defense, Kissinger believed that America should not write a blank check. Israel should have all the weapons it needed, but they should arrive in such a way as to make the Jewish state appreciate fully what the United States was doing on its behalf. The Pentagon believed that military needs should be met firmly without quibbling. As a thoughtful student of American Middle East policy has put it, "U.S. strategy—to end the war without a clear victory for either side and before a resupply of Israel became necessary—was conceived and executed in the NSC without close presidential involvement."[21]

Kissinger derided this attitude as typical American reluctance to think in strategic terms. He thought that the United States should keep Israel on a short leash. He proposed to Nixon that the United States use its military assistance to Israel to make Jerusalem toe the American line. The President leaped at the chance. It gave him an opportunity to demonstrate his toughness versus the Soviets while at the same time play a major role in resolving the problems of the Middle East. They were both assisted in putting pressure on Israel by the attitude of the Western Europeans who feared the wrath of the Arab oil-exporting states. Saudi Arabia and the other Gulf producers threatened a complete embargo on the oil supplies of Western Europe and Japan if they provided military hardware to Israel or let anyone else use their facilities to ship munitions to Israel. If Jerusalem wanted to refurbish its military, it would have to look to the United States. Making use of Portuguese bases in the Azores, the only European NATO airfields made available to the United States, the Pentagon commenced a gigantic airlift to Israel on October 11.[22]

Assured of its sources of resupply, Israel began a counterattack the next day. It pushed Syria beyond the original cease-fire line on the Golan Heights and stopped the Egyptian advance before the strategic Mitla pass. By the 15th Israel's army had marched to within twenty-five miles of Damascus, and later, most dramatically of all, their tanks crossed to the West Bank of the canal. They made a daring sweep south, threatening to surround the Egyptian Third Army. If they succeeded in capturing these 10,000 men, all of populated Egypt stood at their mercy.

At this point the Soviet Union threatened its own intervention. It would not tolerate another humiliation of the Arabs similar to the debacle of 1967. Should that occur, the Soviets, which had encouraged the Arabs to use force against Israel, might be discredited. Arab leaders who had looked to Moscow for support might also be embarrassed before their own people.[23]

Supporters of détente cautioned Kissinger against going too far toward offending the Soviets. "The danger is very real," worried the *Christian Science Monitor*, "that present resupply operations by both sides will escalate into an arms race which will ruin the Nixon–Brezhnev détente." The next day, the *Monitor* expressed a new concern, that the American resupply of Israel bolstered the Soviets' standing with the Arabs. "Every extra American gun and bullet to Israel increases Soviet influence among the Arabs—and opens a wider gulf between Washington and the Arab capitals."[24] Nonetheless, the crisis subsided, as Kissinger pressed Israel now to stop their encirclement of the Third Army, observe the cease-fire, and permit the resupply of the beleaguered Egyptians. Initially, the cease-fire seemed to confirm the value of better relations with the Soviets. On Tuesday, October 23, the *Monitor* reported that "The Soviet Union and the U.S., facing down a challenge to détente, have laid the groundwork for an ultimate settlement of the agonizing conflict in the Middle East."[25]

Kissinger publicly rejected Soviet calls for the dispatch of a joint U.S.–Soviet force to impose their will on Egypt and Israel. It was "inconceivable," he told a press conference, that the two powers could introduce forces in sufficient size to impose a Soviet–American condominium. Moreover, he insisted that "we are opposed to unilateral great power action, especially a nuclear power, to move military forces into the Middle East in whatever guise."[26]

All of this occurred in the midst of the climactic episodes of the Watergate scandal. Trying to regain the initiative, the President looked as always to foreign affairs. He dispatched Kissinger to Moscow to try to arrange a cease-fire in response to a request from Secretary-General Brezhnev. The NSC adviser was surprised to learn enroute to Moscow that Nixon had given him full powers to negotiate. He later noted, "History will not record that I resisted many grants of authority. This one I resented bitterly; it was a classic case of how 'full powers' can inhibit rather than enhance negotiating flexibility." Kissinger wanted the freedom to delay agreement with Brezhnev by pleading that he had to refer matters back to Washington. He telephoned General Haig, Chief of Staff at the White House, to explain the need for greater freedom of action. He recalled that Haig shot back "Will you get off my back? I have troubles of my own." Kissinger wondered "What troubles can you have in Washington on a Saturday Night?"[26] Haig then explained that Nixon had just fired Watergate Special Prosecutor Archbald Cox and that Attorney General Elliot Richardson and Deputy Attorney General William Ruckelshaus had resigned. During this Saturday Night Massacre the FBI sealed off the special prosecutor's office, giving rise to the speculation that the administration sought to destroy evidence. A firestorm of protest spread across the country. The White House received hundreds of thousands of telegrams, phone calls, and letters demanding that Nixon resign or at least appoint another special prosecutor. Members of Congress introduced resolutions of impeachment, referred to the House Judiciary Committee.

Time mattered for Kissinger in Moscow. If the Israelis completed their rout of the Egyptians, the Soviets could make good on their threat to intervene. Moreover, Kissinger saw difficulties for United States policy in the region should Israel be able completely to dominate Egypt once more. He knew how short were memories of gratitude and how deep were the enmities in the Middle East. Israel might very well simply return to its arrogant disregard of Arab sensibilities. Worse still, once the war was won, it could refuse to acknowledge the debt owed to the United States and not take instruction from Washington on the future of the region.

Kissinger hoped that by meeting in Moscow with Brezhnev and Gromyko he could preserve and even expand the boundaries of détente. Instead, détente suffered in the October War. Kissinger asserted that détente consisted in each power recognizing the legitimate interests of the other. That meant not pushing the other too far, shaming it before the world, or blocking all of its efforts at influencing others. The United States and the Soviet Union had a common interest in making certain that the Arab–Israeli problem did not expand so far as to threaten the delicate balance between the two superpowers.[27]

That balance appeared challenged when the cease-fire worked out in Moscow on October 22 broke down within hours. Israel, believing it had a go-ahead from Kissinger to continue the fight, crossed the Canal and encircled Egypt's Third Army. Brezhnev complained directly to Kissinger that Israel had overturned the cease-fire. The Secretary of State cared little for Soviet objections, but he realized that Israel's action threatened the United States' position with other Arab states. He recalled that "If the United States held still while the Egyptian army was being destroyed after an American-sponsored cease-fire and a Secretary of State's visit to Israel, not even the most moderate Arab could cooperate with us any longer."[28]

The Soviets thought the Israelis' continued war on Egypt threatened détente. Believing that the United States had committed itself in the May 1972 Basic Principles to treat Moscow as an equal, the Soviets insisted on participating in the cease-fire. Brezhnev wrote Kissinger that the two nations had the duty to impose the UN Security Council–sponsored cease-fire on Egypt and Israel. Concerned that this might lead to Soviet troops returning to Egypt, Kissinger worked frantically to keep them out. Kissinger believed that Brezhnev threatened "one of the most serious challenges to an American president" when he wrote "I will say it straight that if you find it impossible to act jointly with us in this matter, we should be faced with the necessity urgently to consider the question of taking steps unilaterally."[29]

Receiving news that the Soviets had resupplied Egypt with an airlift on October 24, Kissinger convened a special meeting of the NSC. Present were the principal foreign policy officers of the government: Secretary of Defense James Schlesinger, Director of Central Intelligence William E. Colby, Joint Chiefs of Staff head Thomas Moorer, NSC Deputy Brent Scowcroft, White House Chief of Staff Alexander Haig, and Kissinger. They agreed to a general military alert DEFCON 3 (Defense Condition 3). The alert notified strategic forces stationed in the United States and ground commanders in Europe that the Soviets might move troops to Egypt. It also dispatched three aircraft carriers to the Eastern Mediterranean.

Kissinger had intended the alert to be picked up by Soviet intelligence. He was "shocked," however, to read of it in the newspapers. "This unexpected publicity would inevitably turn the event into an issue of prestige with Moscow, unleashing popular passion at home and seriously complicating the prospects of Soviet retreat." Nonetheless, the crisis subsided as Kissinger pressed Israel to stop their encirclement of the Third Army, observe the cease-fire, and permit the resupply of the beleaguered Egyptians.[30]

Opinion was mixed on the alert. Some considered it significant that "the world did not have another Cuban missile crisis last week. . . . Behind the anxious nine hours was a casebook example of the great powers—U.S.A. and U.S.S.R.—managing a difficult though never dangerous problem in current power politics." Yet other observers believe that "the United States overreacted" by calling the alert. Skeptics called attention to Kissinger's reflections on the effects of Watergate on the conduct of foreign policy. He explained the domestic atmosphere in which the alert was called: "One cannot have crises of authority in a society for a period of months without paying a price somewhere along the line." Editorials believed that "the White House may well have felt that it was necessary to display toughness on a worldwide scale to show that President Nixon was fully in command of foreign policy and in no way weakened by domestic events."[31] The *Los Angeles Times* conceded that "the danger was indeed real, and that President Nixon's firm response—including a worldwide alert of U.S. forces—was both necessary and effective." Still, considering the effects of Watergate the *Times* believed that "a certain amount of skepticism was inevitable."[32]

Kissinger's own position seemed threatened by the growing scandal. An aide to Senator Jacob Javits, a strong Kissinger supporter, informed the Senator that "if, as now seems inevitable, Nixon will soon go under in what is likely to be a nasty, squalid, destructive final spasm of criminal defiance, Kissinger's own constituency—and capacity to operate—will be called into doubt." Representative Thomas P. O'Neill also noticed that the President seemed unstable during the height of the crisis. At a White House briefing in the midst of the war he recalled that Nixon "kept interrupting Kissinger. 'We had trouble finding Henry,' he said. 'He was in bed with a broad.' Nobody laughed." A few weeks later Nixon turned more erratic. O'Neill recalls that "Kissinger had barely opened his mouth when the President interrupted him and started talking to us about the history of Communism in the Soviet Union. He rambled on for almost half an hour. . . . Nobody could understand what, if anything, this had to do with the Middle East war."[33]

After the alert, Kissinger began a process—continued over the next eighteen months—of telling each of the parties exactly what it wanted to hear and subtly shading the meaning of what adversaries said to one another. All the while he advanced the more parochial interests of the United States. He told the Soviets that the United States would not permit Israel to achieve an unqualified victory. While the United States was relieved that Israel had not been overcome by the Syrian and Egyptian onslaught, the United States as well as the Soviet Union had an interest in making sure that the Arabs were not routed.

Kissinger believed that a restoration of Arab pride in its own armed prowess would make them readier to make peace with Israel. If they could recall the thrill of the first days of the war, when Egypt's forces crossed the Suez Canal and captured the Bar Lev line and Syria's forces threatened to cut Israel in two, they might express less fear and hatred of the Israelis. Then they could agree to meet on an equal footing to work out a modus vivendi.

Israel too would have more reasons to reach an agreement settling the issue once and for all if there was a rough equivalency between the two sides. Its military position was not as strong as they might believe at the end of the war. Despite their having crossed the canal and made life miserable for the Egyptians, they had significant exposures of their own. Egyptian troops remained on the east bank of the canal, making it impossible for the Israelis to straighten their lines. Unlike the situation that existed at the end of the 1967 war, the two sides could not now tacitly permit one another to remain in place. Some disengagement of the two nations' forces was necessary from a military point of view, if for no other purpose.

Kissinger questioned the usefulness of Soviet participation in the peace process. As soon as the crisis subsided Kissinger commenced his effort to exclude the Soviets from further involvement. Editorials noted that Kissinger's "strongest single trump card is the fact that only a long-term settlement can keep the Soviets from coming back as a major military force in the Middle East."[34] Moreover, the Soviets might not have the same interest in the outcome as did the United States. Moscow was delighted at the discomfiture of the Americans when the oil-producers made good on their threat to embargo exports to the United States and Western Europe. For Moscow détente did not imply the end of competition between East and West. It demanded only that each side refrain from boxing the other into a corner.[35]

This Soviet definition of détente did not permit Kissinger to welcome the Kremlin as full partners in the search for a solution to the Arab–Israeli impasse. American needs for influence in the region prompted him to follow a more independent course. The most pressing requirement was for an end to the oil embargo against the western nations. The European and Japanese economies depended on imported petroleum for all of their liquid fuel needs. Most of their imports, up to 90 percent in some cases, came from the Middle East. While the United States still produced three-quarters of the petroleum it consumed, imports had risen over the previous decade. Even if the United States could weather the loss of imported oil, its major trading partners could not. Disruption in the world's oil supplies for any length of time might plunge the capitalist world into deep depression. The United States would suffer along with its partners from any dis-

ruption of the supply of petroleum. Economically, the world's mar-
kets were sufficiently interdependent to damage American exporters
when the European economies faltered. The American petroleum supplies also would be strained by the embargo to Europe. United States
producers would export to the blockaded nations. The result would
be higher prices for energy for all.[36]

Shortly after the cease-fire took hold, the Arabs' oil weapon became a reality. The price of the vital liquid, which had remained steady
or even fallen in terms of purchasing power since the end of World
War II, took a fourfold jump. The shah of Iran, long a friend of the
United States, took advantage of the unnatural shortage of supply, to
boost his country's prices. In reply to complaints from the West, he
asserted that he actually helped its client Israel with oil. The West
should be willing to pay the additional price if it wanted to see the
Israelis kept in energy. King Faisal of Saudi Arabia also joined the
embargo. On a trip to Cairo in December Kissinger wrote Nixon that
"Sadat promised me that he would get the embargo lifted during the
first half of January and said that he would call for its lifting in a
statement which praised your personal role in bringing the parties to
the negotiating table and making progress thereafter."[37]

These factors added urgency to the disengagement process. Six
weeks after the cease-fire went into effect, a general peace conference
between Israel and Egypt and Syria convened at Geneva under the
auspices of the United Nations and co-hosted by the United States
and the Soviet Union. The conference met once in one of the chilliest
international gatherings of all time. The two sides refused to acknowledge one another's presence, would not shake hands or even
look one another in the eye. The Israelis refused to permit the seating
of any representatives of the PLO, which offended their Arab opposite
numbers. Syria and Egypt insisted that the principal issue to be discussed was the withdrawal of Israel's armed forces from the occupied
territories and the restoration of the rights of the Palestinians. The
Syrians, unlike the Egyptians, maintained the long-standing Arab position that Israel was an illegitimate state. The Egyptians, on the other
hand, implied that should Israel withdraw and make an overture to
the Palestinians, Cairo could offer recognition. The Soviets backed
the Arab position, but they were troubled by the apparent divergence
between the two allies. Moscow had no influence, however, with
Israel.[38]

That left the United States. Kissinger saw a grand opportunity to
assert American views in the region. The squabbling between Egypt

and Syria, and Egypt and the even more radical state of Libya, suggested that properly applied pressure could separate the major Arab combatants. Since Egypt was the most powerful of the Arab armed forces, its attitude was crucial to the success of the negotiations.[39]

The first frosty meeting among the belligerents was never repeated. Instead Kissinger embarked on an eighteen-month-long mediation effort. It represented probably his greatest temporary success in office. But it also undermined détente and encouraged critics at home. By arranging disengagements of the Egyptian and Syrian forces from the Israelis, he defused for the moment the chances of another war. More important, perhaps, he presided over the end of the Egyptian–Soviet connection. In 1974 Sadat threw the 10,000 Soviet advisers out of his country. From then until the conclusion of the Camp David peace agreement of 1978 and the Washington treaty between Israel and Egypt of 1979 relations between the United States and Egypt soared.

Kissinger set in motion a process that made the United States the major player in the Middle East. If it did not result in a permanent solution to the Arab–Israeli conflict, it did make peace possible. That was an achievement none of his predecessors had accomplished. It was all the more telling as it occurred despite Kissinger having previously demonstrated profound indifference to the fate of the Middle East.

The first disengagement took place between Egypt and Israel; over a period of six weeks at the end of 1973 and the beginning of 1974 Kissinger commenced his shuttle. He flew between the two capitals, with stops in Cyprus, to arrange a troop separation. Even before the shuttle commenced, the two sides had dispatched military representatives to a remote marker along the road to the canal. There, at kilometer 101, they worked out an arrangement for the two sides to pull their troops back from either side of the canal. Three military zones were created on the east bank of the canal—an Egyptian sector closest to the waterway, a middle zone occupied by U.N. forces, and an Israeli zone further east. Egyptian and Israeli forces were to be thinned out in each of the forward zones. One of Kissinger's Israeli detractors, the journalist Matti Golan, claims that the generals at K-101 worked out their own deal, without intermediaries, before Kissinger did.[40]

The view was different in the United States where, by year's end, Kissinger could do no wrong. "The Superstar on His Own" was *Time's* assessment of his latest efforts. "As he whirled through the capitals of Europe and the Middle East last week, Henry Kissinger more than ever before warranted comparison to Metternich, Talleyrand and other great foreign ministers of the past—or, perhaps, to the fast moving comet Kohoutek. No other Secretary of State in U.S. history has ever carried so much power, so much responsibility or so heavy a burden." *Time* gushed over "Kissinger's apparent flair for couscous diplomacy in the Middle East." The editors were just as effusive about his treatment of Europeans. He was "firm but conciliatory, trying to soothe the feelings that had been bruised by his own harsh words, by the surprise alert of American forces in the last days of the Middle Eastern war, and by U.S.–Soviet agreements that the Europeans believe have been made over their heads."[41] The Japanese called him the "Mideast Cyclone." Diplomats who had been frustrated for years by the intractable nature of the Arab–Israeli dispute considered him "virtually a miracle worker." Editorialists praised him for his ability to "recognize and seize the moment when conditions were, for the first time in 26 years, truly favorable to a long-term settlement. This, of course, is the highest statecraft."[42]

Kissinger's contribution was to assure each party of continued United States military and economic support, should they proceed with an agreement. For Israel this represented a substantial change in the pattern of United States assistance. For the first time since the beginning of the Arab–Israeli conflict after Israeli statehood, the United States had become the principal arms supplier to the belligerents. Israel knew that unless Egypt participated in a war against them, they had nothing to fear militarily. Kissinger hammered away at this realization. He informed Meir, Defense Minister Moshe Dayan, and Foreign Minister Abba Eban that binding Egypt to the United States would assure Israel's future security. They responded positively, because they had no other choice. If Israel wanted the backing of the United States, it had to pay attention to American suggestions. They demanded, however, that in return for their accommodation of Washington, the United States maintain Israel's military superiority.

Egypt's interests were exactly the reverse of Israel's. Sadat, looking for another patron after the eviction of Soviet advisers, wanted assurances that the United States would maintain its military forces. He also wanted Kissinger's pledge that the United States would move Israel out of the Sinai. Sadat had despaired of having the Soviets muscle the Israelis, as Moscow had no influence at all with Jerusalem.[43] Kissinger had to deliver before Sadat would feel comfortable as an American ally. The Secretary of State replied that he would indeed encourage Israel to leave the Sinai in return for American guarantees. He suggested that Egypt could enter the international capitalist economy. The United States could provide the development aid necessary for Egypt to become a partner to the Europeans. He also suggested that the United States would find Egypt an even more valuable asset than Israel in the Middle East. A connection between Washington and Cairo would give the United States the credibility it lacked in the Arab world. Sadat told Kissinger that the benefits to the United States from a closer connection to the Arab world would greatly enhance its position throughout the Middle East. Kissinger and Sadat also worked out an agreement for the opening of the canal and the rebuilding of the cities along its banks. Kissinger told the Israelis that Sadat had promised to allow ships bound for Israel to pass through the Canal. Sadat, however, did not mention a specific date.

The ambiguous arrangement over the canal was emblematic of Kissinger's shuttle. As Steven Spiegel wrote in 1985: "This confusion over reopening the canal illustrates Kissinger's tendency to adjust his arguments to a particular moment and his preoccupation with closing a deal. These traits help explain why Kissinger achieved an initial success that proved difficult to sustain. His energies were devoted to specific, highly circumscribed agreements accompanied by secret oral and written understandings often interpreted differently by opposing sides. During the October war, Kissinger had very specific aims and achieved them, but his postwar negotiations were conducted with little consideration for where they might lead."[44]

By January 1974 the Egyptian–Israeli disengagement agreement was in place. Kissinger returned to the United States to nearly universal acclaim. The *New York Times* praised his "extraordinary diplomatic skill" and the "notable achievement" he had wrought. The *Los Angeles Times* hoped that the Egyptian–Israeli arrangement "could well be the prelude to the most significant political development in the last quarter century." The *Chicago Tribune*, though skeptical that the agreement would survive, still cheered Kissinger's "diplomatic coup."[45]

Kissinger had more difficulty arranging the disengagement of Syrian and Israeli forces. In the first place, Syria did not break with the Soviets. Secondly, they refused to meet the Israelis at all, even in the format of armistice talks. Finally, the military situation in the north was different from the one along the Canal. There, the two armed forces were in each others' way, with the Egyptians on the "Israeli side" of the canal and vice versa.

In the North the lines were organized from a military point of view. Israel did, however, hold a strip about ten miles wide of Syrian territory beyond the Golan. Damascus wanted to retrieve that land, if nothing else. The Israelis were willing to exchange that land for ironclad commitments from Syria that they would not permit their territory to be used as a base for guerrilla raids. Israel also had an interest in clearing out of the one inhabited town of Kuneitra. Over the next six months Kissinger worked out a disengagement agreement along this northern border too. He did so by subtly shading what each side said to the other.

Kissinger informed the Syrians that the Israelis would yield everything on the Golan. In Tel Aviv, on the other hand, he implied that the Syrians would offer full recognition once the withdrawal was accomplished. He grew frustrated with the Israelis' quibbling over what seemed to be inches of territory. At one point he exploded at the Israelis: "Such bargaining is not dignified for an American Secretary of State. I am wandering around here like a rug merchant in order to bargain over 100 or 200 meters! Like a peddler in a market! I am trying to save you, and you think you are doing me a favor when you are kind enough to give me a few more meters."[46] At another point he encouraged the Israelis to look on the bright side: "You're always looking at the trees, and you don't see the woods! If we didn't have this negotiation, there'd be an international forum for the 1967 frontiers."[47]

The result was splendid for the peace process. By the middle of 1974, Kissinger had secured a withdrawal agreement in the north. Israel removed its forces back inside the Golan Heights and abandoned Kuneitra. The two agreed that a U.N. force would separate the two sides. He was less successful, however, at turning this military arrangement into the basis for a political solution. The connection of Syria to the Soviet Union and the Ba'ath's implacable opposition to Israel made a political solution seem remote. Syria's rivalry with Egypt for the leadership of the Arab world also blocked further improvement in relations with Israel. Every time Egypt pulled closer to America and made progress in its negotiations with Israel, Damascus denounced Cairo. It could not then turn around and follow the same course. Accordingly, nothing more was done to create a peaceful environment along Israel's northern border.

Kissinger, however, was satisfied with the results of the shuttle. He carefully distinguished between "two broad approaches" in reaching a Mideast agreement. "One was to attempt to solve all problems in one grand negotiation involving all of the parties and all interested outside participants." While noting that this approach was "intellectually very achievable," Kissinger admitted that "it has the defect that it attempts to solve simultaneously problems, any one of which has defied solution for over a generation." He reported to Congress that "it was our judgment that an attempt at such a global solution immediately would lead rapidly to a stalemate." Therefore Kissinger proceeded "step by step." He reported that he "pursued a policy of settling those issues that the participants were prepared to settle in order to create a climate of confidence so the parties could get used to the process of peace. . . . Sooner or later this procedure was certain to merge into an overall settlement."[48]

The United States had become the major actor besides the belligerents themselves. The Arab fantasy of an all-powerful America manipulating Israel had finally become a reality. Perhaps even more important from the point of view of Kissinger's own standing in the White House and the public at large, he had provided a verifiable triumph in the midst of the Watergate scandal. He appeared in a Superman suit on the cover of *Newsweek* magazine and was lionized by the pundits. All in all he had proved what several generations of American diplomats had hoped for. He had become the major mediator in the world's most troublesome region. That alone was enough to lessen the sting of Watergate.

Yet the successes carried seeds of destruction. As Raymond Garthoff writes:

Many politically significant supporters of Israel thus became disenchanted with the policy of détente with the Soviet Union. The lesson of October 1973 was not that U.S.–Soviet détente had *failed*, but that it had *succeeded*. This outcome could lead to a curtailment of Israel's jealously guarded freedom of action to determine unilaterally its own security requirements. . . . What was potentially at stake was not any particular political threat, but the unique and crucial support from the United States that Israel had been able to count on whenever a crunch came, no matter what the Israelis decided to do. . . . The Arabs had never had that advantage from any association with the Soviet Union, as the October war had demonstrated. But if in the future the Arabs could sometimes share the umbrella of America support, Israel's trump card would be gone.[49]

Shuttle diplomacy promised so much that eventual disappointment was almost unavoidable. Kissinger had decided that the process of reaching an agreement was extremely important. Just as he had waived objections from dissenters over SALT to reach an accord, he valued agreement in the Mideast over technical neatness. Kissinger dominated the creation of Mideastern policy as no other diplomat before or since. His commanding presence carried enormous advantages. As Steven Spiegel writes, "This flexibility often made the difference between success and failure. Kissinger's dominance also vastly improved the coherence of American policy."[50] These were splendid assets in getting the parties to withdraw their troops. Kissinger's control of the process was not sufficient, however, to reach a permanent settlement between Israel and its neighbors.

EIGHT

Nixon's Fall
and Kissinger's Triumph

By the beginning of 1974, barely three months after Kissinger had become Secretary of State, the foreign policy landscape had altered beyond recognition. The Watergate scandal combined with a public disillusionment with the war in Vietnam to erode popular support for an assertive foreign policy. Détente with the Soviet Union came under assault. Critics as diverse as AFL-CIO president George Meany and Senator Barry Goldwater challenged Kissinger's relations with the Soviets. They charged that he had abandoned United States interests in return for vague promises. Yet Kissinger retained substantial public admiration, and he used much of 1974 consolidating his position as Richard Nixon ended his presidency in disgrace.

Significantly from Kissinger's point of view most of the criticism was directed at the President rather than the Secretary of State. A Gallup Poll at the end of 1973 ranked Kissinger as the Most Admired Man in the world.[1] Reporters noted that "Nixon now allows Kissinger a new latitude of near autonomy. . . . In foreign affairs, Nixon is still commander-in-chief, but Kissinger has asserted himself as both strategist and tactician with such sweeping command that there is no one in the White House to challenge his power." A cartoonist now depicted Kissinger as Superman soaring above a diminished earthbound Nixon.[2] Kissinger spent New Year's at San Clemente with Nixon where reports marveled at a "dramatically contrasting duo. The President is a politically tattered, isolated man battling to stay in power. The U.S. Secretary of State, fresh from another successful mission, is at the height of his brilliant career. . . . As the new year commences, there seems little doubt that President Nixon is pinning his hopes on more achievements in the field of foreign policy to divert attention from his domestic troubles and help refurbish his tarnished image."[3] David Brinkley, commenting on the NBC evening news, reflected that "it has been a long time since this country had a diplomat cast as a public hero with flowers strewn in his path. . . . In season is Kissinger, at a time when the American people needed somebody they could admire."[4]

His prestige and spirits soared in the late winter and early spring. In late February, "the American magician," as the Egyptians had begun calling him, was off on his fourth trip to the Middle East, this time to arrange a disengagement between Syria and Israel.[5] He won immediate, if premature, praise. "The master of the diplomatic coup has done it again" reported The *Christian Science Monitor* when Syria agreed to supply a list of Israeli prisoners of war.[6] Three months' more hard bargaining was required before a disengagement accord was reached. Actress Gina Lollobrigida photographed and interviewed him for the *Ladies' Home Journal.* She found him "remarkably open, honest and charming. He is much younger, much stronger in person than he appears in photographs. He has confidence in himself."[7] In mid-March he took time off, briefly, and married Nancy Maginnis. Even during a honeymoon in Mexico he kept up a steady stream of cables to the State Department. Then it was back to Moscow at the end of March, in the hopes of finding a "conceptual breakthrough" that would permit the conclusion of a formal SALT-II treaty. All of this globe-trotting led *Newsweek* to swoon "It's Bird, It's a Plane, It's Super K" and picture the indefatigible Kissinger once more in a Superman Cape holding aloft dumbbells in the shape of the hemispheres of the globe.[8] *Saturday Review*'s awestruck summary of Kissinger's "frantic year" since the Paris peace accords maintained that "as far as Henry Kissinger is concerned, *rest* is a four-letter word."[9]

Yet a sour attitude washed over Congress. For the first time since the conclusion of the peace agreement with North Vietnam the previous January, prominent congressional foreign policy spokesmen felt free to assail the conduct of foreign relations. The Vietnam peace seemed illusory, as war between the North and South resumed. Détente with the Soviet Union seemed to fray. Critics became concerned about the cost of détente to the human rights movement within the Soviet Union. Senator Henry Jackson (D.-Wa.), long suspicious of Soviet motives, regretted that the Nixon-Kissinger policy had paid no attention to the tyrannical nature of the Soviet regime. The Washington Democrat challenged the administration to demonstrate the benefits of détente to minorities inside the Soviet Union. Jackson argued that Nixon and Kissinger had exaggerated the economic benefits to be derived from better relations with Moscow. Even if the United States could profit more from traffic with the Soviets, it was immoral for Americans to overlook the deep divisions in the two nations' social systems.[10]

Strains appeared with the March trip to Moscow. Before Kissinger left, Senator Jackson had continued his assault on détente by raising to 100,000 the number of Jews whom the Soviets should permit to emigrate each year. Bringing the subject up immediately before the secretary's trip persuaded many observers that Jackson wanted "an issue for 1976 not a solution." In Moscow, Kissinger was not successful. It appeared that both Soviet and American generals clung to their own services' needs. At home, observers believed that the push for a new summit meeting in June was only an effort to divert attention from President Nixon's Watergate burdens. The *Los Angeles Times* expressed the widespread belief that "a U.S.–Soviet summit this summer is of dubious wisdom."[11]

Jackson's voice was only one of a chorus raised in objection to détente in 1974. Traditional conservatives and the AFL–CIO doubted the worth of the new relationship. George Meany derided Kissinger's conception of détente as "this great idea—this 'conceptual breakthrough' to use one of Henry Kissinger's favorite phrases—is like gossamer. You can't grab hold of it. . . . [H]ow could we have gotten so excited about something that wasn't much of anything anyway?" Meany accused Kissinger and Nixon of misleading the public into believing that "détente meant not just something negative but something positive—not just restraint but cooperation." Even the *New York Times* registered a "reservation to the policy of détente as conceived by Mr. Kissinger" because "this country may find itself settling for minimal tangible benefit for itself in pursuit of a desirable abstraction, while the Soviet leadership successfully extracts real concessions in return for empty lip service."[12]

Kissinger appealed to press and Congress as a master of the subtleties of international relations. He stressed the enduring values of détente as "a continuing process, not a final condition." He found comfort that "the world has been freer of East–West tensions and conflict than in the fifties and sixties." He believed it was "immaterial . . . whether this change [in United States–Soviet relations] should be ascribed to tactical considerations." Regardless of Soviet motives, he told skeptics, "our task is essentially the same, to transform that change into a permanent condition devoted to the purpose of a secure peace and mankind's aspiration for a better life."[13]

Kissinger persuaded some, but not all of the detractors of détente, that improved relations with the Soviet Union allowed the United States to push its own agenda in world politics. He claimed that the United States was better able to husband its resources and pursue its interests in areas other than Europe. He believed that by settling outstanding issues between the United States and the Soviet Union in Europe, the two powers would be able to channel their competitive urges into less explosive regions of the world. He characterized the U.S.–Soviet relationship in the Middle East as "ambiguous, partly competitive, partly cooperative." He offered modest praise for the Soviets' restraint during his Middle Eastern negotiations. "While the Soviet Union gave no active support," he informed the Senate, "it did not block them, as it might have, through a more aggressive policy. Throughout these negotiations we kept in touch with them and we did not find it difficult to stay in touch."[14] Even if the two expressed differences of opinion or backed different sides in disputes in Africa, the Middle East, or Asia, the results would not be as disastrous for world peace.

Yet Kissinger was too hopeful, and the superpowers could not agree on the proper limits of détente. The United States expected that the better relations between the powers would extend beyond Europe to the rest of the world. The Soviet Union, on the other hand, considered détente limited to the original arena of the cold war—the rimland of Soviet territory. For Moscow, détente represented a realistic appreciation of the territorial facts of life. Moscow saw détente as Washington's acknowledgment of rough equality between the two powers. Moreover, Moscow was supposed to have achieved a legitimate position as a major power. No longer would the United States accuse the Soviet Union of trying to disrupt the natural order of world politics.[15]

Accordingly, the Soviets believed that they had the right to participate in determining the future of Africa, the Middle East, and Asia. The Soviets were distressed by Kissinger's shuttle in the Arab–Israeli war. The goal of United States diplomacy seemed to be to evict the Soviets from the region. It appeared that this goal had been reached when Egypt evicted the Soviet advisory force of 10,000 and broke relations with Moscow. At this point, the Soviets came to wonder if the Americans actually wanted to go forward with détente. They came to suspect that Kissinger wanted to ban them from the future of the Middle East. If that was the case, they reasoned, then détente did not indeed extend beyond Europe. Only when there were carefully worked out arrangements, with every "i" dotted and every "t" crossed, could the two sides be said to have reached an accommodation. Otherwise, each power could try to reach its own ends outside of Europe.[16]

The Soviets also became alarmed at the eroding position of the President. In Soviet eyes, the growing Watergate scandal represented the continuous power of right wing enemies of détente. One Soviet official airily dismissed the scandal as "demagoguery . . . all for show. . . . [It] will not amount to anything provided Nixon displays firmness."[17] The initial weakening of the President did not alarm the Soviets who welcomed it as a way of applying additional pressure on the White House. Enough was enough, however. If the President lost so much authority that he no longer could press his better relations with the Soviets, then Moscow would suffer too. The best solution was for the President to be wounded but still in charge. He would then need Soviet assistance.

The Soviets watched in fascination and horror throughout the spring of 1974 as the House of Representatives moved toward an indictment of the President. In May the White House finally succumbed to mounting public pressure and released transcripts of tape recordings of his office and telephone conversations. Instead of stilling the outcry against the President, publication of the record only encouraged the President's detractors.

For the first time, they had the man condemned out of his own mouth. Commentators recoiled in horror at the abusiveness of his language as well as his seeming inability to grasp the essence of issues. Senator Hugh Scott, the Republican Minority Leader, claimed that he was shocked by the coarseness displayed in the tapes.[18] Despite Nixon's carefully orchestrated reputation for understanding of international issues, he came across in the transcripts as tentative and uninformed. He could not make up his mind when confronted with options by his aides. Subordinates had to shield him from the consequences of his actions. If he was as ignorant and tentative in international relations as he seemed to be in dealing with the growing "cancer on the presidency" of Watergate, then he really was not in charge. Opponents could freely deride the President for not controlling the direction of his administration's foreign policy.[19]

Kissinger's travels in behalf of a Mideast arrangement did nothing to revive Nixon's flagging reputation. As the President prepared to embark on his own Mideast swing editorialists remarked that "it is hard to escape the unsettling conclusion that as the Watergate impeachment inquiry inexorably moves forward, Mr. Nixon's strategy is to keep the public spotlight focused on the indisputable strength of his presidency—foreign policy."[20]

In mid-June the story broke that Kissinger had connived in the wire taps of the phones of several subordinates and prominent journalists. Kissinger called a special meeting of the traveling press to denounce their brethren at home who had printed the story. He did not deny the essence of the reports, but he challenged the patriotism of the editors who had dared to print such lèse-majeste. Journalists were stunned by his outburst that "I do not believe it is possible to conduct the foreign policy of the United States . . . when the character and credibility of the Secretary of State is at issue. And if it is not cleared up, I will resign."

An exhausted Henry Kissinger, who deplored sentimentality in others, became maudlin as he decried the press accounts of the taps. "I hope none of you are ever in a position where you have to prove the negative of a knowledge." He never denied that he had known of the surveillance, but he did not accept the charge that his actions had been wrong. "I am supposed to be interested primarily in the balance of power. I would rather like to think that when the record is written, one may remember that perhaps some lives were saved and perhaps some mothers can rest more at ease, but I leave that to history. What I will not leave to history is a discussion of my public honor. I have believed that I should do what I could to heal the divisions in this country. I believed that I should do what I could to maintain the dignity of American values and give Americans some pride in the conduct of their affairs."[21]

Kissinger tried to deflect the scrutiny of the taps away from the specific issue of his staff's privacy. He asserted that the editors who printed the story had overlooked the primacy of foreign policy in the Nixon administration. "My concern was at that time we were preparing the secret trip to China. I was engaged in secret negotiations with North Vietnam that ultimately led to the end of American participation in Vietnam. We were also engaged in secret discussions on strategic arms limitation. I was profoundly concerned and so expressed my views to the President that these initiatives might be aborted if other governments had the idea that the United States Government was not in a position to protect its secrets and that anybody could publish any document and then the proof of its intrinsic significance was left to the government."[22]

Kissinger justified the taps on national security grounds: "I recognize that national security has been abused in recent years, but because there have been abuses does not mean there was not justified concern by honorable people. It did not occur to me in expressing my concern that this might lead to the burglary of a doctor's office. It did occur to me that measures might be taken to protect the government against a recurrence of these leaks."[23]

He continued his campaign to make the press consider him indispensable for the conduct of foreign policy. He had found it necessary to maintain good relations with the conservatives in the White House. They had grave doubts about his earlier career at Harvard. He continued to meet with liberals and transmit information to reporters known to have expressed antiadministration sentiments. A man who spoke regularly with Joseph Kraft could not be trusted with the most important secrets of state. Kissinger told the press corps in Salzburg that he had been compelled to go along with the wire taps to prevent any further erosion of his standing in the White House. He asked the reporters if they really wanted to continue a process that would force him from office. Kissinger pleaded with reporters to continue to bolster his public reputation. They should "spare the United States the indignity and humiliation of having its Secretary of State, while engaged in a trip to the Middle East, constantly exposed to these public charges."[24] Everyone knew that Nixon's days were numbered. Everything he did to extricate himself from the Watergate scandal made matters worse.

Newsweek called the Salzburg press conference "easily the most bizarre scene in his spectacular career."[25] Only two weeks earlier the disengagement on the Golan Heights between Israel and Syria had won him new editorial plaudits for his "virtuoso performance in diplomacy."[26] Another paper concluded: "Secretary of State Henry Kissinger has achieved his long awaited breakthrough in the crucial and climactic negotiations between the Israelis and Syrians." His methods won praise: "Dr. Kissinger has not reached for the moon. He has never tried to end a generation of war in the Middle East in one great, big package." It was "an enormous diplomatic triumph." Even as observers chided him for his "unfortunate and unnecessary" outburst at Salzburg, they took pains to recall that in the Syrian disengagement "his was a monumental diplomatic achievement, a singular contribution to the process of adjusting postwar and postcolonial power balances."[27]

Most observers thought Kissinger had diminished his stature by upstaging Nixon on his upcoming Mideast trip but believed he was indispensable. One of the subordinates whose phone had been tapped told reporters "God, I hope this doesn't bring Henry down. He's the only guy keeping us afloat."[28] Senator J. William Fulbright, chairman of the foreign relations committee and a supporter of détente, was equally concerned. His committee, he said, was "very anxious to assist the Secretary, who is a very valuable man to the country. . . . Kissinger is the symbol of détente. That is why, above all, his resignation would be a body blow to détente, particularly to our policy of normalizing relations with the Soviet Union." Senator Hubert Humphrey thought Kissinger had gotten carried away. "Just cool it, stay with it, you'll get a fair hearing," he advised the overwrought Secretary.[29]

Kissinger weathered the storm over the wiretaps. Congress affirmed its faith in the Secretary of State. Fifty-one senators co-sponsored a resolution expressing their "complete confidence" in Kissinger declaring his "integrity and veracity" to be "above reproach." Senator Fulbright, who supported Kissinger, would not go that far. He pressed ahead with Committee hearings and expressed alarm that "a majority of the Senate are now apparently willing to resolve these issues without seeing a shred of additional evidence."[30] Senator Lowell Weicker (R.-Conn.) also took issue with most members of the Senate. The Secretary, Weicker charged, "is not the victim of a biased news media or of the House Judiciary Committee. He is the victim of his own administration."

Members of the House Judiciary Committee concluded that their investigations implicated Kissinger in originating the wiretaps. Joshua Eilberg (D.-Pa.) decided that either Kissinger or Haig had proposed some of the taps "and if Haig did it, it was under Kissinger's direction." Another member, John Sieberling (D.-Ohio), explained the reasons for the taps: "Kissinger was raising hell because of the leaks and wanted something done to stop them and as a result of that the wiretaps of the 17 were initiated." Sieberling admitted, however, that testimony "doesn't prove Kissinger asked for them [the taps], but at least it's evidence." Richard Holbrooke, editor of *Foreign Policy*, tried to strike a balance. Kissinger was somewhere in between "the one clean man in a school of skunks" and just "another member of the team, involved in some kind of 'White House horror.'" Kissinger should almost be pitied as someone who made a deal with the Devil. He "attempted one of his own delicate balancing acts, in exchange for an opportunity to play an extraordinary role on the world stage."[31]

The Senate Foreign Relations Committee did reopen the case of wiretaps at Kissinger's request. The committee concluded that he had substantially told the truth at his 1973 confirmation. "The committee reaffirms its position of last year that his role in the wiretapping 'did not constitute grounds to bar his confirmation as Secretary of State.' If the committee knew then what it knows now it would have nonetheless reported the nomination favorably to the Senate."[32]

As President Nixon entered the tumultuous last weeks of his administration, his performance on a frantic trip to Egypt and Israel confirmed Kissinger's argument that the Secretary had to retain independent authority over foreign policy. This barnstorm tour of the two principal adversaries in the Middle East made little foreign policy sense. Nixon had nothing to negotiate in the two Mideastern capitals; he appeared only to take credit for Kissinger's earlier achievement. The President's doctors discouraged him from taking the trip because of a flareup of phlebitis in his leg. Nixon went anyway, reasoning that life might not be worth much outside the White House. Rejecting doctors' advice, he stood on the rear platform of the train carrying him and Anwar Sadat from the capital to the port city of Alexandria. As many as two million jubilant Egyptians waved and shouted their approval of the President. He believed that their joy certified his success as a foreign policy leader.

Kissinger, on the other hand, realized that the President had lost touch with what the public thought of him. The Secretary understood that the visit to Egypt was simply a headline grabber. It neither advanced the peace process, nor cemented relations with Israel. These suspicions were confirmed a few days later when the President received a far more subdued reception in Israel. The crowds on the road from Tel Aviv to Jerusalem numbered in the thousands, not millions; they seemed more worried than supportive too. The tumult along the Egyptian rail lines alarmed Israelis who had not fully recovered their nerve from the defeats of the first days of the 1973 war. Signs reading "DON'T SELL US OUT" or, more ominously "MR. PRESIDENT, YOU CAN RUN, BUT YOU CAN'T HIDE" appeared along the motorcade route. The new government of Prime Minister Yitzhak Rabin, formerly ambassador to the United States and perhaps more aware of the nuances of United States politics than that of President Sadat, regarded Nixon as a lame duck.[33]

Israelis were not unhappy to see him go, as long as Kissinger remained in overall charge of United States foreign policy. Since he had injected himself directly into the Mideast negotiations, he had informed Israelis that he, as a Jew, was attentive to their security interests. Without saying so directly, he indicated that the President probably did not share his concern for Israel's interests. The fervid reception of Egyptians who had not agreed to anything more formal than a cease-fire with the Jewish state, raised the prospect of Nixon remaining in power as a friend of Israel's most powerful rival. With Kissinger in charge of foreign policy in a Gerald Ford administration, Israel's anxieties would diminish. As a member of Congress Ford had expressed strong appreciation of Israel's position. Not deeply knowledgeable about foreign policy, the new President was likely to permit the experienced Secretary of State to continue as the major force behind America's Mideast policy.

Kissinger fed these suspicions during the three days the President's party spent in Israel. He indicated that he was aware that Nixon might not be President for long. Not to fear, though, he told his hosts. United States foreign policy was based upon a more profound appreciation of the realities of world power than simply the need of Congress to assert its authority over a badly damaged President. He indicated that once the Watergate scandal ran its full course and Nixon had to leave office, the United States would continue an active role in the Mideast negotiations. He implied that Watergate was a sordid domestic matter, not worthy of the attention of friendly, democratic foreign governments. They should realize, even if the Soviets and the Chinese did not, that public opinion could be fickle, demanding the removal of an official while supporting his public policies.[34]

Nixon also sought to recoup his standing by another summit in the Soviet Union. Leonid Brezhnev had visited Washington in June 1973, so it was Nixon's turn to come to the Soviet Union under the custom of annual summit gatherings. Brezhnev for his part was eager to play host to a beleaguered President desperate for an agreement to recapture public acclaim.[35]

Nixon traveled to Moscow in late June to lay the groundwork for a new arrangement for strategic arms. These conversations were not nearly as productive as those of 1972. Preparations were less comprehensive than they had been for the SALT-I interim agreement. Kissinger preceded Nixon in a meeting with Brezhnev in March. As Secretary of State his visit took place in the glare of publicity. He raised expectations with the claim that the two sides were near a "conceptual breakthrough" over SALT.[36] The Soviets were not so accommodating, and on his departure from Moscow, he reported only that "progress" was being made on SALT. Despite the expectation of

With his wife, Nancy Maginnes Kissinger, on a trip to address the United Nations, September 1974. (Courtesy GRFL)

Cartoonists noticed that some of the magic wore thin during Kissinger's final thirty months in office.

"Oops, Oop, And Away"

Copyright © 1974 by Herblock in the *Washington Post*.

'What's come over you lately?'

LePelley in the *Christian Science Monitor*. Copyright © 1975 TCSPS.

'Listen, next time he cracks the whip, bite him'

LePelley in the *Christian Science Monitor*. Copyright © 1976 TCSPS.

Briefing President Gerald R. Ford. (Courtesy GRFL)

With Brent Scowcroft, President Ford's National Security Adviser, November 1975–January 1977. (Courtesy GRFL)

Secretary of Defense James R. Schlesinger and Kissinger whisper during a National Security Council meeting called to discuss the *Mayaguez* crisis, May 1975. (Courtesy GRFL)

Soviet Communist Party General Secretary Leonid Brezhnev argues his points. (Courtesy GRFL)

Soviet Foreign Minister Andrei Gromyko and Kissinger meet during the Vladivostock summit, November 1974. (Courtesy GRFL)

1972 of a quick SALT-II treaty, obstacles had arisen. The rush of technological developments had made some strategists less eager for an arrangement with the Soviets than they had been before 1972. The United States had proceeded rapidly with the development of independently targeted warheads. This gave the United States strategic force an enormous advantage over the Soviets, whose missiles were far less accurate. Any agreement with the Soviets to limit the deployment of the MIRVed weapons would put the United States at a disadvantage.

Some of these dissents came from politicians who earlier had expressed doubts about the worth of détente. To Senator Henry Jackson the trip to Moscow represented nothing more than Nixon's attempt to recover with foreign travels what he had lost domestically. He expected that any deal struck with the Soviets would only result in the United States losing the technological edge. Since 1972 he had insisted that the United States match the Soviets missile for missile, warhead for warhead. For this the Soviet press indicted him as "the archenemy of détente." Kissinger complained that the effort to match the Soviets weapon for weapon masked a desire for nuclear superiority. "What do you do with superiority?" he wondered. "What does it mean? What value is it?"[37]

Nixon hoped his conversations with Brezhnev would persuade the public that only he was capable of working out an arrangement of differences with the Soviets. No one would want to impeach him and replace him with the new Vice-President, Gerald Ford. The former minority leader of the House of Representatives had no reputation as a foreign policy leader. The public might want to keep Nixon in office to keep relations with the Soviets on an even keel. Otherwise his potential successor might wreck the structure of détente. For Jackson that would not have been a bad idea. He had no use for détente and a weakened President would necessarily rely more upon the normal congressional channels for advice.[38]

His performance at the Moscow summit raised the prospect that "Kissinger is Steering a Reckless Course," according to Joseph Kraft, customarily a friendly columnist. Kissinger raised eyebrows with his tired outburst "what in the name of God is strategic superiority?" and his plaintive plea that "both sides have to convince their military establishments of the need for restraint." These remarks, born of frustration and exhaustion, put Kissinger on a collision course with Secretary of Defense James Schlesinger and would, Kraft believed, "alienate defense-minded senators. John Stennis of Mississippi and other hawks hitherto partial to the Secretary of State would turn against him." Indeed, Schlesinger tartly retorted "we have firm civilian control in this country . . . there is no problem with the military."[39]

With so few substantive results from the Moscow meeting, editorials labeled it "A Meager Summit." It was primarily important, as Nixon noted in his address on July 3, because such get-togethers were "taking place so routinely, so familiarly, as part of a continuing process that would have seemed inconceiveable just a few short years ago." Supporters of détente found satisfaction that "the luster and drama have gone out of summit meetings with the Russians."[40] Kissinger's stop in London on the way back produced further concern that the Nixon administration was desperate for foreign policy diversions. Reporter Joseph Harsch was surprised that "the advantage has changed" from high-level U.S.–European meetings. "It is no longer a political plus to the Europeans, but rather to the Americans. Mr. Nixon finds comfort from being seen working at foreign policy overseas and Dr. Kissinger's presumed indispensability is fortified by being reported about from abroad."[41]

Even if the trip to Moscow did not yield much for the President, it did increase Kissinger's hold on the imagination of the press and public. Back in Washington Kissinger became concerned over Nixon's future. The President concluded that the House Judiciary Committee was conducting a political vendetta against him. He hired James St. Clair, once a member of Joseph Welch's team of legal experts defending the army against Senator Joseph McCarthy's scurrilous charges. St. Clair prepared the President's case before the Judiciary Committee. The President's lawyers had full faith in Nixon's innocence and believed that the charges against him were politically inspired. The President's chief counsel collapsed with a heart attack in the midst of preparing for the appearance before the committee. Kissinger too could tell by the middle of July that the end of Nixon's presidency was near.[42]

Kissinger wanted to keep the government on an even keel in the midst of a transition. Perhaps the worst thing that could happen was a protracted battle with Congress, lasting months or even into 1975. The President had to realize that the world situation was so dangerous that the United States could not afford to endure a prolonged period of uncertainty in foreign affairs. Once more than half the public lost faith in Nixon, fear of Gerald Ford could not prevent Nixon's demise. The President could supply better public service by smoothly turning over power.

The Secretary of State found an incident in the eastern Mediterranean to bring his chief to an understanding for the need for effective leadership. On July 15, a gang of Greek Cypriots led by a notorious plotter named Nikos Sampson overthrew the government of Archbishop Makarios. The archbishop had maintained a precarious balance between the Greek and Turkish Cypriot communities since independence in 1957, thereby incurring the wrath of militants on each side.

All hell broke loose after the 1974 coup. Sampson immediately declared an "enosis," or union, between Cyprus and Greece. The original independence agreement between the two communities and Great Britain, supervised by the United Nations, specifically forbade any political union between the island and either Greece and Turkey. The Greeks, who made up a little more than two-thirds of the population, deeply resented the ban.

The new Cyprus government, made up of unknown men, little better than thugs, found champions within the equally brutal Greek government. Greece had been ruled by a Junta of colonels since a coup in mid-1967. The anti-Communist military officers who took over combined disdain for democrats with a militant Greek nationalism. Having ousted parliament and king to block the rise to power of the Socialist party, the colonels suppressed all political activity and dissent. They banished political leaders and silenced their parties. King Constantine II, who tried unsuccessfully to help the democratic parties with a coup of his own, was banished to Italy. The colonels consolidated popular support with bombastic calls for expanded Greek power in the Mediterranean. They pointed to the position of the Greek Cypriots as an example of the decline of Hellenic influence and accused the Turks of blocking the growth of Greek power. The colonels also attempted to persuade the United States that their Christian anti-Communism helped NATO more than did the Muslim Turks, now ruled by the Social Democratic government of Bulent Ecevit.[43]

The colonels' remarks struck a chord in Washington. President Nixon once blessed the junta with "we in the United States government, particularly in American business, greatly appreciate Greece's attitude toward American investment, and we appreciate the welcome that is given here to American companies and the sense of security that the government of Greece is imparting to them."[44] Kissinger believed that the military government had kept Greece in the alliance as a forceful, anti-Communist member. The Greek Socialists, who might seize power if free elections were to take place, were far more radical than any of the Western European Social Democratic parties.

The Secretary therefore accepted the requirement for the colonels to press their nationalist agenda.[45]

Turkey panicked the new Cypriot government with an armed attack. Sampson expected that either Greece would intimidate the Turks or the United States would discourage Turkey. Instead, Athens found that it could not mount a military operation without the backing of the United States, but Secretary of State Kissinger felt constrained. He worried that a war between two NATO partners in the midst of a constitutional crisis in the United States would devastate American influence in southern Europe. "The overriding consideration in Dr. Kissinger's policy," reported the *Christian Science Monitor*, "is not only to prevent violence but to avoid risking the safety of American military interests in Greece."[46] A beleaguered President Nixon could not control events in the Mediterranean. As an expedient, Kissinger favored permitting the Turks some share of power on Cyprus. Longer-term solutions awaited Nixon's departure.

The Cypriot fiasco brought forth a chorus of denunciation from Greek Americans and their supporters. Conservatives like Representatives Edwin Derwinski (R.-Ill.) or Roman Pucinski (D.-Ill.) who had supported the junta believed that the administration had let the colonels twist in the wind as the United States was consumed with its own constitutional crisis. For liberal Greeks like Representative Paul Sarbanes (D.-Md.) or John Brademas (D.-Ind.), the end of the dictatorship freed them to vent their spleen at past American support for the Greek government and the administration's "tilt" toward Turkey. Sarbanes told a Greek-American gathering that "the consequences of the catastrophic policy of our State Department during this crisis are staggering. . . . Efforts to support the civilian government of Constantine Caramanlis and the restoration of constitutional democracy to Greece have been dealt a serious blow."[47] Brademas reported that he and the other Greek-American congressmen "protested to Secretary Kissinger the failure . . . to voice any public criticism whatsoever of the massive invasion of Cyprus by Turkish forces." He complained that "the sharp rise in anti-American sentiment in Greece at precisely that time when constitutional government is born again there, must stand in sharp rebuke to the shortsightedness of American policy toward Greece."[48] They had not spoken out since 1967 for fear of alarming relatives or friends still in Greece. Once the hold of dictatorship slipped, however, liberal members of Congress denounced the Nixon administration for having supported the colonels. The liberals viewed his support of Turkey's invasion as another example of Kissinger's refusal to look at what happened inside a state and concentrate instead on great power relationships. They introduced legislation banning arms to Turkey.

Kissinger took this criticism in stride, as it only confirmed his judgment that Congress had no business intervening in the proper conduct of foreign policy. He sniffed that "the growing tendency of the Congress to legislate in detail the day-to-day or week-to-week conduct of our foreign affairs" made the United States look ridiculous.[49]

But congressional disquiet enabled him to go to work on President Nixon. By late July, with the Judiciary Committee in full public hearings on what to do about the future of the President, Nixon still wanted to fight the impending impeachment. At this point Kissinger began working with his former deputy, Alexander Haig, now White House Chief of Staff, to persuade Nixon that he had to yield power soon. Kissinger and Haig had grown apart in the fifteen months since the latter had been Chief of Staff. Kissinger worried that his onetime subordinate had established a separate base of power.

Whatever their mutual distrust, Kissinger and Haig came to need one another in the summer of 1974. Both realized that the foreign policy of the country had been held hostage to Watergate. In the long term, a prolonged impeachment trial of the President could only erode further whatever remained of congressional deference in foreign affairs. How could the Senate continue to support presidential initiatives in the relationship with the Soviet Union or with the Middle East nations as it sat as a jury in an impeachment trial? The more revelations of wiretaps, enemies' lists, or tax cheating, the less legislators would want to defer. Moreover, any impeachment would necessarily take up the President's energy. Even if he wanted to devote attention to foreign affairs, he could not.

More likely, Kissinger believed, Nixon would become increasingly erratic in his foreign policy activities. Most of the time he could not pay attention; when he did rouse himself he would go for the dramatic gesture. How many more whirlwind trips to Eastern Europe, the Middle East, or maybe Southeast Asia or Europe could the public abide? He would have to make ever grander gestures to gain any sort of new public support for his flagging presidency.[50]

If Nixon's long-range prognosis was uncertain, the immediate prospect was bleaker. Haig and Kissinger became concerned after the Judiciary Committee voted the first three articles of impeachment with bipartisan support. Until that fateful July 23, Nixon had believed that the Republicans on the committee would remain firm. Dismayed at Republican defections, Nixon might provoke a crisis in the next few weeks to encourage Congress to keep him in power.

Overseas he might involve the United States in new fighting in the Middle East or increase aerial bombardment over Vietnam. The President could even upset the careful balance with the Soviet Union and disturb the NATO allies.

Worst of all from Kissinger's and Haig's point of view might be a President completely unhinged. Concerned, Haig told armed forces commanders to check first with him before acting on unusual orders. Haig considered Nixon capable of directing troops to the Capitol to evict Congress. While Haig knew that the public would react furiously to any attempt to abandon the Constitution, he knew that Nixon had done just that the previous October. His criticism of the Deputy Attorney General for refusing to drop the special prosecutor had all the trappings of an assault on legitimate authority. At that time Haig had helped. He had told William Ruckelshaus that an order from the Commander-in-Chief, Nixon, had to be obeyed. Now, if Nixon tried to use the power of his supreme command of the armed forces Haig worried that other generals, schooled in obedience, might take him at his word. They too might fear that liberals in Congress and the press were attempting to win in an impeachment process what they had lost fairly in the election of 1972. Haig believed, however, that no commander could imagine that Al Haig harbored a soft spot in his heart for liberals. If he signaled that the President's word was not to be accepted without first checking with the general in charge of the staff, there would be some control over the President's worst impulses.[51]

Kissinger, however, could not wait for the President to come unglued. There were important foreign policy issues to be resolved. The Soviets were pressing the United States to participate in a general European security conference that would finally put an end to the division of Europe after the Second World War. Both sides also anticipated some forward momentum in the SALT talks. Europeans also were restless in 1974. The celebrated "year of Europe" of the previous twelve months had not persuaded the Allies that the United States still considered their security equivalent to that of the United States. Most worrisome was the future of the cease-fire in Southeast Asia. The United States had left South Vietnam with the understanding that any breach in the terms of the agreement ending the war would bring the American bombers back to the region. If Nixon continued to resist the rush toward impeachment, Congress would become all the more hostile toward aid to South Vietnam.[52]

For all these reasons Haig and Kissinger maneuvered Nixon into resigning rather than face the prolonged agony of a trial by the Senate. They ushered Senators Barry Goldwater (R.-Ariz.) and John Stennis (D.-Miss.), two of the most conservative members of the upper house, to the Oval Office. They reported that their support remained firm, but they could not vouch for their colleagues. At one point Goldwater announced that fewer than ten senators were likely to vote for acquittal on the impeachment charge.[53]

They nearly begged Nixon to resign for the good of the conservative causes they professed to believe in. For Republicans the longer Nixon remained clinging to office the worse things would be. They hoped that a Ford presidency might insulate them from the wrath of the public deceived. Only if Nixon were out of office long before the congresssional elections of 1974, however, could Republican candidates expect protection from the Watergate explosion. A conservative Democratic Senator like Stennis did not care about the electoral fortunes of the Republican party. As chairman of the Armed Services Committee, however, he worried about erosion of congressional deference for the President, any president. Stennis thought that he could not hold his finger in the dyke much longer if Nixon decided to stay. He also supported many of Nixon's and Kissinger's departures in international relations. Nixon's removal from office, ironically enough, would have a liberating effect upon the President's supporters. Stennis believed that they could legitimately convince their colleagues that the achievements of the administration in foreign policy were bigger than the office holder.

Nixon blanched when he heard from the senators. He considered his support ideological and believed the abuses he had been charged with trivial. Everything he and his subordinates had done since 1970 had been designed to strengthen the President's hand in foreign affairs. He therefore could be moved by appeals to preservation of the gains in foreign affairs.

Kissinger held Nixon's hand. He went to the White House after the senators departed to persuade Nixon that his place in history was assured. He played to Nixon's mawkish side. The two agreed that petty rivals had tried to discredit the President. Kissinger, fed up with liberal academics, concurred with Nixon's view that liberals simply could not stand to see a conservative President effect better relations with the Soviet Union and China. They were equally miserable that Nixon and Kissinger had ended the war in Vietnam. Kissinger reminded Nixon that his place in history depended on the durability of his new direction in foreign policy. The only way to deny his enemies the fruits of their victory was to resign.

Ford, a man without personal enemies, could carry on the tradition. The new President, untutored in foreign affairs, would make the opposition scream. They could not complain that Ford had a compulsion for power, a secretive side, or an obsessive hatred of the Kennedy family—all charges leveled against Nixon. Faced with a hopeless congressional situation but cheered by Kissinger's reassurances that his place in history was safe, Nixon decided to resign on the night of August 8. A session of prayer, with a possibly inebriated and surely distraught President and a highly embarrassed Secretary of State each falling to his knees, sealed the deal. Kissinger was happy that the President had accepted reality, and relieved that a man with a tenuous grip on his own emotions had left office.[54]

A summary of the Nixon years ranked his collaboration with Kissinger as the major positive accomplishment. "With Henry Kissinger's help, Mr. Nixon risked alienating many of his longtime cold war supporters by opening America's door to the Communist world." Another item worthy of praise was "the triumph of Mr. Nixon's emissary Dr. Kissinger in bringing an end to the 1973 Middle East war and laying the groundwork for the difficult continuing negotiations for peace."[55]

Gerald Ford enjoyed a month-long honeymoon with press and public. He appeared Nixon's opposite. Open, friendly, at peace with himself and the rest of the world, he appeared to be a healing figure. The Democratic majority in the House of Representatives had liked Ford, even if they had little respect for his intellectual capacity. From Kissinger's point of view too, Ford made a perfect President, at least until he pardoned Richard Nixon in September. Immediately on taking office, the new President called the Secretary of State and asked for him to stay. "Henry, I need you," he recalled telling Kissinger.[56]

Kissinger's job was made even easier in the last months of 1974. Ford's approval rating suffered a sharp decline as his pardon of Richard Nixon immediately tarnished his appeal. Kissinger's stock rose in the aftermath of the pardon. Joseph Harsch commented that "the foreign policies of the United States have not missed a beat either through or because of the dramatic political events of the past week." Harsch believed that Kissinger had been "the executor and for a long time the originator of American foreign policy." Things were unlikely to change in the Ford administration because the new President was not knowledgeable about foreign affairs and showed "full confidence in Dr. Kissinger's ability to take care of foreign policy matters." For the moment "Dr. Kissinger occupies the kind of position in foreign policy-making in Washington that Dean Acheson enjoyed under President Truman."[57]

Only a few weeks later, however, the adulation changed to "Kissinger Under Fire" as the furor over Chile combined with Republican uneasiness over the reaction to the Nixon pardon. Now prominent Republican members of Congress spoke openly about who would make the best successor to Kissinger, as they urged Ford to make a complete housecleaning of Nixon holdovers. Representative Albert Quie (R.-Minn.) specifically named Kissinger as a cabinet secretary who should go because of "declining credibility." News of Kissinger's difficulties alarmed Moscow, where leaders were reported to "think that the immediate fate of détente depends far more on the person of Dr. Kissinger than upon anything else." When Kissinger went to the U.N. General Assembly later in September, diplomats could speak of little more than Kissinger's travails. One summarized what he thought were the views of his colleagues as: "We see Kissinger doing a tightrope act, with extraordinary skill and style, and we see him being shot at by his American audience. It is easy to say that no man is indispensable, but if he falls we fear the worst for the future of his act." Another diplomat used Kissinger's troubles as emblematic of flaws in the American love of celebrities. "The pity is," he said, "that Americans build up idols to such heights that they cannot be sustained, and when they crash it can be tragic. If Kissinger crashes, it will be an American tragedy, but also a tragedy for the whole world."[58]

Some saw the new scrutiny of Kissinger's record as a healthy return of balance in the aftermath of the "abnormal situation" of Watergate, which had placed "intolerable demands on him," thrusting him "into the unreal role of a miracle worker."[59] In a wide-ranging interview with James Reston, Kissinger likened his position to Dean Acheson's efforts to confront the Soviet Union in the late forties. Now, Kissinger believed, Acheson's work was completed and it was his turn to create a new world order. "I think we are delicately poised right now," he said. "I genuinely think that the next decade will either be a period that in retrospect will look like one of the great periods of human creativity, or it could be the beginning of extraordinary disarray. . . . If we remain strong enough to prevent the imposition of Communist hegemony, then I believe that transformations of the Communist societies is inevitable."[60]

Kissinger's frantic travels in October provoked one professional foreign service officer to wonder "can you really run the State Department that way?" Editorialists were still a bit in awe of "Kinetic Kissinger," as they called him. They cautioned that "Dr. Kissinger seems to be trying to hold the world together singlehandedly—an impossible task." Nonetheless "there is no denying the worthiness and urgency of the goal and his zestful dedication to it." He was described as a "diplomatic dervish . . . a diplomatic superstar . . . a great man who has accomplished much." Ford's inexperience made it "important that Kissinger stay on the job." Still, Kissinger was too much in motion, too personal, too secret, and spread too thin. "It is time to begin institutionalizing those accomplishments. . . . He should spend less time abroad and more in Washington. It also means he should begin delegating more authority to responsible subordinates."[61]

Ford and Kissinger went to Japan and the Soviet Union in late November. The goal was progress on a new SALT agreement. The administration informed Congress that limiting MIRVs would be high on the agenda at Vladivostock. Brent Scowcroft reminded Senators Edward Brooke (R.-Mass.) and Walter Mondale (D.-Minn.) that Kissinger had told the United Nations that the United States "has no higher priority than controlling and reducing the level of nuclear arms." The Secretary had testified to the Foreign Relations Committee that "achieving a first strike capability by either side would represent a major threat to political stability." For his part, Scowcroft noted that "since unconstrained MIRV development and deployment could have a potential disruptive effect on the strategic relationship between the Soviet Union and the United States, the administration considers MIRV limitations an important component of the U.S. approach to SALT."[62]

The presidential party stopped in Tokyo for talks with Prime Minister Tanaka enroute to the meeting with Brezhnev. A French newspaper reported that the "Ford–Tanaka meeting resembled the Nixon–Brezhnev summit in that Mr. Tanaka now needed a successful international meeting as Mr. Nixon had when he went to Moscow." A German newspaper thought that Ford was just as vulnerable. It observed that "the meeting is burdened by both men's domestic political weaknesses. . . . But even if Gerald Ford were simply to sit and gaze at Fuji, he would be fulfilling the main purpose of his trip, which is largely symbolic." An Argentine newspaper stressed Kissinger's trip to China after the Ford–Brezhnev summit. "What the Chinese wish," wrote La Nacion of Buenos Aires, "is to determine whether Ford will have adequate clout on Brezhnev to see that the Nixon–Chou commitment not to tolerate any hegemony in the Asian Pacific is honored. Kissinger will have to be very imaginative in face of Chinese apprehension, because, save for trade ties, relations between the two countries are not very good."[63]

Initial reports from Vladivostock spoke of a "conceptual breakthrough," one of Kissinger's favorite phrases, in measuring the quality of nuclear arsenals. The Secretary of State reported that "we are well down the road" to a SALT-II treaty.[64] Ford's aides were somewhat distressed that Kissinger seemed to be taking the spotlight. On the plane home, Ford's press secretary Ron Nessen pointedly noted that the President had done the negotiating himself. Kissinger, enroute to Beijing, fumed that once more the White House staff was undercutting him. At home, Senator Jackson thought that Vladivostock put the United States at a decided disadvantage in land-based missiles. Jackson promised very careful congressional scrutiny of any treaty. For his part Kissinger warned that a "devisive debate" in Congress could harm U.S.–Soviet relations. Newspapers chided him for once more being high-handed with Congress. "Kissinger seems to be suggesting," wrote the *Los Angeles Times*, "that there should be no substantive debate on the accord to set a ceiling on strategic weapons. . . . [H]e is plainly wrong."[65] The *Wall Street Journal* warned that the " 'breakthrough' at Vladivostock . . . consisted in anything but a new Soviet willingness to deal with a post-Watergate President. The breakthrough consisted of the abandonment of essentials of the American negotiating position." The paper also regretted that Kissinger had acted on his own "without effective consultation within the U.S. government." Secretary of Defense James Schlesinger "was apparently cut in at the last moment, while the presidential party was in Vladivostock and he was in Washington."[66]

Kissinger's NSC staff prepared Ford for a meeting with George Meany to brief the AFL–CIO leader on the Vladivostock arrangement. The President should stress the ten-year duration of the pact, the equal limits of 2400 delivery vehicles, and the equal limits of 1320 MIRVed missiles. He should also point out that the "2400 limit applies to all strategic delivery vehicles," unlike SALT I, which had omitted heavy bombers and mobile land-based ICBM systems.[67]

One of Kissinger's assistants alerted him to Paul Nitze's criticisms of SALT. Nitze, who had resigned from the SALT team, complained about Kissinger's methods. The development of two levels of negotiations (one between the formal delegations and the other conducted by Kissinger) caused "unnecessary difficulties, some of significant consequence, in parrying Soviet strategy and tactics." Nitze also disliked the substance of the Vladivostock agreement, which "does not deal with throw weight—the most useful verifiable measure of relative missile capability. . . ."[68]

In these circumstances Kissinger tried to make good on his earlier promises. Nixon was now out of the way and his replacement had neither the reputation nor the knowledge nor the public popularity to make him an alternative to Kissinger. He was eager to learn about the new relationship between Washington and Moscow. He wanted to attach his own name to an arms control agreement just as Nixon had done. He wanted the structure of peace promised in the first term to be erected with his leadership. Most of all, perhaps, he wanted President Ford to ride to an election victory in 1976 on the strengths of Kissinger's accomplishments. Kissinger found this situation ideal for presenting his foreign policy views. As Ford's mentor he thought he did not have to worry about creating a rival to his authority. For his part, the new President eagerly obliged. He certainly would not deny Kissinger's own role in creating an effective foreign policy.[69]

What this strategy overlooked, however, was that Kissinger's foreign policy had aged. It had created enemies in Congress who jealously wanted to reassert authority over foreign relations. Critics of détente no longer believed that relations could be improved with the Soviet Union. The Republican party, battered by Watergate, no longer offered unquestioned support to the President. Worst of all, the tenuous peace in Southeast Asia unraveled as Ford consolidated his power. As the Republic of Vietnam died in late 1974 and early 1975, what had once appeared to be Kissinger's greatest achievement turned into a major embarrassment. As it grew into a disaster, Kissinger's entire foreign policy came unstuck.

NINE

The End in Vietnam, 1973–1975

The fall of Richard Nixon coincided with the beginning of the end in Vietnam. When Henry Kissinger and Le Duc Tho had signed the peace agreement on January 23, 1973, Kissinger hoped that Southeast Asia would no longer present problems for U.S. foreign policy. He expected that the cease-fire supervised by Polish, Canadian, Indonesian, and Hungarian diplomats would hold. Kissinger believed that the North Vietnamese had been so exhausted by the attrition of the last years of the war that they had welcomed a respite. He decided that the final accords had come because of the weight of United States firepower in the last months of the war. The mining of Haiphong harbor in May 1972 and the Christmas bombing of December–January 1972–1973 had, according to Washington, left the North Vietnamese reeling. They had, in effect, sued for peace. Kissinger believed that without the strong American military actions of 1972, Hanoi would have continued to raise objections.

These assumptions about North Vietnamese behavior overlooked other reasons for the agreement of 1973. The United States had put more pressure on the South than on Hanoi in the last days. During the 1972 election campaigns, the opposition candidate claimed that the Nixon administration had purposely prolonged the war; in order to draw the fangs of the antiwar movement the Nixon administration had pushed forward with an agreement. The settlement of the fall had also come as much from changes in the international environment as from differences in the military situation. Détente with the

Soviet Union and better relations with China had altered American perceptions of international relations.[1]

Now that Kissinger had successfully turned attention away from revolution and nationalism toward state behavior, it did not matter so much what the Vietcong did. The United States had discovered that it could deal directly with Communist governments. They, in turn, expressed far less concern about the state of revolutionary movements. The Vietnam War now appeared to be more of the end of an era of revolutionary enthusiasm rather than the beginning of a worldwide wave of nationalist victories. In other words, Vietnam simply did not mean as much to the United States in the détente era as it had when both the Soviet Union and Communist China appeared to be implacable foes of the United States.

Of course, the South Vietnamese government realized that Kissinger placed low priority on the future of Vietnam. General Thieu's negotiators at Paris had watched in horror as Kissinger made a separate deal to end the war. Saigon had hardly been mollified in the fall of 1972 by General Alexander Haig's assurances that the United States would stand ready to reenter the war if necessary. There had been, however, little that the South could do to prevent the United States from making its own deal with Hanoi. All the South could hope for would be a resumption of American bombing if the situation became worse after the original agreement.

Saigon was not above creating a military situation that would force the United States to come to its aid. Throughout the war itself the ARVN had commenced military operations with the express purpose of drawing the United States along. The invasions of Cambodia and Laos had originated partly in the minds of Saigon's generals who were expecting to include the remaining American combat troops in the fighting. The very incompetence of the ARVN forces had been bait drawing the United States back to the war. Washington had learned that its enthusiasm for Vietnamization of the war had been misplaced. While the Vietnamese were willing to fight the war—something they had avoided since 1965—they could not prevail without United States participation in the fighting. The official historian of the United States delegation to the mixed commission later concluded that "implementing the cease-fire was an impossible task from the beginning—none of the Vietnamese parties was willing to stop fighting. The Americans did not fail for lack of effort. No effort could have succeeded."[2] Saigon's goal throughout the Nixon administration had been to demonstrate just enough military ability to convince

Washington that the cause was not hopeless. At the same time, the ARVN was never able to be and never tried to be strong enough to dominate the North.

In the year after the cease-fire and withdrawal of American forces from the combat zone, Saigon looked for ways to keep the United States interested in the future of the war. In 1974, the ARVN once more began search-and-destroy operations against suspected guerrilla strongholds near Saigon. The South expected that the North would not move to reinforce the NLF. Believing that the enemy had indeed been bled white by the attrition of the war's last year, Saigon doubted that Hanoi had any reserves to move to the South. Moreover, Thieu's generals expected the North to fear the return of the United States as much as the South longed for it.

Kissinger's reputation suffered in early 1975. Liberal columnist Murray Kempton considered him a "magician . . . no longer just a man but, all by himself, a Foreign Office very like those that served the transient governments of the nineteenth century in Europe, being permanent where kings are temporary." Kempton professed "this nagging doubt that all these tricks might not be passing illusions."[3] Another writer believed that "Henry Kissinger has used up his good time." As successful as Dean Acheson or John Foster Dulles, "Kissinger, the grey fox, should have quit when he was ahead." There were "social earthquakes beneath our feet . . . and . . . it is too much for one man to bear. His adopted country is in the psychic workshop for repairs after its Southeast Asian adventure."[4] He retained considerable support among commentators. As he embarked for the Middle East in late February 1975, Joseph C. Harsch praised him: "as nearly as any man is ever indispensable, he is needed for finishing the peace-making role in the Middle East—if it can be finished."[5]

Unfortunately for South Vietnam, Kissinger no longer believed in the military effectiveness of bombing. Combat troops seemed to have been the one thing that could alter the balance of forces in the war. Their removal from the fighting had also been the single accomplishment of the Nixon administration. No high public official desired a repetition of the furious antiwar demonstrations of 1969 and 1970. The only way more United States troops would return to the fighting would be if the South Vietnamese faced impending doom. Those would be precisely the conditions guaranteed to generate angry antiwar outbursts. Resumption of bombing might have greater appeal. It caused fewer American casualties, although the number of prisoners of war rose. Antiwar activists, however, had trouble supporting POWs. The men shot down in bombing raids over the North invariably were officers who fully supported the war. The antiwar movement rarely had the treat of watching one of the pilots directly criticize the American war effort.

But bombing did not destroy the North. It had been useful in encouraging South Vietnamese leaders to believe that the United States stood by them. As such, bombing had improved South Vietnamese morale while it had encouraged allies who had earlier expressed doubts about American willingness to remain in the war. What the bombing had not done was move the North. The economy of North Vietnam was too undeveloped, its road and rail system too rudimentary for bombs to have eroded the North's ability to fight. Pentagon planners estimated that North Vietnam could continue its level of participation in the war forever. Unless the United States had shown a willingness to kill a good proportion of the North Vietnamese population, North Vietnam would continue to supply the South. The only advantages that came from bombing of the North were symbolic and political, not military.[6]

These symbolic payoffs had diminished substantially in the last year. The secrecy of the bombing of Laos and Cambodia had kept public and Congress in the dark. The administration persuaded the public that the war was costing the United States fewer lives and less treasure. Now that news of the attacks had been fully revealed, outsiders no longer could be made to feel that the war did not involve the United States. Any resumption of American bombing would cause more public outcry than it would help the South Vietnamese. Members of Congress could not be persuaded that new bombing would succeed where the earlier bombing had failed. Even conservatives showed little stomach for new American air action. North Dakota Republican Milton Young, a longtime supporter of the war, reminded colleagues that "we have got our prisoners of war out with honor, and what's the point of going on supporting a government that seems to have no will to fight and is corrupt."[7] Senator John McClelland (D.-Ark.), another conservative who chaired the appropriations committee, which would have to approve any new outlays, mused over the danger of seeing new POWs and decided "I have decided to risk the consequences of stopping the bombing."[8] For legislators who opposed the war, nothing the administration could say would alter their opinions.

Kissinger blamed the collapse of his Mideast shuttle on congressional refusal to provide aid to Cambodia. Already, in February, he had said that congressional reluctance to provide military aid for Cambodia generally "could be applied to any country," and Congress's attitude was "no trivial matter" as applied to relations with Israel. Kissinger left the Middle East with a blast at Congress for the prospective "loss of Cambodia." His voice broke as he announced that he was leaving for home. He informed reporters that "we cannot abandon friends in one part of the world without jeopardizing the security of friends everywhere." He went on that failure to provide aid in Southeast Asia could provoke a "massive shift in the policies of other countries, and an ultimate threat to U.S. national security." Opponents of continuing the war drew a different lesson. The *Nation* concluded that "what must have disturbed the Israelis far more than the reluctance of Congress to vote additional aid for Cambodia was the evident fact that the clever Kissinger formulations in the so-called Paris 'peace' agreements had not resulted in a meaningful settlement. Why shouldn't the Israelis be wary of his attempt to use foxy phrases to paper over their basic difference with the Arabs?" The liberal journal thought that Kissinger spent too much time on the road. "The office of the Secretary of State is in Washington and that is where Kissinger belongs."[9]

In March it appeared that "the world of woes seemed to have frayed Ford's and Kissinger's equanimity." The two men talked "as if the U.S. were in danger of becoming a pitiful, helpless giant, immobilized like Gulliver by a swarm of opportunistic adversaries." The period appeared "the gloomiest in Henry Kissinger's tenure as Secretary of State." Another report noted that "U.S. policy in Triple Trouble" in the Mideast, Southeast Asia, and in the NATO alliance. Kissinger "is known to blame Congress for the failures of American foreign policy."[10]

The new Congress defied Kissinger. *U.S. News* observed that "Congress is challenging his conduct of American foreign policy in a campaign that some experienced Washington observers say is unprecedented in its scope." Kissinger plaintively warned that "the growing tendency of Congress to legislate in detail the day-to-day or week-to-week conduct of our foreign affairs raises grave issues." Yet one of his top advisers explained why legislators remained skeptical: "There's a feeling in Congress that they've been 'had' too many times and that Kissinger has played fast and loose with too many laws."[11] The *Christian Science Monitor* warned that "it would be a disservice to the nation if Congress gratuitously tied the Secretary's hands." Yet even this usually supportive newspaper noted that Kissinger had brought some of the problems on himself. After promising early to seek consensus with Congress, "he became too famous perhaps and, in the aftermath of Watergate, the pendulum of adulation finally swung the other way."[12]

As the American position deteriorated, some of the President's aides feared that Kissinger was dragging the President down. One report noted that "the aides wanted a new security affairs adviser on whom Ford could lean and who could counter Kissinger's influence. They feared not so much for Kissinger's wisdom in foreign policy—there is no hint of disagreement with that—but instead the domestic political damage Ford would suffer by keeping a falling Kissinger at his side."[13] Ford dismissed as "a tempest in a teapot" and "not worthy of discussion" a reporter's question regarding "some of your advisers trying to break Secretary Kissinger's strong influence on you." Still, he found himself responding to press speculation about "the popular belief that you are merely a puppet to Secretary Kissinger's foreign policy views." He tried to assert his domination of the process. "When there are key decisions to be made, I make them. . . . I seek the views of all my senior advisers before making a decision. The role of the NSC system in my administration is to insure that I have all points of view presented." Another reporter continued the assault. He asked: "Wouldn't it be a sign that you are running foreign policy yourself if you appointed a new Secretary of State?" The President replied that "there is nothing unusual in American history for such a relationship as we have now. I have full confidence in Dr. Kissinger, and that is all there is to it."[14]

That was not all there was to it. Ford went on television to tell Walter Cronkite "I have never heard anybody on my staff ever make a recommendation to me that Secretary Kissinger should leave." Cronkite persisted: "What about suggestions that perhaps someone else should be National Security Adviser?" Here Ford hedged. He acknowledged that "I think you might make a good argument that that job ought to be divided. On the other hand, sometimes in government you get unique individuals who can very successfully handle a combination of jobs like Secretary Kissinger is doing today as head of the National Security Council and Secretary of State." Under these circumstances Ford "would not recommend, nor would I want a division of those two responsibilities."[15]

Meanwhile, members of Congress who opposed further United States involvement in the fighting could not be moved by demonstrations that the South Vietnamese desperately needed some sort of American assistance. The incapacity of the South Vietnamese to wage war on their own behalf had been a major argument for officials opposed to continued American involvement in the war. If the South Vietnamese government could not preserve itself after the peace agreement of 1973, then there was nothing the United States should do to help them. Antiwar representatives also could not be turned to support additional money for bombing if it were demonstrated to them that the attacks on the Communist forces actually were having an effect. Then the critics of the war would repeat their refrain that the United States was obliterating North Vietnamese society.

The South Vietnamese, however, had never been shrewd observers of the American political scene. They had believed that antiwar American politicians, like their domestic opponents of the war, were active agents of the North Vietnamese. To Saigon the most appropriate course for the United States was to ignore antiwar voices. Unfortunately, the Nixon administration in its last days could not afford to pay no attention to the antiwar movement. The President's principal accusers in the Watergate scandal also had come to despise the war in Vietnam. Lawmakers who had defended the President throughout the war found their support shattered by the revelations of the Watergate prosecutors and the House Judiciary Committee. Antiwar representatives seemed to have been proven correct. The United States government had deceived, committed burglaries, and trampled over constitutional guarantees at home. It probably had done the same thing overseas in the Vietnam war. Once basic confidence in the government's good intentions eroded it could not be restored.

The alignment of antiwar lawmakers and legislators offended by what had happened at Watergate made it impossible for the new Ford administration to do anything to introduce the United States into the war once more. Ford never had acquired the personal appeal in foreign affairs that Nixon had enjoyed at the height of euphoria over détente. What popularity Ford managed to gain evaporated in September when he pardoned Nixon.

Even if Ford and Kissinger had wanted to introduce American forces once more into Vietnam, they would have been blocked by a skeptical and assertive Congress. When Kissinger requested $270 million to aid Cambodia, Congressman Donald Fraser (D.-Minn.) denounced the "bankrupt policy . . . of the Department of State which will lead nowhere, which will cause not only an expenditure of money for no good end, but will lead to the increased loss of life." Representative Bella Abzug traveled to Southeast Asia and reported a "hopeless situation."

"Let us not," she urged, "force Asians to continue killing each other to maintain our false pride."[16]

Ford wanted to avoid dramatic confrontations. He received word from Kissinger that Vietnam was not nearly as important for the future of American foreign policy now that relations had improved with the Communist giants. Kissinger believed that pressing the boundaries of détente surpassed anything that could be accomplished by renewed participation in the war. He had to walk a thin line between committing the United States to returning to the war and caving in to a rebellious Congress. Whatever caused the least opposition at home and abroad would enable the United States to move ahead with its foreign policy.

Kissinger's pragmatic appraisal of current needs of American foreign policy seemed overtaken by events in South Vietnam in late 1974 and early 1975. The South's attempts to bring the United States back into the war had turned into a fiasco. Instead of making certain that the United States resumed the bombing of the North or even reentered the war, Saigon had only provoked Hanoi. The North had not been nearly as devastated as Southern planners had thought. Hanoi could continue to resupply its divisions in South Vietnam. It also was restocking its military supplies. Now that the United States was not bombing the harbors, the North could receive the most advanced types of Soviet equipment. For the first time, the North decided to move modern armor and tanks into the South. Refortified, the North Vietnamese army was poised to confront the ARVN in conventional warfare.[17]

Southern officials begged Washington to provide modern artillery, tanks, and, above all, planes to counter the North's onslaught. Kissinger found himself caught. He did not argue that the future of United States foreign policy in the rest of the world depended on what happened in Vietnam. On the contrary, with the settlement of the war seemingly assured in January 1973, the United States stood ready to get on with its interests in the rest of the world. The peace agreement with the North Vietnamese had appeared to Kissinger to have been proof that the strategy of an orderly withdrawal from the war had worked. He believed that the North had been so exhausted by the war that it had been forced into an agreement with the United States.[18]

This sort of reasoning made Kissinger and Ford reluctant to reenter the fighting. To that end, the United States embassy in South Vietnam sought to restrain the ARVN from military action. It encouraged the South Vietnamese to look on the bright side, invite the

Communists to continue talks on a possible coalition government, and ignore possible Communist violations of the cease-fire. The embassy also indicated that the United States would not easily be pressured into committing more resources to the war. The administration would not provide any additional ground troops, Congress would block any effort at resuming the bombing, and the public would become alarmed at anything that indicated renewed American participation in the fighting.

Kissinger and Ford preferred to maintain public support for foreign policy outside Vietnam. Ironically, this desire to gather public approval for foreign policy initiatives outside of Vietnam encouraged Kissinger and Ford to invest more effort in Southeast Asia. Both believed that they could not leave Southeast Asia under pressure from a disillusioned Congress and public. If Congress was so adamant that the United States could not return to the fighting, for that very reason Kissinger believed that the United States had to make a stand.[19]

Kissinger believed that current congressional opposition to a return of United States forces to Vietnam represented something far more significant than complaints about the future of the South Vietnamese government. It was in fact a defiant assault on executive prerogatives in foreign affairs. More would be lost than simply the future of a non-Communist Vietnam. The President no longer would have the opportunity to set the future course of foreign policy. Instead, the country would return to the foreign policy system that existed before the Second World War.

Kissinger wanted the United States to back the South Vietnamese government's request for additional assistance as a way of stemming the tide of neo-isolationism. The public had to learn, he believed, that there actually was no convenient end to American participation in foreign affairs. He told Congress that "we do not have an enforceable legal obligation [to assist South Vietnam], but we do have moral and political obligations." Unlike the pre-World War II era, however, the United States was not protected from the rest of the world by oceans. Now with nuclear weapons threatening the security of the United States, Americans could not afford to ignore the rest of the world. The modern interdependent world economy also demanded that the United States participate in the full range of international issues. If the United States lost interest in the future of Southeast Asia, its ability to act anywhere else might be affected.[20]

It is hard to know how seriously Kissinger took the threat to United States credibility. He had done as much as anyone to isolate the Viet-

nam War from the remainder of United States foreign policy interests. The relevance of military power had diminished in recent years,
he asserted. The interdependent economic environment was perhaps
the most serious problem facing the United States. He had thought
that Vietnam had diverted American resources from other significant
problems.

Why then did he stress the sanctity of American interests in Vietnam in late 1974 and early 1975? Quite simply, he resented congressional interference in the process. Like a series of foreign policy prac-
titioners since the Second World War, he delighted in exercising control
over the process. Lawmakers' commitment to pressing United States
interests everywhere in the world necessarily could not be as great
as that of the President or Secretary of State.

Kissinger challenged Congress to define a set of American interests. He held that they could only criticize, not present a coherent
view of their own. He believed that the 535 members of Congress responded only to narrow pressures from their constituents. If asked to
define American interests, Congress only seemed able to recount the
slogans of the McGovern presidential campaign—"come home America." For Kissinger this meant that Congress wanted to strip the President of his ability to act independently.[21]

Unfortunately for Kissinger and Ford the final North Vietnamese
offensive coincided with the convening of the Ninety-Fourth Congress, elected in November 1974. This, the most liberal Congress assembled in ten years had little respect for presidential authority. Indeed, the new members had little deference for the seniority system
in use in Congress. New members accused committee chairmen who
had risen to the top of having abandoned their commitment to make
independent judgments in foreign relations. Soon after the new Congress convened in January 1975 several committee chairmen lost their
positions. Moreover, the Democratic party caucuses agreed that committee chairmen would in the future have to stand for reelection at
the beginning of each Congress by the entire party membership. They
further eroded the power of the chairmen by enlarging the number
of subcommittees. Many members who had belonged to the House
for as few as six years became heads of important panels. A similar
process went forward in the Senate where first term senators took
over subcommittees of the foreign relations and armed services committees. Perhaps most significant of all, members of the ninety-fourth
drew a lesson from the Watergate investigations about the benefits
of special committees. The Senate Select Committee on the Watergate scandal (the Ervin Committee) spawned a host of imitators. Both

House and Senate appointed special committees to investigate the actions of the Central Intelligence Agency. Senator Frank Church took over in the Senate and Congressman Otis Pike led a similar panel in the House of Representatives.[22]

This revolution was the work of critics of presidential autonomy in foreign affairs. For Kissinger the task was to nip the rebellion before it overwhelmed him and Ford. The method was to try once more to aid the Saigon government. It presented the administration with a no-lose situation. If Congress relented and released the money needed to support the South Vietnamese government, the administration would have demonstrated once more that it controlled foreign policy. Congress would acknowledge that the President had more information. It would admit that the executive branch had the authority to act most quickly in foreign affairs. Congressional agreement to the request for additional aid to the South also would make Congress a partner in whatever happened. If the South managed somehow to survive the onslaught of the North, then the administration would receive the credit for swiftly moving to the aid of a friend. If, as seemed quite likely in the beginning of 1975, the South did not have the fortitude to resist the North, then Congress, having agreed to additional aid, could not denigrate the administrations' efforts in behalf of Saigon.

Suppose, on the other hand, Congress refused Ford and Kissinger's request for more weapons and money for the South? That too would please the administration—Congress would have the onus of the eventual defeat. Should the South miraculously prevail, then both administration and Congress could take credit for its sturdy independence. That was not very likely, however. It seemed more certain that the South could not make it regardless of the kind of support it had from the United States. Congress might crow, "I told you so," but there would be little joy in its voice.

Kissinger told Ford that "the situation in South Vietnam is critical." The North Vietnamese offensive combined with congressional restrictions on aid and the number of refugees flooding the South "have forced the South Vietnamese to give up large amounts of territory, population, and equipment to the North Vietnamese." These problems might be arrested by a renewal of United States aid. "Without such American assistance, they have no hope," Kissinger feared. Worst of all "America's abandonment of an ally would be unprecedented and would have adverse implications reaching far beyond Indochina."[23]

An air of gamesmanship hung over the final debate on extending aid to South Vietnam and Cambodia. The administration wanted more to have the right to say it had helped than it expected to reverse the Communist victory. For their part, congressional observers like New York Democratic Congresswoman Bella Abzug or Oregon Republican Senator Mark Hatfield, both strong opponents of the war, complained that any new American effort would be wasted. They pointed to continued corruption in the Vietnamese and Cambodian governments. They noted that thousands of rounds of ammunition and hundreds of tanks remained stored in depots and armories. If the anti-Communist authorities were serious about the extent of the threat to their security, they would commit these reserves. Instead, claimed the congressional dissenters, the Thieu government refused to fight in order to make matters appear worse than they actually were. The critics believed that Thieu wanted to force the United States back into the war. They insisted that maybe things were not so bad. If only the South were willing to fight, the anti-Communist cause could prevail. Otherwise Congressman Les Aspin (D.-Wisc.) worried about "the unhappy prospect that a large contingent of U.S. forces will move into South Vietnam followed by fighting, casualties, and maybe, worst of all, American POWs. We would be back in the quagmire." Representative Robert Leggett (D.-Calif.) announced "I am opposed to spending one more U.S. dollar for war in Indochina. . . . By continuing to shower money on the warmaking machines we have created in Indochina, we encourage a profligate style of warfare that is expensive, but not very effective."[24] Representative Richard Ottinger (D.-N.Y.) summarized congressional attitudes toward renewed fighting: "It seems to me that the commitment that the United States made, in entering the Paris agreement [of 1973], was that we were going to get out. . . . For us to continue military activity, and to have the administration and the department of defense come here and indicate quite clearly that they are up to their eyeballs in military activities right now in Cambodia, seems to me to be a clear break of faith with the American people and a breach of law."[25]

A White House aide who accompanied the congressional tour to Cambodia reported "the visit was very helpful and impressed the delegation with the seriousness of the situation there." Congresswoman Bella Abzug "went with a closed mind and came home with a closed mind." Others, however, were more amendable to the administration. Representative Pete McCloskey (R.-Calif.), for example, had "without question the toughest mind on the trip." While McCloskey "will continue to take a public position against political oppression," he could be expected "to support most of the supplemental [appropriation] for South Vietnam." Representative Millicent Fenwick (R.-N.J.) "looked at both sides very carefully" despite spending a great deal of time with Abzug. "A presidental boost may be helpful in her case," the aide believed.[26]

Kissinger helped arrange some friendly persuasion. He told Ford that the congressional "trip was, on balance, a success; three of the four who opposed any supplemental military aid (Representatives Fenwick, Frazer, and McCloskey) have given indications that they may now vote for at least some additional military assistance." Kissinger advised Ford how to encourage the representatives when they met with him on March 5. He suggested that the President explain the disastrous consequences of cutting aid. Instead of spurring negotiations, Kissinger stated, "the opposite will happen. The North Vietnamese and Cambodian Communists will think they can win without negotiations and they will refuse to talk." Kissinger stressed that "the obstacles to negotiations are not in Saigon and Phnom Penh." The Secretary also explained the administration's flexibility. "We are prepared to explore with Congress some formula for limiting our aid to South Vietnam to a period of several years." Several representatives criticized the human rights record of the South Vietnamese government. Kissinger proposed that Ford respond that abuse of prisoners had taken place five years before. "During that time our Embassy in Saigon made quiet representations to the South Vietnamese government. . . . These efforts were largely successful." Kissinger emphasized the dangers of the appearance of outside meddling. "The main point is," he wrote, "that we achieved results because it was done quietly and privately, without publicity. This is how we want to continue to handle it. This is especially true in a country like South Vietnam where the memory of colonial rule is still fresh."

Kissinger went on to remind members of Congress that they could make matters worse in Vietnam by cutting off aid. "All governments," he stated "become less liberal as their security or national existence is threatened. This has happened even in such democracies as the United States and Great Britain." Representatives would be playing with fire if they tried to unseat President Thieu. Kissinger thought he "enjoys the support of a large part of the population. Regardless, even if his position has eroded, I think it would be foolish and presumptuous for us to try to intervene so deeply in internal South Vietnamese politics. Surely the history of our involvement there has taught us that."

Similar reasoning applied to suggestions that the United States oust Lon Nol from the presidency of Cambodia. Kissinger observed that "the Khmer Communists have not just refused to negotiate with Lon Nol. They have also refused to have anything to do with the top seven leaders in the government." The United States could do without Lon Nol. Kissinger commented "we are not wedded to any personality in Cambodia." But the way he left was key to the future. "To ask him to step down even before negotiations is not the way to get talks; it is the way to make the other side think that they do not need to talk because we will meet their conditions without talking." Kissinger desperately wanted Congress to understand the constraints under which the United States operated. Instead of undermining the American position, Congress should either keep still or apply pressure to the Communists. "The problem is," he reiterated, "the other side has shown absolutely no inclination to enter into negotiations or to work for a political settlement. They are not interested in talking to anyone when they think they are winning."[27]

Other White House aides advised Ford to downplay additional money to Cambodia or Vietnam. Press Secretary Ron Nessen, ever alert to domestic political repercussions, predicted "if the President requests more aid for Vietnam and Cambodia, Congress almost certainly will not give it. Thus, the President will be dragged out of the war against his will, while Congress will be seen as leading America out of the war, as the vast majority of Americans wish. It will be more difficult for the President to regain the leadership role in foreign policy." Nessen's preferred course was to cut losses and win praises for realism. "There is no evidence," he asserted, that "President Ford will be able to win the war by any acceptable means. Therefore, his choice is to withdraw from the war, for which he will be overwhelmingly praised by the American people."[28]

Critics of the war had stressed the reluctance of the South Vietnamese to fight for a decade. The terms of the argument did not change much in 1975. The difference was that neither of the two sides in the American debate paid much attention to the claims of the other. Antiwar critics, liberated from charges that their complaints threatened the physical security of American troops, no longer had to restrain their beliefs that the South Vietnamese government was unworthy of United States support. Never shy about hinting that the South Vietnamese could not win, they now claimed that a North Vietnamese victory would not endanger other non-Communist states in the region.

For their part, the administration appeared more eager to pin responsibility for the collapse of the war on congressional opposition than actually to help the South turn back the advancing North Vietnamese armed forces. Kissinger and Ford accepted the content of the opposition's argument, even as they complained that critics undermined the will of the ARVN. Ford sourly complained that "I am frustrated by the limitations that were placed on the chief executive over the last two years. . . . I believe that in any case where the United States does not live up to its moral or treaty obligations, it can't help but have an adverse impact on other allies we have around the globe."[29]

By spring 1975, Washington had concluded that the ARVN was not competent. Its leadership problems had never been solved. Commanders in the central highlands, the first to experience the weight of the Communist spring offensive, failed miserably. They retreated at the first shot, leaving tons of equipment behind. Officers scrambled to get out before their men. Some actually sold their weapons to the advancing Vietcong and North Vietnamese. If nothing else had persuaded Washington that the South was a lost cause, this miserable performance did. Accordingly, the administration did not dispute the critics who held that the South had lost the war on its own. Nor did they differ from the assertion that there was little the United States could have done to stop the North in the spring of 1975. All of this was irrelevant, however, to the domestic debate over the war. Just as Nixon did not want to appear to have been driven out of the war by the strength of the guerrillas, Ford did not want to have to acknowledge the validity of the antiwar movement.

Senators expressed concern when the White House informed them about the use of United States forces to evacuate the embassy in Phnom Penh. Majority Leader Mansfield said "Get 'em out. Why the air cover. . . . There's a lot of worry on the Hill about the Americans in Saigon. Get them out too." Senator Clifford Case (R.-N.J.) wanted to know if the operation was "Just 'in and out.' " Told it was, he said "O.K." He believed that the War Powers Act "does not cover a rescue operation." Minority Leader Hugh Scott thought the operation the "only thing to do now." The most support came from Senator John Sparkman (D.-Ala.), chairman of the Foreign Relations Committee. He was "pleased to hear that it is taking place." He told a White House staff member that the President's speech on the fall of Cambodia was "the best he ever heard—anywhere. He thought his review of the world situation excellent. Great delivery." Senator James Eastland, another conservative Southerner, thought it was "good." He wondered "Why in hell don't we drop a bomb on them."[30]

In fact, however, congressional opposition provided a ready reason to do something that Ford and Kissinger found appealing. They realized first that the North was going to win. Next they had concluded that it did not matter to United States interests in Asia or its relations with the Soviet Union. Vietnam had become an irritating sideshow for the United States. The only way the administration could honorably clear out of South Vietnam, however, was to escape with the prospect of leaving behind a viable government. Because no one in the United States, Europe, or the South itself believed that the Saigon government could make it on its own, or survive without United States assistance, in the spring of 1975, Kissinger would have to look for honor elsewhere. What better way to preserve the fig leaf of United States assertiveness in the region than to claim that America would have acted firmly, if only Congress had not blocked the way? "What kind of people are we?" Kissinger asked when Congress voted not to release $700 million in additional aid to Vietnam and Cambodia in March 1975.[31]

Even if the United States could not turn the tide with more aid, Kissinger hoped to make Congress feel guilty about blocking support. He told a House committee in the last week of the war "one of the themes I have tried to strike in recent months is the absolute necessity of a relationship of confidence between the Congress and the Executive. . . . It is possible that mistakes in judgment are made, or that different people would assess the same problem in a different way. But to suggest that the administration deliberately is keeping Americans hostage to advancing armies is unworthy of the debate." Kissinger promised that the administration "will abide by the verdict of Congress; that we are not seeking to reopen all these wounds—but we do have . . . some profound moral obligations."[32]

Reopening the debate would have been difficult in any event. Congress accurately reflected public disgust with the lengthy, inconclusive nature of the war. Lawmakers were ready to ban further United States involvement in the war only after opinion polls indicated that only an insignificant minority of less than 15 percent favored a resumption of any kind of United States military action in Vietnam or Southeast Asia. President Ford seemed to recognize the altered public mood, even if the Secretary of State did not. He told an audience at Tulane University, a few weeks before the chaotic American evacuation from Saigon, that "the war is finished as far as America is concerned."[33] He went on that the United States would suffer no damages if the North succeeded in displacing the Thieu regime. The ARVN had demonstrated that it could not hold the line, and Ford admitted that it did not matter all that much to the future of American policy in the region.

Enroute back from New Orleans Ford went to the back of the plane, put on a yellow flight jacket, took a drink of bourbon, smoked his pipe and contentedly told reporters why he had spoken out at Tulane. He said "it was decided only yesterday morning" to announce the end of American participation in the war. "It seemed appropriate, if you're going to say it" to have spoken out on a college campus. Ford replied a curt "no" to the question "did Secretary Kissinger play any part in the preparation of the speech?"[34] According to the *New Republic* Nessen wanted to create the impression that "Gerald Ford is able to formulate his foreign policy without always relying upon Henry Kissinger." Despite this effort, Ford's remarks did not differ substantially from Kissinger's own views. A week earlier, Kissinger had said that "the Vietnam debate has now run its course. The time has come for restraint and compassion."[35]

Ford denied that the United States had made any secret promises to Saigon in 1973. "It was," he told Congress, "the openly stated policy of the United States government to maintain the necessary conditions for the validity of the agreement. . . . Since the same policy and intentions contained in these exchanges were declared publicly, there was no secret from the Congress or the American people." Ford went on to claim that neither he nor Nixon "ever invoked any private assurances or commitments as arguments for congressional action."[36]

Kissinger offered a calm assessment of the debacle in Indochina to Hugh Sidey of *Time* who reported that the Secretary "doubts that the American people are going to sustain interest in a recriminatory debate for more than a few months."[37] After the collapse, Anthony Lewis denigrated Kissinger: "[H]e ought to have known better. Impressive intelligence was not enough to save him. He walked on into the trap of Vietnam—and on and on and on. And now it is too late for his reputation. He knows that he will be remembered less as the builder of détente than as the destroyer of Cambodia."[38]

Ford stroked Kissinger before the convention of the National Association of Broadcasters in Las Vegas. As the beaming Secretary looked on the President praised him as "a person of unbelievable wisdom and, I think, the finest background and knowledge in the field of foreign policy of anybody in my lifetime."[39] Ford's other subordinates did not share their chief's enthusiasm. "Ford's Aides Blame Kissinger" proclaimed a column by Peter Lisagor who recorded a "delicate and subterranean" effort by the White House staff to "cut him down to size." Kissinger's detractors believed that he was "more interested in preserving his reputation than in serving the President, especially on the issue of Vietnam."[40]

Speaking as "a high-level source" Kissinger brooded that "the big lesson to be learned from this failure [of the Mideast shuttle] combined with reverses in Southeast Asia is that the United States has been trying to do too much. . . . Perhaps the United States must accept the reality that in 1975 American power and influence cannot achieve the kinds of things it did 20 years ago." Commentators agreed that "American foreign policy has not since the early days of the cold war had at the edges so many actual or threatened losses, so many intractable and unresolved problems, and so much reason for anxiety about some of these problems as today." Friendly editorialists advised Kissinger to calm down. "Dr. Kissinger seems to need a periodic pat on the back," wrote the *Christian Science Monitor.* "He does not live well with failures—his own or the nation's. His professions of concern about America's 'unreliability' are probably genuine. They are also exaggerated." They advised Kissinger to "give up worrying about tactical setbacks and behind-his-back criticisms and devote himself to restoring coherence and purpose to America's role in the world."[41]

Even friends noted the change in his position under the Ford administration. Joseph Harsch commented that "Dr. Kissinger was essential and probably irreplaceable back when Richard Nixon could make foreign policy. Congress usually left policymaking to the White House. And Mr. Nixon increasingly left it all to Dr. Kissinger." Harsch noted that "this is a new and different world. Congress has strong ideas and the determination to enforce them on the administration. It can and will negotiate and compromise with President Ford. But it chooses to deal with him directly rather than through Dr. Kissinger. The Kissinger skills had full play in the Nixon era. He was the right man for that season. But he is not a man for all seasons. And this is a new season. Many leaders on Capitol Hill, of both parties, now regard him as redundant and replaceable." Other voices concluded that while Kissinger was not "indispensable, faultless, infallible," he was "the best man for the moment."[42]

If direct intervention in the war's endgame was politically impossible, Ford and Kissinger could act assertively elsewhere. Two weeks after the final rout of the ARVN and the panicky flight of American personnel from the embassies in Saigon and Phnom Penh, Ford and Kissinger found a way to make a dramatic gesture. An American cargo ship, the *Mayaguez*, strayed too close to the Cambodian shoreline. A patrol of the Khmer Rouge intercepted the wandering vessel and hauled it to the nearest port. The Communist forces interrogated the crew members to find out whether they worked for the CIA. Satisfied they did not, but wanting to embarrass the United States, the Communists held them captive anyway.[43]

This appeared to Kissinger and Ford to be the chance to use force without fear of a permanent involvement in Southeast Asia. Any move to continue U.S. military action for more than a couple of days would invoke the provisions of the War Powers Resolution passed by Congress over Nixon's veto in November 1973. That resolution instructed the President to consult Congress before committing United States forces to combat. If an emergency required the President to act without getting prior approval from Congress, he had to report to Senate and House within forty-eight hours of the deployment of soldiers. After that he had sixty days to use the troops without gaining the consent of Congress. If both houses approved, he could continue to deploy the troops. If they presented objections, however, the President had to begin removing them and have them quit of hostilities within 90 days of their injection into combat.[44]

The President alerted Kissinger to the repercussions of the American defeat upon European public opinion. Arnaud de Borchgrave, a conservative columnist, wrote that "the subliminal impact on European decisionmakers, policy planners and the man and woman in the street has been tremendous." "This is terrific and must be distributed to my top staff," Ford told Kissinger.[45]

Amidst the distrust and despair over the use of force prevailing in the spring of 1975, no President was going to commit American forces for long. But what about a very short demonstration of American power to rescue the crew of the *Mayaguez?* The Communist victory persuaded President Ford that he had to appear in command. An aide said "we must now convince the world that Vietnam was an exception." To that end "Mr. Ford intends to assume personal leadership in foreign policy. . . . Therefore—from now on—his personal diplomacy will be more apparent than Dr. Kissinger's."[46]

Here was exactly the sort of opportunity to show toughness to the world, to Congress, and to the public. It might also undermine the appeal of the War Powers Resolution itself. All of these benefits came to pass within weeks of the action to free the *Mayaguez's* crew. The use of the Marine Corps proved enormously popular with the public. Members of Congress who might have complained that Ford had ignored the notification requirements, kept quiet now that cheers erupted for his swift action.

Congress was chastened by the President's ability to frame the debate. The White House received generally favorable reactions from Congress. Democratic Congressman Carroll Hubbard of Kentucky enthused "It's good to win one for a change."[47] Senator John Sparkman upon being informed said "Thanks. I wonder what those pacifist Swedes are going to do about their vessel." Majority Leader Tip O'Neill was more cautious. "This is getting serious," he told a White House liaison. William Broomfield (R.-Mich.) replied that he was "all for what the President is doing." A White House summary of congressional reaction found that "as expected, most congressional expressions have been very laudatory. With a few exceptions it comes from Republicans and Southern Democrats. Liberal Democrats have been generally silent." Three days after the rescue the White House had received 1436 telegrams in favor of the action and 170 against it.[48] Senator Strom Thurmond (R.-S.C.) said "they are testing us. The President must be firm. The public will back him 100 percent." Senator Robert Byrd (D.-W.Va.) called it a "good initial step. The President should give them a deadline and then go in and get them." Senator John McClelland pledged support and offered "we must be tough with these people and resort to bombing if necessary." Senator Jacob Javits, a principal sponsor of the War Powers Act, told the President that the resolution "stood up well in this crisis." The President's staff dismissed Javits's comments, however. His "note to the President has little relationship to what he said" publicly. Before a House subcommittee Javits had objected that "advance consultation with the Congress fell far short of the intentions of those who drafted the legislation and those who voted for it. . . ."[49]

Kissinger asserted that there had been no time to notify Congress before deployment of the rescue mission. By extension, whatever foreign crisis required presidential attention could not wait for Congress to make up its mind. The *Mayaguez* incident seemed to prove what Kissinger had been unable to show through months of furious lobbying. Congress had not been in a position to respond swiftly enough to the seizure of the ship. Members simply lacked the information to act and displayed little desire to get it. The rescue also validated Kissinger's repeated claims that events abroad moved too fast for legislators.[50]

Even more distressing to congressional dissenters from an assertive international stance for the United States was how the public seemed to turn on a dime and support the use of Marines. Ford's popularity shot up after the rescue mission. He visited the University of Pennsylvania, once a center of the antiwar movement, to receive an honorary degree. He was loudly cheered for having restored American honor after the retreat from Vietnam.

Almost lost in all the tumult over the determination of foreign policy were the facts of the rescue itself. Some thirty-five marines lost their lives in the effort. It turned out that the captured crew had been released by the Khmer Rouge by the time the rescuers reached the island to which the *Mayaguez* had been taken. No matter. The remaining marines triumphantly took custody of the crew and escorted them to safety in Singapore. In Washington the return of the ship and crew greatly boosted the reputation of the Ford administration. To critics who charged that Kissinger and Ford acted billigerently and thoughtlessly, the Secretary replied, "We did not do this to show our macho." Kissinger, of course, could afford to be nonchalant about the success of the rescue. He knew that the public reaction demonstrated that the President still dominated the debate over foreign affairs. The United States had just shown its macho in Southeast Asia, and the friendly response indicated that assertiveness found a sympathetic audience.

Kissinger hoped that the favorable reaction to the *Mayaguez* affair would permit greater freedom of action over the next few months. His strategy of dealing with the legacy of Vietnam was to ignore it. "We do not seek to open wounds," he told the newspaper editors.[51] His experiences with European states in the period after the First World War and with the United States after the Communist victory in China convinced him that losing a war corroded popular faith in leaders. The last thing American politics needed were recriminations over who had "lost Vietnam." If the challenges came from the left of the political spectrum, the result most likely would be an end to any involvement in overseas activities. If, as appeared more likely in the humiliating retreat from Vietnam, the complaints came from the nationalistic right, détente would be jeopardized. The best way to handle the lessons of Vietnam was to stop discussion of responsibility, treat the war as irrelevant to the present conduct of American foreign relations and go on. Kissinger's approach resembled President Nixon's handling of the Watergate investigations. Nixon acknowledged, as had Kissinger, that there was sufficient blame to go around and urged the public to look forward to better days.

Immediately after the fall of Vietnam and Cambodia, Kissinger's staff noted some encouraging disagreements between Moscow and Beijing over the future of Communist Vietnam and Cambodia. China seemed to welcome unity between Vietnam and Cambodia while "Moscow has, interestingly enough, never publicly endorsed the concept of Indochinese solidarity. There is some evidence that Moscow would have preferred a Balkanized Indochina to one dominated by Hanoi."[52]

Kissinger had better success discouraging recriminations over the war in Indochina than Nixon did in discouraging the investigation of Watergate. The two cases were so obviously distinguishable. In one, public anger could focus on the misconduct of one President and his advisers. The Vietnam War was a different matter with leaders of both parties involved in the escalation. For every mistake made by one, there was an equivalent blunder by the other. Accordingly, everybody had an interest in keeping quiet about the direct lessons of Vietnam.

Kissinger was particularly adept at suggesting grim consequences if politicians dwelt on the mistakes of Vietnam. Not only would old scabs be torn off wounds, but Kissinger could threaten each faction with the triumph of the other. During the Nixon administration he stressed his position in the middle ground. If anyone voiced dissatisfaction with the end of American participation in the Vietnam war, Kissinger would threaten the return to power of the complainers' political opponents.

Yet Kissinger's warnings were not enough to stop the erosion of presidential prerogative in 1975 as Congress pressed forward with investigations of the Central Intelligence Agency. The Church Committee in the Senate and the Pike Committee in the House looked into twenty-five years of covert actions by the CIA overseas. Kissinger held no brief for the CIA, which had often dissented from his own efforts at détente with the Soviet Union. What he did worry about, however, was congressional emphasis on its right to control the process. And did Congress ever emphasize its rights. Senator Church described the CIA as a "rogue elephant" which had tried to dominate foreign relations without any oversight. His committee concluded that it had engaged in attempts at assassination of Patrice Lumumba in the recently freed Belgian Congo in 1960, Fidel Castro after the disastrous Bay of Pigs invasion of 1961, and Rafael Trujillo before his death in 1961. The CIA had also been the instrument of suborning foreign political parties. Beginning with the 1948 elections in Italy secret agents had funneled millions of dollars into the coffers of the Italian Christian Democratic Party. The short-term gain of winning the election against a coalition of Communists and Socialists had been more than offset by making the United States a permanent partner in the future of the Christian Democrats. They became pawns of the United States, unable to act on their own. The Socialists, who had no interests in common with the Communists, found themselves painted into a corner by the United States. For the next generation there was no effective non-Communist opposition party in Italy. The Christian Democrats became corrupt, fat, and unable to govern, but there was no effective alternative. The United States became responsible for the growing stalemate in Italian politics.[53]

The investigations of the CIA also revealed numerous domestic activities, which supposedly had been banned to the Agency by the National Security Act of 1947. CIA operatives seemed fascinated by the effects of psychedelic drugs in the 1950s. They had conducted tests on unwitting subjects to determine how they would react to doses of LSD. One man had jumped out of a window after receiving a brandy laced with the mind-altering acid. The CIA had also opened the mail of Americans who had traveled to Communist or leftist countries. Some members of Congress had fallen under its scrutiny.

The investigations ran into a stone wall when they tried to follow Kissinger's career as NSC director or Secretary of State. His memory proved porous when it came to describing what the United States had done to subvert the government of Salvador Allende in 1970 after its election. Only when former CIA director Richard Helms testified that his notes revealed Nixon's demands to "make the economy scream" did Kissinger admit that he might have had some small part in the efforts. Nonetheless, he denied that the initiatives had come from his office in the White House.

Kissinger also balked at describing his or his staff's participation during the overthrow of the government of Cyprus and the Turkish invasion of that island in 1974. The House Intelligence Committee subpoenaed a memorandum by Thomas Boyatt, head of the Cyprus desk, dissenting from Kissinger's "tilt" toward Turkey. The Secretary of State refused to produce it. He lectured the committee:

Our nation today faces serious and unprecedented international challenges. We stand poised for a return to a nuclear arms race and a move forward to a new era of nuclear arms control; our allies and friends around the world continue to look to us for material and moral support to maintain their freedom and independence; our role is crucial in the relationship between developed and developing countries; and the growing problem of interdependence—food, energy, commodities policy, the reformulation of international financial and economic institutions—all demand new, sometimes revolutionary, approaches.

These goals can be achieved only if we preserve the confidence of other governments in us and in our reliability. . . . [Foreign policy's] raw material is actions and statements of American officials. . . . It is our view that junior- and middle-level officers should not be required to testify as to their recommendations to their superiors.[54]

Professional Foreign Service officers, who had sometimes been dismayed by Kissinger's cavalier disregard of their advice and belittling of their expertise, rallied behind him as he preserved the sanctity of their proposals. Unfortunately, the House Committee moved to cite the Secretary for contempt.[55]

Ford supported Kissinger in his battle with Representative Pike. The president wrote the House Committee on Intelligence of his "deep concern" over the effort to find Kissinger in contempt. He asserted that "this issue involves grave matters affecting our conduct of foreign policy."[56]

By the fall of 1975, the revelations of the intelligence committees had damaged everyone. The CIA was shaken, replying gamefully that it had only done what it had been asked to do. Kissinger too had suffered by the exercise in oversight. Congress had insisted that they had the right to set the boundaries of foreign policy. They had dissented from the style and the substance of Kissinger's actions. They accused him of secrecy for its own sake. They believed that he had disregarded morality and human rights in the rest of the world. They had even suggested that he did not have the interests of the country at heart. Instead, they suggested that he had wanted to promote his own ambitions.

But Congress did not emerge unscathed. The public fascination with these hearings never rose to the same level as that shown toward the Watergate hearings. The television networks did not carry them. Moreover, there were calls to keep the results of these investigations secret. The entire House of Representatives voted not to make public the Pike Committee's findings. Only when someone leaked the document to CBS reporter Daniel Shorr, who then turned it over to the *Village Voice*, did the findings see the light of day. Shorr lost his job at CBS for his pains.[57]

The result then was that by the fall of 1975 anyone who tried to grasp the reins of foreign policy was tremendously weakened. Kissinger no longer could point to the end of the war in Vietnam as a success for United States foreign policy. The "lessons" of Vietnam were too diverse to point the way to the future. Kissinger no longer appeared to be a miracle worker who could perceive the true interests of the United States. The CIA stood shamed by its accusers, who seemed reluctant to propose alternatives. Having shown the tawdry side of American foreign policy over a generation, critics worried that there was nothing left. Better dirty tricks than ineptitude, Kissinger argued. Six months after the fall of Saigon, Vietnam hung like an albatross round the neck of the foreign policy establishment.

TEN

The Decline of Détente, 1975–1976

Henry Kissinger's reputation rests on the unfreezing of relations with the Soviet Union. Kissinger managed by 1973 to convince President, Congress, and public that there was not going to be a final triumph of good over evil. Americans had, for the most part, gotten over the immature belief that somehow they would rout the Communists from Russia and Eastern Europe. There would be no final end to the cold war. By 1975, however, popular support for détente eroded.

Kissinger had argued that there was as much that bound the two superpowers together as there was that divided them. He defined détente as "an attempt to work out ground rules and agreed restraints in our relations with the Soviet Union that will lessen the danger of nuclear war and international conflicts in which either party might become involved."[1] As industrial giants each wanted to preserve present economic arrangements. As large naval powers each wanted maximum access of its fleet to all parts of the world. The two superpowers shared an interest in stopping the spread of nuclear weapons beyond the five states that currently possessed them. Both recognized the gradual diffusion of power since the early 1960s.

More difficulties faced Ford and Kissinger as 1975 wore on. The President's trip to Europe in May helped him gain "increased confidence in his ability to deal with the intricacies of foreign policy." According to one editorial, the trip gave "Mr. Ford visibility as he prepares for the 1976 campaign. It confirms his preeminent role in foreign policy at a time when Dr. Kissinger has been coming under criticism." Kissinger spent more time in the summer of 1975 speaking before audiences in the United States trying to generate grassroots support for his "beleaguered foreign policy." Observers noted that he hoped that "Americans, if made aware of the complexity and gravity of U.S. relations with nations overseas, might put pressure on Congress to ease strictures on foreign policy." Kissinger defended détente in face of detractors who wanted the United States to stress the moral deficiencies of the Soviet system. In a Minneapolis speech on "the moral foundations of foreign policy," Kissinger obliquely acknowledged "courageous voices" like that of Aleksandr Solzhenitsyn, but maintained that détente held greater promise for improvement than "blind assertions of moral absolutes." He noted that "there is no alternative to coexistence" when the United States and the Soviet Union had the power to destroy the world.[2] He also discouraged Ford from receiving Solzhenitsyn.

While Kissinger had explained the advantages of détente, his political position was never secure. At the moment of greatest triumph, the Helsinki Conference of August 1975, domestic backing for détente slipped. Never again did the Secretary of State rally a broad consensus of moderates, liberals, and establishment politicians and commentators in favor of better relations with the Soviets.[3]

The Helsinki meeting represented the culmination of Soviet efforts at stabilizing the boundaries of Eastern Europe. The United States had balked at fixing the dividing line between Poland and East Germany. Conservative opposition fell apart after the successful conclusion of Willy Brandt's Ostpolitik in 1969. Then Chancellor Brandt visited Poland and recognized the boundary separating Poland and East Germany. Poland and West Germany established full diplomatic relations. The Brandt government also dropped West Germany's long standing refusal to maintain diplomatic relations with any state that also exchanged envoys with East Germany.[4]

Six years elapsed between Brandt's Ostpolitik and formal acknowledgment of the division of Europe in the August 1975 Helsinki Conference. Most of the delay was taken up with bilateral negotiations between the United States and the Soviet Union. Throughout the conversations over strategic arms and trade, Washington had worked directly with the Soviets, excluding Europeans from the process. Kissinger's success at getting agreements over arms had masked Europeans' disappointment at being ignored. He had chosen the inauspicious year of 1973 as a "year of Europe," expecting European members of NATO to drop their bickering of the past fifteen years.

He could not have picked a worse twelve months. In 1973 Watergate washed over President Nixon, limiting his capacity to generate support for his foreign policy. The Arab–Israeli war of October drove another wedge between the Europeans and the United States. Greatly dependent on petroleum from the Middle East, European NATO members infuriated and frightened Israel when, with the exception of Portugal, they refused to permit American planes to refuel enroute to resupply the embattled Israelis. In the wake of the oil embargo following the war, European economies faltered. The European Economic Community broke with the United States and took a position more favorable to the interests of the Arabs than did Washington. They were rewarded with a lifting of the embargo, but their economies did not revive. In 1974 and 1975 Europeans regarded the United States' preoccupation with Watergate and its support for Israel as reasons for their dismal economic performances. They therefore resented all the more the United States' concentration on the bilateral relations between Washington and Moscow.

Faced with restive allies, Kissinger and Ford turned once more to improving relations with Europe. The Helsinki Conference on Security and Cooperation in Europe (CSCE) became the arena of agreement among the major participants in post–World War II Europe. Thirty-five nations took part in this carefully orchestrated gathering. The United States and NATO allies acknowledged the permanent division of Europe. They promised to establish diplomatic relations with East Germany. Yet Westerners would not go as far as the Soviets wanted in dismantling the alliance systems. The United States took the lead in stressing the need to maintain armies in Europe. Kissinger reminded the Soviets that the Mutual and Balanced Force Reduction (MBFR) talks had been proceeding without visible result for nearly five years. The Soviets had not even agreed with the Americans about the number of troops each side had in Europe. Kissinger considered such stalling designed to wear down the resistance of the western allies. As a sign of continued United States commitment to the Western Europeans' future, Kissinger vowed to keep the troops there until the Soviets agreed to a reduction on both sides of the border.

The Secretary of State also pressed the Soviets to include a declaration of human rights in the final Helsinki document. This statement recognizing the rights of political dissent and free transit across borders did not originate with the State Department. Kissinger always feared that an emphasis on human rights interfered with détente, as American concern for personal liberties could not but block progress on other issues. The Soviets necessarily resented interference in their internal affairs, and Kissinger based improved relations with Moscow on the principle that it did not matter what happened within a state's borders. He thought that the traditional American impulsive excitability over foreign relations would reassert itself if the public dwelled too much on the Soviets' repression.[5]

Why then did Kissinger include the Declaration on Human Rights at Helsinki? Pressing the Soviets to accede to such a demeaning declaration measured the deterioration of American backing for détente. Kissinger hoped to resurrect public support for a relaxation of tensions with the Soviets by including references to human rights. Already ominous voices were raised against détente and Kissinger's conduct. Jack Anderson told Congress that "as chief navigator of our foreign policy since 1969, Kissinger has kept the flag of American idealism deliberately lowered and has sailed the seven seas without a moral rudder. He has been willing to do what must be done to get 'results,' ready to make common cause with any pirate who controlled a useful ship."[6] Kissinger thought that throwing a bone of human rights to the critics of détente might bring them along. He then portrayed the Helsinki agreement as the first means of getting a commitment from the Soviets to major concerns of ordinary Americans. He acknowledged the dangers of cynical "I told you so's" if the Soviets violated the human rights stipulations, but he believed the risks worth the gain. Helsinki might assure support from Americans who otherwise opposed friendly relations with the Soviets.

Ford and Kissinger were defensive about Helsinki. Stopping in Warsaw enroute to the conference, Ford's staff tried to avoid discussion of the Helsinki agreements. When pressed, they told reporters, "they are not legally binding." At the conference itself Kissinger informed reporters that the Soviets now were likely to be more forthcoming on arms control in return for the guarantee of the inviolability of the borders of Eastern Europe. According to observers this was "the only bonus or dividend which Dr. Kissinger is likely to be able to extract in return for American signature on the Helsinki declaration, since American leverage is not quite what some critics back at home have been assuming." Joseph Harsch noted that Kissinger had done little to shape the Helsinki texts. The declarations on human rights had originated with the Europeans. Kissinger "did not early appreciate the possible importance of the matter and did not become personally interested in it."[7] George Ball, once a supporter of Kissinger, denounced him and Ford for yielding too much to the Soviets at Helsinki.[8]

The VFW wired Ford its "sharp disappointment in both the purpose and the pattern of your forthcoming trip to Europe, especially the gratuitous write-off of Eastern Europe implicit in the Helsinki accords." Eastern European immigrants denounced Ford for the "one sided policy of détente initiated by Richard Nixon and continued by you." The administration chose to ignore such objections in light of "the lack of post–CSCE conference critical correspondence, and the fact that some members of the press are now taking a favorable line." Kissinger was a favorite target. One irate New Mexico realtor fulminated, "First it was Vietnam, now it is Kissinger's lovey dovey giveaway attitude of the Panama Canal and shortly we will be bowing to the demands of that illegitimate bastard in Cuba. . . . What price détente? It is the price of lost freedom for millions of Europeans and the very thing which you so proudly proclaim as the right of every American."[9]

Congress continued to quarrel with Kissinger. Henry Jackson tried to summon him to testify on SALT before the Armed Services Committee. In August 1975 he complained that "your persistent failure to appear before the committee in the face of Soviet deployments inconsistent with your assurances raises serious doubts about the manner in which that agreement was negotiated." As Jackson denounced Kissinger publicly, the Senator's assistants undermined the Secretary's position within the White House. Richard Perle of Jackson's staff told the White House that the President had not received "an objective and unbiased presentation of SALT" from Kissinger. Perle reported that Kissinger had tried unsuccessfully to persuade James Schlesinger to support his efforts toward SALT-II. Kissinger's deputy, Lawrence Eagleburger, sent his chief a SECRET cable, explaining that Jackson was incorrect. "You have several times agreed in principle to appear before the Jackson group. . . . Jackson first requested your appearance in March and has since grown increasingly impatient. His staffers have said that 'it is clear we are getting the run around.' This could be the basis for their claim that they know you have decided not to appear."[10]

When Congress tried to limit executive agreements, Kissinger recommended that "the executive branch undertake a concerted effort to counter this movement." Not only should the White House, and the departments of State, Defense, and Justice become involved, but the administration should mobilize "the support of bar associations, prominent legal scholars, and former high-ranking government officials."[11] Kissinger considered the congressional efforts to limit executive agreements "in many ways reminiscent of the defeated Bricker amendment of the 1950s."[12]

In August 1975, just as the Helsinki Conference got under way in the Finnish capital, Ronald Reagan, former governor of California, announced his candidacy for the Republican presidential nomination. He denounced the "Washington buddy system" that had promoted Ford. He accused the "insiders" of forcing détente on a public that did not understand it and would not want it if they could have comprehended its meaning. He accused Ford and Kissinger of bargaining away American military superiority. Reagan lambasted the opening to China, claiming that the United States had turned its back on a friend of long duration when Nixon had shaken hands with Zhou Enlai and left Taiwan to fend for itself.[13]

Reagan revived the issue of the Panama Canal. The governor derided the negotiations going on quietly to return the waterway to Panamanian sovereignty as the culmination of a generation of retreat and appeasement by the United States. Under a nationalist administration the United States would regain the previous position of respect it had held in the western hemisphere.

By the end of the year Reagan presented a grave political threat. The word "détente" itself had become a term of derision for conservatives. They complained that for all of their sophistication Kissinger, Nixon, Ford and their establishment supporters underestimated the Soviet threat. Kissinger defined the American conception of détente again in a press conference in September 1975. "The policy of relations with the Soviet Union, and of attempting to ease the tensions between the two great nuclear superpowers," he explained, "derives from the conditions in which we find ourselves. The United States and the Soviet Union have the capability of destroying humanity. Their conflicts, therefore, are different from the conflicts between nations throughout history. They have a special obligation to conduct their affairs in such a manner that the risk of war is minimized if this is at all possible."[14] Despite Kissinger's claims that he offered a European perspective to American foreign policy, his detractors concluded that he followed the most deadly American tradition in foreign policy—naïveté. The Soviets had led him by the nose, never recognizing linkage and making the United States pay for good relations.[15]

Had this challenge come only from outside the administration Kissinger might have been in a better position to resist. Unfortunately, the endemic squabbling within the bureaucracy revived. Secretary of Defense James Schlesinger, formerly director of the Central Intelligence Agency, continued the tradition of representing the views of the military establishment. Schlesinger traded on his experience as head of intelligence to paint a grim picture of the Soviet menace. He informed Congress that "at the present time the Soviet Union can target any city in the United States that it desires; that there is no protection in nuclear war provided by air defenses so long as the Soviets depend primarily upon ballistic missiles."[16] Having opposed excessive involvement by the United States in the war in Vietnam, the former professor of economics considered his position ideal from which to criticize détente. Schlesinger considered the competition with the Soviets the primary American military mission. The NATO alliance remained the cornerstone of United States military planning. If American leaders consistently minimized the Soviet threat, then NATO countries would be less willing to contribute a fair share to the common defense.

Schlesinger spent much time in 1975 testifying before Congress about the requirement for American vigilance in its military competition with the Soviets. "Despite détente and its opportunities," he observed, "the need for steadfastness is no less great than it was a decade or more ago. Putting aside the shibboleths of the cold war era, it is nonetheless the case that the world remains a turbulent place." He minimized the benefits that could come from agreements over strategic arms. The western alliance still faced serious threats from Soviet military power. He warned that "we are now beginning to witness in the Soviet Union the largest deployment of improved strategic capabilities in the history of the nuclear competition. . . . [T]here is no doubt that these new ICBMs . . . combined with significant improvements in their sea-based missile force will give the Soviets a much more powerful strategic offensive force, even within the constraints of Vladivostock."[17] While the United States had withdrawn its forces from Vietnam, it had not used the "peace dividend" to restore its military power. Instead, he told the Senate Budget Committee, "when converted into 1976 constant dollars there has been a decline in the outlays of the Department of Defense by some 42 percent since the peak year of 1968."[18]

Drawing on experience as head of intelligence, Schlesinger certified that the Soviets had been developing their military machine. While the United States had its equipment "chewed up" in the heaviest fighting of the Vietnam War, the Soviets had learned a lesson from the Cuban missile crisis of 1962. With the ouster of Nikita Khrushchev by the Communist Party's Political Bureau in October 1964, the Soviets embarked upon a major military expansion. Leonid Brezhnev, the new General Secretary of the Communist Party, vowed that his foreign policy would be less bumptious than Khrushchev's, but that he also would provide the means of achieving Soviet ends. He suggested that the problem with Khrushchev had been his inability to back talk with proper strength. As a result, the Soviet Union had experienced the worst of all worlds—ridicule.

According to Schlesinger, the major change under Brezhnev had been the reduction in the fire of Soviet rhetoric. The Secretary of Defense believed that Brezhnev had been more circumspect in his fulminations against the West than had his predecessor only because he was biding his time. Once the Soviets achieved superiority over their western adversaries, Moscow would try to intimidate Europeans. Schlesinger predicted that if the Soviets maintained their current view of the meaning of détente and the United States did not increase its spending for defense then the "worldwide military balance [might] erode which would ultimately result in the eastern hemisphere falling under the hegemony of the Soviet Union."[19]

Schlesinger had Kissinger in a tough spot. The Secretary of State also noted the restlessness of the Europeans. He thought that the best way to calm them was for the United States to join them in opening better commercial and political relations with the Soviets. Loose talk from official Washington about the extent of Soviet military preparations alarmed allies. Europeans, long accustomed to hearing conflicting opinions from Washington, would conclude that the United States had once more become paralyzed over what to do about the Soviet Union. Kissinger believed that if he allowed Schlesinger to go on for too long complaining about the extent of the Soviet threat, his own position within the administration would decline.

By October, Ford found it impossible to make peace between the two principal foreign policy cabinet secretaries. Kissinger informed him that support for détente among the most influential segments of American society had disintegrated in the face of Schlesinger's criticisms. Congress stood on the brink of a major revolt against détente with plans to increase dramatically the expenditures for the Pentagon. Should this reversal take place, Kissinger would lose his preeminent position in foreign affairs. While the Secretary of State demanded Schlesinger's scalp, Ford's political advisers presented the horrifying news that Kissinger himself had become a liability with the most conservative parts of the Republican party. These people, unfortunately for the President, dominated the voting in the Republican primary elections. Were he to capture the nomination, he had to reduce the thunder from the right, without at the same time offending the centrists who had supported Kissinger's foreign policies.

The solution Ford adopted was to reduce Kissinger's visibility while retaining the substance of his policies. The President decided that the word détente itself should not be spoken publicly, even if the kinds of policies implied by the word continued to dominate America's relations with the Soviets. He instructed his staff not to use the word, even when they meant to speak of relaxation of tensions between the United States and the Soviet Union. He also stripped Kissinger of his title as special assistant to the president for national security affairs. He replaced him with Air Force General Brent Scowcroft, who had served as deputy to the NSC head since the departure of General Alexander Haig in 1973.[20]

Ostensibly, Ford wanted Kissinger to concentrate on running the department. He explained to the press that nothing would alter the way in which the architect of détente presented advice to the President. He still would have unlimited access and they would be meeting as often as practical. No longer did Kissinger talk with the President every morning anyway. His globe-trotting shuttle diplomacy had made him absent from Washington for about 30 percent of the time in 1975. But claims that Kissinger's stature remained as high as ever fooled no one. Ford had pushed him out of the limelight.

As a concession indicating the continuing hold Kissinger exercised over the formulation of policy, Ford removed James Schlesinger from the Pentagon, replacing him with Donald Rumsfeld. The President also replaced William Colby with George Bush, formerly representative to China and Chairman of the Republican National Committee, as Director of the Central Intelligence Agency. Ford concluded that Schlesinger's dour warnings about the Soviet military buildup only weakened the President's political appeal. The Defense Secretary's testimony appealed to segments of the public and opinion leaders who looked for ways to break with Ford. Democrats loved Schlesinger's implications that Republican administrations had permitted the country's defenses to slip. Conservatives also found Schlesinger's complaints about the Soviet threat strengthening the political appeal of Ronald Reagan.

Ford praised Kissinger even as he dropped him from the national security post. The President commented that he had "done a superb job as Secretary of State and as my Assistant for National Security Affairs. . . . There will be organizational changes . . . but Secretary Kissinger will have the dominant role in the formulation of and the carrying out of foreign policy." Ford denied any "basic differences" between Kissinger and Schlesinger, a bewildering statement to some observers. He explained, however, that "any president has to have the opportunity to put together his own team."[21]

The *National Review* expressed astonishment in Ford's assertion that "no basic differences" existed between Kissinger and Schlesinger over détente. "The opposite is true," the conservative journal asserted. "Kissinger is a pessimist. . . . In Kissinger's view the United States— and the West—lacks the will to stay the course in the face of the relentless Soviet military buildup and drive for global dominance." Schlesinger, on the other hand, "thinks it may, just possibly, be worthwhile to speak out about it."[22] *Fortune* concurred that "President Ford has badly damaged his own credibility by his curious and stubborn insistence, in the face of overwhelming evidence to the contrary, that no policy issues were involved in last month's dismissal of James R. Schlesinger as Defense Secretary." The *Los Angeles Times* believed that the President was "in danger of losing his reputation for candor without advancing his reputation in other areas." Joseph Kraft cruelly observed that Ford "has stimulated new doubts as to whether he has the brains to be President." George Will called the firing simply "a foolish thing done in a foolish way."[23]

Some commentators supported Ford and denigrated Kissinger. The *Youngstown Vindicator* praised the President. "Mr. Ford has put the good doctor down a peg," they wrote approvingly. "Rarely has the President displayed so firm and emphatic a demeanor." The *Charleston Evening Post* disagreed. It feared that "Mr. Schlesinger's departure will remove the strongest voice for military preparedness from within the Ford administration. It signals the President's determination to follow Kissinger's line." A columnist for the *Wall Street Journal* thought the shakeup signaled that "the end is finally in sight" for Kissinger. "As the election nears," he wrote, "Mr. Ford may be retreating a bit from any statesmanlike ideas he entertained, and becoming ever more of a politician seeking votes." This was too bad, because "Henry Kissinger is a confirmed believer in strong, imaginative leadership. . . . There are few around Washington who would call such traits the hallmarks of Gerald Ford's career, or of those he chooses as associates."

The *New York Times* considered it "highly doubtful" that Ford had "achieved any political gain by dismissing Secretary of Defense James R. Schlesinger and dropping Secretary Kissinger from his National Security Council post." The *Wall Street Journal* hoped that the shakeup meant that "Jerry Ford has seized a firmer control over his own administration." It feared, however, "that Henry Kissinger has seized control." The *Savannah Morning News* also expressed "great misgiving at the Sunday Night Massacre." It was distressed that "Mr. Schlesinger's view of defense and détente" might no longer have a "hearing at the highest level of government." The *Omaha World Herald* concurred. It explained that "the Ford administration's capacity for respecting varying points of view is brought into question."[24]

Ford's advisers portrayed the cabinet shakeup as "another sign" that the President was "getting bolder by the second." Reports held that the removal of Schlesinger left Kissinger "more than ever preeminent in foreign policy, but more exposed on Capitol Hill." One editorial warned that "this 'nonreform' is unlikely to placate congressional and other critics of Kissinger's immense power. In fact it will probably be seen that amid all the reshuffling the one man thought to be the most powerful—and the most secretive—has survived."[25]

In the aftermath of the cabinet shakeup Kissinger's relations with Congress worsened. He refrained from lobbying publicly for aid to Turkey for fear that his efforts would do more harm than good. A newspaper reported that "in unguarded moments congressmen charge Dr. Kissinger with intellectual snobbism. They feel they are being patronized."[26] Congress held hearings on the state of the organization of U.S. foreign policy. Kissinger became the central focus of the conversations. One expert, A. Doak Barnett, a specialist on China testified that "the present juggler" Kissinger, deserves "very good marks" for the way he handled Chinese affairs.[27] Another, Adam Yarmolinski, claimed that "the real victims of President Ford's Sunday night massacre are not the departing officials . . . the real victims are the American people." He went on to characterize the changes as a hawk for a pigeon. (Schlesinger for Donald Rumsfeld), a diplomat for a warrior (Kissinger for Scowcroft), and a professional civil servant for a political partisan (William Colby for George Bush at the CIA).[28] He faintly praised Kissinger's accomplishments: "Whether one agrees or disagrees with Kissinger's the-jet-is-faster-than-the-eye diplomacy, his background and expertise is in the peaceful resolution of international controversy, while General Scowcroft is a professional in what his own profession describes as 'the management of violence.' "[29]

Neoconservatives used the shakeup as proof that Kissinger had failed. Professor Richard Pipes of Harvard, a member of the Committee on the Present Danger and a close adviser to Schlesinger, complained "I am not sure that [Kissinger's] vast power is exactly healthy for us because it allows Mr. Kissinger to conduct a foreign policy which is often very shortranged and which I suspect does more for his popularity or prestige in the world . . . than it does for the interests of this country."[30] Pipes went on to charge that once Kissinger took the job of Secretary of State as well as National Security Adviser "he became so embroiled in domestic politics and the shorterm political interests of the President that he lost sight of his long term views and began to play what I consider a very dangerous game; that is, of actively engaging the United States in major international commitments without a vision where it will all lead to."[31]

Kissinger's and Ford's trips to China in the fall did not revive their flagging standing. Kissinger's October trip brought no dramatic breakthroughs. One editorial commented "it is increasingly clear that there are limitations to the relationship." The Secretary refused Chinese entreaties to abandon détente and join an anti-Soviet alignment with Beijing.[32]

When the President visited China in December Deng Xiaoping, officially vice premier but actually the successor to Mao Zedong, pointed to the Soviet Union as "the country which most zealously preaches peace and is the most dangerous source of war." Deng warned Ford and Kissinger that "rhetoric about détente cannot cover up the stark reality of the growing danger of war." Reporters considered the Chinese warning a veiled assault on Kissinger's belief that U.S.–Soviet relations took precedence over the opening to China. "It will be fascinating to see," predicted one, "whether on his return to Washington the President begins to move away from the Kissinger policy. Such a move would be politically popular in a city in which Dr. Kissinger is coming under increasing criticism from many quarters."[33]

Deng Xiaoping's assault on détente did not provoke Ford, who said he had "no complaint about the toast." Kissinger explained that his expert on China had authorized Ford's mild reaction because Deng's remarks were a "slap at Russia, not at us."[34]

Publicly Kissinger denied that the Chinese had made demands on the United States regarding its relations with the Soviets. "The Chinese did not request anything of the United States with respect to détente, and we did not request anything of the People's Republic of China."[35] Press Secretary Nessen denied "reports that Secretary Kissinger is pushing the President to resume full diplomatic relations with the PRC but that Ford decided to postpone normalization because of the defeat in Indochina and the Reagan threat." Nessen called the charges without foundation and explained that "there is no difference between the President and the Secretary on any aspect of the process of normalization of relations with the PRC."[36]

Kissinger downplayed speculation that the Chinese were "trying to discourage the process of détente between ourselves and the Soviet Union." He explained that China had its interests, while the United States had its own. He promised to "resist hegemony. . . . But the United States will also make every effort to avoid needless confrontations. . . . We will be guided by actions and realities and not rhetoric."[37]

Kissinger needed help with the public. His reputation for political sagacity plunged as the United States tried to put down revolutionary nationalism in the former Portuguese colonies of Africa. In 1974, with the war going badly, the army moved against the Portuguese dictatorship. A bloodless coup in March brought hundreds of thousands of Portuguese to the streets. The crowds cheered the military for its pledge to end the war in Africa, create democracy at home, and redistribute wealth. Within months the new government had concluded negotiations with the nationalists in Guinea and Mozambique. Talks continued with Angola because three groups, each with a different political outlook, vied for power there. By late 1974, however, the colonels in Lisbon had agreed to turn power over to the most radical of the three, the Popular Movement for the Liberation of Angola (MPLA).[38]

In Washington, Kissinger's heart fell as he contemplated the course of the Portuguese revolution. It appeared that what he had tried to avoid in Chile had occurred in Portugal. Kissinger had worried over the past three years about the rise of "Eurocommunism." This movement of the Communist parties of Western Europe tried to steer a middle course between Moscow and Washington. Unlike the rigid Stalinist Communist parties of the immediate postwar era, new leaders in Italy, Spain, and sometimes France broke with the Soviet Union on human rights issues. The revolutionary Portuguese officers took their cues from Eurocommunist parties in the rest of Europe. Kissinger feared that should they be successful, they would set a precedent for potential radicals throughout Europe.[39]

An irritated Henry Kissinger pressed Frank Carlucci, American ambassador in Lisbon, for action against the Portuguese revolution. He bombarded the more restrained Carlucci with requests for information about the connections of the Portuguese revolutionaries with the Soviet Union. Despite Kissinger's pleas, Carlucci advocated nonintervention. Already in late 1974 he saw signs of moderation. The ambassador successfully blocked Kissinger's attempts to circumvent regular processes, something of an accomplishment for an ambassador. The Secretary, preoccupied with the transition from Nixon to Ford, could not throw the full weight of his office behind the efforts to evict the revolutionaries.

The CIA thereupon entered Angolan politics. It supported one faction in the civil war along with China. While China engaged in a balance of power competition worthy of the nineteenth century's most cynical diplomats, the United States Congress had lost its appetite for the old diplomacy of the concert of Europe. Fresh from discoveries of CIA misconduct in Cuba, Latin America, and the Congo unearthed by the special committees, members wanted to make certain that the agency did not spend the next years involving the United States in a guerrilla war in Africa. Senators concluded that the earliest United States participation in the war in Indochina had come about because secret agents had meddled in the French colonial war.

Senators Dick Clark (D.-Iowa) and John Tunney (D.-Calif.) led the opposition to CIA action in West Africa. They attached an amendment to a foreign aid appropriation that effectively banned covert activities in Angola. Before the CIA could operate in a war zone, the President would have to observe the provisions of the War Powers Resolution. In other words, he had to notify Congress of his intentions to deploy combat forces, explain what the United States could gain by having troops there, and point out the conditions under which the United States would leave West Africa. Tunney and Clark had cut the foundation of covert action.[40]

Kissinger exploded when the Senate passed the Tunney amendment. He told a press conference on December 23 that U.S.–Soviet relations "will suffer if we don't find an adequate solution" to the Angola impasse. Failure, he warned, would be "catastrophic."[41] Liberal Senator Jacob Javits's foreign policy adviser cautioned against a strong resolution "drawing the line in Angola." He believed that "Kissinger's rhetoric on Angola sounds like a parody of Dean Rusk's verbal excesses about Vietnam—he claimed that World War III was at stake." Kissinger appeared to be taking a stand to preserve détente. This specialist considered "Kissinger's Angola rhetoric a smokescreen of 'talking tough' about the Russians in order to keep the Reagan and Jackson wings off his back on the really important issue of SALT, where Kissinger is fighting a desperate battle to get an agreement."[42]

Editorials chided Congress for tying Kissinger's hands in Southern Africa. The very policy of détente was at stake, and Congress, by publicly airing its disagreements with the Secretary of State, made it difficult to maintain a steady course with Moscow. The *Christian Science Monitor* agreed with Kissinger's position. It wrote that "the Angolan affair most surely violates the spirit of bilateral understandings reached when Richard Nixon met with Leonid Brezhnev in Moscow in 1972." While hoping to avoid "a public slanging match with the

Russians," the paper urged Kissinger to pursue "quiet, firm diplomacy that puts it on the line to the Russians: If they insist on fomenting trouble in Southern Africa, the relationship of détente—already under strain—will suffer even more."[43]

A weakened Secretary of State visited Moscow in January 1976, trying to patch together a SALT-II agreement before the presidential election campaign took over. After one day of talks with Andrei Gromyko, Kissinger told the press that "progress has been made" and "both delegations . . . have worked seriously to find a new basis for an agreement." That was the reassurance. Yet in a public toast to the Soviet delegation he obliquely raised Angola. He warned that the United States would oppose "efforts to achieve unilateral gains" one power sought from "instabilities in other parts of the world." When Kissinger left Moscow, he explained "we settled some important issues which will be passed on to Geneva. We made good progress on other issues. The Soviet side introduced some significant new ideas last night which we now have to study in Washington, and we will come back with our answer in a few weeks."[44]

Upon his return Kissinger faced a restless Congress "toes tapping with impatience—and devising new schemes to further restrict the administration's freedom of action in Angola." The House voted 323 to 29 to stop further covert aid to the rebels in Africa. That was bad enough, and a new storm emerged when Daniel Patrick Moynihan, ambassador to the United Nations, erupted. The combative representative cabled Kissinger a lengthy defense of his U.N. methods. He had responded publicly to every assault on United States positions and had threatened cutoffs of economic aid to Third World countries casting U.N. votes against positions taken by the United States. Moynihan was enormously popular at home, and deeply resented by professionals in the Department. His outbursts put Kissinger in a tight spot. Politically he had to back Moynihan, but Kissinger saw him emerge as a potential replacement for James Schlesinger as a champion of antidétente voices. The Secretary and Ford voiced full support of the ambassador, but by early February Moynihan resigned. Observers believed that a clash with Kissinger forced Ford's hand. As one editorial observed "if, as seems likely, President Ford found himself in the predicament of being unable to reconcile clashes between two strong personalities in his official family, he had little alternative" to accepting Moynihan's resignation.[45]

Faced with opposition to presidential action, the Ford administration entered the election year 1976 severely weakened. The controversy over the negotiations ending U.S. control of the Panama Canal made Ford and Kissinger especially uncomfortable. The Secretary had shown little interest in affairs in the western hemisphere. Even the effort to oust the government of Salvador Allende in Chile derived more from bureaucratic rivalry and a desire to send a message to other states in the world, than from any real fear that the Soviet Union might make significant gains in the western hemisphere.

The negotiations over the canal, however, did attract some attention from Kissinger. He did not wonder about the legalities or the morality of previous United States action in the Canal Zone. Nor did he express much interest in the use other Latin nations might make of continued American control over the canal. What perplexed Kissinger, however, was the use that Panamanian leader Omar Torrijos could make of an American refusal to return the canal. The former general, who had come to power in the Central American republic in 1968, had provided a mixture of nationalism, anti-Americanism, flirtation with Fidel Castro, and a measure of local capitalist development. Kissinger knew enough about the outlook of nationalist leaders around the world to consider Torrijos fairly typical of heads of neutral states. He clearly did not take orders from Moscow. His admiration for Castro did not mean that the Panamanian leader wanted to develop his country into a one-party state. Torrijos's rule was too much based on the appeal of one man, connections with the army, and support among the country's business leaders eagerly to embrace Castro's sort of government.[46]

Although Torrijos had no natural affinity for Castro or the Soviet Union, Kissinger feared what might happen if the issue festered. Torrijos might embrace the Soviets, or, even worse, more radical leaders might come to the fore in Panama. The Secretary understood that the Johnson administration had begun the process of negotiations over the canal. Democrats had reasoned that the United States had little to gain by retaining sovereignty over the waterway. It had almost everything to lose, though, if the isthmus erupted into violence. The worst possible outcome, of course, would be the destruction of the intricate lock system. The American navy worried that its ships could not easily go back and forth between the two main oceans. Shipping rates from the eastern United States to the Pacific might become prohibitive. On the other hand, a change in sovereignty that retained the viability of the canal could only work in the favor of the United States. As operator of the Canal, Panama would have an interest in having it remain a safe passage. The new operator also would face the prospect of competition from large tankers and a new sea-level canal across Nicaragua. In other words, the canal was a wasting asset. Every year the operator of the waterway, whatever country it was, had to do more for the customers. The Johnson administration believed that the sooner the United States yielded control to Panama, the better it would be for the long-range interests of the U.S. Navy and American commerce.

Kissinger also believed that the canal issue needed speedy resolution. The United States lost nothing by permitting Panama to operate the waterway. In the back of the Secretary's mind he feared that Central America could erupt into another Vietnam if the issue were not properly defused. Torrijos made an unlikely Ho Chi Minh, and Kissinger believed that the Panamanian leader wanted to say to his countrymen that he had redeemed a seventy-year-old debt of honor.[47]

If, however, the Canal did not come back to Panama, the potential for a nationalist explosion was limitless. The best thing for the United States to do then was to conclude a treaty as quickly as possible. If it retained rights for the United States to return to the Zone and protect the canal from outsiders, Kissinger believed that it could only abet American naval and commercial interests. He also believed that Torrijos could become a major supporter of United States interests in Central America. A successful negotiation with a nationalist power like Panama would send a beneficial signal to other countries flirting with Castro. Kissinger could demonstrate that there was more to be gained from cooperation with the United States than from tweaking Uncle Sam's nose.

Accordingly, Kissinger felt concerned when President Ford decided that the Panama Canal negotiations had to wait until the 1976 election. From the President's point of view, however, there was no choice. After barely defeating Ronald Reagan in the New Hampshire, New York, and Pennsylvania primaries in March and April, Ford suffered a series of embarrassing defeats. Reagan triumphed in the more conservative southern and southwestern states on a platform of denouncing the "accommodationist" policies of détente and Kissinger's approach. He mocked the Secretary of State for his vaguely sinister foreign accent. He implied that the European Kissinger had forsaken traditional American values. His willingness to seek a compromise with the Soviets indicated that he no longer cared about prevailing over an inhumane adversary. Negotiations over the Panama Canal revealed to Reagan that the Secretary had no understanding of American nationalism. The challenger used the canal as a symbol of what he considered to be America's loss of control over the world. He predicted, moreover, that turning the canal over to Omar Torrijos's control would embolden Communists and revolutionaries throughout the hemisphere. Reagan ridiculed Kissinger for paying so much attention to European developments that he overlooked the revolution brewing on the southern doorstep of the United States.[48]

Meanwhile, Eastern Europe remained a problem. Garbled reports that State Department Counselor Helmut Sonnenfeldt had noted an "organic union" between the Soviet Union and Eastern Europe created a furor. Ethnic communities told the White House they had met to "plan a strategy to voice their protests." Ford's staff advised that "the President discuss the Sonnenfeldt position and disavow it as totally nonrepresentative of American foreign policy." The President's first comments to reporters held that Sonnenfeldt "clearly does not represent my view. . . . The United States strongly supports the aspirations for freedom and national independence of people everywhere, including Eastern Europe. I am totally opposed to spheres of influence by any power."[49]

Conservative Senator James Buckley of New York demanded that Kissinger repudiate the Sonnenfeldt doctrine. If he did not, the New Yorker threatened Ford, "I shall have to 'go public' on the issue as forcefully as I know how." Kissinger assured Buckley that "our policy in no sense accepts Soviet 'domination' of Eastern Europe, nor is it in any way designed to seek the consolidation of such 'dominion.'"[50]

The White House drafted a form letter to members of Congress who objected to Sonnenfeldt's assessment. It stated that "There is no 'Sonnenfeldt Doctrine' embodied in U.S. policy toward Eastern Europe. In fact the administration opposes the views alleged in various press accounts. They most certainly do not reflect the President's policy toward Eastern Europe. Both Secretary Kissinger and Mr. Sonnenfeldt have made this clear."[51]

Détente and Kissinger were prominent issues in the presidential primary campaigns. Ronald Reagan savaged the decision to drop the word détente and replace Secretary of Defense Schlesinger. "Mr. Ford says détente will be replaced by 'peace through strength,'" Reagan said in late March. "Well, now that slogan has a nice ring to it, but neither Mr. Ford nor his new Secretary of Defense will say that our strength is superior to all others. . . . I believe former Secretary of Defense James Schlesinger was trying to speak the truth frankly and boldly to his fellow citizens. And that's why he is no longer Secretary of Defense."

Reagan also denounced the "negotiations aimed at giving up our ownership of the Panama Canal Zone." The California governor declared that "the Canal Zone is not a colonial possession. It is not a long-term lease. It is sovereign U.S. territory. . . . We should end those negotiations and tell the General: We bought it, we paid for it, we built it and we intend to keep it."[52]

Reagan accused Kissinger of "giving away our own freedom." He quoted the Secretary as saying that "the day of the U.S. is past and today is the day of the Soviet Union. . . . My job as Secretary of State is to negotiate the most acceptable second-best position available." Ford rebutted Reagan whose "so-called quotes from Secretary Kissinger are a total and irresponsible fabrication." Kissinger himself went to Dallas to rebut Reagan. "I do not believe that the United States will be defeated. I do not believe that the United States is on the decline. I do not believe that the United States must get the best deal it can."[53]

Reagan charged that "under Messrs. Kissinger and Ford this nation has become number two in military power in a world where it is dangerous—if not fatal—to be second best." The challenger blamed the Soviets for doublecrossing Kissinger by tearing up the 1973 Paris peace agreements. Even as they "inflicted upon the United States the worst humiliation in its history, Mr. Ford and Dr. Kissinger said in chorus: 'we must not let this interfere with détente.' " Soviet actions in Angola also provoked Reagan, "yet Ford and Kissinger continue to tell us that we must not let this interfere with détente." Fed up, Reagan demanded "the time has come for Mr. Ford and Dr. Kissinger to tell us, the American people, what we are getting out of détente." He indicted the administration for moral cowardice. "At Kissinger's insistence, Mr. Ford snubbed Aleksandr Solzhenitsyn, one of the great moral heroes of our time. At Brezhnev's insistence, Mr. Ford flew halfway around the world to sign an agreement at Helsinki which placed the American seal of approval on the Soviet empire in Eastern Europe." Kissinger had failed. "Despite Henry Kissinger's sophistication and wit, his recent stewardship of U.S. foreign policy has coincided precisely with the loss of U.S. military supremacy." Détente produced only "the peace of the grave," Reagan warned.[54]

Reagan also denounced the Sonnenfeldt doctrine as telling the "captive nations" of Eastern Europe to "give up any claim of national sovereignty and simply become a part of the Soviet Union." Kissinger presented the administration rebuttal before Congress. "We do not accept a sphere of influence of any country, anywhere, and emphatically we reject a Soviet sphere of influence in Eastern Europe."[55]

Reagan condemned détente to Ohio voters before that state's primary. "Despite concessions granted by our government to the Soviet Union while pursuing détente, the Soviets' belligerent attitude toward us and our allies has not changed. Now, our friends and allies throughout the world question not only our military capability, but also our will to resist Communist aggression and to reassert effective moral leadership."[56]

As Reagan excoriated Kissinger, reporters asked Ford "don't you think Dr. Kissinger is becoming something of a problem, if not a liability?" In Texas, Ford defended him as "an excellent Secretary of State. He has implemented the policies which I have directed." In North Carolina he invited Kissinger to remain in the cabinet for a "long, long, long time." Again he walked a fine line between praising Kissinger's genius and stressing his own command of foreign policy. "Secretary of State Kissinger," he announced, "working with me at my direction has done some of the most outstanding diplomatic work on behalf of the United States and world peace, I think, of any Secretary of State in the history of the United States."[57]

The Republican challenge alarmed Ford's aides, some of whom considered Kissinger a liability. Ten Republican representatives wrote Ford in March complaining about Kissinger's use of the press to advance his own strategic conceptions and undermine those of the military. Articles in which Kissinger "openly derides the American cruise missile and lends support to the Soviet rationale on the Backfire bomber are damaging to our position in SALT and deprive us of much-needed negotiating strength." The letter languished for three months at the White House before a staff member prepared a cool, noncommittal response. At that point a congressional liaison complained "the letter from the 10 M.C.'s is almost *three months* old. After that period of time, to dispatch their serious concerns with a two paragraph slap is inconceivable. Many of these M.C.s are great friends and supporters of the President. But they wouldn't remain so upon receipt of the proposed response."[58]

During the primary campaign some White House staff members revived the issue of a meeting with Aleksandr Solzhenitsyn. The situation had changed in the ten months since Kissinger had persuaded the President that meeting the Soviet exile would undermine delicate relations with the Soviets. Now "détente is attacked daily in the press. Kissinger is criticized continually by Reagan who occassionally brings up the Solzhenitsyn issue. The administration is attempting to take a stronger line on defense matters. What could be a better *symbol* of our awareness of the Soviet threat than our willingness to hear the warnings of a Nobel Laureate who is widely respected as a man of principle." Such a meeting might prove enough to tip the balance to Ford in the crucial Texas primary. In the end, however, the White House decided that too decisive a break with Kissinger and détente would alienate more moderates than it would attract conservatives.[59] After the Republican convention of August 1976 conservatives still complained that "hostility toward Solzhenitsyn within the policy-making machinery headed by Secretary of State Henry Kissinger has not subsided since 1975, when it convinced President Ford he should snub the Nobel Laureate."[60]

Outsiders also complained about Kissinger. A former Republican congressman wrote the White House that he was "frankly appalled by the new turn in policy recently enunciated by Secretary Kissinger while in Africa." He thought that "the sooner the President disso-ciates himself from these views . . . the better for his sake, for the sake of the Republican Party, and for that of the country."[61] Senator Barry Goldwater threatened to withhold support for Ford if the administration officially recognized the PRC. The Senator reminded Kissinger that "on numerous occasions you have told me that rec-ognition of Red China was not even being considered. I heard on the news this morning that it is being considered and that we will rec-ognize her after the elections." An alarmed White House staff learned that "Goldwater has sent Henry an ultimatum: either respond to his China letter within 24 hours or he will publicly announce he cannot support Ford." Kissinger called Goldwater and "turned him off," he reported to the White House. Goldwater also wrote Kissinger "I don't mind telling you if we are going to sell Taiwan down the river, it's going to have a decided effect on what I do for the rest of the cam-paign."[62]

China policy remained a political problem for Ford in the summer of 1976. His press secretary advised him to refuse to be drawn into a debate with Reagan. Instead Ford should quote Kissinger's latest exposition of policy toward China. The United States, he told a Se-attle audience, seeks "durable and growing ties. . . . Both sides de-rive benefits from constructive relations, improved prospects for maintaining a global equilibrium. . . . The new relationship be-tween the U.S. and the PRC is an enduring and important feature of the international scene, and we are determined to work to improve it further."[63]

Throughout the presidential campaign Democratic candidate Jimmy Carter waged a two-pronged assault on the Ford administration's handling of foreign affairs. Kissinger became the target from opposite directions. On the one hand the Democrat blasted Ford for removing himself from foreign affairs. Carter claimed that the President had abdicated the field to Kissinger, who traded on his experience as a way of continuing to dominate American foreign policy. "As far as foreign policy goes," Carter wryly observed in one debate with Ford, "Mr. Kissinger has been President of this country. Mr. Ford has shown an absence of leadership." Carter claimed that the public deserved better than a part-time President, especially one who had never been elected to the office. Where was the accountability if the President took no interest in the process and permitted the Secretary of State to imply that he alone knew the nation's interests?[64]

The White House noted with delight that Carter earlier had professed great admiration for Kissinger's accomplishments. "He's a remarkable man and a very good friend of mine," he told the B'nai Brith. "He's the kind of person who has a tremendous sense of humor and who, I think, is preserving the character of his nation in a superlative way during the times that are so trying to us all." Later he told a Georgia newspaper "I think Dr. Kissinger deserves the gratitude of the American people." He explained in Chicago "there is no way I would keep Kissinger as Secretary of State, but as a personal diplomat, in a particular circumstance, I would certainly call on Kissinger either for a confrontation or perhaps as a negotiator."

Carter changed tactics dramatically during the fall campaign. He decried "the Nixon-Kissinger-Ford policy" as "covert, manipulative, and deceptive in style. It runs against the basic principles of this country, because Kissinger is obsessed with power blocs, with spheres of influence. This is a policy without focus. It is not understood by the people or the Congress." Carter's most damaging charge attacked Ford's competence. "The President is not really in charge," he declared. "Our policies are Kissinger's ideas and his goals, which are often derived in secret." Carter assailed Kissinger for having "oversold détente." He decried the Helsinki accords and the Sonnenfeldt doctrine for conceding "Eastern European freedoms to the Soviets. We should either not have gone at all to Helsinki, or drove [sic] a harder bargain."[65]

Carter told the Foreign Policy Association that "under the Nixon-Ford administration, there has evolved a kind of secretive, 'Lone Ranger' foreign policy, a one-man policy of international adventure." The problem with entrusting so much to Kissinger was that "a foreign policy based on secrecy inherently has had to be closely guarded and amoral."[66]

Carter also accused Presidents Nixon and Ford and Secretary Kissinger of lacking control of the competing factions in the government. The Republican administration, he complained, had been "almost all style and spectacular and not substance. . . . We've ignored or excluded the American people and Congress from shaping our foreign policy. It's been one of secrecy and exclusion."[67] This charge, particularly wounding to Kissinger who had tried to seize power in the NSC, reflected two years of incessant warfare between the Secretary, the CIA, and the defense department.

Ford prepared detailed defenses of Kissinger and the policy of détente for his debates with Carter. The President underlined key passages regarding U.S.–Soviet relations in the briefing material put together by the NSC staff. He noted an obligation to "reduce the danger of *confrontation and nuclear war.*" He portrayed himself as alert to the Soviet danger. *"We have deep differences, we have fundamental differences, but from a position of strength,* we can seek to reduce tensions. . . . "* He reminded his listeners of the bad old days. *"We will not go back to the Cold War. Relations with the Soviet Union require hard bargaining. . . . [W]e will seek to reduce tensions so that every issue does not lead to dangerous confrontation.*"

He readied himself for questions about Kissinger's role in SALT. "Many people say that the SALT agreements were hastily negotiated by Kissinger so that Nixon could use them for the election of 1972." To which Ford rejoined: "Both sides have lived up to the agreements. . . . It is not surprising that there have been some uncertainties and ambiguities. As a matter of fact, the 1972 agreement foresaw just such problems and established a joint commission to deal with them. It has worked well."[68]

Ford rebutted Carter on secrecy. "Diplomacy can't be conducted without confidentiality during negotiations, and Governor Carter knows it." He defended Kissinger as a "strong Secretary of State" who "has been enormously successful. Respect for the United States internationally has never been higher. We are the acknowledged and respected political, military and economic leader of the free world. Our strength is unsurpassed." Kissinger deserved much of the credit. "Any strong man will be criticized," the President moralized. "This is not the issue. The important questions are, is he good, is he effective? On those central questions, Henry Kissinger is second to none."[69]

Ford also braced for questions about the Sonnenfeldt doctrine. His staff briefed him for a question about Carter's declaration that "at Helsinki you endorsed Soviet domination of Eastern Europe and he cites the Sonnenfeldt doctrine as proof of this." Ford was supposed to reply, "As far as dealing with the Soviets is concerned, Governor Carter seems to have a confusing, contradictory idea. First he advocates cutting the defense budget. . . . Then he says he will be a tough bargainer." Ford assailed Carter's criticism of the Helsinki accords as "a deep insult to the leaders of the free nations. . . . We have established certain standards of conduct." The NSC advised Ford to say he was "baffled about this talk about a Sonnenfeldt doctrine in Eastern Europe. You can't have it both ways. I have visited Poland, Romania and Yugoslavia as President. Our relations with and support for the countries has never been stronger. I don't see how you can talk about conceding Soviet domination in light of this record. . . ."[70]

Ford prepared notes to himself about how the Helsinki Accords "established standards for human rights" in Eastern Europe. The final act declared that borders were not to be changed by force. "Who wants to change them by force?" he asked. Regarding the Sonnenfeldt doctrine "there is none," he stressed. He visited Romania and Hungary to "symbolize their independence and autonomy." Carter should remember that "no Democratic president has visited Eastern Europe." Ford also scribbled that there had been "two Democrats since World War II. Both got us into wars." Truman and Kennedy "increased commitments, reduced our strength." On the other hand, "two Republican administrations ended wars. I can tell every mother, we are at peace."[71]

Ford anticipated charges that Kissinger had been too secretive. He noted the record number of "speeches and press conferences" Kissinger had conducted. All the while he emphasized that Ford, not the Secretary of State, had made the decisions as President.[72]

Ford expected to praise Kissinger as "a superb international negotiator—the best in the world, so far as I can tell." The President wanted the electorate to know that Kissinger was the messenger, Ford the architect of foreign policy. "The final responsibility," he wanted to say, "rests in the Oval Office. . . . It is the President—and only the President—who can decide where to send our troops, who can decide how many missiles and bombers and ships we need to protect our security, and who can decide whether the moment of truth has arrived in the nuclear age. . . . If elected, Mr. Carter will be the first President in this century with virtually no foreign and defense policy experience. Therefore, I believe he should tell the people—in this debate—who his Secretary of State and Secretary of Defense will be."[73] Ford mocked Carter's insistence on openness in foreign relations. He explained that "there are times when diplomacy cannot be conducted fully in the open. For example, negotiations with our allies or our adversaries on arms reductions involve weapons systems that defend our very security. Mr. Carter may believe that such negotiations can be conducted in the open, but I don't."[74]

Ford defended his banishment of the use of the term détente. He favored a "better approach" than the "'peace at any price' philosophy" Carter advocated. "Something happened to U.S.–Soviet relations early this year," he recalled. "What happened was that the Soviet Union intervened massively with military equipment and Cuban troops in Angola. I warned them publicly and also sent Secretary Kissinger to Moscow in January in part to convey directly and in private the depth of our concern." Carter, he charged "does not know what he is talking about" when he "says we have made no progress" on SALT.[75]

Ford also considered noteworthy Kissinger's standards for a successful Secretary of State. Public opinion polls were too ephemeral to matter, especially now that Kissinger's numbers had slipped. "I think the ultimate test of a Secretary of State—the obligation of a Secretary of State is to give his best judgment to the President as to what is in the national interest. And if he is responsible, he'll understand that the national interest cannot be separated from the world interest. The President then has to make the political decision as to how this judgment can be carried out within the American political context. It's the President who has to make that decision."[76]

Kissinger joined Ford in asserting that the President had the last word on foreign policy. He told a press conference in October that "Dean Acheson used to say that there can be a strong President and a strong Secretary of State as long as the Secretary of State knows who is President. The final decisions are always made by the President. I see the President three or four times a week. I am on the telephone with him constantly. There is no major decision that is taken that is not made by the President." The President noted approvingly Kissinger's explanation that "President Ford and I have had a very close working relationship and it is in the nature of such a relationship that the points of view of the two partners merge. But it is always clear who is the senior partner and who is the junior partner."[77]

During his second debate with Carter, Ford stumbled into saying "there is no Soviet domination of Eastern Europe, and there never will be in a Ford administration." The press pounced on Kissinger, trying to draw him into the dispute over the President's faux pas. A reporter asked "isn't it true that when President Ford admittedly made a blunder during the second debate with Jimmy Carter on the Eastern European situation, that that indicated that he was not on top of the situation—that he wasn't aware fully of certain foreign policy issues?" Kissinger defended the President as well as he could, in words Ford underlined: "No. That indicated that under the pressure of a debate he did not make the point as felicitously as he might have made it—as he has since admitted. Nobody who knows his record could believe that on this particular issue he did not know exactly what the facts were. He had one thing in mind and he expressed it in a manner that created the wrong impression and he has stated that publicly and has clarified it."[78]

Carter managed to eke out a narrow, two-million-vote margin over President Ford in the general election in November. He had squandered a huge lead in the process. Most voters did not have foreign policy issues on their minds when they decided to punish the Republican party for Watergate and the sorry state of the economy. Insofar as international relations did intrude on the consciousness of the electorate, Kissinger proved a liability. He could maintain a grip on the public as long as he produced results. Once those stopped and the world appeared still to be a complicated and even threatening place, his appeal diminished. He had never thought much of public opinion anyway. He preferred to believe that the era of the expert left little room for public action. All this was fine, so long as there appeared to be progress. Once the United States seemed again on the defensive, Kissinger lacked a base of support. Throughout the campaign Carter turned Kissinger's words back on the man who spoke them. While the election's outcome did not depend much on foreign affairs, it appeared that the verdict of 1976 had gone against Kissinger.

The public had decided that for all of his sophistication, he had not made them happier with his foreign policy. He had come to power with diplomacy in disarray, the product of the least common denominator of warring groups within the bureaucracy. He had taken office when the United States was in the midst of its longest, most divisive war, with the western alliance a shadow of its former self. When he left in 1977, the end in Vietnam had been a debacle. The allies still wondered about the steadfastness of the United States. At home, the squabbling had not stopped within the government. His NSC system had served primarily to annoy and intimidate other professionals. Leaks from various foreign policy officials reached new heights as

Kissinger's rivals looked for their own allies in Congress or the press. Most of all, Kissinger could not offer the public a sense of security or well-being. His pleas for patience had themselves turned into wails that he had been misunderstood. When Carter promised that he would restore order and a sense of purpose to United States foreign policy he received an attentive hearing.

ELEVEN

Kissinger in Retrospect

Henry Kissinger was the most prominent and celibrated American diplomat since the early cold war. He stands with Dean Acheson as one of the two "realist" architects of post–World War II United States foreign policy. The position of the United States changed as dramatically during the eight years from 1969 to 1976 as it did during any comparable period in the post–World War II era. Direct confrontation between the United States and the Soviet Union eased temporarily as steps toward détente raised hopes that the cold war had ended. Kissinger presided over the end of the United States' role as military policeman in Asia and the unhappy end of the war in Vietnam. He supervised the beginning of new relations with China. He also brought the United States into the Middle East as *the* major actor.

Kissinger changed for a time the way the United States conducted foreign policy. He came as close as anyone to concentrating power in the White House. Not since Woodrow Wilson drafted diplomatic dispatches on his own battered Underwood typewriter had United States foreign policy appeared to be as centralized as it was in the Kissinger years. His dominance of the process and his mastery of the press that covered foreign policy left a legacy that none of his successors as National Security Adviser or Secretary of State have approached.

Indeed, his very domination of the process of foreign policy hung like a cloud over the national security establishment in the Carter and Reagan administrations. Each tried to match and surpass Kissinger's record. Each failed.

In the Carter years Secretary of State Cyrus Vance hoped to go beyond the old-fashioned commitment to great power rivalry. Vance's own rival, National Security Adviser Zbigniew Brzezinski, attacked Kissinger from the other direction, claiming that his predecessor's achievements had been insufficiently grounded in geopolitics. Instead, Brzezinski argued that Kissinger had substituted flash and style for a deep appreciation of the realities of Soviet–American conflict. Carter wavered between each position and eventually aligned himself with Brzezinski. The war between Secretary of State and National Security Adviser far exceeded anything that happened in the Kissinger years. In the end Carter could not convince a skeptical electorate that he had created a coherent foreign policy.[1]

The problem of the organization of foreign policy persisted under the Reagan administration, which came to power in 1981 promising to reverse fifteen years of decline in American power. At first Ronald Reagan's diplomats distinguished their approach from Kissinger's by proclaiming the death of détente and the revival of military power. Kissinger was back, however, in June 1983, as head of a special bipartisan commission on Central American policy. The promise to end the endemic bureaucratic rivalry also quickly withered. Within two years the foreign policy apparatus had suffered more upheavals than any predeccessor. Both National Security Adviser Richard V. Allen and Secretary of State Alexander Haig resigned within six months of one another. In eight years, Reagan went through six different National Security Advisers.

A major scandal engulfed the National Security Council staff in late 1986 when Attorney General Edwin Meese revealed that it had secretly arranged for the sale of weapons to Iran and the transfer of profits to the counterrevolutionaries in Central America. Secretary of State George P. Shultz, angry at having been excluded from the process, told Congress that the memory of Kissinger's achievements had goaded the Reagan NSC into conducting dramatic and flawed operations. But, Shultz told lawmakers, the newcomers were not up to the job. "There's only one Henry Kissinger. They broke the mold after they made him."[2]

How then to judge the legacy of Henry Kissinger? If the standard is the endurance of a program, Kissinger was not completely successful. Indeed, many of his apparent achievements already had broken down before the election of 1976. The "peace" in Indochina collapsed in 1975, and détente with the Soviet Union did not survive the Ford administration. The opening to China did, but the Carter administration may have accomplished more. The same may be said of the new American role in the Middle East, and the 1980s were notable for their lack of success in resolving the Arab–Israeli conflict. As Steven Spiegel writes about Kissinger's efforts in the Middle East in words that apply to much of Kissinger's diplomacy, "Bold in style, Kissinger was extremely cautious in policy. His entire approach was to maintain a process, he had neither the vision nor the courage to transform the issue, to make a 'psychological breakthrough' of the sort Sadat would later achieve in Jerusalem."[3] It is hard to identify a single policy of the Kissinger years that survived intact for a decade.

But is longevity the proper standard? One of the best lessons that Kissinger offered was the persistence of foreign policy. If the United States had permanent interests in the rest of the world, it is hard to imagine that a single policy would be successful for all time. Kissinger always believed that the measure of a diplomat was the ability to adjust to changing environments.

Maybe a better gauge of his contributions is the extent to which he changed the ways Americans thought about foreign affairs, the way they set priorities, their ability to see the whole picture. Kissinger had been an academic before entering government who argued that the way foreign policy operators asked questions determined their answers. May not the appropriate way of judging Kissinger be to measure his policies against the theories of international relations and American foreign policy he elaborated before coming to power?

Under this standard the record is mixed, with dazzling promises leading to less revolutionary accomplishments. Kissinger's approach pledged that the United States would follow a plan, a strategy. The United States should create structures and politicians should think strategically. Kissinger in power claimed to act in accordance with a conceptual framework different from that Americans had previously fit over their foreign relations. He won praise at the time for seeing connections others missed. His triangular diplomacy among the Soviet Union, China, and North Vietnam reflected a genuine grand design. His efforts on behalf of arms control also displayed enormous command of a complicated subject, not to mention phenomenal physical stamina.

The practice, however, was less revolutionary than the promise. Kissinger often reacted to events rather than molded them. His foresight dimmed because he neglected what went on inside other countries. His lack of interest in transnational processes, in economics, in morality, in human rights, in the fate of poorer nations opened him to charges of offering only the shopworn clichés of the nineteenth century. He behavior toward Chile and the Angolan revolution encouraged the belief that he did not care about the sensibilities of other peoples or that he betrayed some precious American values. When Jimmy Carter ran for President in 1976 he accused Kissinger of having conducted secret diplomacy unworthy of the United States.

Moreover, Kissinger contributed to the dissipation of support for his foreign policy. He oversold the benefits of détente. When they did not materialize, critics questioned the value of a fresh start with Moscow. Kissinger promised too much from the peace agreement with North Vietnam. When it collapsed, the Secretary of State blamed Congress for hamstringing the President with the Watergate investigations. His peace shuttle in the Middle East provoked similar disappointment. Despite the Herculean efforts of the shuttle, Kissinger did not arrange a final peace between Israel and the Arabs. Israel's supporters in the United States considered some of his proposals detrimental to their interests. His opening to China also ran out of steam by 1976. The United States and the PRC had not yet established diplomatic relations, and critics wondered if the opening had been more illusory than real.

More disturbing questions arise regarding Kissinger's personal conduct in office. He went to great lengths promoting the needs of the NSC against those of other government agencies. He was a relentless boss: For those whose loyalty he questioned, he was impossible; while for those who supported him, he was difficult. He dissembled his role in the wiretapping of his staff and became surly when it was revealed. A man who scored sentimentality in others, he became maudlin about his own needs to retain control over foreign policy.

Kissinger's efforts to keep the spotlight focused on his own accomplishments also eventually haunted him. To that end, he assiduously kept Secretary of State William P. Rogers out of the picture before 1973. Once Kissinger became Secretary of State in his own right in September of that year, he feuded with Secretary of Defense James Schelesinger over the nature of détente and Soviet–American relations.

Hard on subordinates, competitive with other cabinet officers, Kissinger understood that his power derived from his presidents. Richard Nixon and Gerald Ford became the vehicles through which he exercised real influence. As such, he told them directly that their views were subtle and sophisticated. To subordinates and favored members of the press, however, Kissinger questioned his superiors.

He gave the impression that only he had the proper grasp of the intricate nature of modern foreign policy.

Kissinger's diplomacy was personal. He became a celebrity during his time in power and maintained that status for years after leaving office. Much of the appeal was carefully calibrated to enhance the reputation of an expert in foreign affairs. Yet Kissinger's personal style also caused many of the problems associated with a successful new diplomatic course. Kissinger sometimes acted as if only he possessed the wisdom, knowledge, access to the President, awareness of other leaders, and strategic conception needed to design a new foreign policy.

By keeping others out of the process, Kissinger guaranteed that he was the center of attention, but he assured that his diplomacy would not be fully successful. For example, the exclusion of the permanent State Department bureaucracy created resentments. Kissinger did not mind that and, indeed, believed that leaving the bureaucracy out enhanced the ability to reach spectacular agreements with the Soviets. On the other hand, where follow-through was called for, Kissinger lacked the support of other parts of the government. For a while Kissinger could dismiss the concerns of the permanent members of the State Department, as self-interested technical quibbles. As time wore on, however, Kissinger had to demonstrate concrete results. For this he needed the assistance of permanent staff members. Distrustful of them, however, he could not make use of their advice. For their part, professionals by 1975 were reluctant to exert themselves on his behalf.

Similarly, Kissinger could not build a structure that would endure beyond his term. Jealous of sharing power with others, it became nearly impossible to bequeath a legacy to successors, especially from the other political party. During the Carter administration, Brzezinski and Vance were determined to exceed Kissinger's record rather than follow his path.

Kissinger made the expert a celebrity, but his personal diplomacy also called expertise into question. When his predictions failed and détente collapsed he blamed others: Congress, the press, the Democrats, or a fickle public. It became harder and harder to determine the core of Kissinger's foreign policy beliefs as time went on. As criticism mounted, it appeared that Kissinger's domination of the foreign policy process was all that mattered. In 1975 and 1976, Kissinger insisted that he alone should conduct negotiations. This certainly kept the spotlight focused on him, but it failed to produce something lasting.

Kissinger began his public career with the proposition that Americans had failed properly to understand the way international relations should work. As an academic, he had outlined five basic principles of international relations: 1) The United States had permanent interests; 2) Excessive legalism and moralism had marred American foreign relations; 3) Negotiations should be seen as a process in which speaking to one's adversary was as important as concrete results; 4) The United States and the Soviet Union had a permanent relationship; 5) Power had diffused beyond the two superpowers of the Cold War.

These were sensible opinions, the standard fare of professional writers on international relations in the mid-sixties. For the most part, Kissinger maintained them in office—but not all the time. As his power eroded late in the Ford term, he stressed more popular themes about the Soviet danger. It became difficult at the end of the Ford administration to determine what was distinctive about Kissinger's contributions.

Kissinger's diplomatic career represented the triumph and limits of the academic expert. His theories developed in the fifties and sixties reflected a widespread academic view that the United States had finally become a world power but American leaders were unsure how to apply their might. He had a mature appreciation that Americans often were impatient with their diplomacy. In office Kissinger discovered just how impatient Americans were. Many of his dramatic moves beguiled the public. Then Kissinger was trapped; he had to keep pulling rabbits from a hat. The performance seemed to matter more than results. Instead of building a structure, Kissinger created a personality. He became the wise, mature advocate of a foreign policy that had lost public appeal.

Kissinger's fate seemed to parallel that of the United States in world affairs in the sixties and seventies. The country's political leaders came to recognize that America's global ambitions of the first twenty years of the Cold War had become too great a burden. Americans wanted release from Vietnam and the costs of confrontation with the Soviets. Kissinger tried to serve these desires, but he found that shedding the burden had costs. United States foreign policy in the mid-seventies confronted a much more turbulent world than before, so Washington's policy-makers found it difficult to maintain American standing in that world according to the principles of the past twenty years. Kissinger too discovered that he lost his control over foreign policy. In that sense, his diplomacy represented the end of an era more than it heralded a new beginning in American foreign relations.

ABBREVIATIONS USED IN NOTES AND BIBLIOGRAPHY

BSUL	Boise State University Library, Boise, Idaho
CF	Confidential Files
CSM	*Christian Science Monitor*
GRFL	Gerald R. Ford Library, Ann Arbor, Michigan
HAK	Henry A. Kissinger
LAT	*Los Angeles Times*
LBJL	Lyndon Baines Johnson Library, Austin, Texas
NOTP	*New Orleans Times Picaynue*
NP, NA	Nixon Presidential Materials Project, National Archives, Alexandria, Virginia
NYT	*New York Times*
POF	President's Office Files
SMOF	Staff Members' Office Files
WHCF	White House Central Files
WHSF	White House Special Files
WHY	Henry Kissinger, *White House Years* (Boston: Little, Brown, 1979)
YU	Henry Kissinger, *Years of Upheaval* (Boston: Little, Brown, 1982)

NOTES

Introduction: Henry Kissinger's Record

1. *NOTP*, 1/3/73, p. 1; 12/27/74, p. 1. "The Return of the Magician," *Time*, 3/11/74, p. 26; "Miracle Worker Does It Again," *ibid.*; "Superstar Statecraft: How Henry Does It," *ibid.*, 4/1/74. "Travels with Henry," *Newsweek*, 2/14/74, pp. 76–77; "It's a Bird, It's a Plane, It's Super K," *ibid.*, 4/1/74, pp. 33–34. Gina Lollobrigida, "Kissinger Close Up," *Ladies' Home Journal*, 7/74, pp. 68–69; Diane Hunnebelle, "Henry Kissinger and Me," *ibid.*, 8/72, p. 48; Kandy Stroud, "The New Mrs. Kissinger," *ibid.*, 3/74, p. 28; Marvin Kalb, "Nancy Kissinger: My Life with Henry," *ibid.*, 4/75, pp. 75–76; Richard Valeriani, "That Kissinger Dog," *ibid.*, 6/76, p. 126. Jerrold Schechter, "Henry Kissinger: Not So Secret Swinger," *Life*, 1/28/72, pp. 70b–71. J. Steward, "The New Mrs. Kissinger," *McCall's*, 3/74, p. 28. "People are Talking About . . .," *Vogue*, 6/74, pp. 106–107.

For representative cartoons, see *Newsweek*, 4/1/74, p. 33; 4/29/74, p. 42. *LAT*, 1/6/76, II, p. 7; 2/16/76, II, p. 7. *Chicago Tribune*, 2/25/72, p. 10; 1/4/73, p. 20; 10/30/77, p. 12. *CSM*, 4/17/74 ed., 4/1/75 ed., 4/25/75 ed. For literary representations see, for example, the novel, Joseph Heller, *Good as Gold* (1973); the story, Saul Bellow, "Him with His Foot in His Mouth" (1984); the play, Wallace Shawn, *Aunt Dan and Lemon* (1985); and the opera *Nixon in China* (1987).

2. *LAT*, 5/2/76, IA, p. 6.

3. Reston, *NYT*, 1/20/77, p. 1; "Kissinger's View of History," *National Review*, 4/2/76, pp. 310–11; Charles Mee, Jr., "Terminal Madness," *Horizon* (Autumn 1976), 18:104–5.

4. "Miracle Worker or Stuntman? Size-up of the Kissinger Record," *U.S. News and World Report*, 1/10/77, pp. 35–36.

5. Seymour Hersh, *The Price of Power*.

6. Richard Nixon, *RN: The Memoirs of Richard Nixon*.

7. John Ehrlichman, *Witness to Power*; H. R. Haldeman with Joseph DiMona, *The Ends of Power*; William Safire, *Before the Fall: An Inside Look at the Pre-Watergate White House*, pp. 156–170.

8. Raymond Garthoff, *Détente and Confrontation: American–Soviet Relations from Nixon to Reagan*.

9. Gerard Smith, *Doubletalk: The Untold Story of SALT*.

10. U. Alexis Johnson with Jef O. McAllister, *The Right Hand of Power*.

11. Marvin Kalb and Bernard Kalb, *Kissinger*; William Hyland, *Mortal Rivals: Superpower Relations from Nixon to Reagan*.

12. Report of the Bipartisan Presidential Commission on Central America (Washington: GPO, 1984).

13. For admiring portraits of HAK written at the time of his greatest public appeal, see Marvin Kalb and Bernard Kalb, *Kissinger*; John Stoessinger, *Henry Kissinger: The Anguish of Power*; and Stephen Graubard, *Kissinger: Portrait of a Mind*. A more critical account appeared in David Landau, *Kissinger: The Uses of Power*. More balanced approaches appeared shortly after Kissinger left office in Stanley Hoffmann, *Primacy or World Order: Foreign Policy Since the Cold War*; Hoffmann, "The Doctor of Foreign Policy"; Seyom Brown, *The Crises of Power: An Interpretation of United States Foreign Policy During the Kissinger Years*; and Brown, *The Faces of Power: Constancy and Change in United States Foreign Policy from Truman to Reagan*; pp. 321–448.

14. The basic texts of foreign policy realism are Hans Morgenthau, *Politics Among Nations: The Struggle for Power*; Morgenthau, *In Defense of the National Interest: A Critical Examination of United States Foreign Policy*; George F. Kennan, *American Diplomacy, 1900–1950*; Kennan, *Realities of American Foreign Policy*; Reinhold Niebuhr, *The Irony of American History*; Niebuhr, *The Children of Light and the Children of Darkness*; and Michael Joseph Smith, *Realist Thought from Weber to Kissinger*.

15. Richard Stevenson, *The Rise and Fall of Détente*.

16. Thomas Franck and Edward Wiesband, *Foreign Policy by Congress*; pp. 3–13.

17. Garthoff, *Détente and Confrontation*.

18. Anthony Lewis, *NYT*, 1/13/77, p. 37; Hersh, *The Price of Power*, pp. 636–42.

19. Lewis, *NYT*.

20. Hersh, *Price of Power*, pp. 55–64, 258, 276, 363–82; Bob Woodward and Carl Bernstein, *The Final Days*, pp. 469–72, 479.

21. William Shawcross, *Sideshow: Kissinger, Nixon and the Destruction of Cambodia*, pp. 128–87; Paul Sigmund, *The Overthrow of Allende and the Politics of Chile, 1964–1976*, pp. 3–13.

22. See Richard Nixon, *U.S. Foreign Policy for the 1970s: The Emerging Structure of Peace*, pp. 2–9. This was the third of four reports to Congress on the state of U.S. foreign policy prepared by Kissinger's staff at the National Security Council. Kissinger designed them to parallel the annual economic report of the President to Congress, but the Ford administration did not continue the practice. See HAK to President-elect, 12/27/68, WHSF, SMOF, Ehrlichman files, box 19, Foreign Policy, 1970 [1]. NP, NA.

23. U.S. House, Committee on Foreign Affairs, *Hearings on Arms Sales to Iran*, December 8, 1986, testimony of Secretary of State George P. Shultz; Lewis, *NYT*, 6/23/84, p. 32.

1. The Adviser

1. Kalb and Kalb, *Kissinger*, pp. 31–40; Harvey Starr, *Henry Kissinger: Perceptions of International Politics*, pp. 17–22; Dana Ward, "Kissinger: A Psychohistory," *History of Childhood Quarterly* (1975), 2:287–93, 310–13; David Landau, *Kissinger: The Uses of Power*, pp. 16–20, 80–85.

2. "The Other Kissinger," *Newsweek*, 4/1/74, p. 62.

3. Kalb and Kalb, *Kissinger*, p. 40; B. Collier, "The Man who Discovered Kissinger," *SR Arts* (March 1973), 1:14–15.

4. Kalb and Kalb, *Kissinger*, p. 42.

5. Stoessinger, *Kissinger: The Anguish of Power*, p. 2.

6. Stephen Graubard, *Kissinger: Portrait of a Mind*, p. 6; Landau, *Kissinger: The Uses of Power*, p. 11.

7. Peter Dickson, *Kissinger and the Meaning of History*, p. 153. See also Brown, *The Faces of Power*, pp. 441–42.

8. Quoted in Starr, *Henry Kissinger: Perceptions of International Politics*, p. 23.

9. Henry Kissinger, *A World Restored: Metternich, Castlereagh and the Restoration of Europe, 1812–1822*, p. 319.

10. Gordon Dean, "Foreword" to Henry A. Kissinger, *Nuclear Weapons and Foreign Policy*, p. vi.

11. Study Group on Nuclear Weapons and United States Foreign Policy, November 8, 1954, January 10, 1955, Council on Foreign Relations File. Hanson W. Baldwin Papers, Yale University Library.

12. Kissinger, *Nuclear Weapons and Foreign Policy*, p. 405.

13. Edward Teller review of Henry Kissinger, *Nuclear Weapons and Foreign Policy*, *New York Times Book Review*, July 7, 1957. See also Ralph E. Lapp review of same, *New York Herald Tribune Book Review*, June 30, 1957, p. 1; Robert Osgood review of same, *Chicago Sunday Tribune*, July 7, 1957.

14. Henry A. Kissinger, "Reflections on American Diplomacy," *Foreign Affairs* (October 1956), 35(1):37–57; Kissinger, "Strategy and Organization," *Foreign Affairs* (April 1957), 35 (3):379–94.

15. Ralph Blumenfeld et al., *Henry Kissinger: The Private and Public Story* (New York: New American Library, 1974), p. 120.

16. Dean Acheson to HAK, 2/16/60, 3/14/60, Acheson Papers, Series 1, box 18, folder 226. Yale University Library.

17. HAK to McGeorge Bundy, 6/1/61, POF, box 31. HAK, June 1–August 28, 1962, folder. HAK to Bundy, 7/15/61, National Security Files, box 320. HAK, June–July 1961, folder. HAK memcon with Conway 11/17/61. Charles E. Johnson, memo for the record, 11/28/61. *Ibid.*, HAK, November–December 1961, folder. Lucius Battle to Bundy, 1/10/62. *Ibid.*, HAK, January 1962, folder. Bundy to Battle, 2/3/62, National Security Files, box 321. HAK, February–May, 1962. John F. Kennedy Library, Boston, Mass.

18. Henry Kissinger, *The Necessity for Choice: Prospects of American Foreign Policy*, pp. 1–101.

19. HAK to Dean Acheson, 12/31/64, Series 1, box 18, folder 226, Acheson Papers, Yale University Library.

20. Henry Kissinger, *The Troubled Partnership: A Reappraisal of the Atlantic Alliance*, p. 97.

21. HAK's Notes of Conversation of 3/23/66, WHCF, CF, box 8, CO81 France, 1966. LBJL.

22. HAK to Acheson, 12/14/66, Acheson Papers, Series 1, box 18, folder 226. Yale University Library.

23. HAK's Notes of Conversation of 3/23/66, WHCF, CF, box 8, CO81 France 1966. LBJL. McNamara to LBJ, 3/23/66; Bundy to HAK, 11/26/65, Confidential Name File, box 5, CF KI folder. Bundy to HAK, 12/30/63; HAK to Bundy, 2/7/64; Bundy to HAK, 10/1/64; HAK to Bundy, 11/24/64; same to same, 5/11/65; Bundy to HAK 5/29/65; HAK to Bundy, 8/3/65; same to same, 8/17/65; Bundy to HAK, 1/4/66; Moyers to HAK, 4/26/66; same to same 5/4/66; same to same 5/21/66; HAK to Rostow, 7/17/68. White House Name file, box 164, HAK folder. LBJL.

24. John Newhouse, *DeGaulle and the Anglo-Saxons*, p. 292.

25. HAK's Notes of Conversation of 3/23/66, WHCF, CF, box 8, CO81 France, 1966. LBJL.

26. Hersh, *The Price of Power*, p. 46. Kalb and Kalb, *Kissinger*, p. 66–72.

27. HAK to Bundy, 11/23/65, WHCF, CF, box 12, CO312 Vietnam, 1964–65. LBJL.

28. HAK to Bundy, 10/7/65; Clifford to President, 11/4/65; Moyers to HAK, 11/12/65. See also Roche to President, 6/7/67; President to HAK, 10/4/67. White House Name File, box 164, HAK folder. LBJL.

29. George C. Herring, ed., *The Secret Diplomacy of the Vietnam War: The Negotiating Volumes of the Pentagon Papers*, pp. 520, 727, 740.

30. Hersh, *The Price of Power*, pp. 12–13.

31. Hamilton Fish Armstrong, "Power in a Sieve," *Foreign Affairs* (July 1968), 46(3):468–69.

32. HAK, "The Vietnam Negotiations," *Foreign Affairs* (January 1969), 47(2):211–34.

33. Robert Blum, *The United States and China in World Affairs*, p. 145.

34. Richard M. Nixon, "Asia after Vietnam," *Foreign Affairs* (October 1967), 46(1):11–26.

35. J. William Fulbright, *Old Myths and New Realities*, pp. 3–46. See also William Berman, *William Fulbright and the Vietnam War: The Dissent of a Political Realist*.

36. Godfrey Hodgson, *America in Our Time*, pp. 263–73; Allen J. Matusow, *The Unraveling of America: A History of Liberalism in the 1960s*, pp. 377–82; Alonzo Hamby, *Liberalism and Its Challengers*, pp. 266–78.

37. Herbert Parmet, *JFK: The Presidency of John F. Kennedy*, pp. 61–82. Richard Neustadt, *Presidential Power*, pp. 171–84.

38. Arthur M. Schlesinger, Jr., *A Thousand Days: John F. Kennedy in the White House*, pp. 420, 435–36. Thomas Schoenbaum, *Waging Peace and War: Dean Rusk in the Truman, Kennedy, and Johnson Years*, p. 287. U.S. Senate, Committee on Government Operations, Subcommittee on National Security Policy Machinery, *Organizing for National Security*, Interim Report, 86th Cong., 2d Sess., January 18, 1960, pp. 5–10.

39. Theodore H. White, *The Making of the President, 1960*, pp. 335–58. Stephen E. Ambrose, *Nixon: The Education of a Politician, 1913–1962*, pp. 584–608.

40. *WHY*, pp. 7–16; Hersh, *The Price of Power*, pp. 11–24; Kalb and Kalb, *Kissinger*, pp. 14–30.

41. C. L. Sulzberger, *The World and Richard Nixon*, p. 180.

42. HAK, 10/18/67 and 12/5/68, Diary Cards. LBJL.

43. *National Review*, 12/17/68, p. 1251; *Business Week*, 12/7/68, p. 34; *The New Republic*, 12/14/68, p. 10.

44. *Time*, 12/13/68, p. 18.

45. *Newsweek*, 12/16/68, p. 30.

46. HAK to President-elect, 12/27/68, WHSF, SMOF, Ehrlichman files, box 19, Foreign Policy, 1970 [1]. NP, NA.

47. U.S. Senate, Committee on Government Operations, Subcommittee on National Security, *The National Security Council*, Comment by Henry A. Kissinger, 91st Cong., 1st sess., March 3, 1970, p. 1.

48. *Ibid.*, p. 2.

49. *Ibid.*, pp. 6–7.

50. *Ibid.*, p. 4.

51. Richard Nixon, *RN: Memoirs of Richard Nixon*, pp. 340–41.

52. John Ehrlichman, *Witness to Power: The Nixon Years*, pp. 68–69.

53. Harry R. Haldeman with Joseph DiMona, *The Ends of Power*, p. 58.

54. Kalb and Kalb, *Kissinger*, p. vi.

2. Grappling With Vietnam

1. *WHY*, pp. 38–48; Hersh, *The Price of Power*, pp. 25–36; Kalb and Kalb, *Kissinger*, pp. 78–99.

2. Alan E. Goodman, *The Lost Peace: America's Search for a Negotiated Settlement of the Vietnam War*, p. 81; Nixon, *RN*, pp. 323–26; *WHY*, 226–39.

3. Dean Acheson to Pamela Berry, 6/24/69, box 3, folder 33; Acheson to J.H.P. Gould, 3/12/70, box 13, folder 13, Acheson Papers. Yale University Library. Gregory T. D'Auria, "Present at the Rejuvenation: The Association of Dean Acheson and Richard Nixon," *Presidential Studies Quarterly* (Spring 1988), 18(2):396–97.

4. Joan Mellen, *Privilege: The Enigma of Sasha Bruce*, pp. 30–34.

5. *WHY*, pp. 282–86.

6. Garthoff, *Détente and Confrontation: American Soviet Relations from Nixon to Reagan*, pp. 248–54.

7. Robert Randle, *Geneva, 1954: The Settlement of the Indochinese War*, pp. 134, 261; Herring, *America's Longest War*, pp. 34–72.

8. Herring, pp. 220–24, *WHY*, pp. 269–76.

9. Donald Zagoria, *Vietnam Triangle: Moscow, Peking, Hanoi*, pp. 63–98; Robert G. Sutter, *China Watch: Toward Sino-American Reconciliation*, pp. 1–9, 63–70.

10. *WHY*, pp. 226–64.

11. I. M. Destler, *Presidents, Bureaucrats and Foreign Policy*, pp. 95–153; Destler, "The Nixon System: Another Look," *Foreign Service Journal*, February 1974, p. 24.

12. Roger Morris, *Uncertain Greatness: Henry Kissinger and American Foreign Policy*, pp. 146–47.

13. "Man with the Pressure Cooker Job," *U.S. News and World Report*, 12/14/69, p. 16.

14. Gerald Astor, "Strategist in the White House Basement," *Look*, 8/12/69, p. 53.

15. John Osborne, "White House Who's Who," *The New Republic*, 10/18/69, p. 14.

16. "Mr. Nixon's Professor," *Newsweek*, 12/22/69, p. 21.

17. Nora Beloff, "Professor Bismarck Goes to Washington," *Atlantic*, 12/69, p. 80.

18. John Osborne, "Henry's Wonderful Machine," *The New Republic*, 1/31/70, p. 12.

19. James McCarthy, "One-Third of Kissinger Staff Has Quit," *Houston Chronicle*, 10/19/69. Copy in Post-Presidential Name File, Kissinger file, box 33. LBJL.

20. U.S. Senate, Committee on the Judiciary, Subcommittee on Separation of Powers, *Hearings*, July 22–29, August 4–5, 1971, 92d Cong., 1st sess., pp. 21–23.

21. *Ibid.*, p. 259.

22. *Ibid.*, p. 348.

23. *Ibid.*, p. 363.

24. *WHY*, p. 138.

25. *Ibid.*, pp. 140–47.

26. Shawcross, *Sideshow*, p. 19.

27. Herring, *America's Longest War*, p. 147; Larry Berman, *Planning a Tragedy: The Americanization of the War in Vietnam*, pp. 31–78; Leslie Gelb with Richard K. Betts, *The Irony of Vietnam: The System Worked*, pp. 156–70; George McT. Kahin, *Intervention: How America Became Involved in Vietnam*, pp. 366–98.

28. Wheeler to Laird, 3/13/69, 4/9/69, 4/11/69, 4/21/69, 5/1/69, 5/19/69, 6/5/69, 6/17/69, 6/21/69, 6/27/69, 7/9/69, 8/9/69, 8/18/69, Laird to Wheeler, 10/19/69, Wheeler to Laird, 3/12/70, *Declassified Documents Reference Service*, 1979, 372B, 385A–404B.

29. Shawcross, *Sideshow*, pp. 390–92.

30. *Ibid.*, p. 140.

31. *Ibid.*, pp. 129–30.

32. *Ibid.*

33. Butterfield to Haldeman and Harlow, 4/28/69, WHSF, CF, box 42, ND18/CO165, Vietnam Jan.–April 1969, NP. NA.

34. President to HAK, 9/22/69; *ibid.*, Aug. 69–Feb. 70. NP, NA.

35. Charles DeBenedetti, *The Peace Reform in American History*, pp. 183–92; DeBenedetti, "On the Significance of Citizen Peace Activism: America, 1961–1975," *Peace and Change* (Summer 1983), 9(2/3):6–20; Milton S. Katz, *Ban the Bomb: A History of SANE, the Committee for a Sane Nuclear Policy, 1957–1985*, pp. 135–52; Melvin Small, *Johnson, Nixon, and the Doves*, pp. 162–92.

36. *NYT*, 4/6/69, p. 9.

37. H. R. Haldeman, *The Ends of Power*, p. 100; John Ehrlichman, *Witness to Power*, p. 274.

38. Haldeman, *The Ends of Power*, pp. 101–2. "Abstracts of News Analysis Regarding the Alleged Role of Henry Kissinger in Wiretaps of Government Officials and Newsmen," Congressional Research Service to Senate Foreign Relations Committee, 7/8/74, p. 8. Javits Papers, Series 4, subseries 2, box 64. Kissinger wiretapping—1974 folder, Melville Library, SUNY, Stony Brook.

39. Ken Cole to Kissinger, 9/19/69; HAK to President, 9/22/69; WHSF, CF, box 14, FG6-6, NSC file. NP, NA.

40. Garry Wills, *Nixon Agonistes*, pp. 547–50.

41. U.S. Senate, Committee on Foreign Relations, *Dr. Kissinger's Role in Wiretapping*, 93d Cong., 2d sess., July 23, 1974, p. 173.

42. U.S. House, Select Committee on Intelligence, *Intelligence Agencies and Activities*, 94th Cong., 2d sess., pp. 1205–06.

43. *Dr. Kissinger's Role in Wiretapping*, p. 247.

44. *Ibid.*, pp. 184–85.

45. *Ibid.*, p. 245.

46. *Ibid.*, p. 193.

47. Henry Brandon, *The Retreat of American Power*, p. 96; Safire, *Before the Fall*, pp. 181–86.

48. Morris, *Uncertain Greatness*, p. 147.

49. Haldeman notes, 5/1/70. WHSF, SMOF, Haldeman files, box 41. NP, NA.

50. *Ibid.*, 5/11/70.

51. *Ibid.*, 5/20/70.

52. Gerald Astor, "Strategist in the White House Basement," *Look*, 8/12/69, p. 53.

53. Brandon, *The Retreat of American Power*, p. 106.

54. Nora Beloff, "Professor Bismarck Goes to Washington," *Atlantic*, 12/69, p. 88.

55. Joseph Kraft, "In Search of Kissinger," *Harper's*, 1/71, pp. 54, 58.

56. Derek Shearer, "An Evening with Henry," *Nation*, (212) 3/8/71, pp. 296–97.

57. John Osborne, "More about Kissinger," *The New Republic*, 4/3/71, p. 13.

58. Haldeman notes, 7/17/71. WHSF, SMOF, Haldeman files, box 44. NP, NA.

59. John Osborne, "More about Kissinger," *The New Republic*, 4/3/71, p. 13.

60. *WHY*, p. 514.

61. Brandon, *The Retreat of American Power*, p. 101.

62. U.S. Senate, Committee on Foreign Relations, *U.S. Security Agreements and Commitments Abroad*, May 25–July 15, 1970, 91st Cong., 2d sess., p. 311.

63. Butterfield to HAK, 8/8/69, WHSF, CF, box 42, ND18/CO165, Vietnam, August 1969–February 1970. NP, NA.

64. Safire, *Before the Fall*, pp. 335–37.

65. *Ibid.*, p. 338.

66. News summary 4/13/71, WHSF, POF, Box 33, News summaries, April 1971, NP, NA. Richard M. Nixon, *U.S. Foreign Policy for the 1970s: A New Strategy for Peace*, pp. 62–76.

67. Haldeman notes, 5/25/71. WHSF, SMOF, Haldeman files, box 43. NP, NA.

68. *Ibid.*, 5/24/71.

69. *Ibid.*, 6/22/71.

70. News summary, 4/14/71; WHSF, POF, box 33; News summaries, April 1971. NP, NA.

71. Italics original. Haldeman notes, 6/13/71, WHSF, SMOF; Haldeman files, box 43. NP, NA.

72. *Ibid.*, 7/8/71, Haldeman, box 44.

73. *Ibid.*, 7/1/71.

74. *Ibid.*, 6/23/71. Haldeman notes, box 43. Ehrlichman notes, 6/21/71, WHSF, SMOF, Ehrlichman files, box 21. *New York Times* folder, 6/71 [1]. NP, NA.

75. Haldeman notes, 6/30/71, Haldeman files, box 44. Scali to HAK, 6/16/71, Ehrlichman files, box 21. *New York Times* folder, 6/71 [2]. NP, NA.

76. Haldeman notes, 7/7/71, Haldeman files, box 44.

77. *Ibid.*, 7/19/71.

78. *Ibid.*, 7/13/71.

79. Herring, *America's Longest War*, pp. 244–46; Gareth Porter, *A Peace Denied: The United States, Vietnam, and the Paris Agreement*, pp. 98–101; Goodman, *The Lost Peace*, pp. 111–15; *WHY*, pp. 1016–48; Szulc, *The Illusion of Peace*, pp. 226–29.

3. The Perils of Détente

1. Walter Hixson, "From Containment to Neoisolationism: The Diplomacy of George F. Kennan," Ph.D. dissertation, University of Colorado (1986), ch. 4.

2. Kissinger, *The Troubled Partnership: A Reappraisal of the Atlantic Alliance*, p. 49.

3. Newhouse, *DeGaulle and the Anglo-Saxons*, pp. 184–212.

4. Garthoff, *Détente and Confrontation*, pp. 5–8, 108–10.

5. Kissinger, *The Troubled Partnership*, p. 234; Stanley Hoffmann, *Gulliver's Troubles: Or the Setting of American Foreign Policy*, p. 539. See also Harvey Starr, *Henry Kissinger: Perceptions of International Politics*, pp. 93–126.

6. Garthoff, *Détente and Confrontation*, pp. 25–36.

7. U.S. Senate, Committee on Armed Services, *Authorization for Military Procurement, Research and Development, FY 1970, and Reserve Strength*, Part 2, April 22 and 23, 1969, 91st Cong., 1st sess.

8. Kissinger, *The Necessity for Choice: Prospects of American Foreign Policy*, p. 296.

9. Mason Willrich, *Non-Proliferation Treaty: Framework for Nuclear Arms Control*, p. 9.

10. Kissinger, *Nuclear Weapons and Foreign Policy*, p. 426.

11. Butterfield to HAK, 4/25/69 and 4/12/69, WHSF, SMOF, Haldeman files, box 50, Memos (HAK). NP, NA.

12. John Newhouse, *Cold Dawn: The Story of SALT*, pp. 66–102; Alton Frye, *A Responsible Congress: The Politics of National Security*, esp. pp. 15–46.

13. *WHY*, p. 207.

14. *Ibid.*, p. 210.

15. *Ibid.*, p. 212.

16. *Ibid.*, p. 203.

17. Schedule Proposal and memo, David Parker to H. R. Haldeman, April 8, 1971, WHSF, CF, FG 239-USACDA, 1971–74. NP, NA.

18. Smith, *Doubletalk*, pp. 60–64.

19. *Ibid.*, p. 84.

20. Roger Labrie, "Overview," in Labrie, ed., *SALT Handbook*, p. 13.

21. Huntsman to HAK, 6/1/71; WHSF, POF, box 33, NP, NA.

22. Haldeman notes, 4/13/71. WHSF, SMOF, Haldeman files, box 43, notes, April–May 19, 1971, part 1, folder. NP, NA.

23. *Ibid.*, 5/20/71.

24. *Ibid.*, 6/7/71.

25. *Ibid.*, 7/23/71, and 8/10/71, box 44.

26. Garthoff, *Détente and Confrontation*, pp. 90–93.

27. *YU*, p. 252. See also *ibid.*, pp. 235–246 for Kissinger's criticism of liberal dissenters from détente as practiced in the Nixon administration.

28. U.S. Senate, Committee on Finance, *Emigration Amendment to the Trade Reform Act of 1974*, 93d Cong., 2d sess., December 5, 1974, pp. 51–52.

29. Brandon, *The Retreat of American Power*, pp. 235–38.

30. C. Fred Bergsten to Council on Foreign Relations, Washington, D.C., April 7, 1982, "Henry Kissinger's Non-economics," *Business Week*, 1/19/74, p. 21.

31. Walt Rostow to President Johnson, 9/16/71, Post-presidential Name File, box 88. LBJL. Brandon, *The Retreat of American Power*, p. 235.

32. *Ibid.*, p. 236.

33. Smith, *Doubletalk*, pp. 62–63.

34. *Ibid.*

35. *WHY*, p. 1217.

36. Smith, *Doubletalk*, p. 222.

37. *Ibid.*

38. *Ibid.*, p. 459.

39. *Ibid.*, p. 376.

40. *WHY*, p. 1243.

41. Peter Flanigan to the President, 4/26/72, WHSF, CF, CO158, USSR, 1971–74. NP, NA.

42. Haldeman notes 10/2 and 10/26/71. WHSF, SMOF, Haldeman files, box 44. NP, NA. Raymond Price, *With Nixon*, pp. 305–6.

43. Haldeman notes, 10/4/71, 11/2/71, 10/28/71. Haldeman files, box 44; notes 1/14/72, Haldeman files, box 45.

44. "Eyes only" memorandum, President to HAK, 3/11/72. Haldeman files, box 44; Haldeman notes, Feb.–March, 1972, part 2. NP, NA.

45. Haldeman notes, 5/23, 25, 26/72. Haldeman files, box 45. NP, NA. Nixon, *RN*, pp. 609–21.

46. Garthoff, *Détente and Confrontation*, p. 189; "Basic Principles of Relations Between the United States of America and the Union of Soviet Socialist Republics," *Department of State Bulletin* (6/26/72), 898; Richard M. Nixon, *U.S. Foreign Policy for the 1970s: The Emerging Structure of Peace*, pp. 16–25; Nixon, *U.S. Foreign Policy for the 1970s: Shaping a Durable Peace*, pp. 26–41.

47. Gary Sick, *All Fall Down*, pp. 16–17.

48. *Ibid.*; James Bill, *The Eagle and the Lion: The Tragedy of American–Iranian Relations, 1941–1979*, pp. 200–210.

49. President's News Summaries, 6/20/72, p. 6. WHSF, POF, box 40; News Summaries, June 7–23, 1972, part 2. NP, NA.

50. "President Nixon and Dr. Kissinger Brief Members of Congress on Strategic Arms Limitations Agreements," *Department of State Bulletin*, 7/19/72, p. 42.

51. U.S. Senate, Committee on Foreign Relations, *Strategic Arms Limitation Agreements*, June 19–22, 1972, 92d Cong., 2d sess.

52. Congressional briefing by HAK, 6/15/72, Church papers, box 166, folder 14, BSUL.

53. U.S. Senate, Committee on Foreign Relations, *Strategic Arms Limitation Agreements*, June 19–22, 1972, 92d Cong., 2d sess.

54. U.S. Senate, Committee on Armed Services, *Military Implications of the Treaty on Limitations of Anti-Ballistic Missiles and the Interim Agreement on the Limitations of Strategic Offensive Arms*, June 20–July 8, 1972, 92d Cong., 2d sess. See also Henry M. Jackson, "A Senator Questions U.S. Concessions," *LAT*, June 25, 1972, p. F7.

55. Public Law 92-448 as amended by Sen. Jackson, approved by House on September 25 and Senate on September 30, 1972.

56. U.S. Senate, *Congressional Record*, 92d Cong., 2d sess., 1972, vol. 118, no. 138, p. 514280.

57. *Ibid.*

4. Breaching the China Wall

1. Nancy Bernkopf Tucker, *Patterns in the Dust: Chinese–American Relations and the Recognition Controversy, 1949–1950*, pp. 173–94.

2. Warren Cohen, *Dean Rusk*, p. 280.

3. Memo, President to HAK, 9/22/69. WHSF, CF, box 6, CO34, China, 1969–70. NP, NA.

4. "China: U.S. Policy Since 1945," *Congressional Quarterly*, p. 202.

5. Garthoff, *Détente and Confrontation*, pp. 243–45.

6. Donald Zagoria, *The Sino–Soviet Conflict, 1956–1961*, pp. 225–342.

7. Kissinger, *The Troubled Partnership*, p. 211.

8. Cohen, *Dean Rusk*, p. 280.

9. U.S. Senate, Committee on Foreign Relations, *U.S.–Chinese Relations*, March 1966, 89th Cong., 2d sess.

10. Walter Hixson, "From Containment to Neoisolation: The Diplomacy of George F. Kennan," Ph.D. dissertation, University of Colorado (1986), pp. 167–72.

11. "China: U.S. Policy Since 1945," p. 33.

12. *Ibid.*, p. 37.

13. Robert D. Schulzinger, *The Wise Men of Foreign Affairs: The History of the Council on Foreign Relations*, pp. 178–93. The eight volumes of the United States and China in World Affairs series, all published by McGraw-Hill, were: A. M. Halperin, ed., *Policies Toward China: Views from Six Continents* (1965); Robert Blum (A. Doak Barnett, ed.), *The United States and China in World Affairs* (1966); A. T. Steele, *The American People and China* (1966); Alexander Eckstein, *Communist China's Economic Growth and Foreign Trade: Implications for U.S. Policy* (1966); Lea A. Williams, *The Future of the Overseas Chinese in Southeast Asia* (1966); Samuel B. Griffith II, *The Chinese People's Liberation Army* (1967); Fred Greene, *U.S. Policy and the Security of Asia* (1968); Kenneth T. Young, *Negotiating with the Chinese Communists: The United States Experience, 1953–1967* (1968).

14. Garthoff, *Détente and Confrontation*, pp. 200–43.

15. Howard K. Beale, *Theodore Roosevelt and the Rise of America to World Power*, p. 187; Michael H. Hunt, *The Making of a Special Relationship: The United States and China to 1914*, pp. 189–200.

16. Congressional Quarterly, *China: U.S. Policy Since 1945*, p. 184.

17. *Ibid.*, p. 321.

18. Richard Nixon, "Asia after Vietnam," *Foreign Affairs* (October 1967), 46(1):111–26.

19. Alexis Johnson with Jef O. McAllister, *The Right Hand of Power*, pp. 516–17.

20. Szulc, *The Illusion of Peace*, pp. 405–14.

21. Garthoff, *Détente and Confrontation*, pp. 254–56; Robert G. Sutter, *China Watch: Toward U.S.–China Reconciliation*, pp. 65–70.

22. *Time*, 3/23/71.

23. "China: U.S. Policy Since 1945," p. 164.
24. Haldeman notes, 4/13/71. WHSF, CF, Haldeman files, box 43; notes April–May 19, 1971, part 1. NP, NA.
25. *WHY*, p. 711.
26. *Ibid.*, p. 1094.
27. Garthoff, *Détente and Confrontation*, pp. 243–45, 262–66; *WHY*, pp. 698–708, 733–42; Jack Anderson with George Clifford, *The Anderson Papers*, pp. 205–70; Szulc, *Illusion of Peace*, pp. 442–44.
28. Haldeman notes, 6/28/71, box 43.
29. *Ibid.*, 6/28/71, box 44; June 27–30, July 1, 1971.
30. *Ibid.*, 6/24/71, box 43.
31. *Ibid.*, 7/10/71, box 44.
32. *Ibid.*, italics original, 7/14/71, box 44; also 7/1/71.
33. "Secret Voyage of Henry K," *Time*, 7/26/71, p. 13. "Nixon: I Will Go to China," *Newsweek*, 7/26/71, pp. 16–21. Also, "Blazing the Trail to Peking," *U.S. News and World Report*, 8/2/71, p. 17.
34. *U.S. News and World Report*, 7/26/71, p. 53; *ibid.*, 11/1/71, p. 26. "With Henry Kissinger in China," *Ladies' Home Journal*, March 1972, p. 78.
35. Haldeman notes, 6/8, 5/25, and 6/10/71. WHSF, SMOF, Haldeman files, box 43. NP, NA.
36. *Ibid.*, 7/12/71.
37. *WHY*, p. 745.
38. *WHY*, pp. 745–55.
39. *WHY*, pp. 770–84.
40. Garthoff, *Détente and Confrontation*, pp. 254–56.
41. Zagoria, *Vietnam Triangle*, pp. 63–99.
42. Szulc, *Illusion of Peace*, pp. 410–14.
43. Haldeman notes, 7/13/71. WHSF, SMOF; Haldeman files, box 44. NP, NA.
44. Memo, David Parker to H. R. Haldeman, 3/13/72; H. R. Haldeman to HAK, 8/3/71, WHSF, CF, box 6, CO34, China 1971–74. NP, NA.
45. Acheson to HAK, 7/19/71, Acheson Papers, box 18, folder 226. Yale University Library. Haldeman notes, 7/16/71, WHSF, SMOF, Haldeman files, box 44. NP, NA.
46. President's News Summary, 7/19/71, p. 4, WHSF, POF, news summaries, July 1971. NP, NA.
47. *Ibid.*, p. 3.
48. Haldeman notes, 7/19/71. WHSF, SMOF, Haldeman files, box 44. NP, NA.
49. *Ibid.* Nixon, *U.S. Foreign Policy for the 1970s: The Emerging Structure of Peace*, pp. 26–31.
50. Memo, Colson to President, 7/20/71. WHSF, CF, box 65. NP, NA.
51. Haldeman notes, 7/20/71. WHSF, SMOF, Haldeman files, box 44. NP, NA.
52. *Ibid.*, 6/7/71, box 43.
53. *Ibid.*, 8/11/71, box 44. *NYT*, 8/11/71, pp. 2, 37; *ibid.*, 8/27/71, p. 5.
54. Johnson, *The Right Hand of Power*, p. 520.
55. Kissinger, *The Troubled Partnership*, p. 97.
56. Chapin to Haldeman, 10/1/71, "Eyes Only." See also Chapin to Haldeman, 7/17/71, 11/19/71, 1/28/72, WHSF, SMOF, Dwight Chapin files, box 33. NP, NA.
57. Haldeman notes, 10/14/71. WHSF, SMOF, Haldeman files, box 44. NP, NA.
58. *Ibid.*, 7/19/71, 10/27/71, 10/1/71, 10/3/71, 10/4/71, Haldeman files, box 44. NP, NA.

59. *Ibid.*, 10/30/71.
60. John Osborne, "Toilet Training," *The New Republic*, 1/1,8/72, pp. 16–17.
61. Haldeman notes, 8/6/71, 12/16/71, 12/24/71. WHSF, SMOF, Haldeman files, box 44. NP, NA.
62. *Ibid.*, 1/14/72 and 1/10/72, box 45. Anderson, *The Anderson Papers*, pp. 224–29; Nixon, *RN*, pp. 527–30.
63. *WHY*, pp. 1074–87.
64. Haldeman notes, 2/17/72, box 45.
65. Memo, administratively confidential, Higby to Chapin, 3/7/72. WHSF, CF, box 65, TR 24, China, 1971–74. NP, NA.
66. Haldeman notes, 11/2, 11/3/71. WHSF, SMOF, Haldeman files, box 44. NP, NA.
67. Hersh, *The Price of Power*, pp. 489–503.
68. "China: U.S. Policy Since 1945," p. 323.
69. *Ibid.*, p. 39.
70. Haldeman notes, 2/28/72, WHSF, SMOF; Haldeman files, box 45. NP, NA.
71. Price, *With Nixon*, p. 8.
72. Haldeman notes, 3/2, 3/21/72, WHSF, SMOF; Haldeman files, box 45. NP, NA.
73. "China: U.S. Policy Since 1945," p. 39.
74. Italics original. Haldeman notes, 7/15/71, WHSF, SMOF; Haldeman files, box 44. NP, NA. Nixon, *U.S. Foreign Policy for the 1970s: Shaping a Durable Peace*, pp. 18–21.

5. Liquidating Vietnam, 1972–1973

1. Haldeman notes, 1/1 and 1/25/72. WHSF, SMOF, Haldeman files, box 45. NP, NA.
2. James J. Best, "Kent State: Answers and Questions," Thomas R. Hensley and Jerry M. Lewis, eds., *Kent State and May 4th: A Social Science Perspective*, pp. 17–22.
3. *WHY*, pp. 282–88; Garthoff, *Détente and Confrontation*, pp. 256–61.
4. Garthoff, *Détente and Confrontation*, pp. 280–83.
5. Herring, *America's Longest War*, pp. 226–29; Dorothy C. Donnelly, "A Settlement of Sorts: Henry Kissinger's Negotiations and America's Extrication from Vietnam," *Peace and Change* (Summer 1983), 9(2/3):55–60.
6. "The Church–Case Amendment," Church Papers, box 47, folder 1. BSUL.
7. News release, 4/27/72, Church Papers, box 2, folder 9. BSUL.
8. Donnelly, "A Settlement of Sorts," p. 61.
9. *WHY*, pp. 984–1002.
10. John W. Garver, *China's Decision for Rapprochement with the United States, 1968–71*, pp. 77–83.
11. Garthoff, *Détente and Confrontation*, pp. 240–43.
12. *WHY*, pp. 1016–31.
13. Donnelly, "A Settlement of Sorts," pp. 66–70; Porter, *A Peace Denied*, pp. 79–83.
14. *WHY*, pp. 1186–97; Garthoff, *Détente and Confrontation*, p. 289–91.
15. *WHY*, pp. 505–9.
16. Haldeman, *The Ends of Power*, p. 98.

17. *WHY*, pp. 1108–24.

18. *WHY*, pp. 1197–1201; Garthoff, *Détente and Confrontation*, p. 289; Nixon, *RN*, pp. 605–8.

19. *WHY*, p. 1187.

20. Donnelly, "A Settlement of Sorts," pp. 65–67; Porter; *A Peace Denied*, p. 153.

21. *The Gallup Poll, 1972*; Theodore H. White, *The Making of the President, 1972*, pp. 235–38.

22. Herring, *America's Longest War*, pp. 250–51; Szulc, *The Illusion of Peace*, pp. 621–28.

23. Haldeman notes, 8/14 and 8/15/72. WHSF, SMOF; Haldeman files, box 46. NP, NA.

24. *Ibid.*, 8/14/72.

25. *WHY*, pp. 1301–31.

26. Szulc, *The Illusion of Peace*, pp. 611–12; Donnelly, "A Settlement of Sorts," pp. 68–70; *WHY*, p. 1304.

27. *WHY*, pp. 1301–05; Donnelly, "A Settlement of Sorts," p. 68.

28. *WHY*, pp. 1331–60.

29. L. Higby to Bart Porter and Pat O'Donnell, 7/25/72, WHSF, CF, FG 6/11/1, Kissinger folder, 1971–74. NP, NA.

30. Murrey Marder, "Kissinger Goes Public," *Washington Post*, 9/16/72, A15. Memo. David Parker to Charles Colson, 8/14/72. WHSF, CF, box 15, FG 6-11-1/Kissinger, Henry. NP, NA.

31. Herring, *America's Longest War*, p. 245.

32. *WHY*, pp. 1366–74.

33. Herring, *America's Longest War*, p. 247.

34. Stanley Karnow, *Vietnam: A History*, pp. 649–51.

35. *WHY*, pp. 1378–92; Karnow, *Vietnam*, p. 651.

36. *Department of State Bulletin*, October 30, 1972.

37. Haldeman notes, 10/15/72. WHSF, SMOF; Haldeman files, box 46. NP, NA.

38. Haldeman, *The Ends of Power*, p. 94; *WHY*, pp. 1406–08.

39. *WHY*, pp. 1406–11.

40. Oriana Fallaci, *Interview with History*, p. 41.

41. Haldeman, *The Ends of Power*, p. 117.

42. Hamilton Fish Armstrong, "Isolated America," *Foreign Affairs*, October 1972, copy with President's handwriting in WHSF, POF, box 19, November 1972. NP, NA.

43. Fallaci, *Interview with History*, p. 30.

44. Haldeman notes, 1/14/73. WHSF, SMOF; Haldeman files, box 47. NP, NA.

45. *WHY*, pp. 1411–15; Arnold R. Isaacs, *Without Honor: Defeat in Vietnam and Cambodia*, pp. 5–7; Nguyen Tien Hung and Jerrold Schechter, *The Palace File*, pp. 107–19; Porter, *A Peace Denied*, pp. 138–44.

46. Herring, *America's Longest War*, p. 253; Szulc, *The Illusion of Peace*, pp. 635–36.

47. Nixon, *RN*, p. 735.

48. Karnow, *Vietnam*, p. 653; *Nation*, 1/5/83, p. 2.

49. *Nation*, 216, 1/1/73, p. 2; Martin F. Herz assisted by Leslie Rider, *The Prestige Press and the Christmas Bombing, 1972: Images and Reality in Vietnam*, pp. 15–21.

50. *Time*, 1/1/73, p. 13.

51. U.S. House, Committee on International Affairs, Subcommittee on Asian and Pacific Affairs, *U.S. Aid to North Vietnam*, 95th Cong., 1st sess., July 19, 1977, p. 5; Hung and Schechter, *The Palace File*, pp. 120–26.

52. U.S. House, Committee on Foreign Affairs, *The Situation in Indochina*, 93d Cong., 1st sess., February 6–March 6, 1973, p. 101.

53. *Ibid.*, pp. 102–03.

54. Memorandum for the President, Herbert Klein to President, 2/3/73. WHSF, SMOF, Ziegler files, box 27, Vietnam, 2/73, part 1. NP, NA.

6. Securing the Prize: Kissinger as Secretary of State

1. George Ball, "A Vote for Kissinger," *Newsweek*, 11/20/72, p. 21.

2. Stephen Ambrose, *Eisenhower: The President*, 2:423–26; Ambrose, *Nixon*, pp. 525–27; Herbert Parmet, *Jack*, pp. 499–523; Henry Jackson, ed., *The Organization of United States Foreign Affairs*.

3. Haldeman, *The Ends of Power*, p. 120; Ehrlichman, *Witness to Power*, p. 330; *WHY*, p. 1409.

4. *YU*, pp. 3–5, 414–23; John Dean, *Blind Ambition*, pp. 194–205; Woodward and Bernstein, *All the President's Men*, p. 282.

5. *Time*, 1/27/73; *Newsweek*, 1/27/73.

6. White, *Breach of Faith*, pp. 222–49.

7. *CSM*, 8/24/73, p. 3; Elizabeth Drew, *Washington Journal, The Events of 1973– 1974*, pp. 4–5.

8. Garthoff, *Détente and Confrontation*, p. 335.

9. *Ibid.*, p. 341.

10. *Time*, 9/3/73, p. 14; *Newsweek*, 9/3/73, p. 14; *U.S. News and World Report*, 9/3/73 p. 21. See also *Chicago Tribune*, 8/24/73, p. 16.

11. *CSM*, 8/24/73, ed. and p. 1; *ibid.*, 8/30/73, ed.; *ibid.*, 9/5/73, ed. *New Yorker*, 9/17/73, p. 20.

12. U.S. Senate, Committee on Foreign Relations, *Nomination of HAK to be Secretary of State*, 93 Cong., 1st sess., part 1, September 7, 10, 11, and 14, 1973; p. 4; *YU*, p. 425–33.

13. *CSM*, 9/8/73, p. 1.

14. Stanley Karnow, "Secretary Kissinger," *The New Republic* (169) 9/22/73, p. 19.

15. Church in re HAK nomination, 9/20/73, Church Papers, box 154, folder 3. BSUL.

16. "The Talk of the Town," *New Yorker*, 9/17/73, p. 21.

17. U.S. Senate, *Nomination of HAK*, p. 151.

18. *Newsweek*, 12/10/73, p. 62.

19. Benjamin Welles, "Revival at State," *CSM*, 10/25/73, ed.

20. *CSM*, 10/6/72, p. 1; *ibid.*, 9/26/73, ed.

21. Franck and Wiesband, *Foreign Policy by Congress*, p. 13.

22. *YU*, p. 356.

23. U.S. Senate, *Nomination of HAK*, p. 313.

24. Paul Sigmund, *The Overthrow of Allende and the Politics of Chile*, p. 113; HAK to Secretary of State and Defense, Director of Central Intelligence, Chairman

of Joint Chiefs of Staff, NSSM97, 7/21/70, *Declassified Documents Reference System*, 1978, 244D.

25. *WHY*, pp. 653, 670–78; Hersh, *The Price of Power*, pp. 277–96; Thomas Powers, *The Man Who Kept the Secrets: Richard Helms and the CIA*, p. 227.

26. Sigmund, *The Overthrow of Allende*, p. 120; Powers, *The Man Who Kept the Secrets*, pp. 225–26. U.S. Senate Select Committee on Intelligence, *Alleged Assassination Plots Involving Foreign Leaders*, Interim report, 94th Cong., 1st sess., November 20, 1975, pp. 225–54.

27. U.S. Senate, Select Committee on Intelligence, *Covert Action in Chile, 1963–1973*. Staff report, 94th Cong., 1st sess., December 18, 1975, *passim*.

28. Korry to William Rogers, 9/29/71, *Declassified Documents Reference System*, 1978, 397A; Sulzberger, *The World and Richard Nixon*, p. 63.

29. Sigmund, *The Overthrow of Allende*, pp. 188–201.

30. David F. Cusack, *The Internal and International Dynamics of Conflict and Confrontation in Chile, Monograph Series in World Affairs*, Graduate School of International Studies, University of Denver (1976), 14:4, pp. 35–38.

31. *WHY*, p. 683.

32. Jerome Levinson and Juan de Onis, *The Alliance that Lost Its Way*, pp. 215–306.

33. Anthony Sampson, *The Sovereign State of ITT*, pp. 284–313.

34. *Ibid.*, pp. 301–13.

35. White, *Breach of Faith*, pp. 178, 200.

36. *WHY*, pp. 678–83; William Bundy, "Who Lost Patagonia? Foreign Policy in the 1980 Election Campaign," *Foreign Affairs* (Fall 1979) 58 (1):1–3.

37. William Colby and Peter Forbath, *Honorable Men: My Life in the CIA*, pp. 302–06; Cusack, "The Internal and International Dynamics of Conflict and Confrontation in Chile," pp. 51–53.

38. Richard Fagen, "The U.S. and Chile: Roots and Branches," *Foreign Affairs* (1975), 53 (2):300–4.

39. *WHY*, pp. 681–83.

40. *NYT*, 10/17/73, p. 11; 10/24/73, p. 3.

41. Trudy Rubin, "Nobel Award Draws Fire," *CSM*, 10/18/73, p. 7.

42. "Honoring the Cause of Peace," *LAT*, 10/17/73, II6.

7. America Enters the Middle East

1. Steven Spiegel, *The Other Arab–Israeli Conflict: Making America's Mideast Policy from Truman to Reagan*, p. 220.

2. Garthoff, *Détente and Confrontation*, pp. 385–93, 405–8; Spiegel, *The Other Arab–Israeli Conflict*, pp. 220–83.

3. *WHY*, pp. 341–80; William B. Quandt, *Decade of Decisions: American Policy Toward the Arab–Israeli Conflict, 1967–76*, pp. 72–77.

4. Quandt, *Decade of Decisions*, pp. 65–70; Seth Tillman, *The United States in the Middle East*, pp. 56–57.

5. Michael Brecher, *Decisions in Crisis: Israel 1967 and 1973*, pp. 254–85.

6. Quandt, *Decade of Decisions*, pp. 128–37.

7. *WHY*, pp. 558–94.

8. Quandt, *Decade of Decisions*, p. 138.

9. *Ibid.*, pp. 140–64.

10. *Ibid.*, pp. 152–64; Tillman, *United States Policy in the Middle East*, p. 56; Spiegel, *The Other Arab–Israeli Conflict*, pp. 166–200.

11. Alan Dowty, *Middle East Crisis: U.S. Decision-Making in 1958, 1970 and 1973*, pp. 182–98, 334–38.

12. Chaim Herzog, *The War of Atonement*, pp. 11–15.

13. Quandt, *Decade of Decisions*, pp. 72–104.

14. Abba Eban, *An Autobiography*, pp. 461–69; Quandt, *Decade of Decision*, pp. 76–71.

15. Herzog, *The War of Atonement*, p. 15–18.

16. Jean LaCouture, *Nasser*, pp. 347–50; Anwar Sadat, *In Search of Identity*, pp. 208–11.

17. Sadat, *In Search of Identity*, p. 228; Mohammed Heikal, *The Road to Ramadam*, pp. 160–65.

18. Sadat, *In Search of Identity*, pp. 233–37; Garthoff, *Détente and Confrontation*, pp. 361–62.

19. Golda Meir, *My Life*, pp. 422–24. Herzog, *The War of Atonement*, pp. 55–77.

20. *YU*, pp. 450–76.

21. Spiegel, *The Other Arab–Israeli Conflict*, pp. 256–57.

22. *YU*, pp. 507–15.

23. Galia Golan, *Yom Kippur and After: The Soviet Union and the Middle East Crisis*, pp. 65–73.

24. "Some Middle East Facts," *CSM*, 10/16/73, ed.; "Moscow Recoups Its Losses," *ibid.*, 10/17/73, ed.; *ibid.*, 10/23/73, p. 1.

25. *Ibid.*, 10/26/73, p. 1.

26. *YU*, p. 552; Garthoff, *Détente and Confrontation*, pp. 368–71.

27. Garthoff, *Détente and Confrontation*, pp. 370–75.

28. *Ibid.*, p. 375; *YU*, p. 571.

29. *YU*, p. 583.

30. *YU*, p. 591; Garthoff, *Détente and Confrontation*, p. 380.

31. *CSM*, 10/27/73, pp. 1, and ed.

32. "The People Should Be Told," *LAT*, 10/30/73, II, 6; "Right Action in the Middle East," *ibid.*, 10/26/73, II, 6.

33. Peter Lakeland to Jacob Javits, 11/27/73, Javits Papers, series 9, subseries 4, box 9, folder, Javits autobiography, Middle East, 1969–1980, Javits Papers. Melville Library, SUNY, Stony Brook, Thomas P. O'Neill with William Novak, *Man of the House: The Life and Political Memoirs of Speaker Tip O'Neill*, pp. 253–54.

34. "Mr. Kissinger's Trumps," *CSM*, 11/1/73, ed.

35. Garthoff, *Détente and Confrontation*, pp. 393–98.

36. Richard B. Mancke, *Squeaking By: U.S. Energy Policy since the Embargo*, pp. 47–66, 93–104; Neil de Marchi, "Energy Policy under Nixon: Mainly Putting out Fires," in Craufurd D. Goodwin, ed., *Energy Policy in Perspective: Today's Problems, Yesterday's Solutions*, pp. 456–65; *YU*, pp. 866–96.

37. Spiegel, *The Other Arab–Israeli Conflict*, p. 271.

38. Matti Golan, *The Secret Conversations of Henry Kissinger: Step by Step Diplomacy in the Middle East*, pp. 27–70.

39. *YU*, pp. 614–23, 747–49.

40. *YU*, pp. 750–54; Golan, *The Secret Conversations of Henry Kissinger*, pp. 101–05.

41. *Time*, 12/24/73, pp. 32, 33.
42. "The Road of Neighbors," *CSM*, 11/12/73, ed.
43. Sadat, *In Search of Identity*, p. 219.
44. Spiegel, *The Other Arab–Israeli Conflict*, p. 274.
45. Quoted in *ibid.*, p. 275.
46. Golan, *The Secret Conversations of Henry Kissinger*, p. 195.
47. Edward Sheehan, *The Arabs, Israelis and Kissinger: A Secret History of American Diplomacy in the Middle East*, p. 124.
48. U.S. House, Committee on International Relations, *Middle East Agreements*, 94th Cong., 1st sess., September 8, 1975, p. 4.
49. Garthoff, *Détente and Confrontation*, p. 406.
50. Spiegel, *The Other Arab–Israeli Conflict*, p. 312; Ishaq I. Ghanayem and Alden H. Voth, *The Kissinger Legacy: American Middle East Policy*, pp. 159–65.

8. Nixon's Fall and Kissinger's Triumph

1. *NOTP*, 1/1/74, p. 1.
2. "Kissinger: Less Fun but More Awe," *Time*, 12/24/73, p. 36.
3. "Nixon on Kissinger's Coattails," *CSM*, 1/2/74, p. 1.
4. *CSM*, 2/5/74, ed.
5. The Return of the Magician," *Time*, 3/11/74, p. 41.
6. "Kissinger Breaks Syria Stalemate," *CSM*, 2/28/74, p. 1.
7. Gina Lollobrigida, "Kissinger Close-up," *Ladies' Home Journal*, 3/74, p. 68.
8. *Newsweek*, 4/1/74, p. 33. See also *Chicago Tribune*, 3/31/74, p. 1; 4/3/74, p. 20.
9. David Alpern, "Henry's Frantic Year," *SR/World*, 4/20/74, p. 14.
10. Garthoff, *Détente and Confrontation*, pp. 409–13, 435–37; *YU*, 979–85.
11. *LAT*, 3/29/74, II, p. 6.
12. U.S. Senate, Committee on Foreign Relations, *Détente*, 93d Cong., 1st sess., August 15, 20, and 21, September 10, 12, 18, 19, 24, and 25, and October 1, and 8, 1974, pp. 373, 377.
13. *Ibid.*, pp. 257–58.
14. *Ibid.*, p. 265.
15. Garthoff, *Détente and Confrontation*, pp. 431–35.
16. *Ibid.*, pp. 393–98; Harry Gelman, *The Brezhnev Politburo and the Decline of Détente*, pp. 137–51.
17. Adam Ulam, *Dangerous Relations: The Soviet Union in World Politics*, p. 100.
18. Woodward and Bernstein, *The Final Days*, pp. 106–7.
19. John Dean, *Blind Ambition*, pp. 16–17.
20. "Nixon to the Mideast," *CSM*, 6/5/74, ed.
21. U.S. Senate, Committee on Foreign Relations, *Dr. Kissinger's Role in Wiretapping*, July 10, 15, 16, 23, and 30, and September 10, and 17, 1974, 93d Cong., 2d sess., p. 9; *YU*, pp. 1111–23.
22. U.S. Senate, *Dr. Kissinger's Role in Wiretapping*, p. 7.
23. Ehrlichman, *Witness to Power*, pp. 260–65; Jonathan Schell, *The Time of Illusion*, pp. 101–15; U.S. Senate, *Dr. Kissinger's Role in Wiretapping*, p. 7.
24. U.S. Senate, p. 9.
25. "Kissinger Blows his Cool," *Newsweek*, 6/24/74, p. 24.
26. "A New Possibility in the Mideast," *LAT*, 5/30/74, IIp. 6.
27. "Mideast Peace Breakthrough," *CSM*, 5/21/74, ed.; "Mideast Peace Op-

portunity," *CSM*, 5/31/74, ed.; "Kissinger Inquiry, Not Ingratitude," *LAT*, 6/12/74, II, p. 6.

28. "Kissinger Blows His Cool," *Newsweek*, 6/24/74, p. 26.

29. "Congress Support of Kissinger Rising," *CSM*, 6/13/74, p. 1; "The Kissinger Crisis," *CSM*, 6/13/74, ed.; *Chicago Tribune*, 6/14/74, p. 16.

30. Statement by Sen. J. W. Fulbright, 6/14/74. Church Papers, box 2, folder 9. BSUL.

31. "Abstracts of News Analysis Regarding the Alleged Role of HAK in Wiretaps," Luella Christopher, Congressional Research Service, to Senate Foreign Relations Committee, 7/8/74. Javits Papers, Series 4, Subseries 2, box 64, Kissinger wiretapping folder, 1974. Melville Library, SUNY, Stony Brook.

32. U.S. Senate, *Dr. Kissinger's Role in Wiretapping*, p. x.

33. Sadat, *In Search of Identity*, p. 277; Richard Valeriani, *Travels with Henry*, pp. 248–280.

34. Valeriani, *Travels with Henry*, pp. 201–47; Garthoff, *Détente and Confrontation*, pp. 436–37; *YU*, pp. 1101–09.

35. Garthoff, *Détente and Confrontation*, pp. 416–31; *YU*, 1020–28.

36. *Department of State Bulletin* (April 8, 1974), 70:353.

37. Ulam, *Dangerous Relations*, pp. 122–23; Committee on Foreign Relations, *Détente*, 1974, p. 212.

38. Garthoff, *Détente and Confrontation*, pp. 425–31.

39. Joseph Kraft, "Kissinger is Steering a Reckless Course," *LAT*, 7/15/74, II.5; Joseph Harsch, "Kissinger Warns the Big Powers," *CSM*, 7/9/74, p. 1.

40. "A Meager Summit," *CSM*, 7/5/74, ed.; "The Third Summit," *ibid.*, 6/25/74, ed.; *Chicago Tribune*, 7/4/74, p. 11.

41. Joseph Harsch, "Why U.K. Hardly Noticed Kissinger," *CSM*, 7/9/74, p. 1; "New Start with Old Allies," *ibid.*, ed.

42. *YU*, pp. 1179–87.

43. Laurence Stern, *The Wrong Horse: The Politics of Intervention and the Failure of American Diplomacy*, pp. 63–73.

44. *Ibid.*, p. 64.

45. *YU*, pp. 1187–93.

46. *CSM*, 7/19/74, p. 1.

47. U.S. House, Committee on Foreign Affairs, *Cyprus–1974*, August 19–20, 1974, 93d Cong., 2d sess., p. 80.

48. *Ibid.*, p. 82.

49. *YU*, p. 510; Roger Morris, *Haig, The General's Progress*, pp. 287–88.

50. Woodward and Bernstein, *The Final Days*, pp. 236–37; *YU*, pp. 1193–1200.

51. Woodward and Bernstein, *The Final Days*, pp. 341–43.

52. *YU*, pp. 128–95.

53. White, *Breach of Faith*, pp. 309–13; Woodward and Bernstein, *The Final Days*, pp. 454–55; New York Times, *The End of a Presidency*, p. 276; Nixon, *RN*, pp. 1076–78.

54. *YU*, pp. 1204–14.

55. "The Nixon Years," *CSM*, 8/12/74, ed.

56. Gerald R. Ford, *A Time to Heal: The Autobiography of Gerald R. Ford*, pp. 229–30.

57. Joseph Harsch, "Kissinger Keeps U.S. Policy Course in Domestic Storm," *CSM*, 9/13/74, pp. 1, 8.

58. Harsch, "Kissinger under Fire," *CSM*, 9/20/74, p. 1; Dev Muraka, "Soviets Fret over Future of Kissinger," *ibid.*, 9/23/74, p. 1, Dana Adams Schmidt, "Diplomats Worry about Kissinger," *ibid.*, 9/24/74, pp. 1, 10. "Harris Poll on HAK," *Chicago Tribune*, 8/18/74, p. 22.

59. "Balance on Kissinger," *CSM*, 9/24/74, ed.

60. Reston interview, *NYT*, 10/16/74, p. 1.

61. Dana Adams Schmidt, "Diplomacy on the Run," *CSM*, 10/18/74, p. 2; "Kinetic Kissinger," *ibid.*, 10/23/74, ed. "Kissinger as Diplomatic Dervish," *LAT*, 11/11/74, II.4.

62. Scowcroft to Brooke, 11/16/74. WHCF, box 32, FO6-2 SALT, 8/9/74–10/31/75, executive folder. GRFL.

63. Ed Savage to Ron Nessen, 11/18/74. Ron Nessen Papers, box 59, 11/17–24/74, Alaska, Japan, Korea, USSR, wire stories. GRFL.

64. "Ford–Brezhnev 'Breakthrough'" *CSM*, 11/25/74; William Hyland, *Mortal Rivals: Superpower Relations from Nixon to Reagan*, pp. 90–97.

65. "Danger in an Arms Debate?" *LAT*, 12/10/74, II.6.

66. "Whose Triumph?" *Wall Street Journal*, 12/2/74. In Ron Nessen Papers, box 29, SALT folder. GRFL.

67. Meeting with George Meany, Top Secret, 11/27/74. WHCF, box 32, FO6-2 SALT, 8/9/74–10/31/74, executive folder. GRFL.

68. Lodal to HAK, 1/22/75. WHCF, box 32, FO6-2, SALT, 8/9/74–10/31/75, executive folder, GRFL.

9. The End in Vietnam

1. Garthoff, *Détente and Confrontation*, pp. 256–62.

2. Karnow, *Vietnam: A History*, p. 659; Hung and Schechter, *The Palace File*, p. 246.

3. Murray Kempton, "The Magician," *Progressive*, (2/75), 39: 47.

4. "Death of a Salesman," *Commonweal*, 3/14/75, p. 444.

5. Joseph Harsch, "Keeping Kissinger," *CSM*, 2/27/75, ed.

6. Isaacs, *Without Honor*, pp. 101–53; Hung and Schechter, *The Palace File*, pp. 246–49.

7. Franck and Wiesband, *Foreign Policy by Congress*, p. 19.

8. *Ibid.*, P. Edward Haley, *Congress and the Fall of South Vietnam and Cambodia*, pp. 28–47.

9. "Kissinger on Aid to Cambodia, Israel," *CSM*, 2/26/75, p. 1, "Kissinger Moves to Shore Up U.S. World Influence," *CSM*, 3/27/75, p. 1. "Home to Roost," *Nation* (4/5/75) 220(2):338. "Kissinger's Peace Mirage," *Newsweek*, 3/31/75; pp. 40–41; "A World of Woes," *Newsweek*, 4/7/75, p. 20.

10. "A World of Woes," *Newsweek*, 4/7/75, pp. 18–20. "US Policy in Triple Trouble," *CSM*, 3/24/75, pp. 1, 4.

11. "Can Kissinger Tame Congress?" *U.S. News and World Report*, 2/17/75, p. 30.

12. "Kissinger and Congress," *CSM*, 1/22/75, ed. See also Joseph C. Harsch, "Kissinger Congress Struggle: an Analysis," *CSM*, 2/7/75, p. 1.

13. *Miami Herald*, 4/15/75, p. 20-A, Copy in WHCF, box 4, CO1-Indochina. GRFL.

14. Press secretary's Q and A, 4/21/75, Ron Nessen Papers, box 123, HAK folder, GRFL.

15. Cronkite interview, 4/21/75; *ibid.*

16. U.S. House, Committee on International Relations, *The Vietnam–Cambodia Emergency, 1975,* 94th Cong., 1st sess., March 6, 1975, pp. 291, 302; Haley, *Congress and the Fall of South Vietnam and Cambodia,* pp. 116–24.

17. Gelb and Betts, *The Irony of Vietnam,* pp. 324–31.

18. *YU,* pp. 9–13.

19. Ford, *A Time to Heal,* pp. 270–73.

20. Committee on International Affairs, *The Vietnam–Cambodia Emergency, 1975,* p. 313.

21. Franck and Wiesband, *Foreign Policy by Congress,* pp. 61–82; *YU,* pp. 510–14.

22. Franck and Wiesband, *Foreign Policy by Congress,* pp. 13–19; Haley, *Congress and the Fall of South Vietnam and Cambodia,* pp. 156–63.

23. "NSC Talking Points," 4/75. WHCF, box 4, CO 1 Indochina. GRFL.

24. U.S. House, Committee on Appropriations, Subcommittee on Foreign Assistance, *Aid to Cambodia and Vietnam,* 94th Cong., 1st sess., February 3, 1975, p. 97.

25. *Ibid.,* p. 111.

26. Wolthuis to Friedersdorf, 3/3/75. John Marsh files, box 43, Vietnam, congressional trip 2–3/75. GRFL.

27. Kissinger, "Meeting with Members of Congress," 3/5/75 (administratively confidential). WHCF, box 15, FO3-2 3/1–3/24/75, Executive. GRFL. Gary Hart to constituents, March 28, 1975 (on aid to Vietnam and Cambodia), Gary Hart Papers, Office administration, box 3, memo #31, Gary Hart Papers. Western History Collection, Norlin Library, University of Colorado, Boulder. Haley, *Congress and the Fall of South Vietnam and Cambodia,* pp. 80–92, 147–48.

28. Nessen to Rumsfeld, 4/8/75. Richard Cheney files, box 13, Vietnam, general, 3/25–4/8/75. GRFL.

29. Franck and Wiesband, *Foreign Policy by Congress,* p. 39; HAK, Interview, *LAT,* 4/28/75, p. 1.

30. Kendall to Friedersdorf, 4/12/75, WHCF, box 36, ND18/CO165, executive, 4/15–4/23/75. GRFL.

31. Isaacs, *Without Honor,* pp. 313–20.

32. Committee on International Affairs, *The Vietnam–Cambodia Emergency, 1975,* pp. 134–35.

33. *Time,* 4/15/85, p. 31.

34. Pool Report with AF 1, New Orleans–Washington, 4/23/75. Ron Nessen Papers, box 62, New Orleans (1). GRFL.

35. John Osborne, "Footnotes," *The New Republic,* 5/3/75, p. 11.

36. Ford to Sparkman, 4/25/75. WHCF, box 36, ND18/CO165, 4/24/75–4/30/75, executive. GRFL.

37. "Henry Makes the Best of It," *Time,* 5/12/75, p. 19.

38. Anthony Lewis, "Hubris, National and Personal," *The New Republic,* 5/3/75, p. 19.

39. John Osborne, "Kissinger and Ford," *The New Republic,* 4/26/75, p. 6.

40. Peter Lisagor, "Ford's Aides Blame Kissinger," *LAT,* 4/13/75, XI.6.

41. Dana Adams Schmidt, "U.S. Reappraising Basic Strategies," *CSM,* 3/25/75, p. 1; Joseph Harsch, "Kissinger and the Era of U.S. Pullback," *ibid.,* 3/27/75, p. 1; "Redefining America's Role," *ibid.,* 4/1/75, ed.

42. Joseph Harsch, "Dr. Kissinger's Environment," *CSM*, 7/29/75. "The Need for Kissinger," *LAT*, 4/20/75, VI.2.

43. Richard G. Head, Frisco W. Short, and Robert C. McFarlane, *Crisis Resolution: Presidential Decision Making in the Mayaguez and Korean Confrontations*, pp. 102–5.

44. Franck and Wiesband, *Foreign Policy by Congress*, pp. 68–71; Jacob Javits, "War Powers Reconsidered," *Foreign Affairs* (1985) 64:1, pp. 130–40. Harold Hyman, *Quiet Past and Stormy Present? War Powers in American History; Bicentennial Essays on the Constitution*, pp. 50–59; *YU*, pp. 510–14; U.S. Senate, Committee on Foreign Relations, *War Powers Legislation*, 92d Cong., 1st sess., March 8, 9, 24, 25, April 23, and 26, May 14, July 26, and 27, and October 6, 1971, pp. 135–37.

45. Jerry Jones to HAK, 5/6/75. James Connor files, box 30, Brent Scowcroft (NSC) 1975 (1). GRFL.

46. Godfrey Sperling, "Ford to Assume Role as Top Foreign Policy Maker," *CSM*, 5/5/75, p. 1.

47. Carroll Hubbard news release, 5/15/75. Ron Nessen Papers, box 14, Mayaguez, general. GRFL.

48. Friedersdorf to Ford, 5/14/75 and 5/16/75; Jones to Rumsfeld, 5/15/75. WHCF, box 32, ND18/CO26, executive, 8/9/74–5/15/75. GRFL.

49. Kendall to Friedersdorf, 5/13/75, 6/12/75. John Marsh files, box 20, Mayaguez 5–8/75. GRFL.

50. Head, Short and McFarlane, *Crisis Resolution*, p. 104.

51. Committee on International Affairs, *The Vietnam–Cambodia Emergency, 1975*, p. 345.

52. William Stearman to HAK, 4/30/75, WHCF, box 4, CO-1, Indochina. GRFL.

53. James E. Miller, "Taking Off the Gloves: The United States and the Italian Elections of 1948," *Diplomatic History* (Winter 1983), pp. 35–56. U.S. Senate, Select Committee on Intelligence, *Alleged Assassination Plots Involving Foreign Leaders*. Colby, *Honorable Men*, pp. 389–424.

54. U.S. House, Select Committee on Intelligence, *U.S. Intelligence Agencies and Activities*, 94th Cong., 1st sess., October 31, 1975, pp. 840–41.

55. *NYT*, 10/14/75, p. 5; U.S. Senate, Committee on Foreign Relations, *Foreign Service Promotion List*, 94th Cong., 2d sess., February 5, 1976, pp. 26–33, *YU*, pp. 442–46.

56. Ford to Pike, 11/19/75, WHCF, box 38, FG 6-11-1, HAK, GRFL.

57. Daniel Shorr, *Clearing the Air*, pp. 193–95; "The CIA Report the President Doesn't Want You to Read," *Village Voice*, 2/16/76, pp. 21–44.

10. The Decline of Détente, 1975–1976

1. U.S. House, Committee on Appropriations, Subcommittee on Foreign Operations, *Foreign Assistance Appropriations for 1976*, 94th Cong., 1st sess., November 14, 1975, p. 51.

2. "What European Trip Has Done for Ford," *CSM*, 6/2/75, p. 1. "Mr. Ford Goes to Europe," *ibid.*, 5/27/75, ed. "Why Kissinger Woos Grass-Roots Support," *ibid.*, 6/25/75, p. 1; "Kissinger Goes to People to Strengthen His Hand," *ibid.*, 7/17/75, p. 4.

3. Garthoff, *Détente and Confrontation*, pp. 468–73.

4. *Ibid.*, pp. 473–82. Remarks on East–West Trade for Use by the President at

the Economic Summit, 5/6/76. William Seidman files, box 189, HAK, 5/6/76 folder, WHCF. GRFL.

5. Garthoff, *Détente and Confrontation* pp. 473–79; John J. Moresca, *To Helsinki: The Conference on Security and Cooperation in Europe*, pp. 21–28.

6. "The Press and Foreign Policy," Panel Discussion before Subcommittee on Future Foreign Policy Research and Development, Committee on International Relations, House, 94th Cong., 1st sess., Sept. 24, 1975, pp. 4, 46.

7. "Ford Aides Play Down Helsinki," *CSM*, 7/29/75, p. 3; "Helsinki Agreement: Something for All," *ibid.*, 7/30/75, p. 1; "The Helsinki Texts," *ibid.*, 8/5/75, ed; "Kissinger Looking Beyond Helsinki to SALT II," *ibid.*, 8/1/75, p. 26.

8. "Henry in Decline," *Newsweek*, 3/1/76, p. 84; George W. Ball, "Kissinger's Paper Peace," *Atlantic*, 2/76, 237:43.

9. Tele. VFW to Ford, 7/25/75. Dennis Clift to Jeanne Davis, 8/25/75. WHCF, box 57, TR34–3, Helsinki, executive, 7/29–8/2/75. Tele. Americans to Free Captive Nations to President, 7/23/75. Wayne Adams to Ford, 7/26/75, WHCF, box 58, TR34–3, Helsinki, general. GRFL.

10. Jackson to HAK, 8/22/75; Les Janka to Marsh, 9/9/75; Marsh to the Files, 2/10/76; Eagleburger to Secretary, 8/23/75. Secret, John Marsh Files, box 31, SALT folder. GRFL.

11. HAK to Ford, 5/11/75. John Marsh files, box 84, NSC 9/74–2/76 folder. GRFL.

12. HAK to Ford, 5/2/75. John Marsh files, box 93, Brent Scowcroft 11/74–5/75 folder, GRFL.

13. *NYT*, 8/15/75, p. 1.

14. HAK press conference, 9/9/75. Ron Nessen Papers, box 26, State–HAK press conferences (1). GRFL.

15. Garthoff, *Détente and Confrontation*, pp. 453–71.

16. U.S. Senate, Committee on Armed Services, *FY 1975 Authorization for Military Procurement*, Hearings before the Senate Committee on Armed Services, 93d Cong., 2d sess., February 5, 1974, p. 9.

17. U.S. Senate, Committee on Armed Services, *FY 1975 Authorization for Military Procurement*, 94th Cong., 1st sess., March 21, 1975, p. 1084.

18. *Ibid.*, p. 1115.

19. *Ibid.*

20. Garthoff, *Détente and Confrontation*, pp. 441–42.

21. Press conference, 11/3/75. Gergen files, box 5, HAK folder, GRFL.

22. "Kissinger vs. Schlesinger," *National Review*, 11/21/75, p. 1281.

23. *Fortune* 12/75, p. 91. "The Shadow over Ford," *LAT*, 11/11/75, II.6; "Ford's Sunday Massacre: The New Doubts," *ibid.*, 11/5/75, II.5; cf. "The Pushout," *ibid.*, 11/4/75, II.4. "The Case Against Kissinger," *Aviation Week and Space Technology*, 12/8/75, p. 7.

24. *Youngstown Vindicator*, 11/4/75. *Charleston Evening Post*, 11/4/75, "Exit for Kissinger?" *Wall Street Journal*, 11/5/75; "Halloween Massacre," *ibid.*, 11/4/75. *Savannah Post*, 11/4/75. "Kissinger Prevails," *Omaha World Herald*, 11/4/75, Ron Nessen Papers, box 1, administration shakeup, 11/75, media reaction (1). GRFL.

25. "Behind the Shake-up: Ford Tightens Grip," *CSM*, 11/4/75, p. 1, 2; "Ford's Shake-up," *ibid.*, 11/5/75, ed. Colby, *Honorable Men*, pp. 7–11.

26. "Why Kissinger Stays Away from Congress," *CSM*, 11/17/75, p. 3.

27. U.S. House, Committee on International Relations, Subcommittee on Fu-

ture Foreign Policy Research and Development, *The Future of U.S. Foreign Policy*, 94th Cong., 1st sess., November 1975, p. 22.

28. *Ibid.*, p. 28.

29. *Ibid.*, p. 29.

30. *Ibid.*, p. 55.

31. *Ibid.*, p. 57.

32. "Coolness in Peking," *CSM*, 10/24/75, ed.

33. "Teng Warns Ford on Risk of Détente with Soviets," *CSM*, 12/2/75, p. 1; *ibid.*, 12/3/75, p. 1, 11; "Questions about U.S.–China Triangle," *ibid.*, 12/5/75, p. 1.

34. Nessen notes, 12/1/75. Ron Nessen Papers, box 73, 11/22–12/8/75, China-General, (1). GRFL.

35. HAK press conference, 12/4/75, *ibid.*

36. "Kissinger Pushing Ford on China," n.d. [1975], Nessen Papers, box 122, China 8/9/74–1/20/77.

37. China, 10/20/75. Nessen Papers, box 122, China, 8/9/74–1/20/77. See also First Line Report, 10/24/75. Nessen Papers, box 133, Donald Rumsfeld, 7/75–11/75 (2) folder, Secretary in Tokyo to Secretary of State, 10/18/75. GRFL.

38. John Marcum, *The Angolan Revolution*, vol. 2: *Exile Politics and Guerrilla Warfare (1962–1976)*, pp. 245–46.

39. Garthoff, *Détente and Confrontation*, pp. 519–26.

40. U.S. Senate, Committee on Foreign Affairs, Subcommittee on African Affairs, *Hearings on Angola*, 94th Cong., 2d sess., January 29, February 3, 4, and 6, 1976, pp. 23–26, Henry Kissinger, "Building an Enduring Foreign Policy," *Department of State Bulletin*, (12/15/75), 1903:843. Roger Morris, "The Proxy War in Angola: Pathology of a Blunder," *The New Republic*, 1/31/76, p. 20; Nathaniel Davis, "The Angola Decision of 1975: A Personal Memoir," *Foreign Affairs* (Fall 1978):111–14; John Stockwell, *In Search of Enemies: A CIA Story*, p. 67; "Secretary Kissinger's News Conference of December 23, 1975," *Department of State Bulletin* (1/19/76), 1908:76; Colin Legum, "Angola and the Horn of Africa," in Stephen S. Kaplan, *Diplomacy of Power: Soviet Armed Forces as a Political Instrument*, pp. 593–94.

41. "Kissinger Takes Angola Policies to Public," *CSM*, 12/24/75, p. 1.

42. Peter Lakeland to Javits, 2/5/76, Javits Papers, Series 4, Subseries 2, box 63, HAK folder. Melville Library, SUNY-Stony Brook. See also Gary Hart to John Stennis, March 25, 1976. Hart Papers, Personal Office, box 11, Armed Service Committee folder, Western History Collection. Norlin Library, University of Colorado, Boulder.

43. "Angola and Détente," *CSM*, 12/24/75, ed.

44. "Cautious Hope for SALT Pact," *CSM*, 1/23/75, p. 3. Kissinger press conference, 1/23/76. Ron Nessen Papers, box 26, State—Kissinger press conferences (3). GRFL.

45. "Moynihan Salvo Rekindles UN Dispute," *CSM*, 1/29/76, p. 5; "Moynihan—Exit the Gladiator," *ibid.*, 2/4/76, ed.

46. Walter LaFeber, *The Panama Canal: The Crisis in Historical Perspective*, pp. 160–95; J. Michael Hogan, *The Panama Canal in American Politics: Domestic Advocacy and the Evolution of Policy*, pp. 57–82, 114–16. Stephen Rosenfeld, "The Panama Negotiations," *Foreign Affairs* (October 1975), 54 (1):1–13.

47. George Moffett III, *The Limits of Victory: The Ratification of the Panama Canal Treaties*, pp. 19–47.

48. Jules Witcover, *Marathon, 1972–1976: The Pursuit of the Presidency*, pp. 410–21.

49. Myron Kuropas to Jack Marsh, 3/26/76; Scowcroft to Marsh, 3/26/76. Marsh files, box 13, Eastern Europe folder. GRFL.

50. Buckley to Ford, 3/22/76; Scowcroft to Cheney, 3/27/76; Janka and Cliff to Scowcroft, 3/30/76. Marsh files, box 84, NSC 3/4–31/76. GRFL.

51. Proposed reply regarding Sonnenfeldt doctrine, 4/20/76; Scowcroft to Buckley, 6/18/76, WHCF, box 5, CO1-4, Communist bloc 4/1/76–1/20/77; Charles Leppert to Henry Helstoski, 4/23/76; WHCF, box 5, CO1-5 Eastern Europe folder. GRFL.

52. Reagan's TV address, 3/31/76. WHSF, box 6, Panama Canal, April 17, 1976 (3) folder. GRFL.

53. Reagan—Issues, Foreign Affairs, Ron Nessen Papers, box 3. GRFL.

54. Statement by Ronald Reagan at Orlando, Florida, 3/4/76. Robert Hartmann Files, Box 26, Ronald Reagan folder. Bud McFarlane, NSC, Response to Reagan Speech, *ibid.*, box 40, Reagan speech 3/31/76 folder. GRFL.

55. *Ibid.*

56. Reagan to Ohio voters, 6/76. WHCF, box 16, PL-Reagan, 4/1/76–1/20/77. GRFL.

57. Press conference transcripts, 3/12, 3/13, 4/9/76. David Gergen files, box 5, HAK folder. GRFL.

58. William Broomfield et al. to Ford, 3/3/76; Russ Rourke to Marsh, 6/1/76, John Marsh files, box 85, NSC6/76 folder. GRFL.

59. Stef Halper to David Gergen, 4/20/76. Gergen files, box 8, Solzhenitzyn folder. GRFL. Robert T. Hartmann, *Palace Politics: An Inside Account of the Ford Years*, p. 338.

60. "The Hostility Toward Solzhenitsyn," n.d. [8/75]. Ron Nessen Papers, box 26, Solzhenitsyn folder, GRFL.

61. John Davenport to Marsh, 5/8/76. John Marsh files, box 108, Davenport folder. GRFL.

62. Goldwater to HAK, 5/28/76; Marsh to Cheney [n.d.], John Marsh files, box 7, China, PRC folder. Goldwater to HAK, 4/29/76. John Marsh files, box 93, Scowcroft folder, 3/76–6/76. GRFL.

63. U.S. China Policy, 7/26/76. Nessen Papers, box 122, China 8/9/74–1/20/77. GRFL.

64. Sidney Kraus, ed., *The Great Debates: Carter vs. Ford, 1976*, p. 477.

65. Carter on the conduct of foreign policy, Carter's basic attack, 9/76. David Gergen files, box 16, debate background, foreign policy folder. GRFL.

66. UPI, issues—Kissinger, 10/3/76, the president has seen. WHSF, box 2, HAK as Issue folder. GRFL.

67. Kraus, ed., *The Great Debates*, p. 480.

68. NSC debate briefing book (1), WHSF, box 2. GRFL.

69. HAK, n.d. [10/76], *ibid.*

70. NSC debate briefing book (2), *ibid.*

71. Ford notes on briefing, 9/76. WHSF, box 2. GRFL.

72. Ford notes on briefing, *ibid.*, and briefing cards. WHSF, box 3. GRFL.

73. Ford's briefing cards, 9/76. WHSF, box 3. GRFL.

74. Debate briefing cards, 9/76. *ibid.*

75. SALT, Q and A, 9/76. WHSF, box 3, 3d debate issue papers. GRFL.

76. HAK PC, 10/15/76. WHSF, box 3, 3d debate issue papers. GRFL.
77. *Ibid.*
78. *Ibid.*

11. Kissinger in Retrospect

1. Gaddis Smith, *Morality, Reason and Power: American Diplomacy in the Carter Years*, pp. 34–45.
2. U.S. House, Committee on Foreign Affairs, *Arms Sales to Iran*, 99th Cong., 2d sess., December 8, 1986, testimony of Secretary of State George P. Shultz.
3. Spiegel, *The Other Arab–Israeli Conflict*, p. 311.

BIBLIOGRAPHY

Manuscript Collections

Dean Acheson Papers, Sterling Memorial Library. Yale University, New Haven, Connecticut

Hanson W. Baldwin Papers, Sterling Memorial Library. Yale University, New Haven, Connecticut

Patrick Buchanan Files. NP, NA

Dwight Chapin Files. NP, NA

Richard Cheney Files. GRFL

Frank Church Papers. BSUL

James Connor Files. GRFL

Council on Foreign Relations, Records of Groups. Council on Foreign Relations Archives, New York

Diary Cards. LBJL

John Ehrlichman Files. NP, NA

David Gergen Files. GRFL

H. R. Haldeman Files. NP, NA

Gary Hart Papers, Western History Collection. Norlin Library, University of Colorado, Boulder

Robert Hartmann Files. GRFL

Jacob Javits Papers. Melville Library, State University of New York, Stony Brook

William Kendall Files. GRFL

John Macy Files. LBJL

John Marsh Files. GRFL

National Security Files. John F. Kennedy Library, Boston

Ron Nessen Files. GRFL

Ron Nessen Papers. GRFL

Post-Presidential Name File. LBJL

Presidential Handwriting Files. GRFL

President's Office Files. NP, NA

President's Office Files. John F. Kennedy Library, Boston

President's Personal Files. NP, NA

William Seidman Files. GRFL

Special Files Unit. GRFL
White House Central Files. GRFL
White House Central Files. LBJL
White House Central Files. NP, NA
White House Special Files. NP, NA
Ronald Ziegler Files. NP, NA

Published Government Documents

Bi-partisan Presidential Commission on Central America. *Report.* Washington, D.C.:
GPO, 1984.
Declassified Documents Reference System. Aberdeen, Md. Carrolton Press, 1978–1987.
Nixon, Richard M. *U.S. Foreign Policy for the 1970s: A New Strategy for Peace.*
Washington, D.C.: GPO, 1970.
—— *U.S. Foreign Policy for the Seventies: Building for Peace.* Washington, D.C.:
GPO, 1971.
—— *U.S. Foreign Policy for the 1970s: The Emerging Structure of Peace.* A Report
to Congress, February 9, 1972. Washington, D.C.: GPO, 1972.
—— *U.S. Foreign Policy for the 1970s: Shaping a Durable Peace.* Washington, D.C.:
GPO, 1972.
U.S. Congress. Joint Economic Committee. *The 1974 Economic Report of the
President.* 93d Cong., 2d sess., 1974.
U.S. Department of State. *Bulletin* (1969–1977).
U.S. House. Committee on Appropriations. *Foreign Assistance and Related Agencies
Appropriations for 1975.* 94th Cong., 1st sess., 1975.
—— *Foreign Agencies and Related Appropriations for 1976.* 94th Cong., 1st sess.,
1975.
—— *Department of Defense Appropriations for 1976.* 94th Cong., 1st sess., 1975.
U.S. House. Committee on Armed Services. *Department of Defense Energy Re-
sources and Requirements.* 93d Cong., 2d sess., 1974.
—— *Military Posture, 1974.* 93d Cong., 2d sess., 1974.
—— *Military Posture, 1976.* 94th Cong., 2d sess., 1976.
—— *Inquiry into the Alleged Involvement of the Central Intelligence Agency in the
Watergate and Ellsberg Matters.* 94th Cong., 1st sess., 1974.
U.S. House. Committee on the Budget. *FY 1976 Budget and Economic Report.* 94th
Cong., 1st sess., 1975.
U.S. House. Committee on Foreign Affairs. *Agreement on Limitations of Strategic
Offensive Weapons.* 92d Cong., 2d sess., 1972.
—— *Hearings on Arms Sales to Iran.* 99th Cong., 2d sess., December 8, 1986.
—— *Cyrpus, 1974.* 93d Cong., 2d sess., 1974.
—— *FY 1975 Foreign Assistance Request.* 93d Cong., 2d sess., 1974.
—— *Foreign Assistance Act of 1972.* 92d Cong., 2d sess., 1972.
—— *Situation in Indochina.* 93d Cong., 1st sess., 1973.
—— *To Amend the Foreign Assistance Act of 1961.* 91st Cong., 2d sess., 1970.
—— (Congressional Research Service, Library of Congress). *U.S. Foreign Policy for
the 1970s.* 92d Cong., 2d sess., 1972.
—— *U.S. Forces in NATO.* 93d Cong., 1st sess., 1973.
U.S. House. Committee on International Relations. *Middle East Agreements and the
Early Warning System in Sinai.* 94th Cong., 1st sess., 1975.
—— *The Press and Foreign Policy.* 94th Cong., 1st sess., 1975.

—— *Report of Secretary of State Kissinger on His Trip to Latin America.* 94th Cong., 2d sess., 1976.

—— *U.S. Aid to North Vietnam.* 95th Cong., 1st sess., 1977.

—— *United States-Soviet Union-China: The Great Power Triangle.* 94th Cong., 1st and 2d sessions, 1975–1976.

—— *The Vietnam-Cambodia Emergency, 1975.* 94th Cong., 2d sess., 1976.

—— *The War Powers Resolution, 1976.* 94th Cong., 2d sess., 1976.

U.S. House. Committee on the Judiciary. *Nomination of Nelson A. Rockefeller to be Vice President of the United States.* 93d Cong., 2d sess., 1974.

U.S. House. Select Committee on Intelligence. *U.S. Intelligence Agencies and Activities: Domestic Intelligence Programs.* 94th Cong., 1st sess., 1975.

—— *The Performance of the Intelligence Community.* 94th Cong., 1st sess., 1975.

—— *Risks and Control of Foreign Intelligence.* 94th Cong., 1st sess., 1975.

U.S. Senate. Committee on Armed Services. *FY 1975 Authorization for Military Procurement.* 93d Cong., 2d sess., 1974.

—— *FY 1976 Authorization for Military Procurement.* 94th Cong., 1st sess., 1975.

—— *Military Manpower Issues of the Past and Future.* 93d Cong., 2d sess., 1974.

—— *Nomination of James R. Schlesinger to be Secretary of Defense.* 93d Cong., 1st sess., 1973.

—— *Transmittal of Documents from the National Security Council to the Chairman of the Joint Chiefs of Staff.* 93d Cong., 2d sess., 1974.

U.S. Senate. Committee on Appropriations. *Department of Defense Appropriations, FY 1975.* 93d Cong., 2d sess., 1974.

—— *Department of Defense Appropriations, FY 1976.* 94th Cong., 1st sess., 1975.

—— *Foreign Assistance and Related Programs, FY 1973.* 92d Cong., 2d sess., 1972.

—— *State, Justice, Commerce, the Judiciary and Related Agencies Appropriations, FY 1975.* 93d Cong., 2d sess., 1974.

U.S. Senate. Committee on the Budget. *1976 First Concurrent Resolution on the Budget.* 94th Cong., 1st sess., 1975.

U.S. Senate. Committee on Finance. *Emigration Amendment to the Trade Reform Act of 1974.* 93d Cong., 2d sess., 1974.

U.S. Senate. Committee on Foreign Relations. *Briefing on Counterforce Attacks.* 93d Cong., 2d sess., 1974.

—— *Briefing on Major Foreign Policy Questions.* 93d Cong., 1st sess., 1973.

—— *Détente.* 93d Cong., 2d sess., 1974.

—— *Dr. Kissinger's Role in Wiretapping.* 93d Cong., 2d sess., 1974.

—— *Effects of Limited Nuclear Warfare.* 94th Cong., 1st sess., 1975.

—— *Nomination of Henry A. Kissinger to be Secretary of State.* 93d Cong., 1st sess., 1973.

—— *Nuclear Weapons and Foreign Policy.* 93d Cong., 2d sess., 1974.

—— *U.S. Forces in Europe.* 93d Cong., 1st sess., 1973.

—— *U.S.-USSR Strategic Policies.* 93d Cong., 2d sess., 1974.

—— *War Powers Legislation.* 93d Cong., 1st sess., 1973.

U.S. Senate. Committee on Government Operations. *The National Security Council* (Comments by Henry A. Kissinger). 91st Cong., 2d sess., 1970.

—— *Oversight of U.S. Government Intelligence Functions.* 94th Cong., 2d sess., 1976.

—— Subcommittee on National Security Policy Machinery. *Organizing for National Security* (Interim Report), 86th Cong., 2d sess., 1960.

U.S. Senate. Committee on the Judiciary. *Crisis in Cyprus, 1975.* 94th Cong., 1st sess., 1975.

—— *Executive Privilege: The Withholding of information by the Executive.* 92d Cong.,
1st sess., 1971.
U.S. Senate. Select Committee on Presidential Campaign Activities. *Presidential
Campaign Activities of 1972.* 93d Cong., 1st sess., 1973.
U.S. Senate. Select Committee Intelligence. *Alleged Assassination Plots Involving
Foreign Leaders.* 94th Cong., 1st sess., 1975.
—— *Covert Action in Chile.* 94th Cong., 1st sess. 1975.

Newspapers, Newsmagazines, and Journals of Opinion

Chicago Tribune (1969–1977)
Christian Science Monitor (1969–1977)
Los Angeles Times (1969–1977)
The Nation (1968–1977)
National Review (1968–1977)
New Orleans Times Picayune (1969–1977)
The New Republic (1968–1977)
Newsweek (1968–1977)
New York Times (1969–1977)
Time (1968–1977)
U.S. News and World Report (1968–1977)
Washington Post (1969–1977)

Books and Articles

Alpern, David. "Henry's Frantic Year." *SR/World*, April 4, 1974.
Ambrose, Stephen E. *Eisenhower: The President*, vol. 2. New York: Simon and
Schuster, 1984.
—— *Nixon: The Education of a Politician, 1913–1962.* New York: Simon and
Schuster, 1987.
Anderson, Jack with George Clifford. *The Anderson Papers.* New York: Random
House, 1973.
Armstrong, Hamilton Fish. "Power in a Sieve." *Foreign Affairs*, July 1968.
Astor, Gerald. "Strategist in the White House Basement." *Look*, August 12, 1969.
Ball, George W. "Kissinger's Paper Peace." *Atlantic*, February 1976.
Barnds, William. *China and America: The Search for a New Relationship.* New York:
New York University Press, 1977.
Beale, Howard K. *Theodore Roosevelt and the Rise of America to World Power.*
Baltimore: Johns Hopkins University Press, 1956.
Bellow, Saul. *Him with His Foot in His Mouth.* New York: Viking, 1984.
Beloff, Nora. "Professor Bismarck Goes to Washington," *Atlantic*, December 1969.
Bender, Gerald. "Kissinger in Angola: Anatomy of a Failure." In René Lemardine,
ed., *Africa: The Stakes and the Stance.* 2d ed. Washington: University Press of
America, 1981.
Bergsten, C. Fred. *The Dilemmas of the Dollar.* New York: New York University
Press, 1976.
Berman, Larry. *Planning a Tragedy: The Americanization of the War in Vietnam.*
New York: Norton, 1982.
Berman, William. *William Fulbright and the Vietnam War: The Dissent of a Political
Realist.* Kent: Kent State University Press, 1987.

Best, James J. "Kent State: Answers and Questions." In Thomas A. Hensley and Jerry M. Lewis, eds., *Kent State and May 4th: A Social Science Perspective*, pp. 17–22. Dubuque: Kendall Hunt, 1978.

Bill, James. *The Eagle and the Lion: The Tragedy of American–Iranian Relations.* New Haven: Yale University Press, 1988.

Blum, Robert (A. Doak Barnett, ed.). *The United States and China in World Affairs.* New York: McGraw-Hill, 1966.

Blumenfeld, Ralph et al. *Henry Kissinger: The Private and Public Story.* New York: New American Library, 1974.

Brandon, Henry. *The Retreat of American Power.* New York: Norton, 1973.

Brecher, Michael. *Decisions in Crisis: Israel, 1967 and 1973.* Berkeley: University of California Press, 1980.

Brown, Seyom. *The Crises of Power: An Interpretation of United States Foreign Policy in the Kissinger Years.* New York: Columbia University Press, 1979.

—— *The Faces of Power: Constancy and Change in United States Foreign Policy from Truman to Reagan.* New York: Columbia University Press, 1983.

Bundy, William P. "Who Lost Patagonia?: Foreign Policy in the 1980 Campaign," *Foreign Affairs*, Fall 1979.

"The Case Against Kissinger." *Aviation Week and Space Technology*, December 1975.

Cohen, Warren. *Dean Rusk.* Totowa, N.J.: Cooper Square, 1980.

Colby, William and Peter Forbath, *Honorable Men: My Life in the CIA.* New York: Simon and Schuster, 1978.

Congressional Quarterly. *China: United States Policy Since 1945.* Washington: Congressional Quarterly, 1980.

Cusak, David F. *The Internal and International Dynamics of Conflict and Confrontation in Chile.* Monograph Series in World Affairs. Graduate School of International Studies, University of Denver, 1976.

Dallek, Robert. *The American Style of Foreign Policy: Cultural Politics and Foreign Affairs.* New York: Knopf, 1983.

D'Auria, Gregory T. "Present at the Rejuvenation: The Association of Dean Acheson and Richard Nixon." *Presidential Studies Quarterly*, Spring 1988.

Davis, Nathaniel. "The Angola Decision of 1975: A Personal Memoir." *Foreign Affairs*, Fall 1978.

Dean, John. *Blind Ambition.* New York: Simon and Schuster, 1975.

"Death of A Salesman." *Commonweal*, March 14, 1975.

DeBenedetti, Charles. "On the Significance of Civilian Peace Activism: America, 1961–1975." *Peace and Change*, Summer 1983.

—— *The Peace Reform in American History.* Bloomington: Indiana University Press, 1980.

de Marchi, Neil. "Energy Policy Under Nixon: Mainly Putting Out Fires." In Crauford D. Goodwin, ed., *Energy Policy in Perspective: Today's Problems, Yesterday's Solutions.* Washington, D.C.: Brookings Institution, 1981.

Destler, I.M. *Presidents, Bureaucrats and Foreign Policy.* Princeton: Princeton University Press, 1971.

—— "The Nixon System, Another Look." *Foreign Service Journal*, February 1974.

"Détente Study Fueled Kissinger/Schlesinger Feud." *Aviation Week and Space Technology*, November 10, 1975.

Dickson, Peter. *Kissinger and the Meaning of History.* New York: Cambridge University Press, 1979.

Donnelly, Dorothy C. "A Settlement of Sorts: Henry Kissinger's Negotiations and America's Extrication from the War in Vietnam," *Peace and Change,* Summer 1983.

Dowty, Alan. *Middle East Crisis: U.S. Decisionmaking in 1958, 1970 and 1973.* Berkeley: University of California Press, 1984.

Drew, Elizabeth. *Washington Journal: The Events of 1973–1974.* New York: Random House, 1975.

Eban, Abba. *An Autobiography.* New York: Random House, 1977.

Eckstein, Alexander. *Communist China's Economic Growth and Foreign Trade: Implications for U.S. Policy.* New York: McGraw-Hill, 1966.

Ehrlichman, John. *Witness to Power.* New York: Simon and Schuster, 1982.

Fagen, Richard. "The U.S. and Chile: Roots and Branches." *Foreign Affairs,* Spring, 1975.

Fallaci, Oriana. *Interview with History.* New York: Liverwright, 1976.

Ford, Gerald R. *A Time to Heal: The Autobiography of Gerald R. Ford.* New York: Harper and Row, 1979.

Franck, Thomas and Edward Wiesband. *Foreign Policy by Congress.* New York: Oxford University Press, 1979.

Frye, Alton. *A Responsible Congress: The Politics of National Security.* New York: McGraw-Hill, 1975.

Fulbright, J. William. *Old Myths and New Realities.* New York: Random House, 1964.

Garthoff, Raymond L. *Détente and Confrontation: American-Soviet Relations from Nixon to Reagan.* Washington: Brookings Institution, 1985.

Garver, John W. *China's Decision for Rapprochement with the United States, 1968–1971.* Boulder: Westview Press, 1982.

Gelb, Leslie with Richard K. Betts. *The Irony of Vietnam: The System Worked.* Washington: Brookings Institution, 1979.

Gelman, Harry. *The Brezhnev Politburo and the Decline of Détente.* Ithaca: Cornell University Press, 1984.

Ghanayem, Ishaq I. and Alden H. Voth. *The Kissinger Legacy: American Middle East Policy.* New York: Praeger, 1984.

Golan, Galia. *Yom Kippur and After: The Soviet Union and the Middle East Crisis.* Cambridge: Cambridge University Press, 1977.

Golan, Matti. *The Secret Conversations of Henry Kissinger: Step by Step Diplomacy in the Middle East.* New York: Bantam, 1976.

Goodman, Alan E. *The Lost Peace: America's Search for a Negotiated Settlement of the Vietnam War.* Stanford: Hoover Institution Press, 1978.

Graubard, Stephen. *Kissinger: Portrait of a Mind.* New York: Norton, 1973.

Greene, Fred. *U.S. Policy and the Security of Asia.* New York: McGraw-Hill, 1968.

Griffith, Samuel B. II. *The Chinese People's Liberation Army.* New York: McGraw-Hill, 1967.

Haldeman, H. R. with Joseph DiMona. *The Ends of Power.* New York: Times Books, 1978.

Haley, P. Edward. *Congress and the Fall of South Vietnam and Cambodia.* East Brunswick, N.J.: Farleigh Dickinson University Press, 1982.

Hallett, Douglas. "Kissinger *Dolossus*: The Domestic Politics of SALT." *Yale Review,* December 1975.

Halperin, A. M., ed. *Politics toward China: Views from Six Continents.* New York: McGraw-Hill, 1965.

Hamby, Alonzo. *Liberalism and Its Challengers.* New York: Oxford University Press, 1985.

Hartmann, Robert T. *Palace Politics: An Inside Account of the Ford Years.* New York: McGraw-Hill, 1980.

Head, Richard G., Frisco W. Short, and Robert C. McFarlane. *Crisis Resolution: Presidential Decisionmaking in the Mayaguez and Korean Confrontations.* Boulder: Westview Press, 1978.

Heikal, Mohammed. *The Road to Ramadam.* New York: New York Times Books, 1975.

Heller, Joseph. *Good as Gold.* New York: Viking, 1973.

"Henry Kissinger's Non-economics," *Business Week,* January 19, 1974.

Herring, George C. *America's Longest War: The United States and Vietnam, 1950–1975.* 2d ed. New York: Knopf, 1985.

—— *The Secret Diplomacy of the Vietnam War: The Negotiating Volumes of the Pentagon Papers.* Austin: University of Texas Press, 1983.

Hersh, Seymour. *The Price of Power: Kissinger in the Nixon White House.* New York: Summit Books, 1983.

Herz, Martin F., assisted by Leslie Rider. *The Prestige Press and the Christmas Bombing, 1972: Images and Reality in Vietnam.* Washington: Ethics and Public Policy Center, 1980.

Herzog, Chaim. *The War of Atonement.* Jerusalem: Steinmatzky, 1975.

Hodgson, Godfrey. *America in Our Time: From World War II to Nixon.* New York: Random House, 1976.

Hoffmann, Stanley. "The Doctor of Foreign Policy." *New York Review of Books,* December 5, 1979.

—— *Gulliver's Troubles: Or, the Setting of American Foreign Policy.* New York: McGraw-Hill, 1966.

—— *Primacy of World Order: Foreign Policy Since the Cold War.* New York: McGraw-Hill, 1978.

Hogan, J. Michael. *The Panama Canal in American Politics: Advocacy and the Evolution of Policy.* Carbondale: Southern Illinois University Press, 1986.

Hung, Nguyen Tien and Jerrold Schechter. *The Palace File.* New York: Harper and Row, 1986.

Hunnebelle, Diane. "Henry Kissinger and Me." *Ladies' Home Journal,* August 1972.

Hunt, Michael. *The Making of a Special Relationship: The United States and China to 1914.* New York: Columbia University Press, 1984.

Hyland, William G. *Mortal Rivals: Superpower Relations from Nixon to Reagan.* New York: Random House, 1987.

Hyman, Harold. *Quiet Past and Stormy Present?: War Powers in American History.* Washington: American Historical Association, 1986.

Isaacs, Arnold R. *Without Honor: Defeat in Vietnam and Cambodia.* Baltimore: Johns Hopkins University Press, 1983.

Jackson, Henry. *The Organization of United States Foreign Affairs.* New York: Praeger, 1961.

Javits, Jacob. "War Powers Reconsidered." *Foreign Affairs,* Fall, 1985.

Johnson, U. Alexis with Jef O. McAllister. *The Right Hand of Power.* Englewood Cliffs: Prentice-Hall, 1984.

Kalb, Marvin. "Nancy Kissinger: My Life with Henry." *Ladies' Home Journal,* April 1975.

Kalb, Marvin and Bernard Kalb. *Kissinger.* Boston: Little, Brown, 1973.

Karnow, Stanley. *Vietnam: A History.* New York: Viking, 1983.

Katz, Milton S. *Ban the Bomb: A History of SANE, the Committee for a Sane Nuclear Policy.* Westport: Greenwood Press, 1986.

Kempton, Murray. "The Magician." *Progressive,* February 1975.

Kennan, George F. *American Diplomacy, 1900–1950.* Chicago: University of Chicago Press, 1951.

—— *Realities of American Foreign Policy.* Princeton: Princeton University Press, 1954.

"Kissinger Deliberately Concealed SALT Violations, Zumwalt Claims." *Aviation Week and Space Technology,* December 8, 1975.

Kissinger, Henry A. *A World Restored: Metternich, Castlereagh, and the Restoration of Europe, 1812–1822.* Boston: Houghton Mifflin, 1957.

—— *The Necessity for Choice: Prospects for American Foreign Policy.* New York: Harper and Row, 1961.

—— *Nuclear Weapons and Foreign Policy.* New York: Harper and Row, 1957.

—— "Reflections on American Diplomacy." *Foreign Affairs,* (October 1956).

—— "Strategy and Organization." *Foreign Affairs,* April 1957.

—— *The Troubled Partnership: A Reappraisal of the Atlantic Alliance.* New York: Harper and Row, 1965.

—— "The Vietnam Negotiations." *Foreign Affairs,* January 1969.

—— *White House Years.* Boston: Little, Brown, 1979.

—— *Years of Upheaval.* Boston: Little, Brown, 1982.

Kraft, Joseph. "In Search of Kissinger." *Harper's,* January 1971.

Kraus, Stanley, ed. *The Great Debates: Carter versus Ford, 1976.* Bloomington: Indiana University Press, 1979.

Labrie, Roger, ed. *SALT Handbook.* Washington: American Enterprise Institute, 1979.

LaCouture, Jean. *Nasser.* New York: Knopf, 1970.

LaFeber, Walter. *The Panama Canal: The Crisis in Historical Perspective.* New York: Oxford University Press, 1979.

Landau, David. *Kissinger: The Uses of Power.* Boston: Houghton Mifflin, 1972.

Legum, Colin. "Angola and the Horn of Africa." In Stephen S. Kaplan, ed., *Diplomacy of Power: Soviet Armed Forces as a Political Instrument.* Washington: Brookings Institution, 1981.

Levinson, Jerome and Juan de Onis. *The Alliance that Lost its Way.* Chicago: Quadrangle, 1970.

Litwak, Robert S. *Détente and the Nixon Doctrine: American Foreign Policy, 1969–1976.* New York: Cambridge University Press, 1984.

Lollobrigida, Gina. "Kissinger Close Up." *Ladies' Home Journal,* July 1974.

Luttwak, Edward and Walter Lacquer. "Kissinger and the Yom Kippur War." *Commentary,* December 1974.

Mancke, Richard B. *Squeaking By: U.S. Energy Policy Since the Embargo.* New York: Columbia University Press, 1976.

Marcum, John. *The Angolan Revolution.* Vol. II. *Exile Politics and Guerrilla Warfare.* Cambridge: MIT Press, 1978.

Matusow, Allen J. *The Unraveling of America: A History of Liberalism in the 1960s.* New York: Harper and Row, 1984.

Mee, Charles L., Jr. "Terminal Madness." *Horizon,* Autumn 1976.

Meir, Golda. *My Life.* New York: Putnam, 1975.

Mellen, Joan. *Privilege: The Enigma of Sasha Bruce.* New York: NAL Books, 1982.

Moffett, George III. *The Limits of Victory: The Ratification of the Panama Canal Treaties.* Ithaca: Cornell University Press, 1985.

Moresca, John J. *To Helsinki: The Conference on Security and Cooperation in Europe.* Durham: Duke University Press, 1987.

Morgenthau, Hans J. *In Defense of the National Interest: A Critical Examination of U.S. Foreign Policy.* New York: Knopf, 1951.

—— *Politics Among Nations: The Struggle for Power.* 6th ed. New York: Knopf, 1985.

Morris, Roger. "Kissinger and the Media: A Separate Peace." *Columbia Journalism Review,* May–June 1974.

—— *Haig: The General's Progress.* New York: Harper and Row, 1982.

—— *Uncertain Greatness: Henry Kissinger and American Foreign Policy.* New York: Harper and Row, 1976.

Neustadt, Richard. *Presidential Power.* New York: Wiley, 1960.

Newhouse, John. *DeGaulle and the Anglo-Saxons.* New York: Viking, 1970.

—— *Cold Dawn: The Story of SALT.* New York: Holt, Rinehart, and Winston, 1973.

New York Times. *The End of a Presidency.* New York: Bantam, 1974.

Niebuhr, Reinhold. *The Children of Light and the Children of Darkness.* New York: Scribner's, 1944.

—— *The Irony of American History.* New York: Scribner's, 1952.

Nixon, Richard M. "Asia After Vietnam." *Foreign Affairs,* October 1967.

—— *RN: The Memoirs of Richard Nixon.* New York: Grosset and Dunlap, 1978.

O'Neill, Thomas P., with William Novak. *Man of the House: The Life and Political Memoirs of Speaker Tip O'Neill.* New York: Random House, 1987.

Osgood, Robert E. et al. *Retreat from Empire? The First Nixon Administration.* Baltimore: Johns Hopkins University Press, 1973.

Parmet, Herbert S. *Jack: The Struggles of John F. Kennedy.* New York: Dial Press, 1984.

—— *JFK. The Presidency of John F. Kennedy.* New York: Penguin, 1984.

"People are Talking About . . ." *Vogue,* June 1974.

Porter, Gareth. *A Peace Denied: The United States, Vietnam and the Paris Agreements.* Bloomington: Indiana University Press, 1975.

Powers, Thomas. *The Man Who Kept the Secrets: Richard Helms and the CIA.* New York: Knopf, 1979.

Price, Raymond. *With Nixon.* New York: Viking, 1977.

Quandt, William B. *Decade of Decisions: American Policy Toward the Arab–Israeli Conflict, 1967–1976.* Berkeley: University of California Press, 1977.

Randle, Robert. *Geneva, 1954: The Settlement of the Indochina War.* Princeton: Princeton University Press, 1969.

Rosenfeld, Stephen S. "The Panama Negotiations: A Close Run Thing." *Foreign Affairs,* October 1975.

Sadat, Anwar. *In Search of Identity.* New York: Harper and Row, 1977.

Safire, William. *Before the Fall: An Inside Look at the Pre-Watergate White House.* Garden City, N.Y.: Doubleday, 1975.

Sampson, Anthony. *The Sovereign State of ITT.* New York: Fawcett, 1974.

Schechter, Jerrold. "Henry Kissinger: Not So Secret Swinger." *Life,* January 28, 1972.

Schell, Jonathan. *The Time of Illusion.* New York: Knopf, 1976.

Schlesinger, Arthur M., Jr. *A Thousand Days: John F. Kennedy in the White House.* Boston: Houghton-Mifflin, 1965.

Schoenbaum, Thomas. *Waging Peace and War: Dean Rusk in the Truman, Kennedy, and Johnson Years.* New York: Simon and Schuster, 1988.

Schulzinger, Robert D. *The Wise Men of Foreign Affairs: The History of the Council on Foreign Relations.* New York: Columbia University Press, 1984.

Shawcross, William. *Sideshow: Kissinger, Nixon and the Destruction of Cambodia.* New York: Simon and Schuster, 1979.

Shawn, Wallace. *Aunt Dan and Lemon.* New York: Grove Press, 1985.

Sheehan, Edward. *The Arabs, Israelis and Kissinger: A Secret History of American Diplomacy in the Middle East.* New York: Reader's Digest Press, 1976.

Shorr, Daniel. *Clearing the Air.* Boston: Houghton Mifflin, 1977.

Sick, Gary. *All Fall Down: America's Tragic Ecounter with Iran.* New York: Penguin, 1986.

Sigmund, Paul. *The Overthrow of Allende and the Politics of Chile.* Pittsburgh: University of Pittsburgh Press, 1977.

Small, Melvin. *Johnson, Nixon, and the Doves.* New Brunswick: Rutgers University Press, 1988.

Smith, Gaddis. *Morality, Reason and Power: American Diplomacy in the Carter Years.* New York: Hill and Wang, 1986.

Smith, Gerard. *Doubletalk: The Untold Story of SALT.* Garden City, N.Y.: Doubleday, 1981.

Smith, Michael Joseph. *Realist Thought From Weber to Kissinger.* Baton Rouge: Louisiana State University Press, 1986.

Spiegel, Steven. *The Other Arab–Israeli Conflict: Making America's Middle East Policy from Truman to Reagan.* Chicago: University of Chicago Press, 1985.

Starr, Harvey. *Henry Kissinger: Perceptions of World Politics.* Lexington: University Press of Kentucky, 1983.

Steele, A. T. *The American People and China.* New York: McGraw-Hill, 1966.

Stern, Laurence. *The Wrong Horse: The Politics of Intervention and the Failure of American Diplomacy.* New York: Times Books, 1977.

Stevenson, Richard. *The Rise and Fall of Détente.* Champaign: University of Illinois Press, 1985.

Steward, J. "The New Mrs. Kissinger." *McCall's,* March 1974.

Stockwell, John W. *In Search of Enemies: A CIA Story.* New York: Norton, 1978.

Stoessinger, John. *Henry Kissinger: The Anguish of Power.* New York: Norton, 1976.

Stroud, Kandy. "New Mrs. Kissinger." *Ladies' Home Journal,* March 1974.

Sulzberger, C. L. *The World and Richard Nixon.* New York: Prentice-Hall, 1987.

Sutter, Robert G. *China Watch: Toward Sino–American Reconciliation.* Baltimore: John Hopkins University Press, 1978.

Szulc, Tad. *The Illusion of Peace: Foreign Policy in the Nixon–Kissinger Years.* New York: Viking, 1979.

"The Talk of the Town." *New Yorker,* September 17, 1973.

Tillman, Seth. *The United States in the Middle East.* Bloomington: Indiana University Press, 1985.

Tucker, Nancy Bernkopf. *Patterns in the Dust: Chinese–American Relations and the Recognition Controversy, 1949–1950.* New York: Columbia University Press, 1983.

Ulam, Adam. *Dangerous Relations: The Soviet Union in World Politics.* New York: Oxford University Press, 1983.

"Unraveling Issues in the Schlesinger Firing." *Fortune*, December 1975.

Valeriani, Richard. *Travels with Henry*. Boston: Houghton Mifflin, 1979.

—— "That Kissinger Dog." *Ladies' Home Journal*, June 1976.

White, Theodore H. *Breach of Faith: The Fall of Richard Nixon*. New York: Reader's Digest, 1975.

—— *The Making of the President, 1960*. New York: Atheneum, 1962.

—— *The Making of the President, 1972*. New York: Atheneum, 1973.

Williams, Lea A. *The Future of the Overseas Chinese in Southeast Asia*. New York: McGraw-Hill, 1966.

Willrich, Mason. *Non-Proliferation: Framework for Nuclear Arms Control*. Charlottesville: Michie, 1969.

Wills, Garry. *Nixon Agonistes*. New York: NAL Books, 1979.

Witcover, Jules. *Marathon, 1972–1976: The Pursuit of the Presidency*. New York: Viking, 1977.

"With Henry Kissinger in China." *Ladies' Home Journal*, March, 1972.

Woodward, Bob and Carl Bernstein. *All the President's Men*. New York: Simon and Schuster, 1974.

—— *The Final Days*. New York: Simon and Schuster, 1976.

Young, Kenneth T. *Negotiating with the Chinese Communists: The United States Experience, 1953–1967*. New York: McGraw-Hill, 1968.

Zagoria, Donald. *The Sino–Soviet Conflict, 1956–1961*. Princeton: Princeton University Press, 1962.

—— *Vietnam Triangle: Moscow, Peking, Hanoi*. New York: Pegasus, 1967.

INDEX